I0419093

VISUALLY SPEAKING

VISUALLY SPEAKING

MASTERING THE ART OF PHOTOGRAPHY

TED FORBES

CONTENTS

Foreword

WHEN TED ASKED ME TO WRITE an introduction to this book, I immediately warmed to the idea. Now, after a few week's reflection, I realize that what has made him such a successful advocate for photography is his broad ecumenical relationship to the medium itself. From cameras to content.

This is how he structures his embrace of the medium. The passionate photographer, whether amateur or professional, knows that at the end of the process, which is the photograph itself, there remain areas or aspects of unexplained meaning to the image. The medium itself seems to have taken over. And we ask ourselves, Why and how are we responding to this visual power?

Enter Ted. He too wants to know and wants to share his quest. At this point I recall a line from Roland Barthes in which he stated that the author of a book is only half of the content of the book, the reader being the other half. Each reader brings their own unique response to the work, thus multiplying its authorship. I find this to be true of photography to the extent that the viewer becomes a part of the content of the photograph as well. Of course the great questions often remain unanswered. But where this book assumes its importance is in the fact that Ted has *defined* the major questions in an infinitely more interesting way. This is his gift and his thanks to the medium.

Bon Voyage,
Ralph Gibson
May 5, 2023

INTRODUCTION

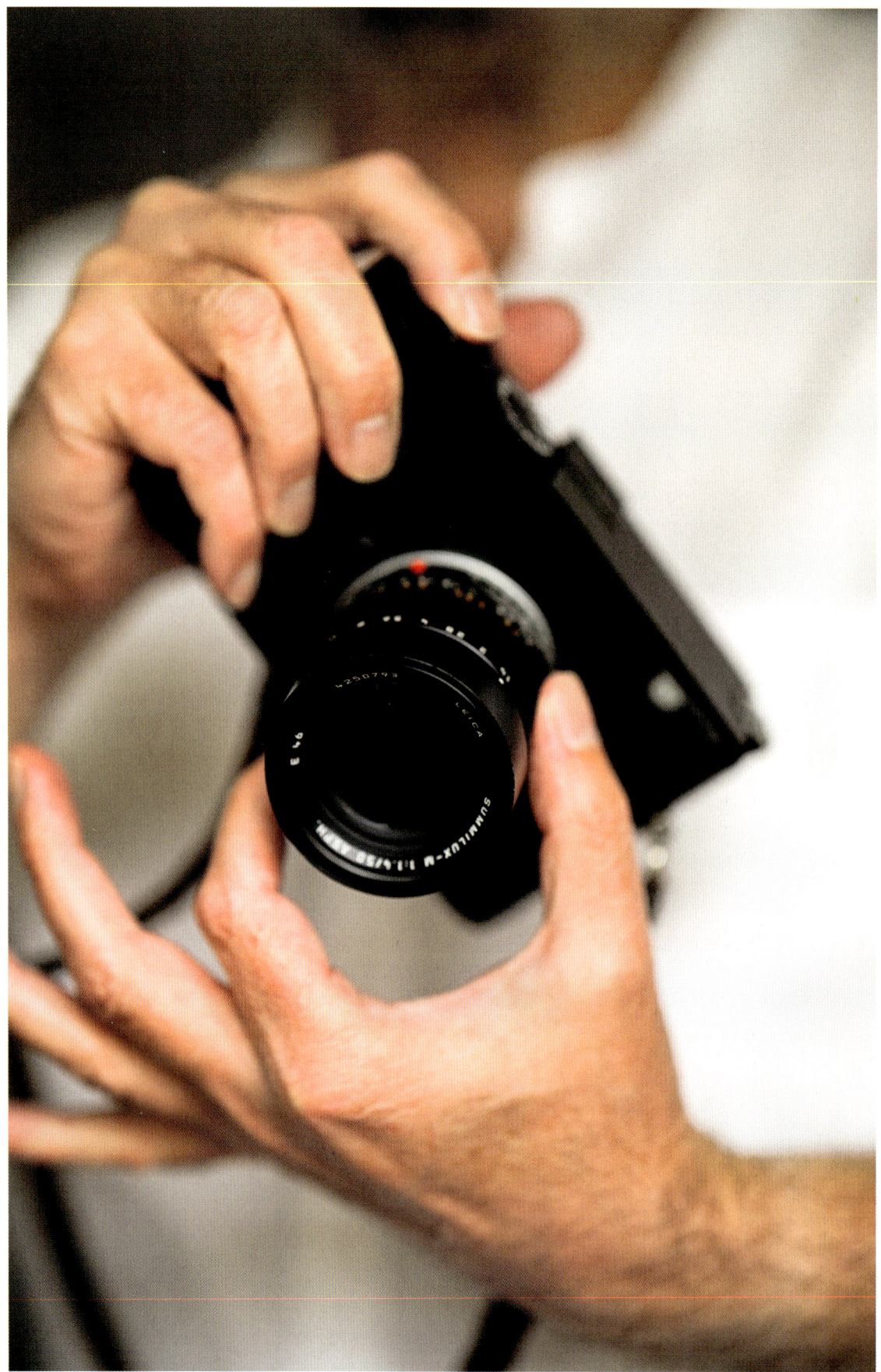

Why This Book Is Different

THE IDEA THAT MAKES photography so interesting is how it requires many disciplines to produce the final image. It brings together art, physics, optics, chemistry, and digital technology, in addition to what's in front of the lens in any given photograph. There is no shortage of books on photography. You're holding this book in your hands right now, so you know this.

I am largely self-taught as a photographer. My formal training is in music, which I devoted myself to through college. When I started taking photography seriously, I turned to the canon of books on the topic. I found there were way too many books, especially in the last twenty years, most over explaining how to get an exposure correct. There are a lot of books on how to break into the wedding industry and how to shoot portraits for a living. There are books explaining software and how to edit your images. There are books on how to develop film, how to print in a darkroom, even books on how to revive early photography practices. There are books on lighting, books on toy cameras, and books on making a pinhole camera. There are books on the history of photography and picture books of amazing work from famous photographers. And then there are countless self-published books by amateur photographers (some of them quite good, others not so much) and even photography zines. There are books on just about every aspect of photography, except for the actual act of photography itself.

Photography is a visual language—a universal and powerful language. Every photograph communicates something to the viewer. Photography has the power to express beauty and emotion. Photography also has the power to say something more provocative. It has the power to be controversial and uncomfortable. In some ways we interpret photography differently than we do the spoken word.

Art is a reflection of culture in time. The time we are in now concerns me. At the risk of sounding like I'm trying to say "you kids get off my lawn"—I do believe that over the last two decades photography has changed. Mainly thanks to a small handful of major camera companies, the tools that we use have matured substantially. However, those companies have turned to technology to "solve problems" that humans inherently exhibit. In other words, they automate certain tasks that are not difficult to learn and master as a means to sell more cameras and lenses.

To be clear I have no problem with this at all. It's exciting. It's a time of unbelievable leaps in possibilities. But there is no emphasis on the creative side. There is no encouragement other than going online and arguing in various forums over what model is better than another. It becomes the theory rather than the practice.

Some of this technology is very exciting. I am not a hater of technology at all. But the magic happens when we combine artistic intention with what is available. Sadly, I feel like there is much available, but the idea of artistic intention is profusely overlooked.

Another problem is that it's no longer the 1960s—the famous era of experimentation and the attitude of "anything goes." And the hardest part for anyone artistically minded is that, literally, everything has been done.

I was discussing this once with Ralph Gibson, and he made the sobering point that every sub-genre had already been undertaken in the first few years of photography as a medium. Landscape, portraits, abstract, events, photojournalism, street, even "optical illusions," later synonymous with "photoshopping," had all already been explored. Enter the late 1960s and we have a whole new level of experimentation that exceeds everything that came before it and then some.

So here we are today. We're making technological bounds only to all be producing the same types of snapshots. Let me be clear: there are excellent practitioners in photography today, but it is the exception, not the norm. The world is a smaller place thanks to social media and the internet, but the development of ideas is not there to meet it.

This Book Is about Visual Communication

My goal with this book is simple: I want you to understand how to communicate an idea that resonates with the person who views the image.

One of the great joys for me is the idea of showing someone how to do something, then watching them take that concept in a whole new direction. If you teach with intention, you become your student's biggest fan. You see yourself in the early stages, but then you see how the student makes it their own. What's strange is that I'm not sure if my teachers ever saw this in me—I'd like to think that they did. But this is the phenomenon that drew me to teach. Fifteen years ago, I was teaching at a local college and quit because of the political side of higher education. I went on to start a YouTube channel and now, fifteen years later, it's been a fabulous journey and career.

There is a fine line between over analyzing theory and actually making photographs. This book will teach you how to communicate through photography by understanding the structure and syntax that will give you the tools to make intelligent work. It is learning how to speak a visual language. In order to understand this visual language, we do need to establish elements of structure and logic to define how (and why) concepts work.

There is a point where one can take analysis too far. Over analysis can become a vehicle to explain obvious macro elements of a composition, treat unintended visual coincidences as planned, or worse, to justify a work of art by avoiding subjective opinion.

I caution you as the reader because my goal is to provide you with the tools and structure to improve your skills and create stronger work. I want you to achieve the level of mastery that you desire as an actual practicing photographer.

Art is not "paint by numbers"; it is an act of creativity. Intelligent art has structure, and the challenge is what you decide to create within that structure. Just like literature, dance, music, architecture, or any other creative medium, photography must evolve to represent the culture we live in currently.

Finally, I want to say this: everything I'm going to give you in this book is a starting point. Know that you have to put the work in, which takes time and patience. But more importantly, please take this information and make it your own. Then use it as the proverbial "jumping off" point to expand these ideas into new ones. That is where the real magic happens. Yes, learning is understanding concepts, but understanding is when your learning turns into new ideas and possibilities.

My desire is for you to set the world on fire, then write your own book one day to inspire others. You've got this!

CHAPTER 1

WHAT IS A VISUAL
LANGUAGE?

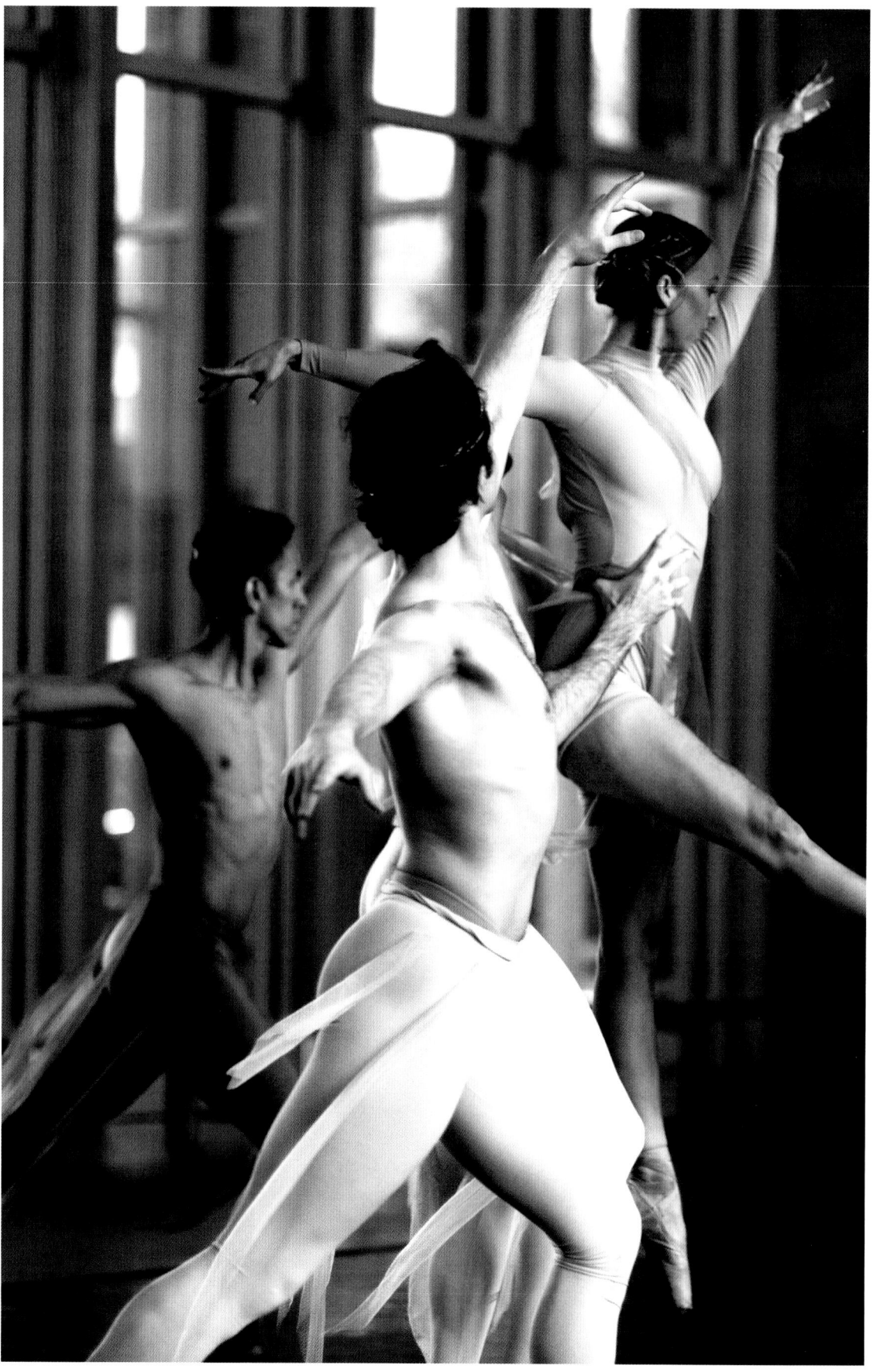

THE IDEA OF COMMUNICATION is fundamental to our experience as humans. It's how we express our wants and needs. It's how we show affection and express emotion. It's a tool we use to express support, empathy, disagreement, and even disdain. Humans do not inherently exist in isolation, therefore the ideas of "showing" and "sharing" are part of our existence, as well as where our passion for life originates.

While most of us consider language to be the default method of communicating, visual imagery is sometimes more powerful in how it can transcend a localized, spoken language. This is why iconography is used so heavily in public signage. Understanding traffic lights, directions, warnings, or even how to find the bathroom—these ideas are expressed using universal iconography that can be understood no matter what country you're from or what language you speak.

Art has this function as well but can take the viewer even further. Art can often command more of one's attention, and it certainly lends itself to interpretation. For example, you and I might absolutely love the same painting, but that painting means something different to each of us. The best art makes us think. Visual art is, at its core, an important and powerful form of communication.

There is a great deal of evidence that suggests that visual art predates language as a form of communication. We can begin by considering the very earliest examples of visual expression, which were usually drawn on rocks or on the walls of caves. Note that caves are insulated and protected. They survived the millennia and are here today. But there is plenty that hasn't survived.

The evidence we do have, however, has created a debate in modern paleontology. At what point did humans begin to exhibit "modern" behaviors of communicating or creating? This is typically studied through the artifacts—objects such as stone tools or markings left behind on rocks or caves. A tool certainly indicates problem-solving, at least for one's self. But a strong case for using visual pictures to communicate is currently being made with the Blombos Cave complex on the Cape coast of South Africa (70,000 BCE) and the Bhimbetka rock shelters in Central India (at least 290,000 BCE).

The Blombos Cave features line renderings composed in rock. The Bhimbetka renderings feature stick figures of humans and animals in various configurations. Abstract ideas such as the ordering and stacking of stones or the outlines of handprints suggest at least the idea of expression. Some archeologists interpret this imagery as the markings of places in caves thought to be special. Oftentimes these hand stencils are found in hard-to-reach spaces that would suggest the preparation of materials was involved before going into the cave. They also suggest symbolism and perhaps a crude level of compositional thinking—in other words, the ability to have language and communicate.

Moving through our pre-written history by means of archeological discoveries, we start to reveal a record of time. What we consider to be "cave art" certainly evolves in terms of hand skills and drawing ability. But most importantly, we begin to see the expression of narrative.

Now the connection I'm making between today and early humans is quite simple. There is a visual language that exists in art. Today we speak and notate this visual language whether we realize it or not. If I show you something you recognize, then I've made a statement. If I imply action in a photograph, then I'm starting to make you think. In fact, if you have no idea why I showed you anything in the first place—if it is questionable or mysterious—then you might be inclined to solve it, if it draws you in.

Imagery is powerful and important, and these visual statements transcend us as individuals. The early humans who left these drawings are long gone. We do not know them as individuals. But the idea of leaving behind an idea that lasts longer than our own existence is extraordinarily powerful.

When we photograph, we are possibly leaving statements as visual records. I would guess those early humans painting on cave walls probably had no sense of the impact they were having on discussions many centuries later. Who's to say the volume of images uploaded to social media every day won't be a point of discussion later in a time we can't even comprehend right now?

Or perhaps it's more complex than that. The materials we work with now—paper or even digital media—are extremely fragile compared to the idea of a cave protected from light and weather. This idea should make us all think. Paper has a lifespan. Digital media is dependent completely on backups and electricity, both of which need to be paid for. It's something sobering to realize. Our ideas and statements are very finite.

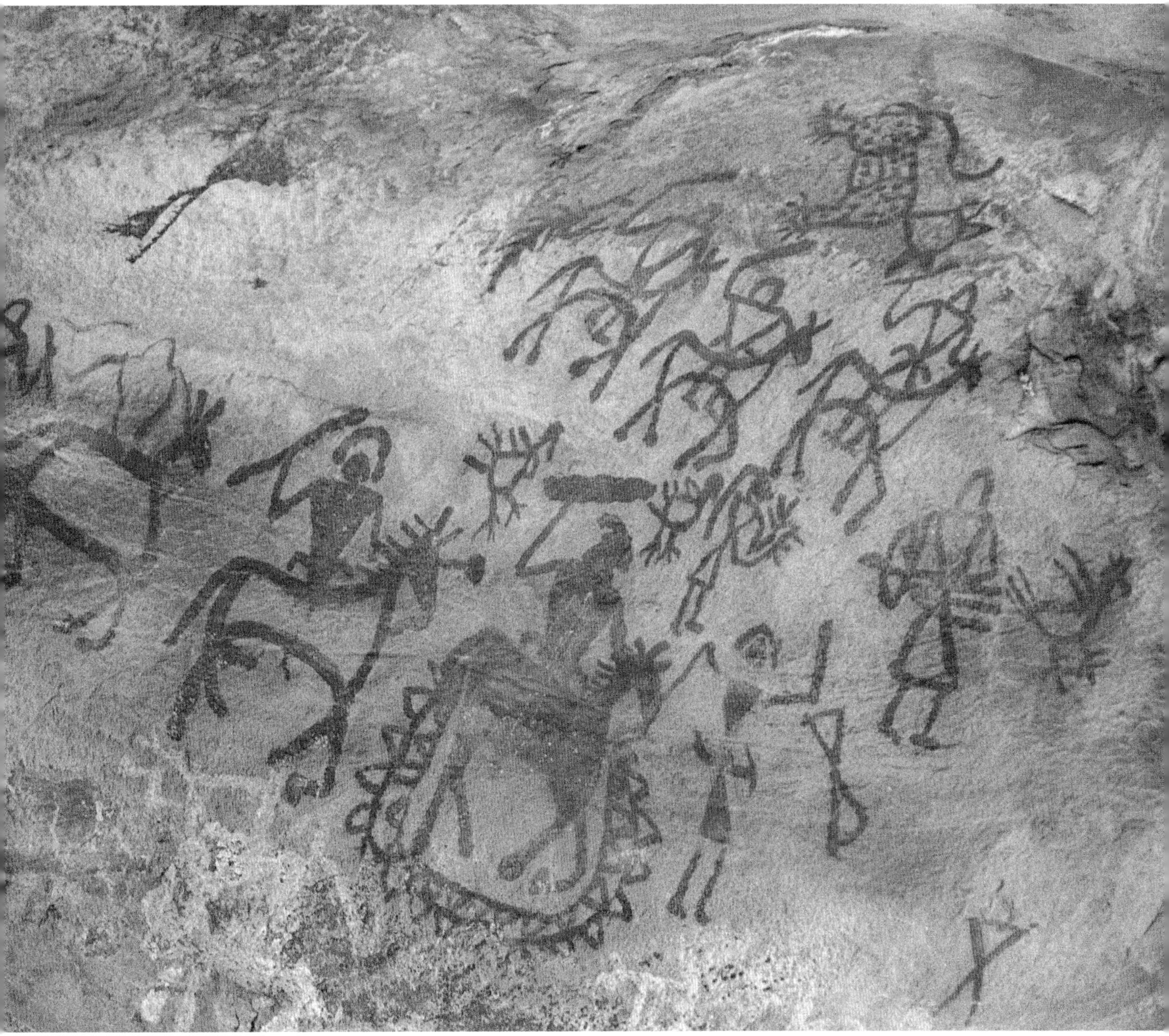

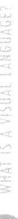

Paintings from the Rock Shelters of Bhimbetka in Madhya Pradesh, India; used under official license from Shutterstock.com.

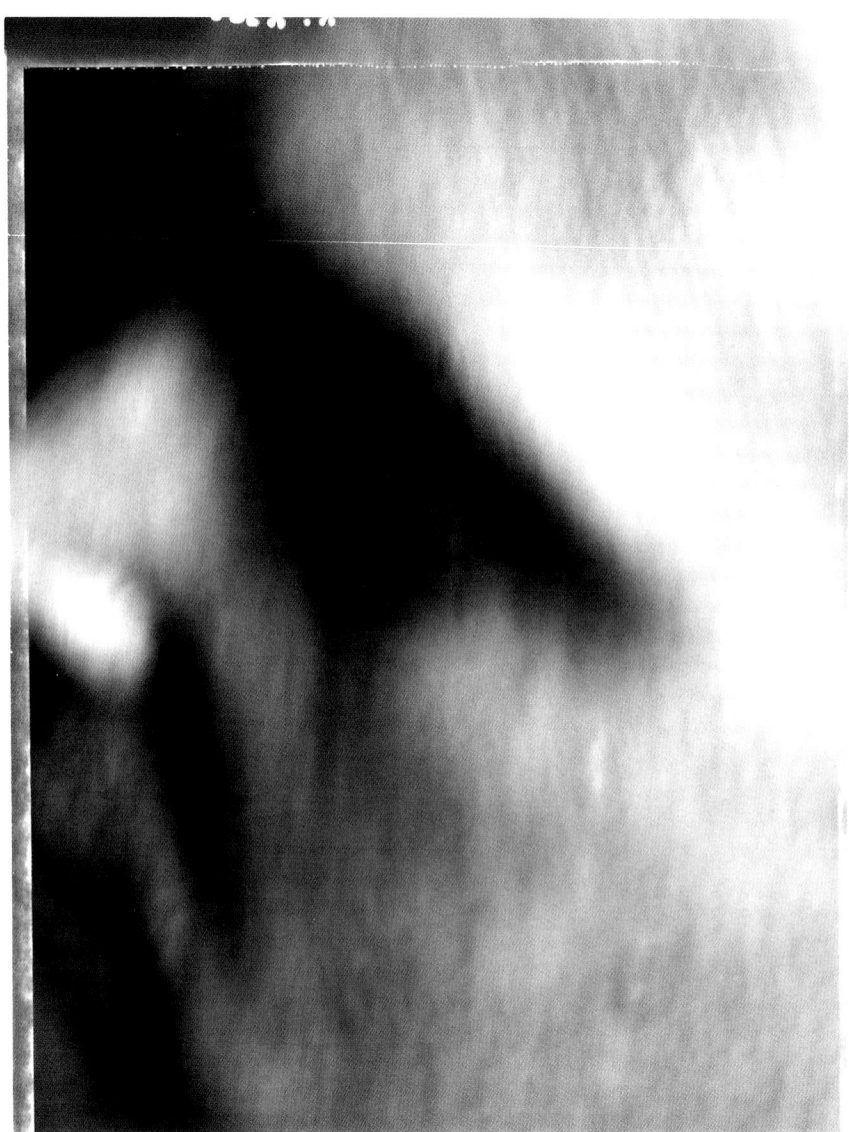

Photography vs. Art

The making of photography is inherently different from other visual media in that the process is somewhat inverted. The essential idea to understand as we begin is that most visual arts are created as the result of some type of "additive" process. A painting is made and designed completely by the artist's hand. Layers are created, objects are placed—all by the mind, intention, and hand of the artist. Hand skills are also required to render the aesthetic quality of the picture.

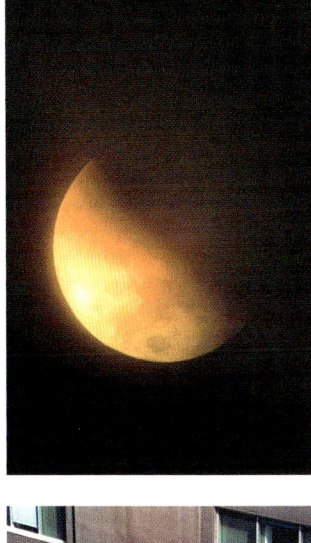

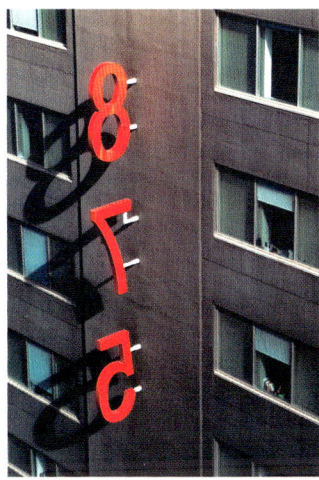

Photography is different in that we are using a combination of optics and digital or analog recording to fix an image in time. At its defining core, photography is a way of capturing something that exists in light in front of the camera. Therefore there is nothing "additive." Using a camera, we capture what exists in a fleeting moment.

Throughout its entire history, photography has been questioned to this degree. Some see the practice as no more than pressing a button, and, yes, this does enable certain "practitioners" who unfortunately don't put much more effort into their craft.

This is always what's fascinated me. Photography is a beautiful compound technology that brings together elements of optics, physics, chemistry, and most recently electronics, engineering, and even artificial intelligence. These are the building blocks of photography, and they have their own sets of rules and limitations. These are the technical sides to the craft. Practicing the craft is then way more complex than grabbing a pencil and making a mark. It requires an understanding of all of the technological elements to exercise an expression of intention. Hand skills are replaced with an understanding of the field of focus, exposure, contrast, the dynamic range limitations of the equipment, timing, shadow, and light. The photographer "draws" in a fraction of a second.

This book is about you, the creator. It's about understanding how to express an idea or your feelings or make a statement. Photography is an art form. Ironically photography is rarely addressed with this approach, and most photographers get lost in the technical details.

Photography is more of a "subtractive" process. Photography is more about what you're leaving out of the picture than what you are choosing to include. By this thinking, photography has as much in common with sculpture as it does with painting. You are removing objects, details, elements, etc. to get to the intended expression.

Intention

When we think of photography as an art form, we define it as using visual imagery to communicate an idea to the viewer. The ideas being communicated are unique to each photographer, but we all share a common visual language. This language is how the photographer uses the image to express something to the viewer. How you choose to say it visually is your intention.

Visual elements are constant—your own intention is not. But intention is supported by the arrangement and portrayal of visual elements, so this is where we begin. I can't tell you how to express your own intention, but I can tell you how you arrange visual elements to get you there.

There are two types of visual elements: the literal and the abstract. For example, we easily recognize and define the human figure, a spoon, a tree, or a chair. I'm randomly throwing out objects, but you would identify them immediately. This is literal symbolism. But what about an undefined shape, a random line, a shadow, or a blurred object? These are not so easily identified, though our brain will attempt to draw conclusions. These are abstract. But they are important because our brain will try to draw the conclusions.

There is also the dividing line between the literal and the abstract. What if we ask, "How much of the object needs to be shown in the image before it's no longer recognizable?" For example, I can crop out parts of the chair in the image and the remaining shapes might lead you to see it as a chair. This begins to introduce a layer of abstraction. Of course, you can continue cropping until we no longer have enough visual information to understand we're looking at a chair, and the communication either stops or takes on new meaning.

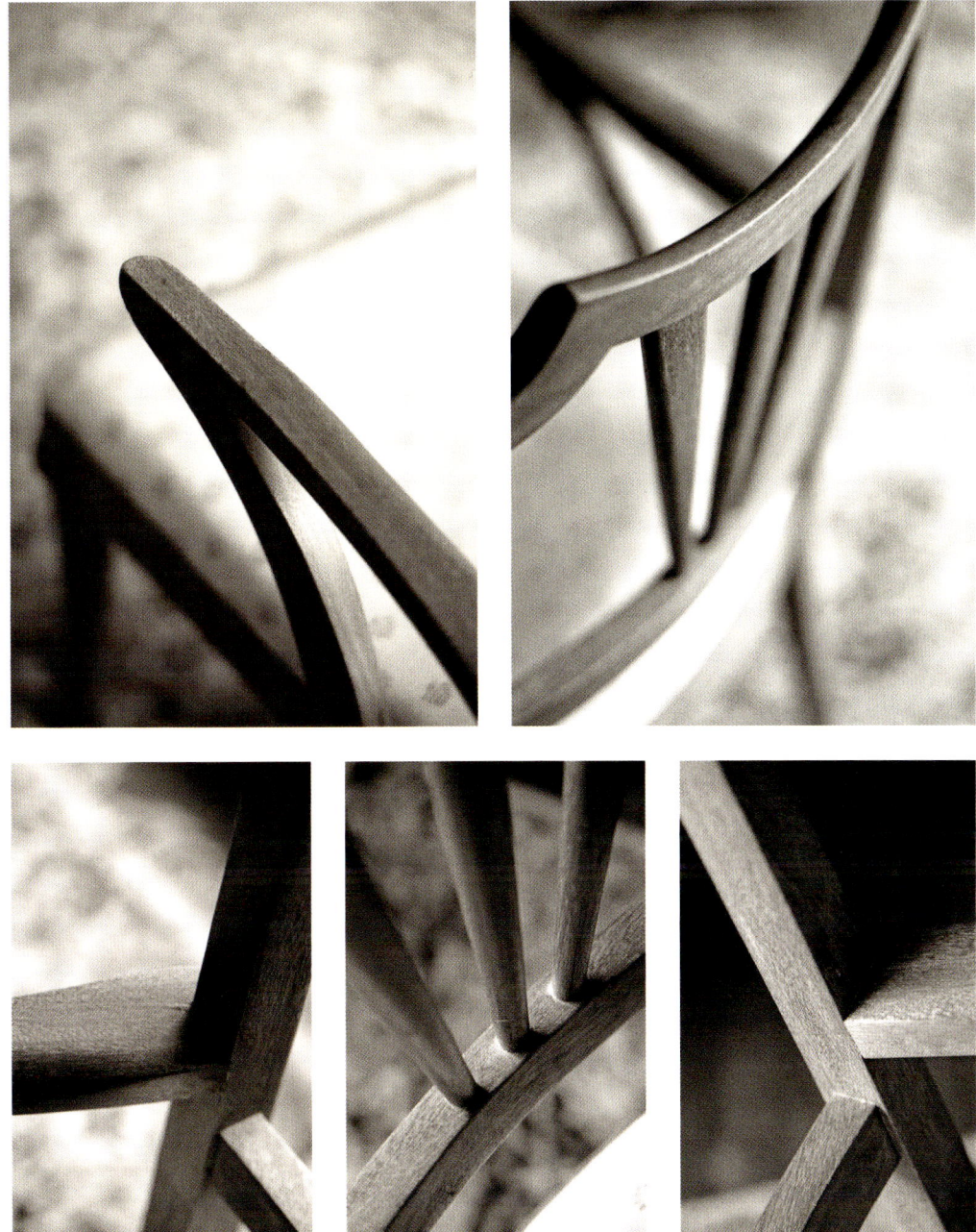

Let's consider the abstract. Shapes and lines are good examples of abstraction. A triangle might not mean much to us at a glance, but as children, it is a shape we're all taught to recognize. Put this in a context and it might start to take on some form of meaning. Perhaps it's creating balance or tension within an image. Maybe a line is used to divide the image or lead one's eye to something visually important.

But how do we put this in the form of language to communicate an idea? What is it that we have to say? Sometimes statements are dramatic and thought through. Other times they are simple visuals that offer a beauty of time and place. These are both complex ideas. So, how do we communicate them?

Language is made up of words and a structure for how they work together. Sounds by themselves are abstract, but we make sense out of them based on patterns we recognize. The same can be said of visual elements.

What is the shape of a face? This might seem silly to ask, but it's not a geometrical concept in that there are variations of every human being in existence. Even if you find your doppelganger, there is a difference.

We know the basic outline; we know where the eyes are expected to be seen, the nose and the mouth. There are criteria for definition, but then how do we account for expression? Expression is an abstract. The face we are seeing implies joy, sorrow, happiness, sadness, or even horror. These expressions are only defined if we have felt them ourselves. The idea of a portrait then indicates communication through a perceived layer that is abstract.

This is the essence of visual communication. It is indeed a language. It is combining the elements of what we understand with those that we might not understand to make a statement, communicate an idea or a memory, render a moment of beauty, or even make the viewer uncomfortable.

We learn to speak by emulating sounds from those who are raising us. Our brain recognizes patterns; we recognize them to understand and we emulate them verbally to express. After five years or so, we get to the point where we can analyze what is being said, and we are taught the formalities in school. We learn to read and write these abstractions because the patterns are now ingrained in our subconscious.

Art is no different. There is a language of visual elements that we are learning how to speak. These elements are made up of what we know and the abstract. As an artist you must internalize these concepts because the making of art is not academic or theoretical. It is organic and comes from the artist.

The objective of this book is to get you to understand the concepts of using a visual language. Just like learning any new language, the most efficient way to master it is through full immersion—be around people who speak the language and use it yourself constantly. The same holds true for photography. Spend time with people who share the passion, practice, and photograph as much as you possibly can.

I want to stress that this is an iterative process. It takes a lot of work combined with time, patience and practice. But just like a spoken language, the idea is to internalize it.

When you're photographing you should not be recalling theoretical information. You're only concentrating on the image at hand. The concepts are in the subconscious. Review the work afterward and learn for the next time.

One of my favorite quotes on this very topic is from Keith Carter. Keith is a brilliant photographer and an excellent teacher. Once I was asking him about one of his well-known photographs. We were analyzing why it worked so well and what it meant. It's a great image filled with symbolism, metaphor, and advanced composition ideas.

Keith abruptly stopped talking, looked at me, and explained how he had none of that in mind when he made the image. He said, "You have the rest of your life to figure out what it means, just make the picture."

Fireflies by Keith Carter (1992); used with permission from the artist.

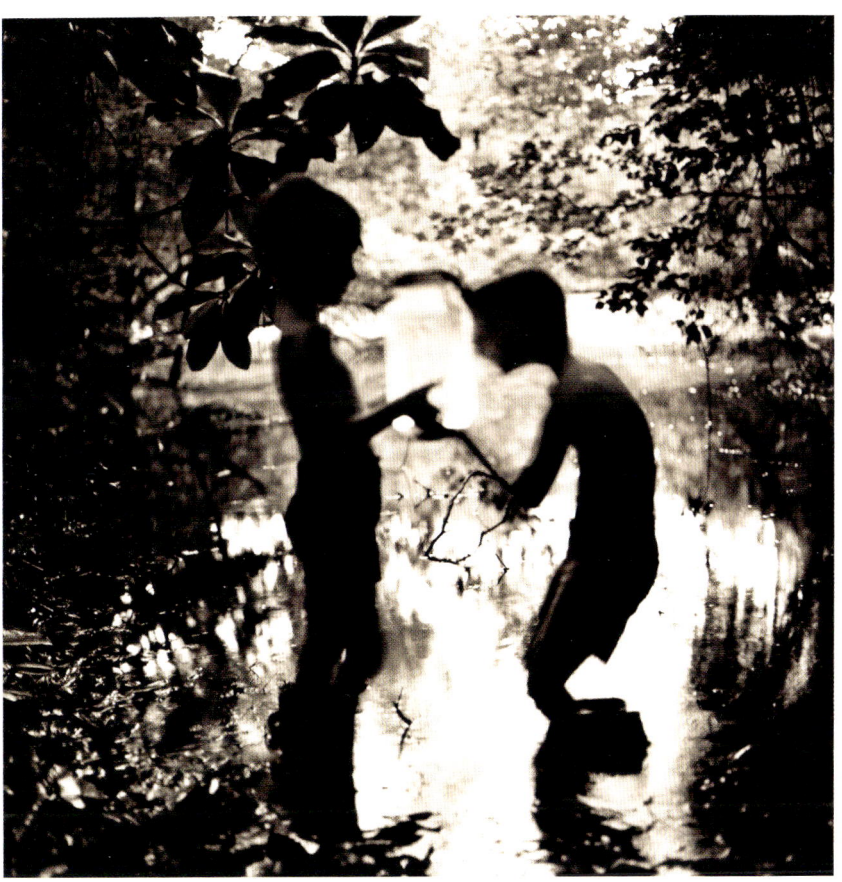

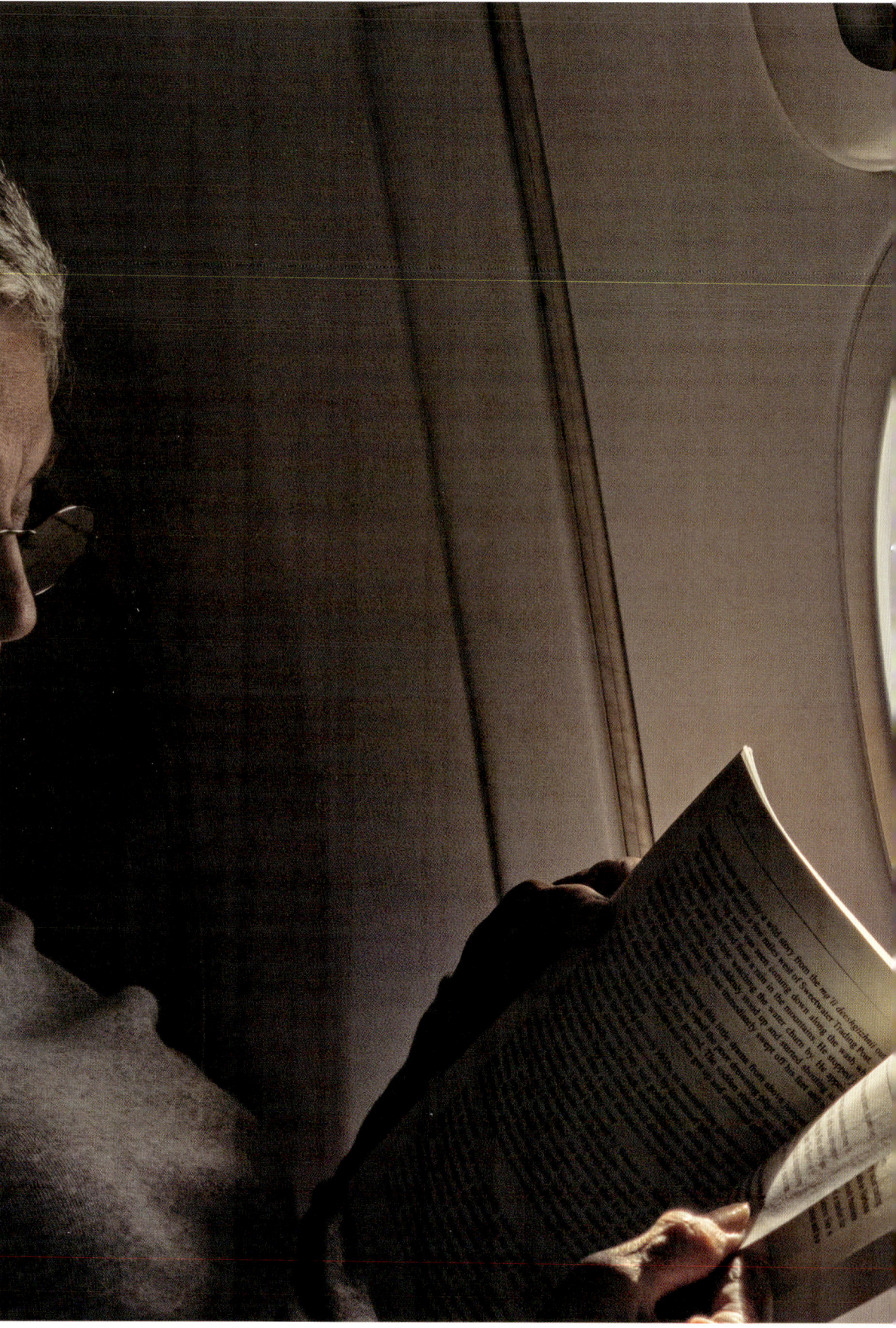

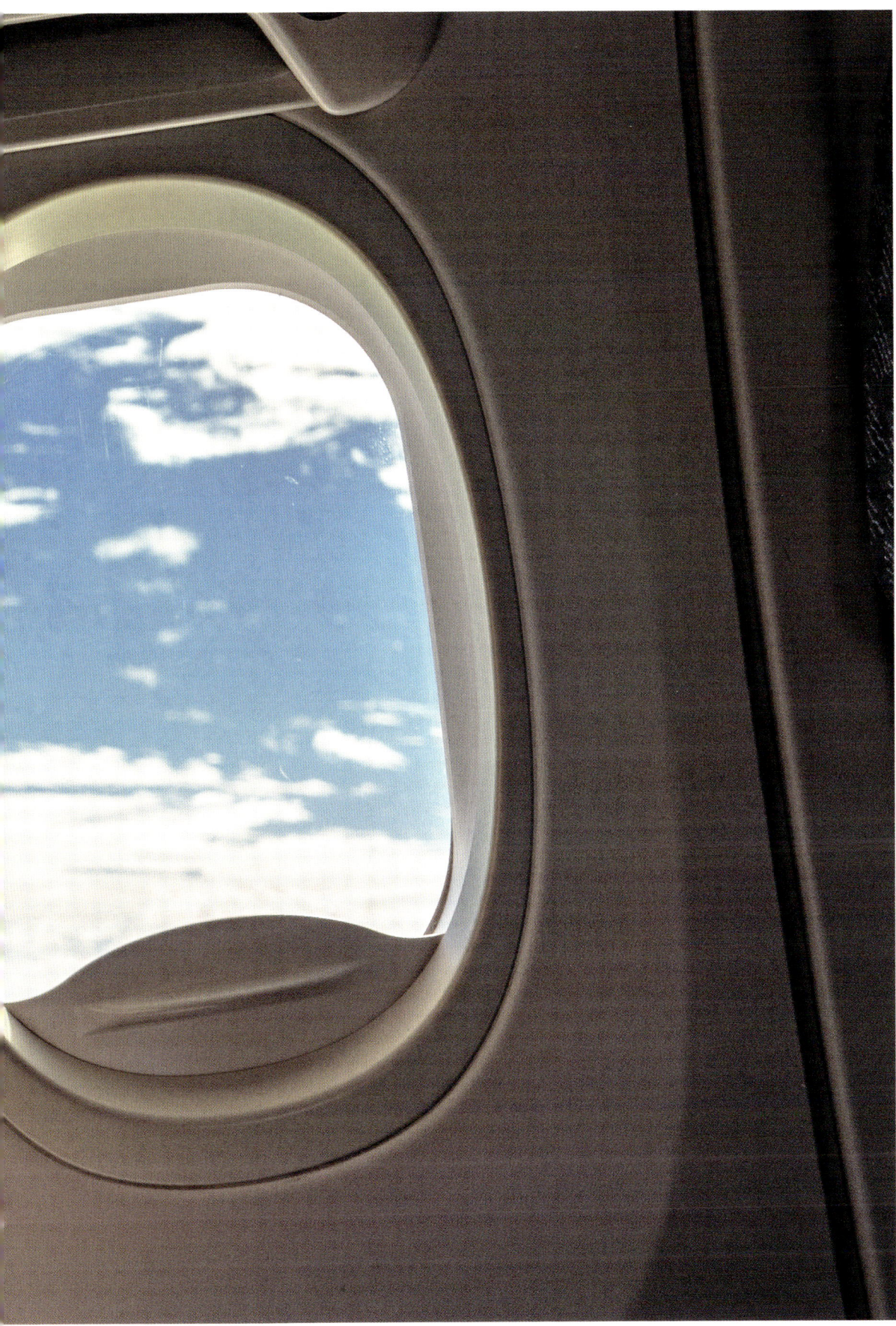

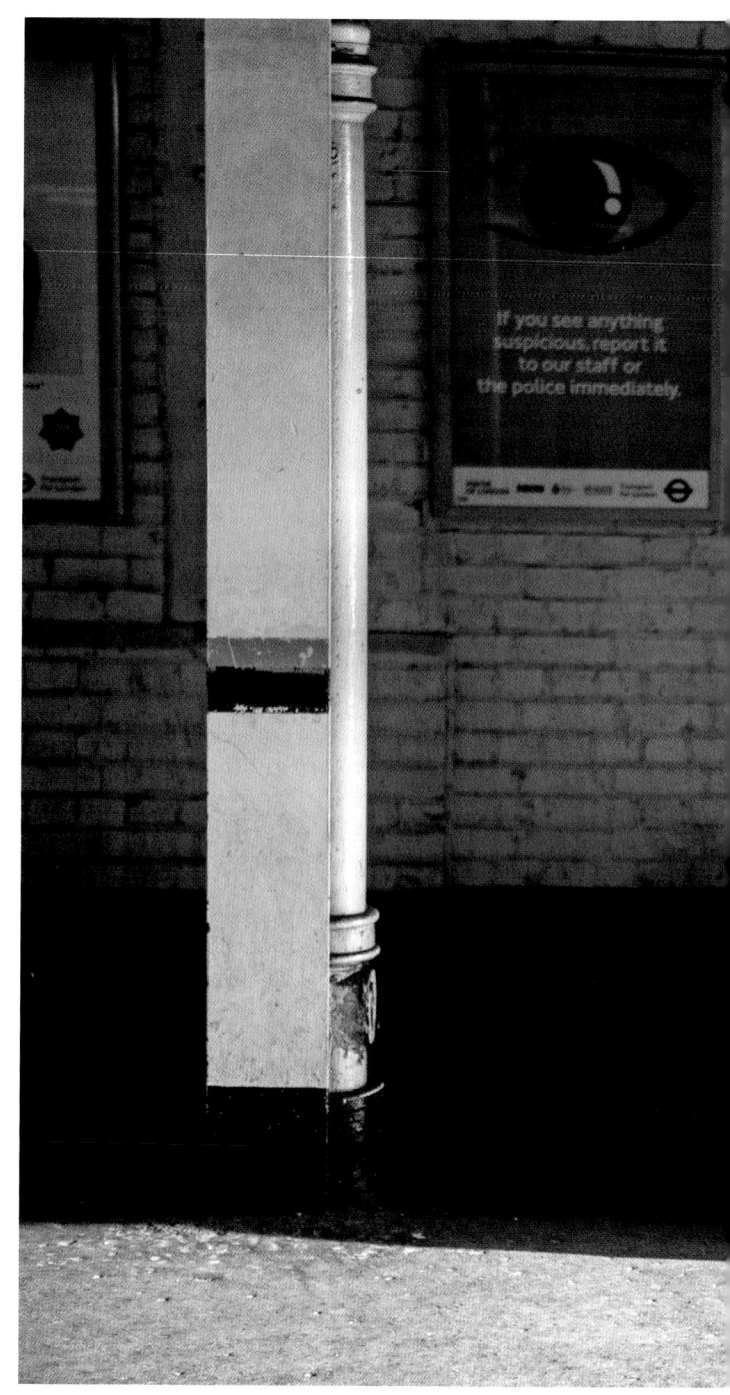

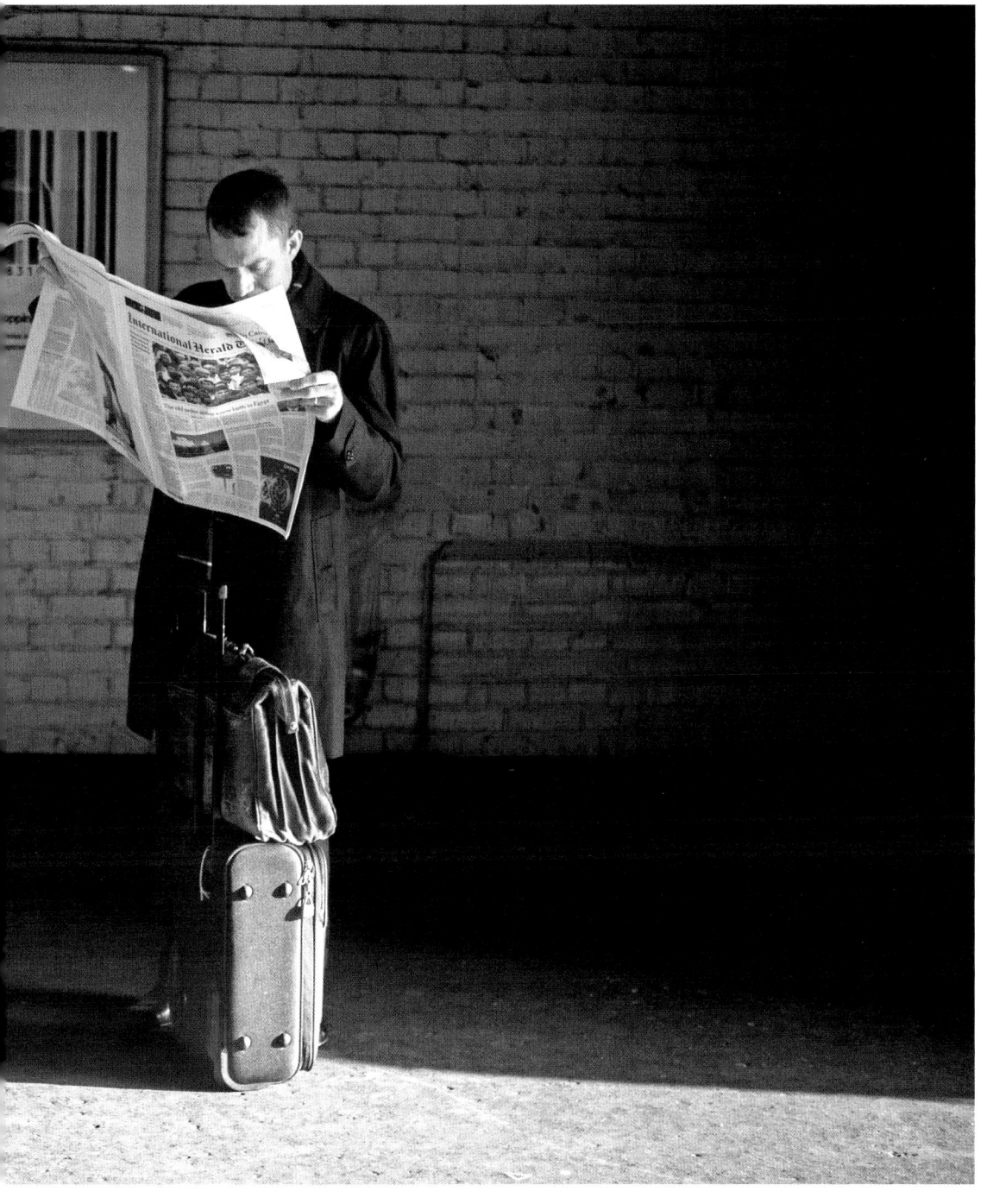

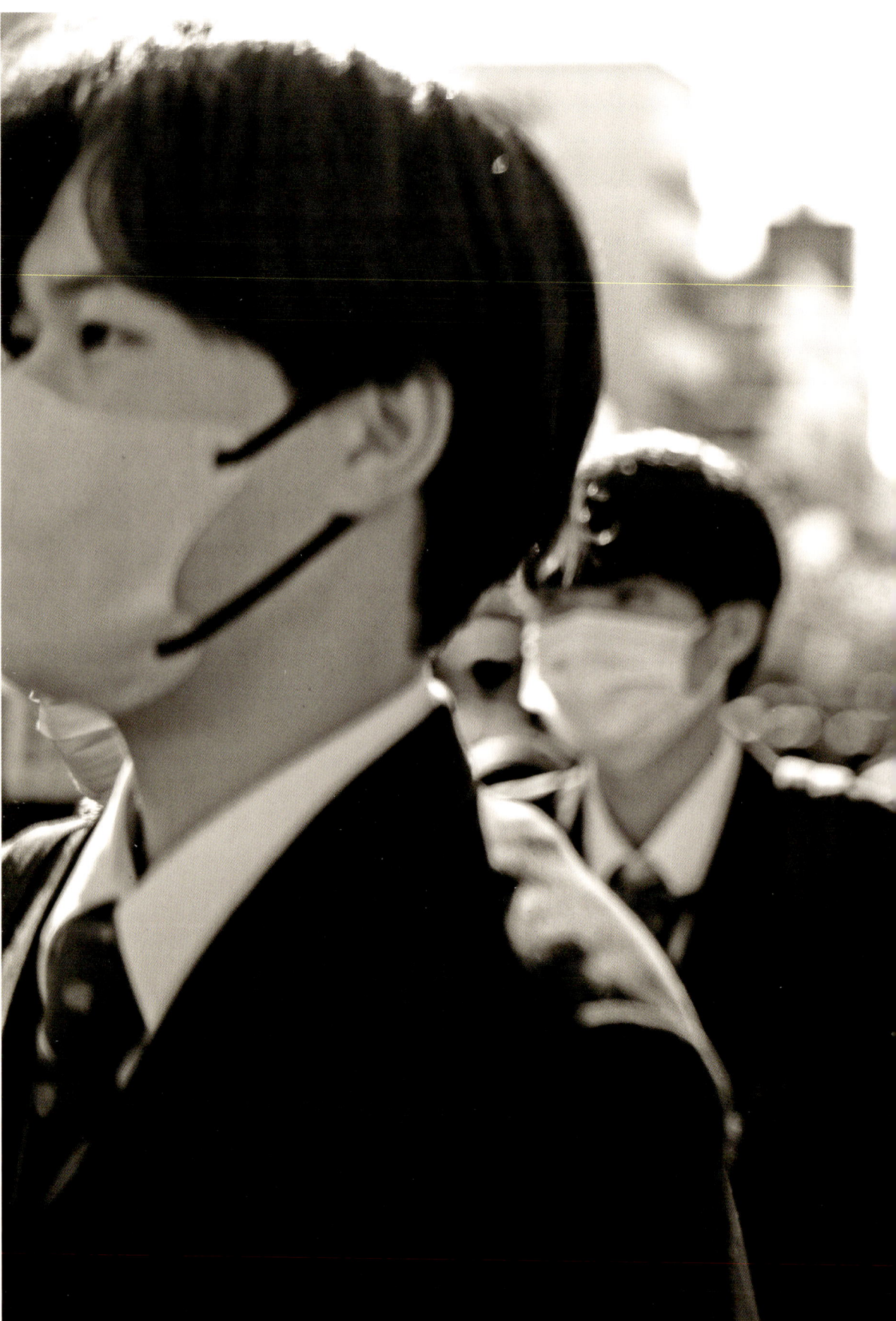

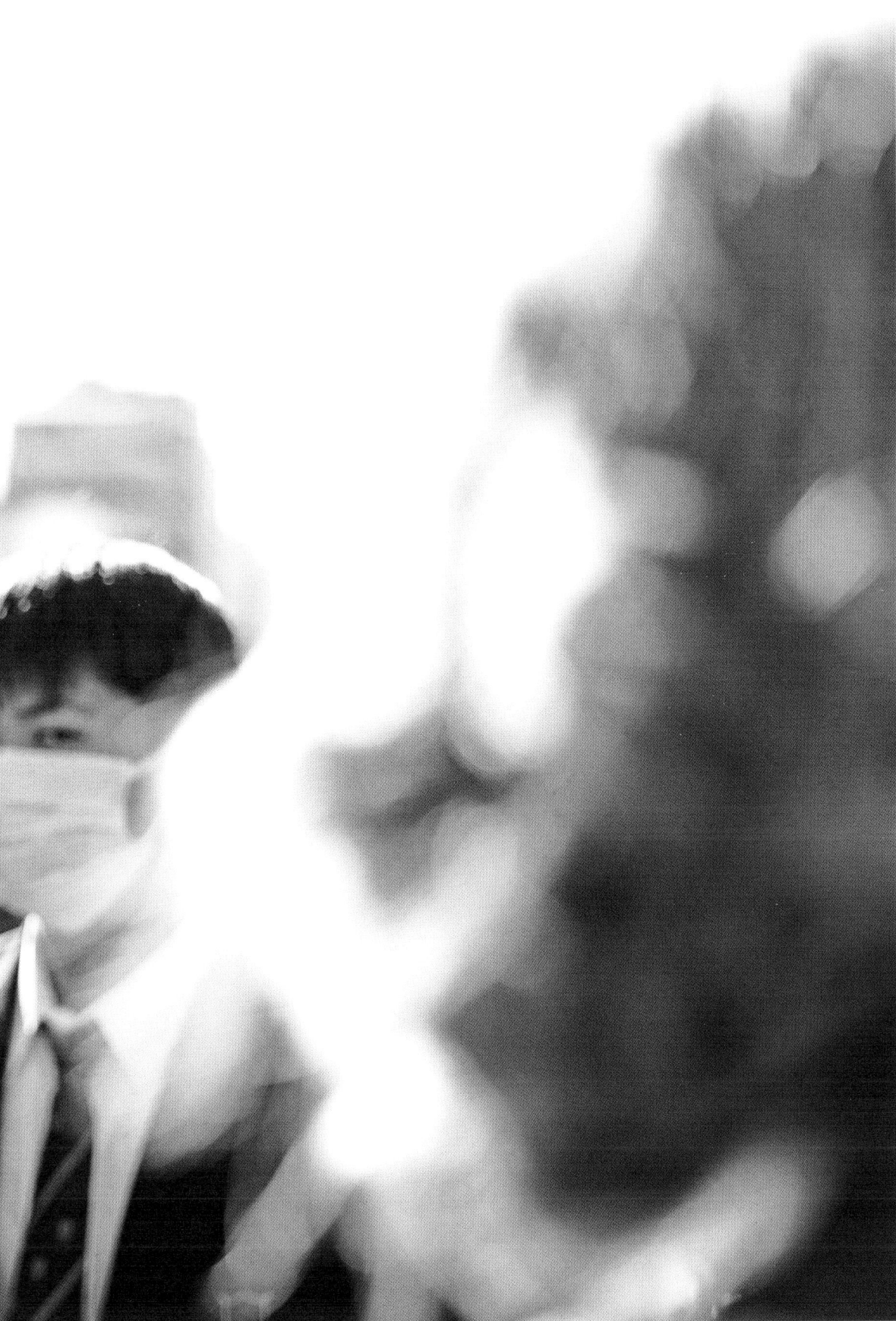

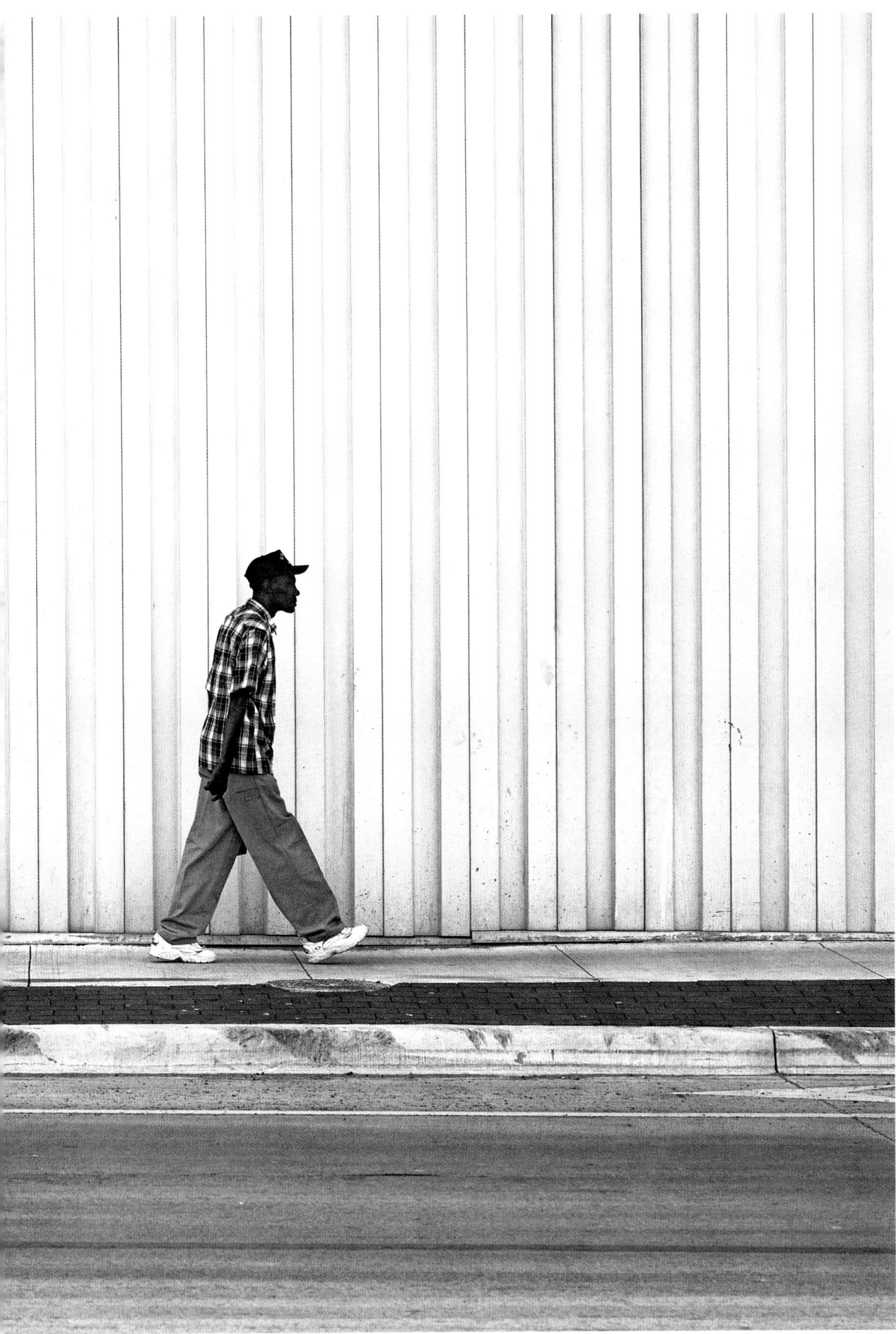

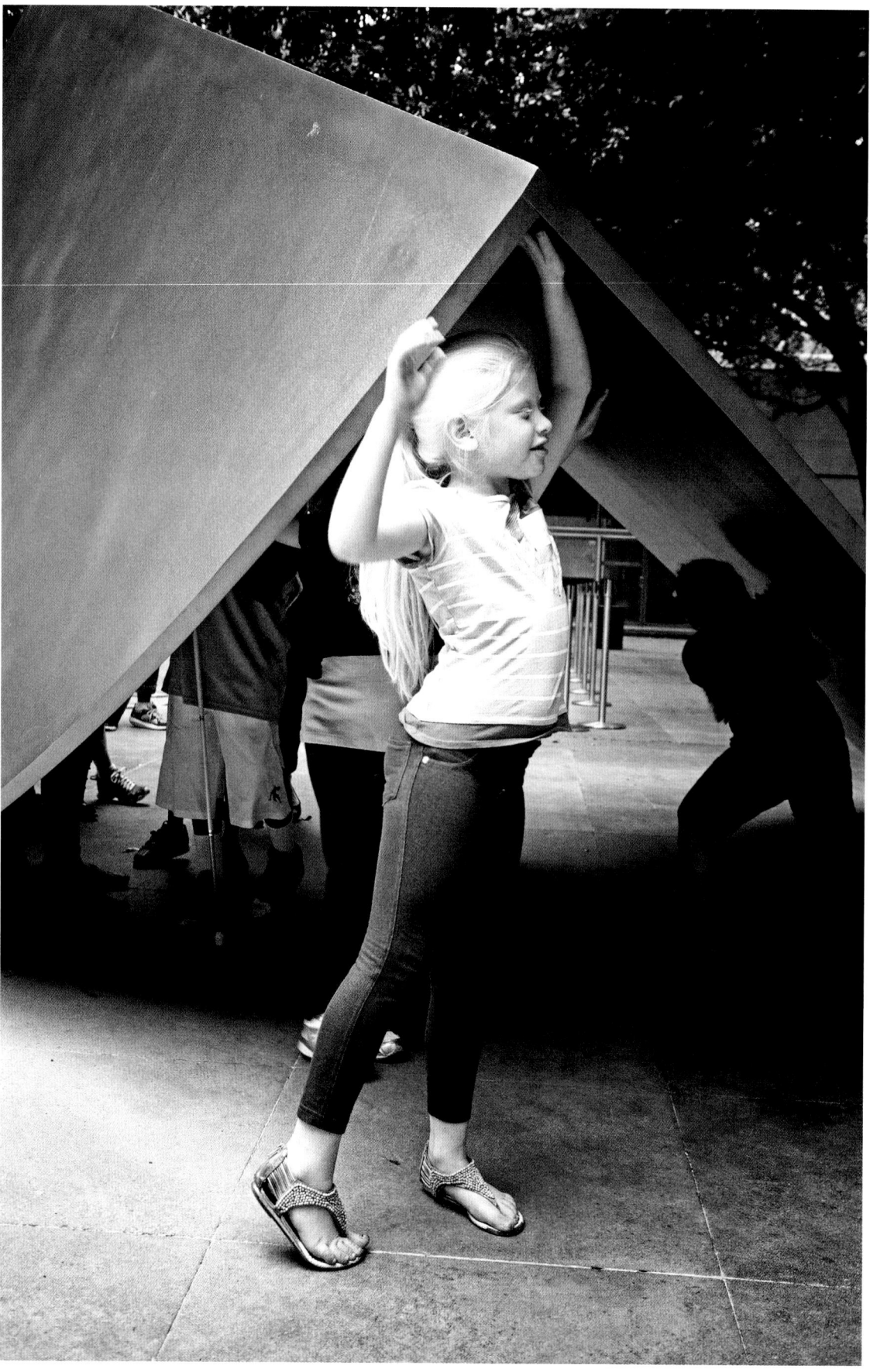

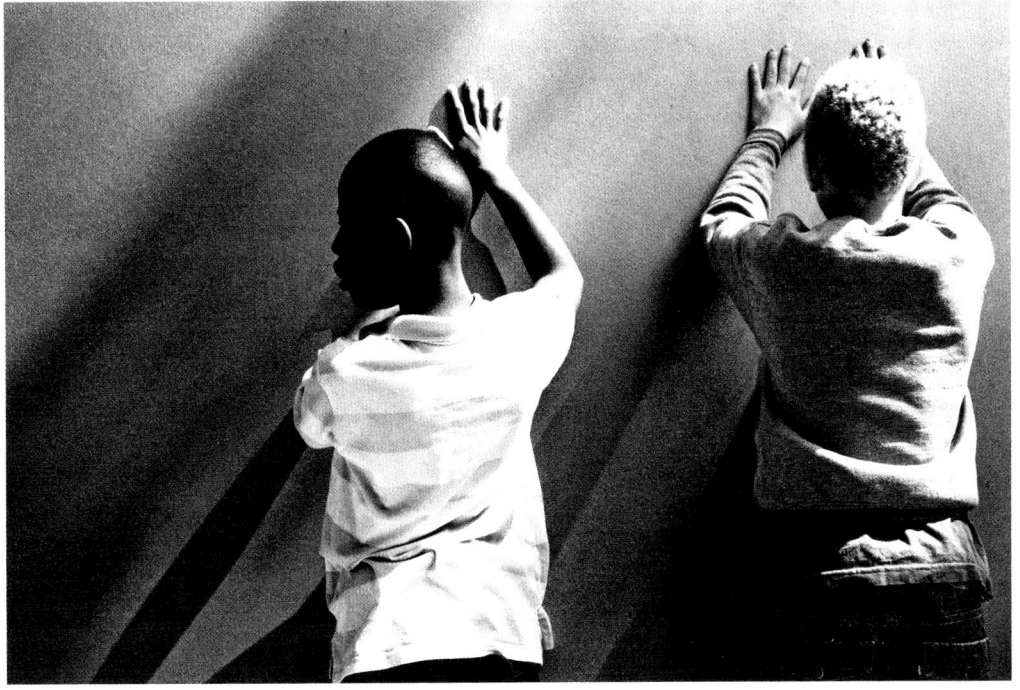

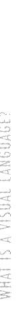

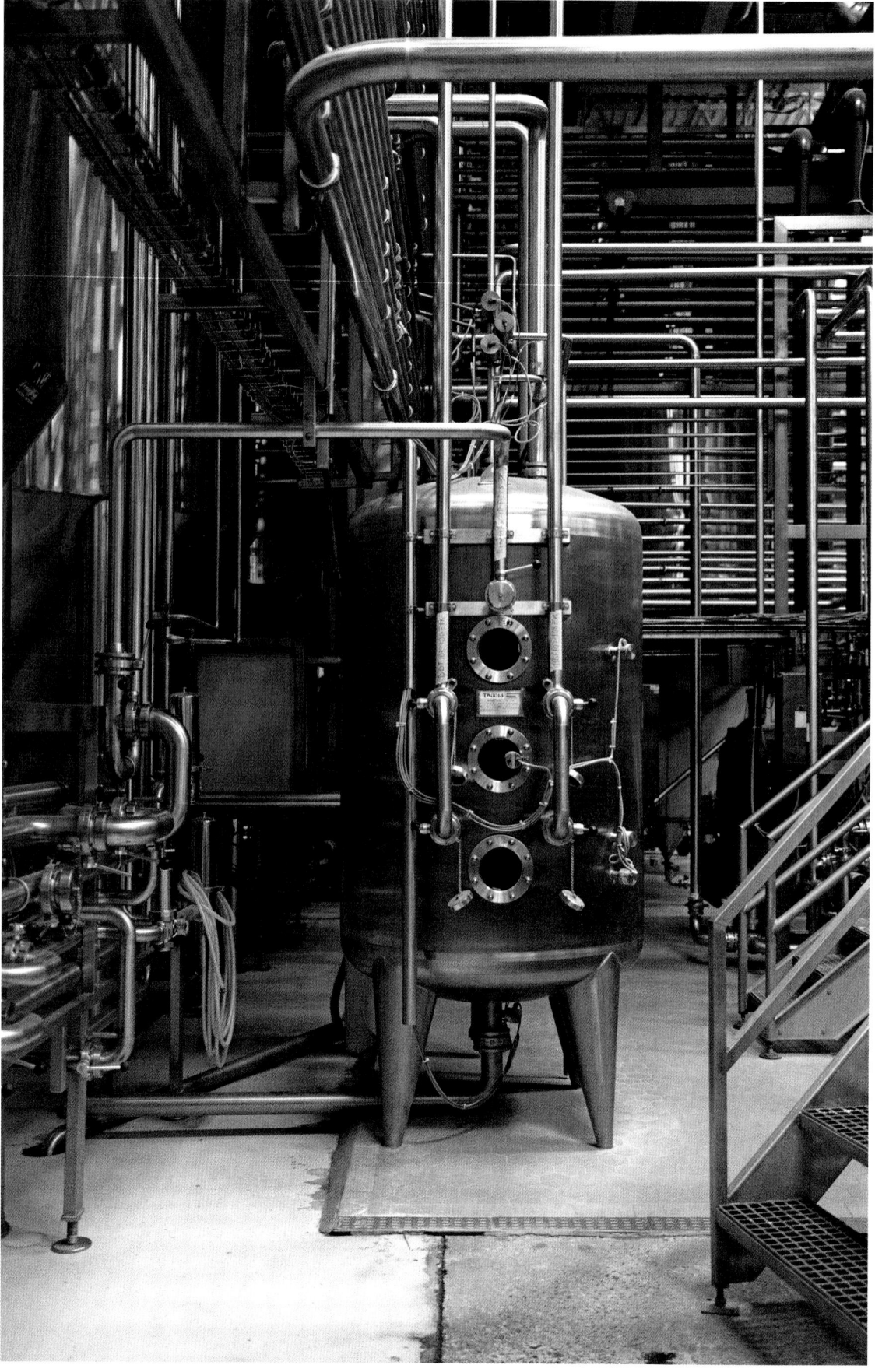

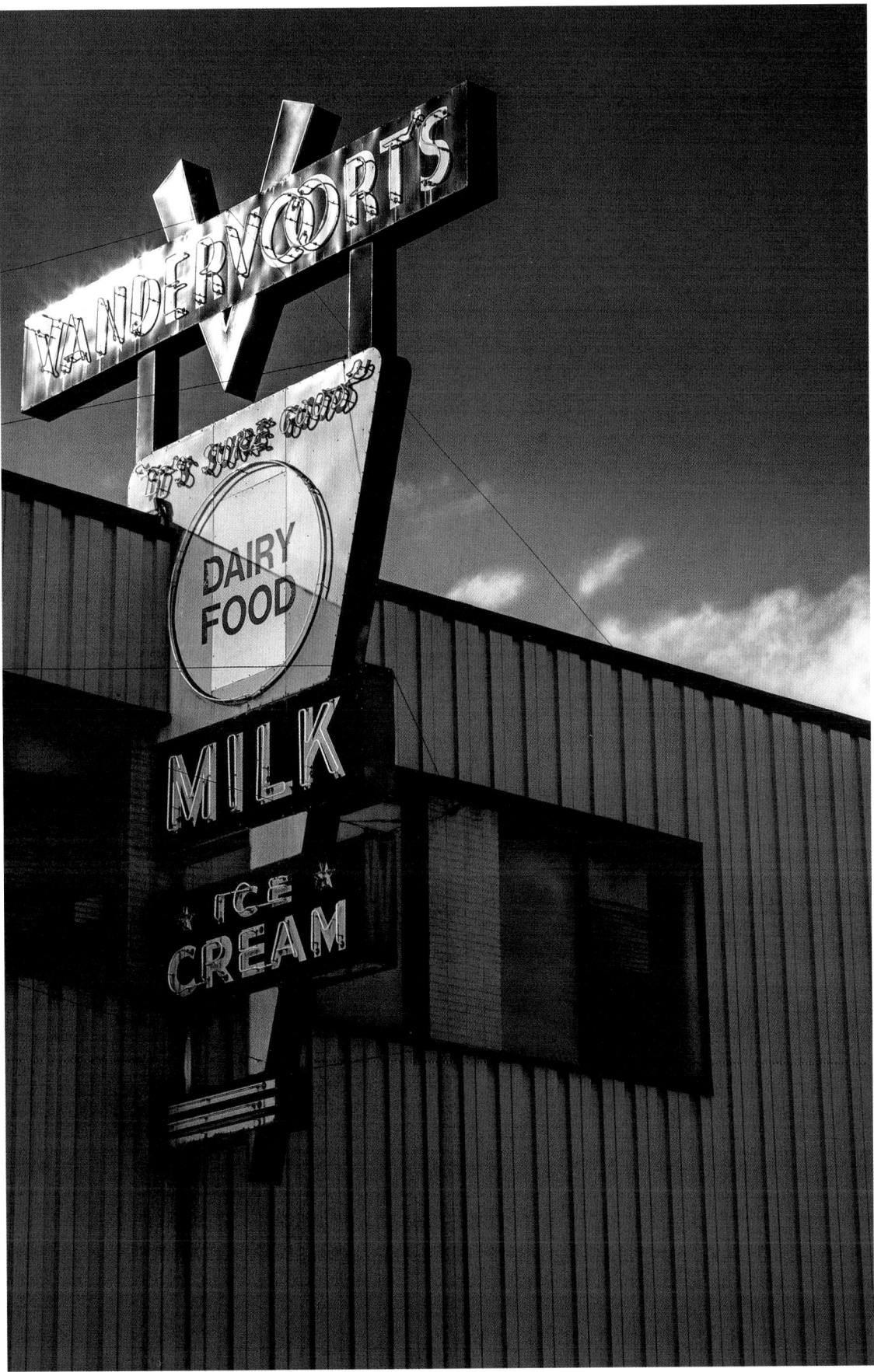

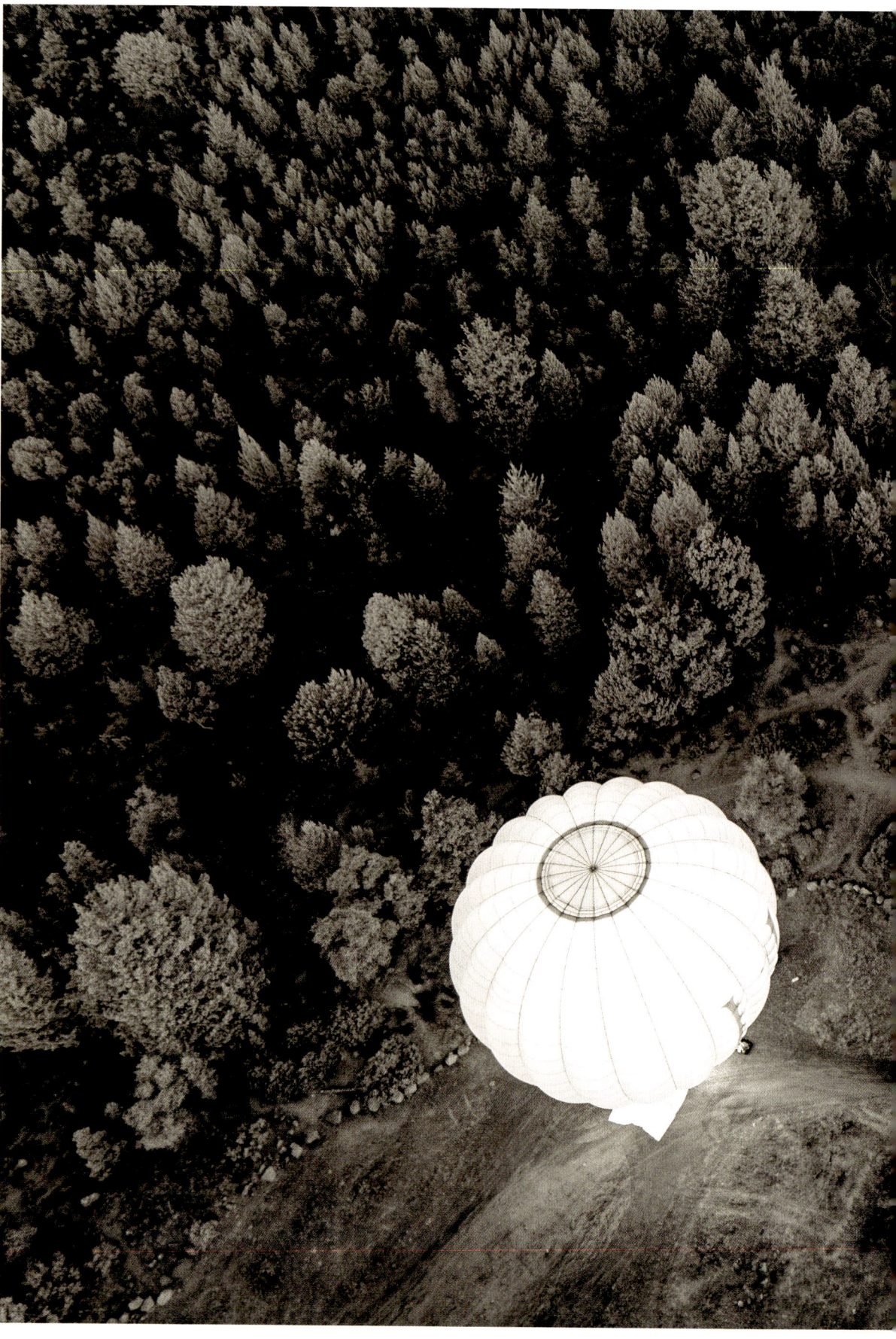

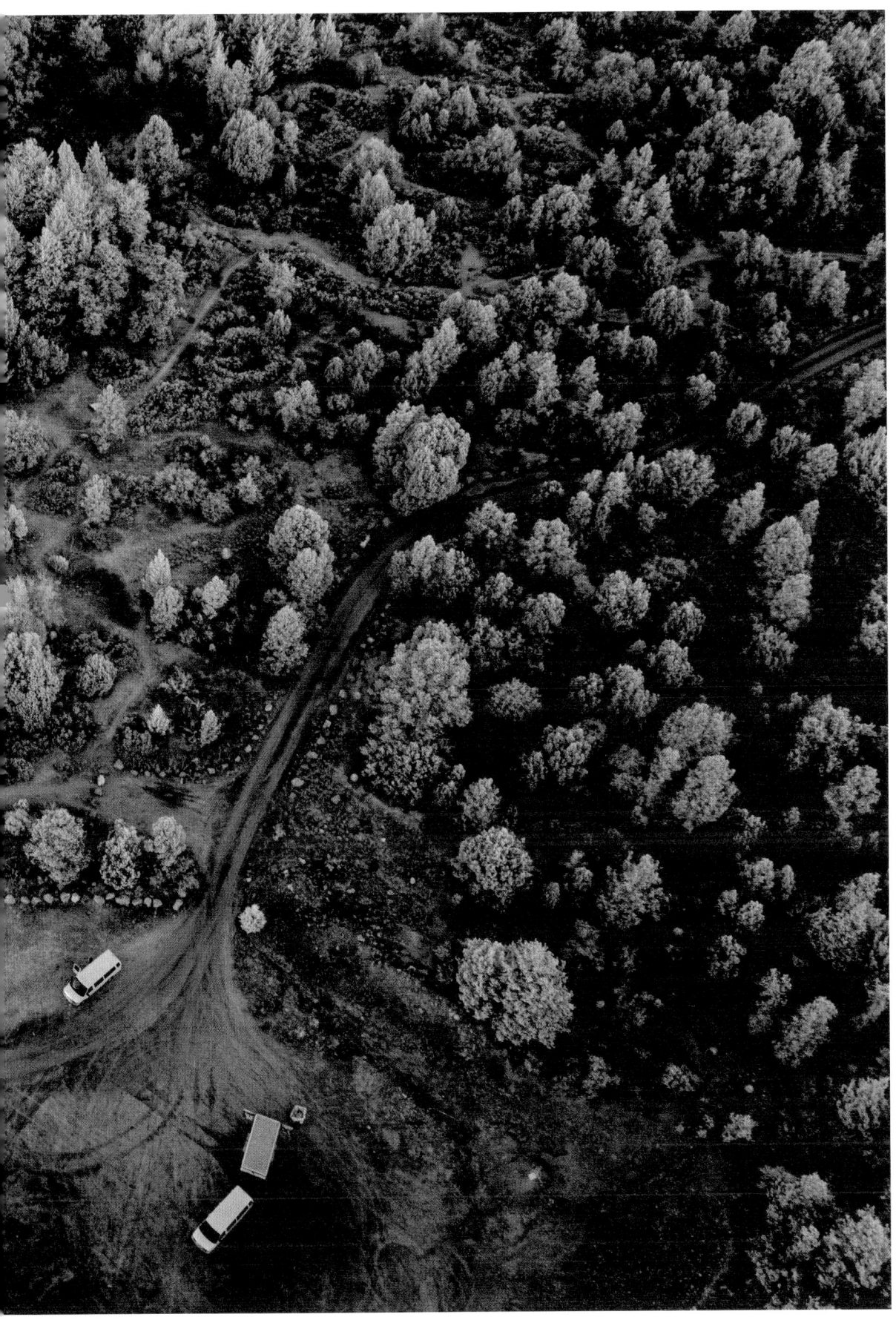

WHAT IS PHOTOGRAPHY?

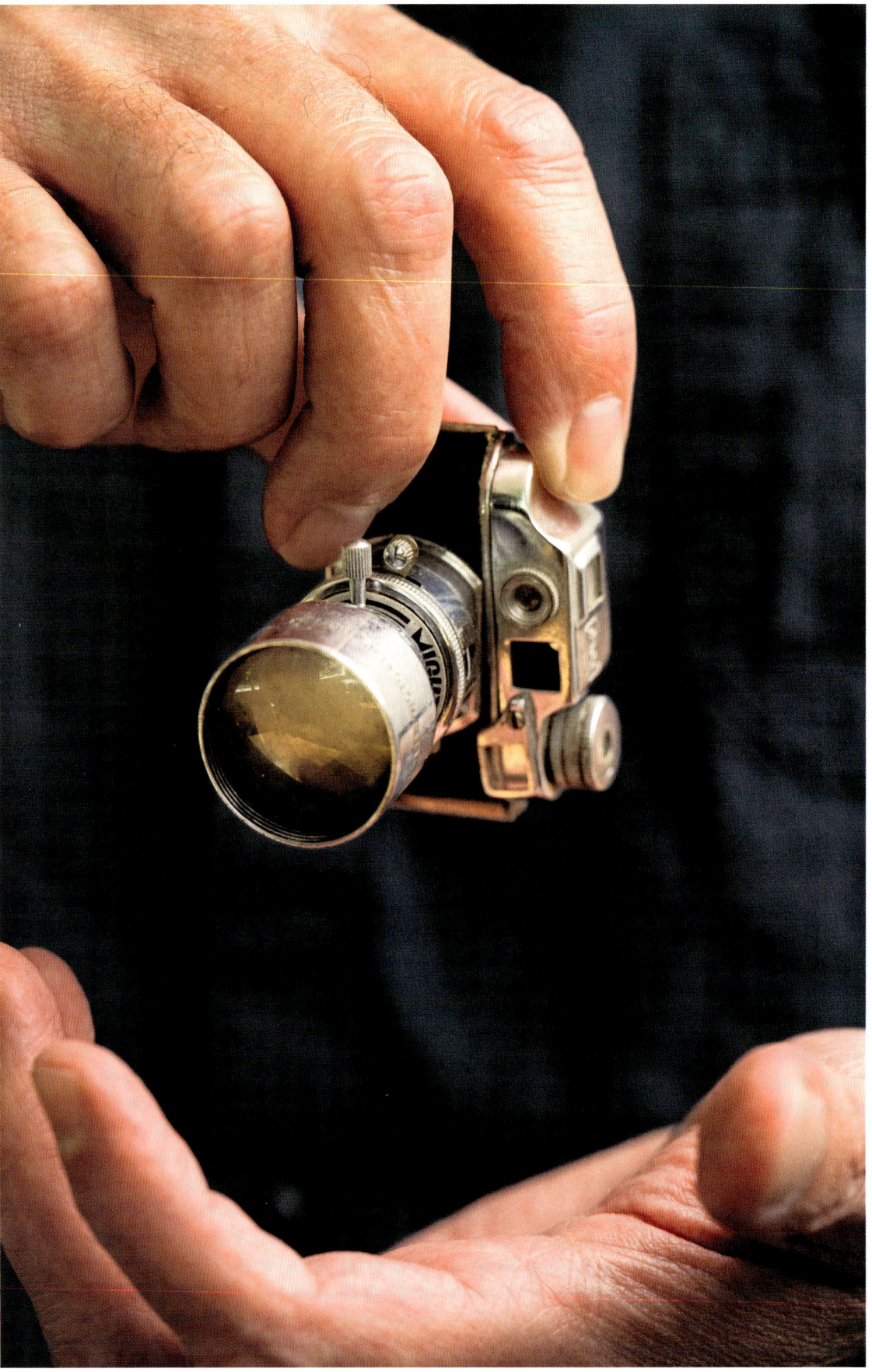

I CLEARLY REMEMBER THE PHOTOGRAPH that made me fall in love with photography.

I was eight years old. My parents took me and my sister over to another family's home for dinner. We were all close friends—my father was a commercial illustrator and his friend Greg Booth was, at the time, one of the most successful photographers in the commercial world. He spent about 250 days out of the year traveling the world to exotic photoshoots. He also owned a studio in Dallas that employed six other photographers who did product and magazine work while he was on the road. His wife, Carol, oversaw the studio. They were great people and had two kids that were much younger than me. My sister and their daughter Christi are still close to this day.

They had a beautiful home filled with amazing art: African sculptures, an amazing wall of masks collected from various places, and a ton of black and white photographs.

Now, at the age of eight, I knew nothing about photography. But I remember "discovering" this one photograph near the living room of a man sitting at a piano. It was black and white,, and I remember being drawn to several features of the image. The piano was largely cropped, revealing only the lid. I remember finding it interesting that you could identify an object by only a portion of it being revealed. The other thing I found fascinating is that I assumed the man in the portrait was a musician. He was sitting at the piano, but he wasn't playing it, so maybe he was a composer or even a conductor.

I loved that photograph and would seek it out any time we were at the Booth's home. It sparked my interest in photography, and a few years later, for my birthday, my parents gave me my first Kodak 110 pocket camera.

Of course, this was the famous 1946 portrait of Igor Stravinsky sitting at the piano, by the great Arnold Newman.

That image is a classic example of Arnold Newman's environmental portraits. It also contains many of the concepts and ideas that I'll be sharing with you in this book. But most importantly, that image made me realize that a photograph is more than just a cool picture to look at. I understood that the man in the photograph was a composer. I had no idea who Stravinsky was at that time. Newman's photograph had communicated something.

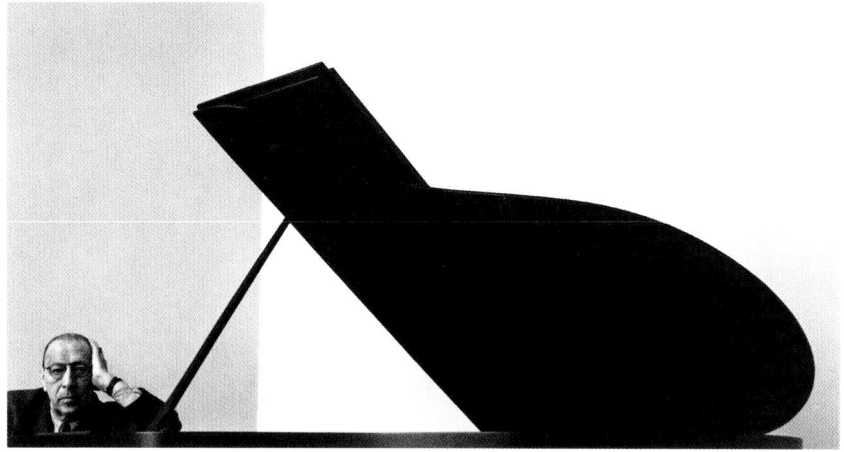

Portrait of Russian composer Igor Stravinsky, December 1, 1946, in New York City.
(Photo by Arnold Newman Properties/Getty Images).

This was the moment I was introduced to the concept of visual communication.

Another fascinating thing about this piece (the final print is cropped from the 4x5 negative) is that it made me realize that photography is a subtractive process. Most art forms are additive. In other words, the artist begins with a blank canvas and adds all of the elements. Photography uses a camera to capture what exists in front of it. You can see this with the Stravinsky example—it's about taking elements away until the composition works. In the case of this image, it's just about as perfect as you can get.

The history of photography contains many styles and genres. Certainly, some lend more control over the "canvas" than others. For example, still life images, or even portraits, are typically controlled. The photographer can place elements in the frame. But even as you can see in the Stravinsky example, it's still about refining what's excluded from the picture to enhance what *is* the picture.

In more improvisational types of photography, such as photojournalism, street photography, and even sports photography, the photographer has very little control of the scene unfolding in front of the camera. The act of photography becomes more of, as the great Henri Cartier-Bresson called it, the Decisive Moment. The photographer must be aware of not only where things are but the moment the picture will be made. Photography, in the improvisational sense, is about understanding not only the current moment but also an anticipation of what might happen in the next. Photography is part arranging and part psychic.

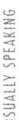

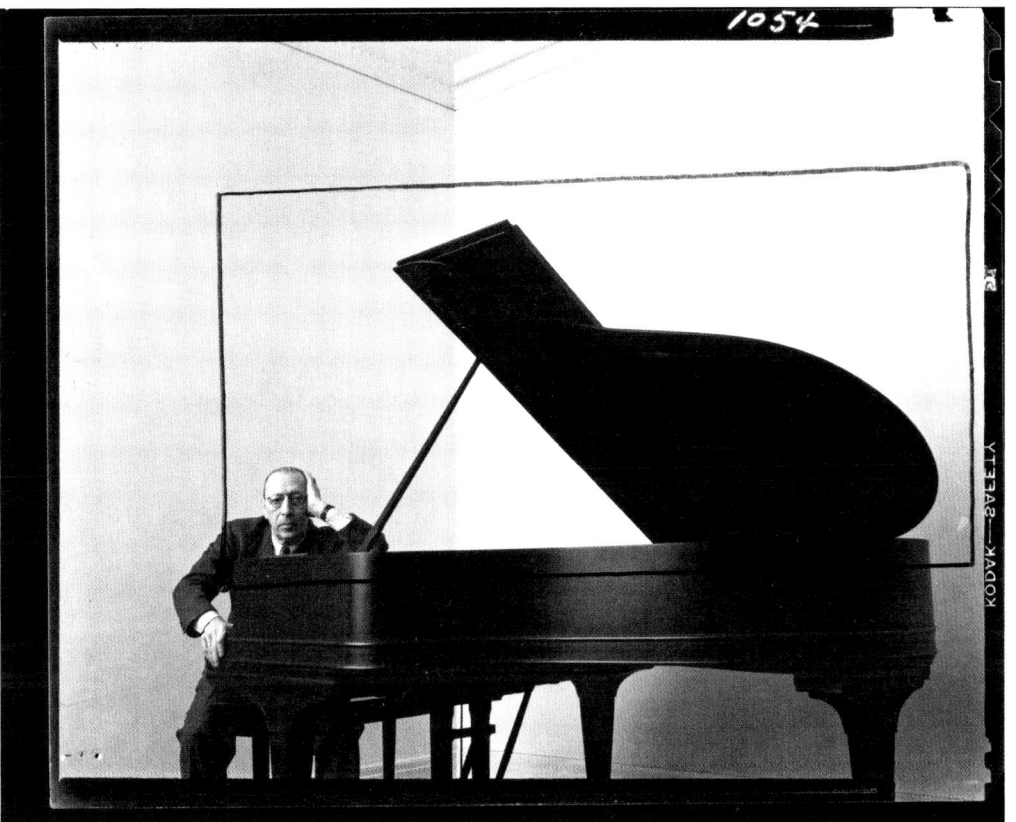

Portrait of Igor Stravinsky as he sits at a piano with editing marks on the image. (Photo by Arnold Newman Properties/Getty Images).

Photography is three dimensions being shown in a two dimensional space. Prints and digital screens are flat, so this leaves us with height and width. The human brain will register depth when viewing a picture, but there are ways to accentuate this, such as leading lines, shadow, proportion, lighting, and many other compositional techniques included in this book.

Photography is about showing, but it can also be about not showing. How many times have you looked at a family photo of someone you know? Everyone is smiling and looking perfect, and you know it was during a time when the marriage was falling apart and one of the kids was dealing with substance abuse. I know that's outrageously dark, and I made up that example, but it's not off base. In fact, I've seen versions of that. The photograph by nature allows a space where things can exist outside of reality, but could it also imply an external reality by what the photographer decides to show?

This is where we begin to understand the power of visual communication. Knowing that, we can also clearly see the irony of photography as evidence. The photograph is just seeing what the lens captures, so it must be true, right? I'd like to think the reader understands that photographs can be manipulated without ever being opened in Photoshop. Moments, facial expressions, even cropping and lighting, can start removing an image from what's real. It becomes an interpretation.

I firmly believe that all photography is interpreted to one degree or another. The idea that photography represents reality and must be true belongs to the early days of the camera in the 1830s and 1840s. This is what makes me really appreciate great photojournalists—because they constantly walk this line.

I think what I love the most about photography in my journey at this point is that it's about everything I've mentioned here. It's about the reveal, the logic, the interpretation, the challenge, the arrangement, the composition, the subtractive process, and it's about what's being shown as well as the possibility of what's not.

Photography can sell shoes, show you what's happening across the world, or make you think. It can record our memories, commemorate our loved ones, freeze time in our, or even provide a facade.

Photography is visual communication.

THE ROLE OF CAMERAS AND LENSES

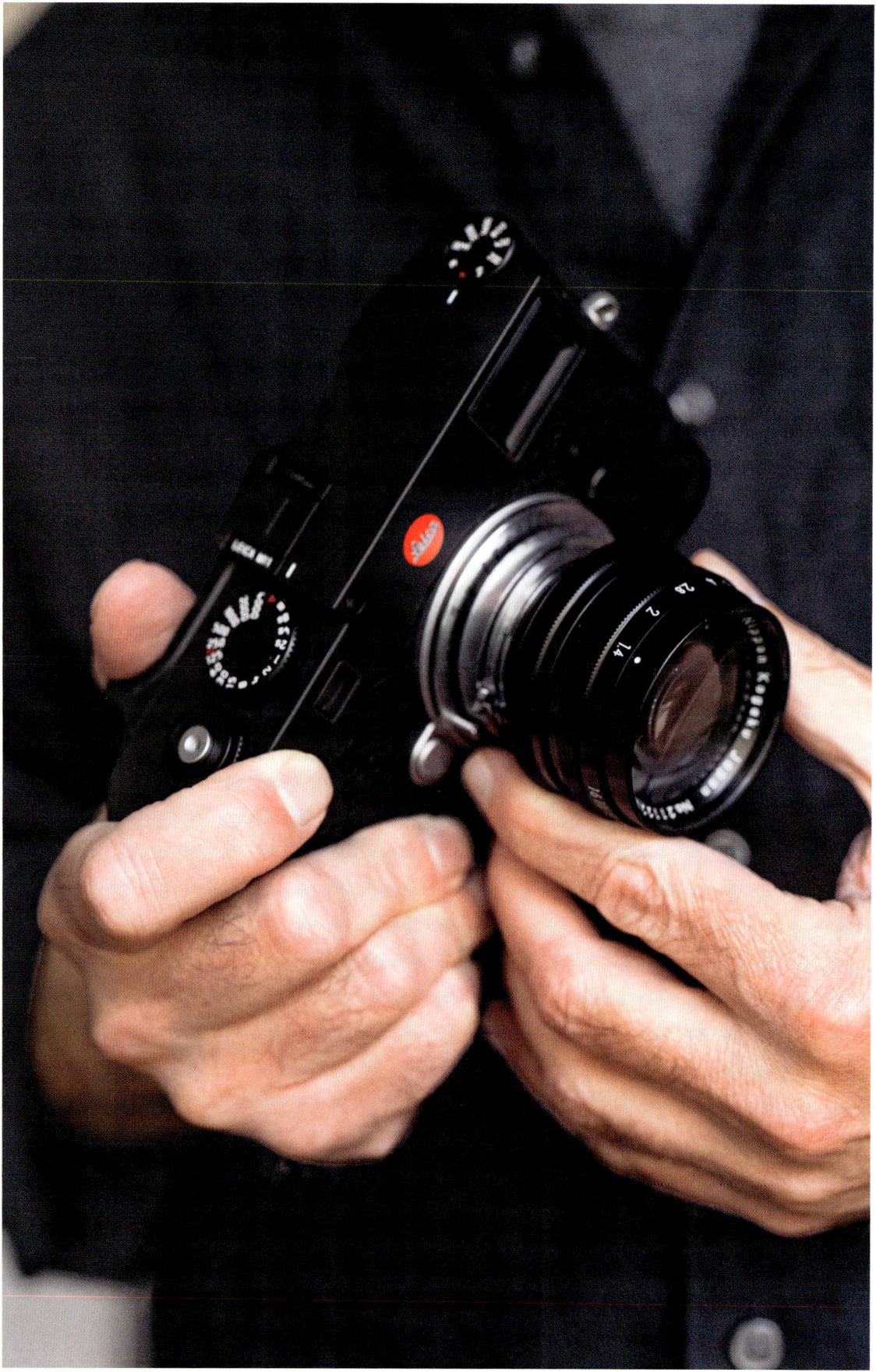

CAMERAS AND LENSES MUST BE discussed in the context of photography, as they are the tools we use. But my views go a little bit against the grain from the modern conversation of the digital era.

If you're reading this book, chances are that you have some kind of camera and some kind of lens—even if it is your smartphone. I'm also guessing you've taken some photographs. My goal here is to show you the possibilities of photographing with any equipment—especially what you've already got. Having said that, this next section is surprisingly controversial to some.

Your Gear Doesn't Matter

Once, during a trip to Germany, I had an amazing opportunity to meet Peter Karbe. Peter is the head of the lens department at Leica and is one of the most brilliant optical designers alive today. He designed the famous 50mm f/1.4 Summilux-M ASPH, the 50mm f/0.95 Noctilux-M, and countless other high-end, modern designs. He's in a rare position, working for a company that gives him design credit (Leica is the only company that does this), and he's often the voice of Leica in marketing videos and presentations. Leica refers to him as "the non-quantifiable human element." I was somewhat nervous to meet Peter, as I have a tremendous amount of respect for him. I've followed his work for a long time and his 50mm Summilux is one of my favorite lenses ever. Peter was a photographer before he became an optics designer and has an understanding of both the visual aesthetic and the complex math that governs the optical formula to create it.

When we met he came right out and told me he had seen a few of my videos on lens design and that I had "most of it correct." Then he went on to explain a few physics-related details where I was slightly off.

Then he paused, put his hand up, and with a large smile said, "There is one thing I absolutely agree with you on though. The best lens is the lens that works for you."

Think about that. This is the man who designed a $13,000 50mm Noctilux and he's the first one to say that what's really important is finding what works for you. I started my photography journey on thrift store cameras and learning how to develop film. I had challenging equipment, but when I got something to work, I felt a sense of accomplishment because I realized that I am greater than the equipment I'm using. If you have an idea, there's a way to realize it no matter how bad the tools are that you are using. You just have to think openly and figure it out. It's problem-solving. The tools exist to serve you, even if they take a little bit of creative management.

Here is where this book goes against the grain of 90 percent of the photography industry today. I'm going to get very real with you and put this bluntly: gear doesn't matter.

I could just end the chapter here.

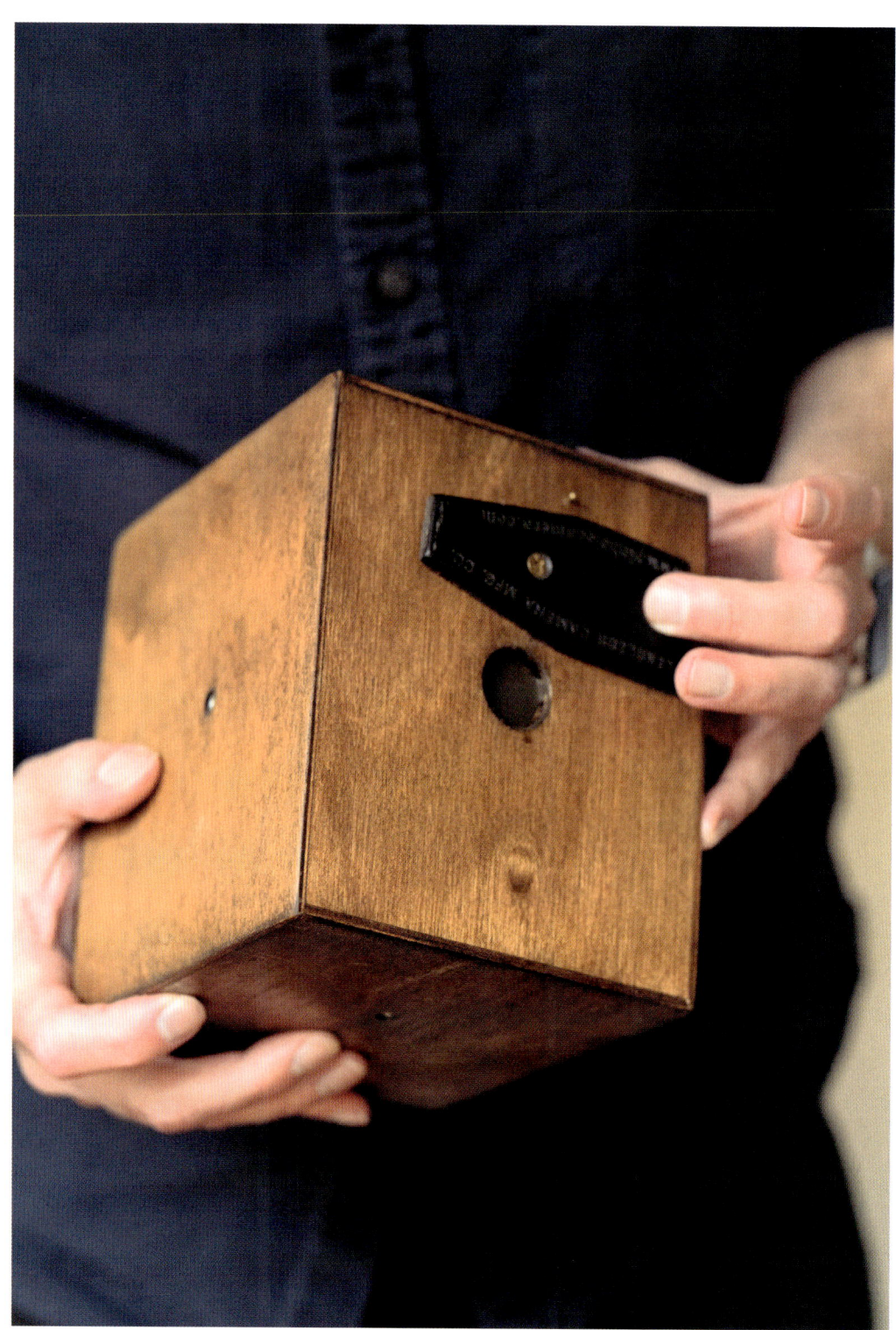

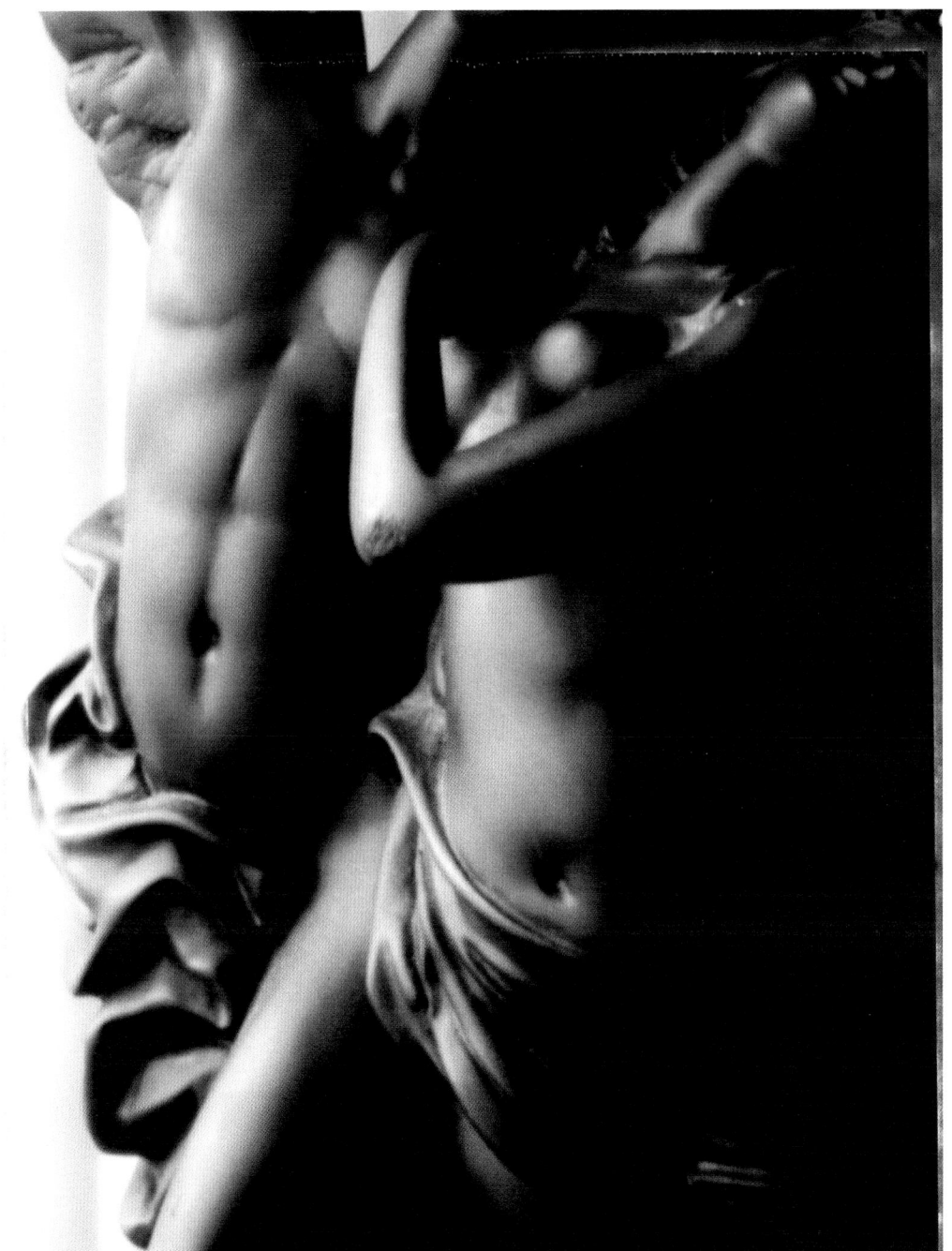

There isn't much technology in a pinhole camera. It's a dark box with a small "pinhole" aperture which projects light to the back side of the box. This camera accepts 4x5 sheet film. Exposures are typically long with an f-stop of around f/256 or so.

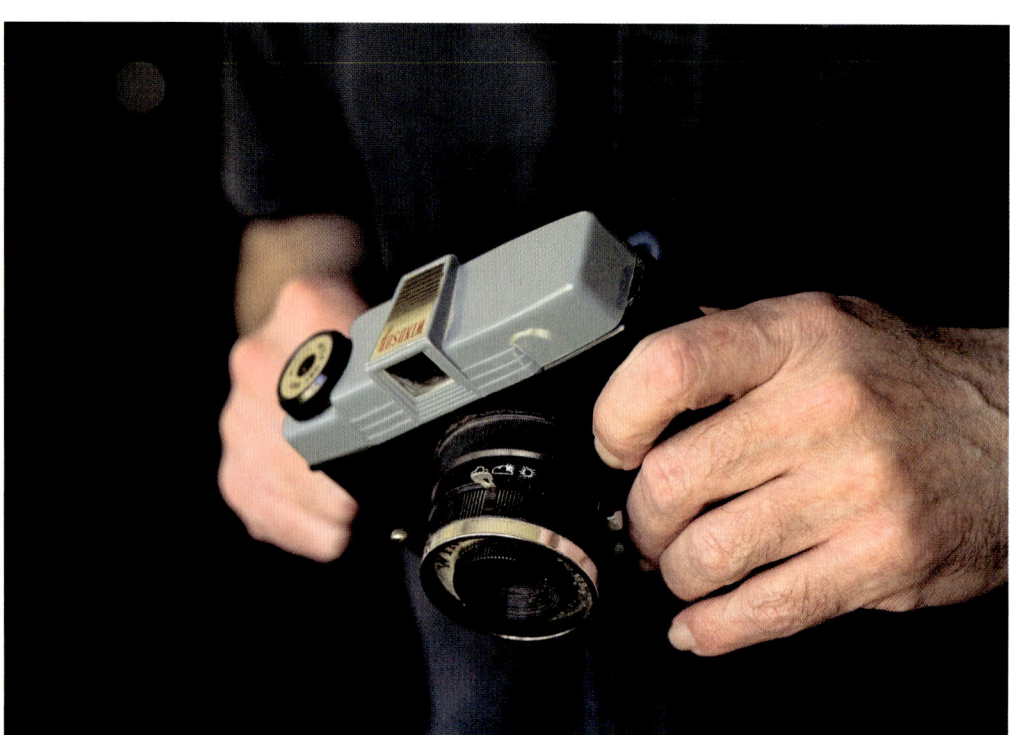

This is a small plastic camera often referred to as a "Diana." These cameras were made in Hong Kong in the 1960s and sold as inexpensive novelties. The lens is a single element meniscus lens made out of plastic. Most of these green plastic cameras say Diana on the nameplate—but there are variants. This one uses "Windsor" as its logo.

Since there is such poor optical correction in the lens, the images produced are soft focus with a somewhat dream like quality to them.

These cameras had no production consistency either, so each one has a slightly different "look". I ended up owning five of these for that very reason. The "Windsor" is my favorite.

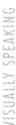

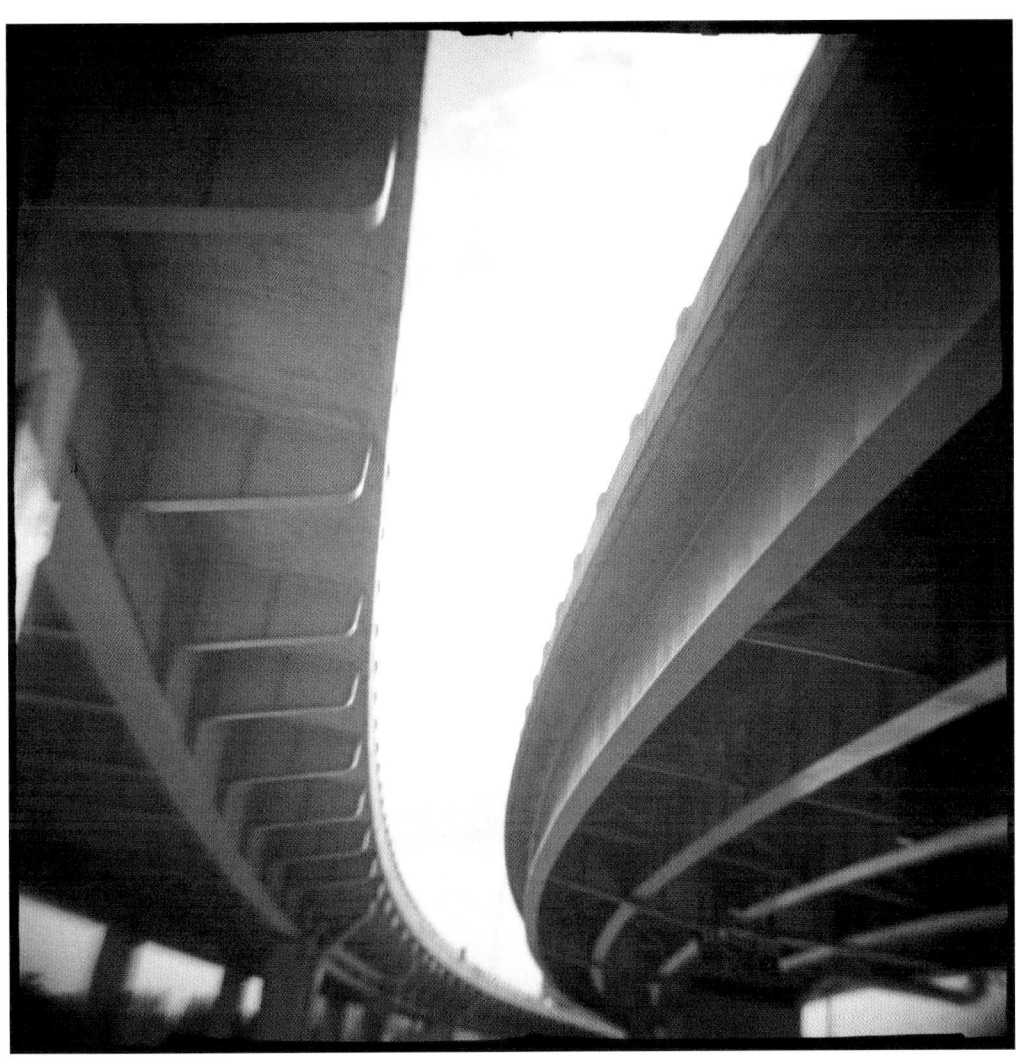

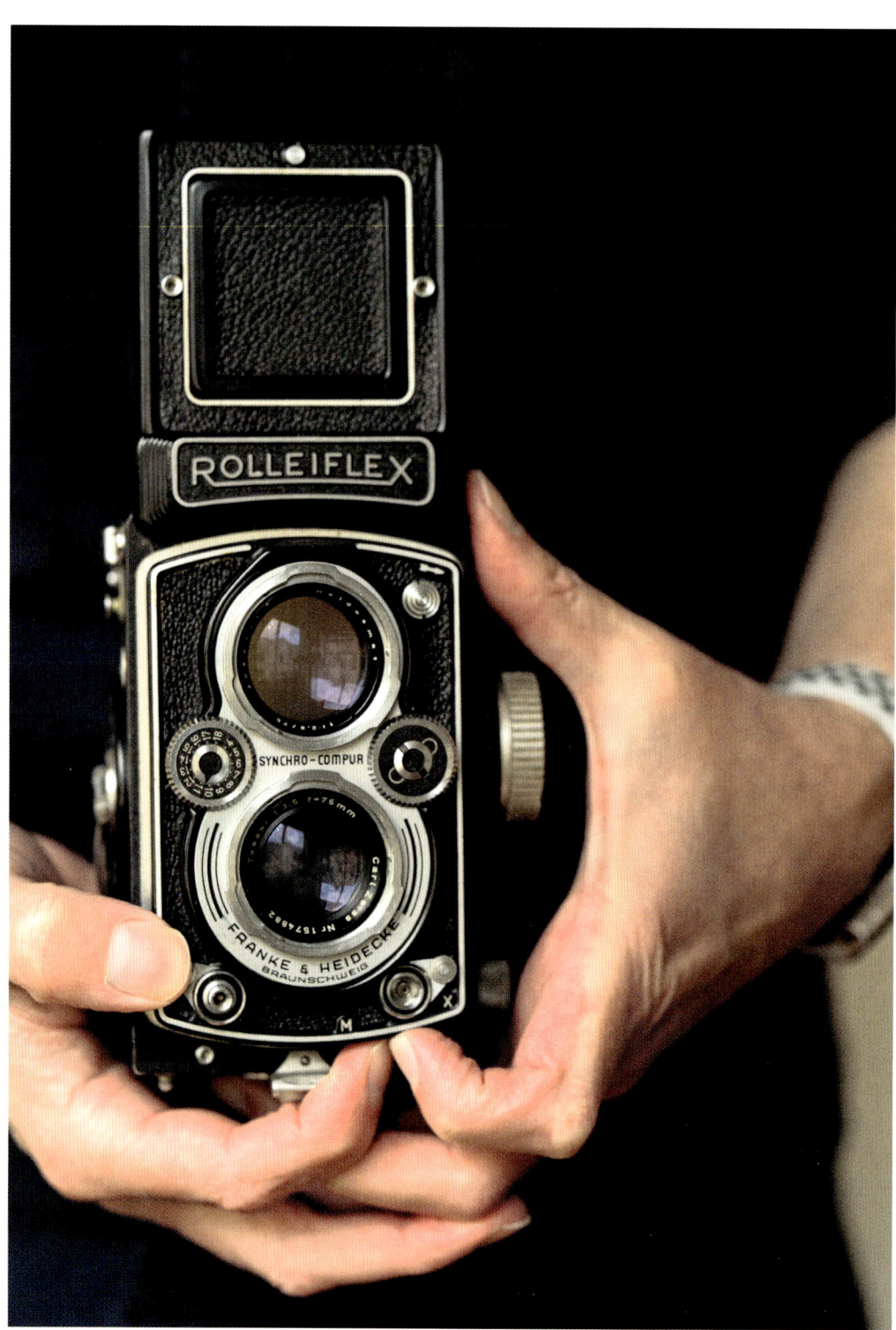

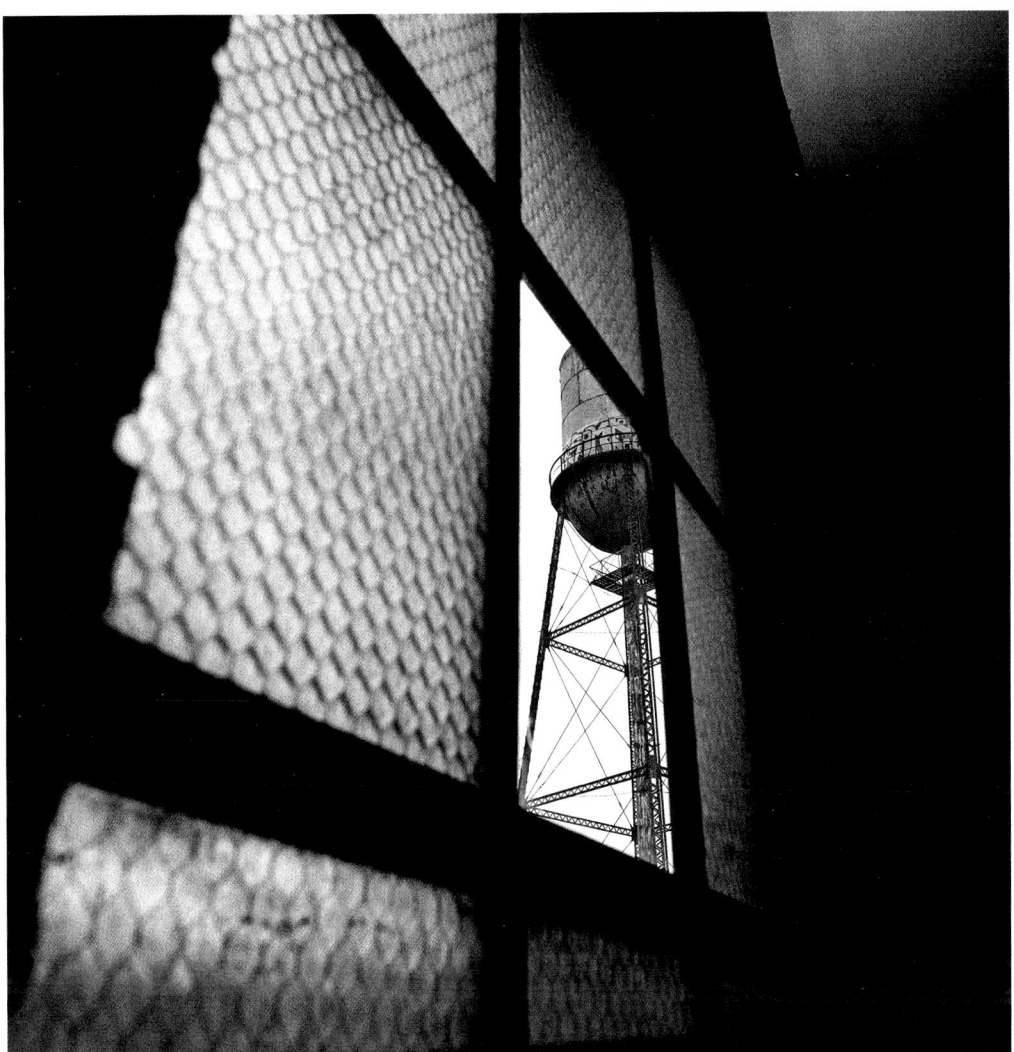

The Rolleiflex MX-EVS is in many ways the opposite of the cheaper toy cameras, as these cameras were developed for precision and optical performance. These cameras use a Twin Lens Reflex or TLR design. The top lens is used to frame the composition and achieve focus while the bottom lens is a higher-quality variant that projects the image onto the film. This particular model is the MX-EVS, which features a locking "Exposure Value System." This was not Rolleiflex's top of the line by any stretch, but it was one I could afford. They were produced between 1954 and 1956, and for me this was the gateway to a higher quality camera on a budget.

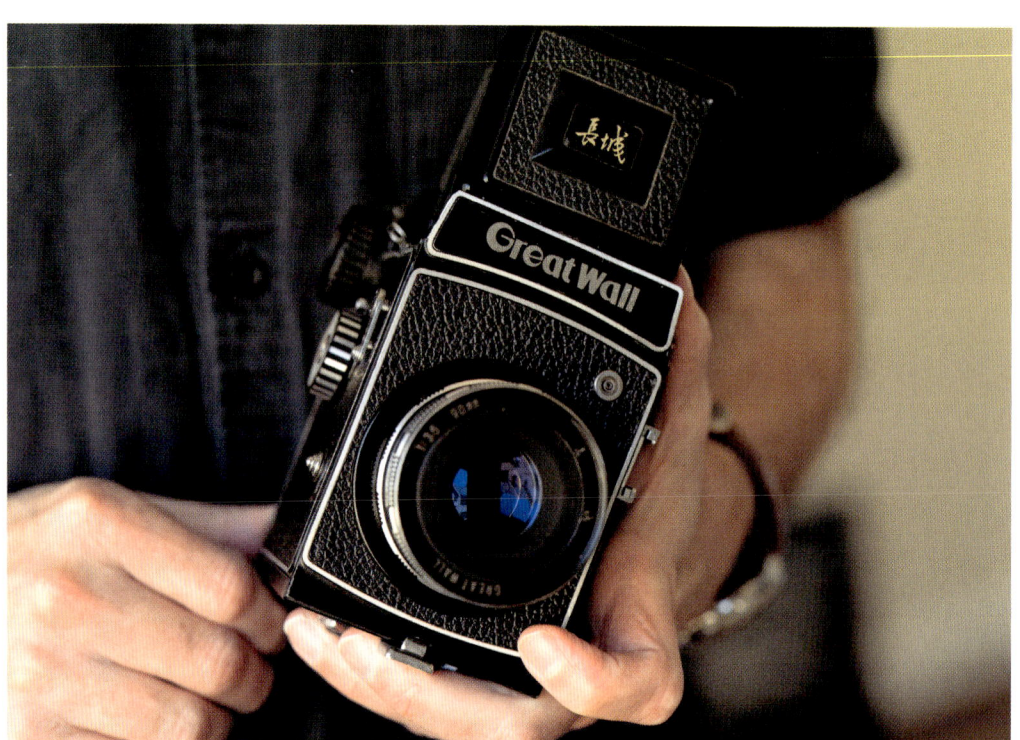

Great Wall was a Chinese manufacturer in the 1980s that made about four different models of medium-format cameras. I fell in love with this camera, as it lived somewhere between the Rolleiflex and the cheaper plastic cameras I loved using.

The lens is removable, though to my knowledge Great Wall only made this one lens. I've read theories that it was repurposed from a print enlarger.

I actually incorporated the removable lens into my own technique. I would unscrew the lens and tilt it to "throw" the focus off of the film plane in order to get a selective focus. Note the windows on the side are in focus, but the rest of this image is not. This is not possible with the lens mounted flush to the camera at this distance.

The Great Wall is poorly made and it tends to fall apart. But it is one of my favorite cameras ever made. You have to earn your images, but when they come together the results are very unique.

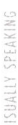

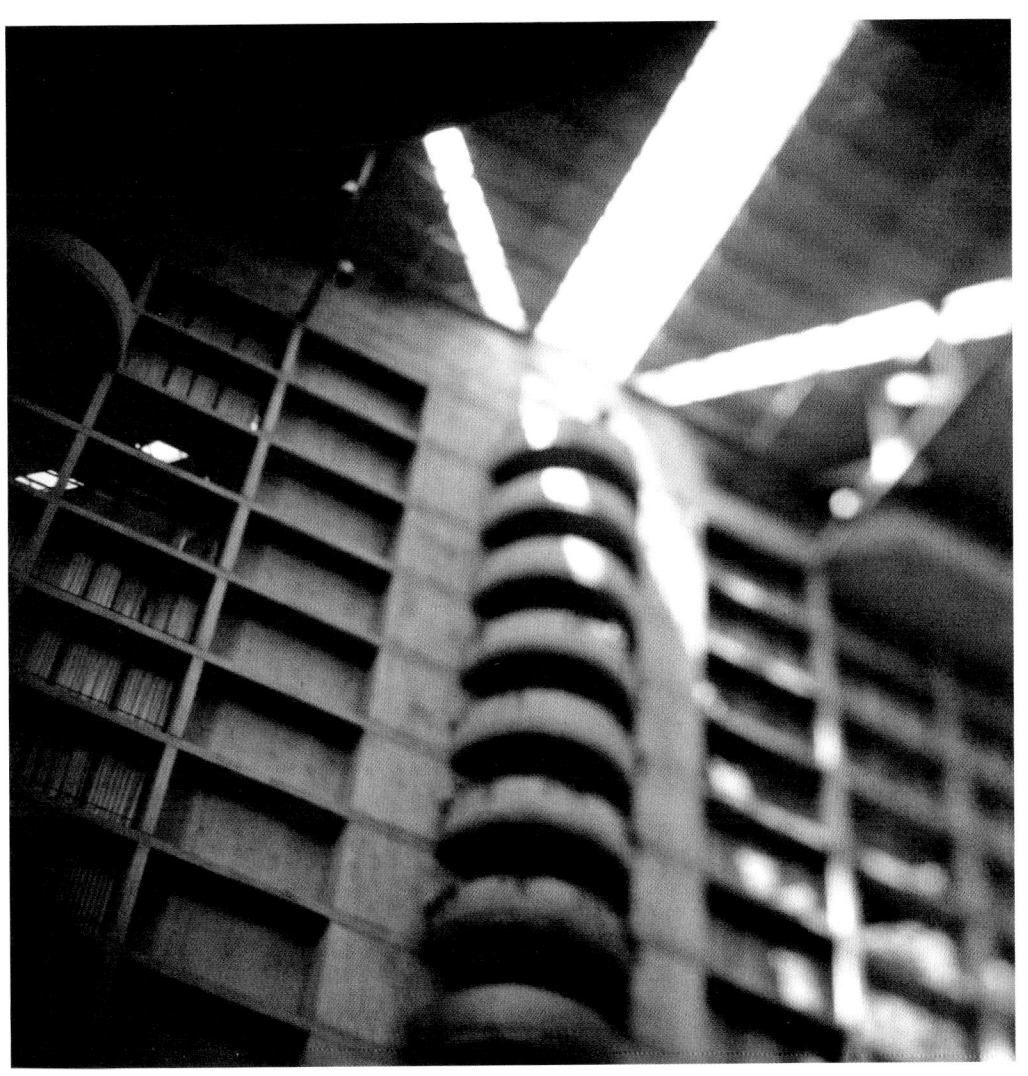

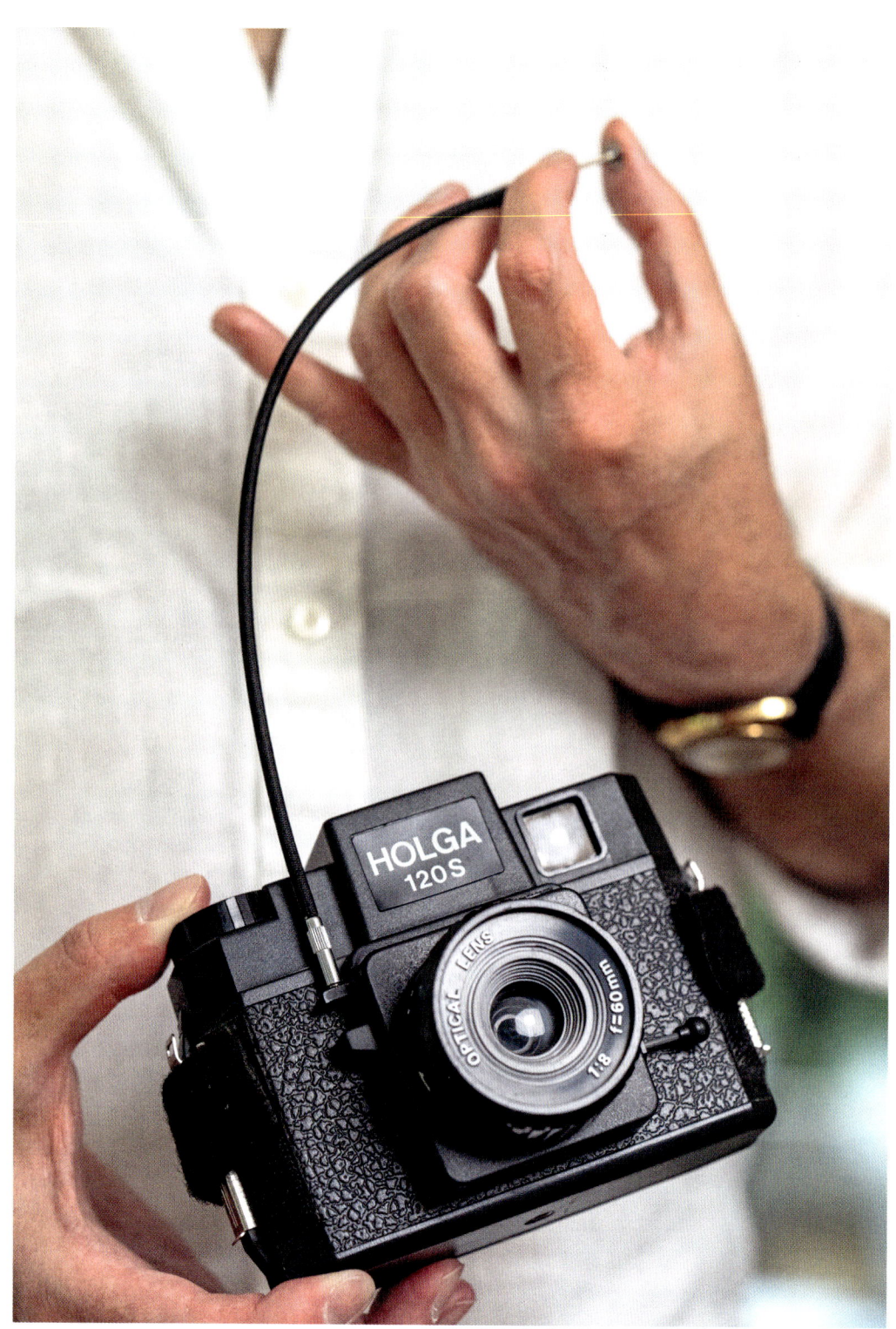

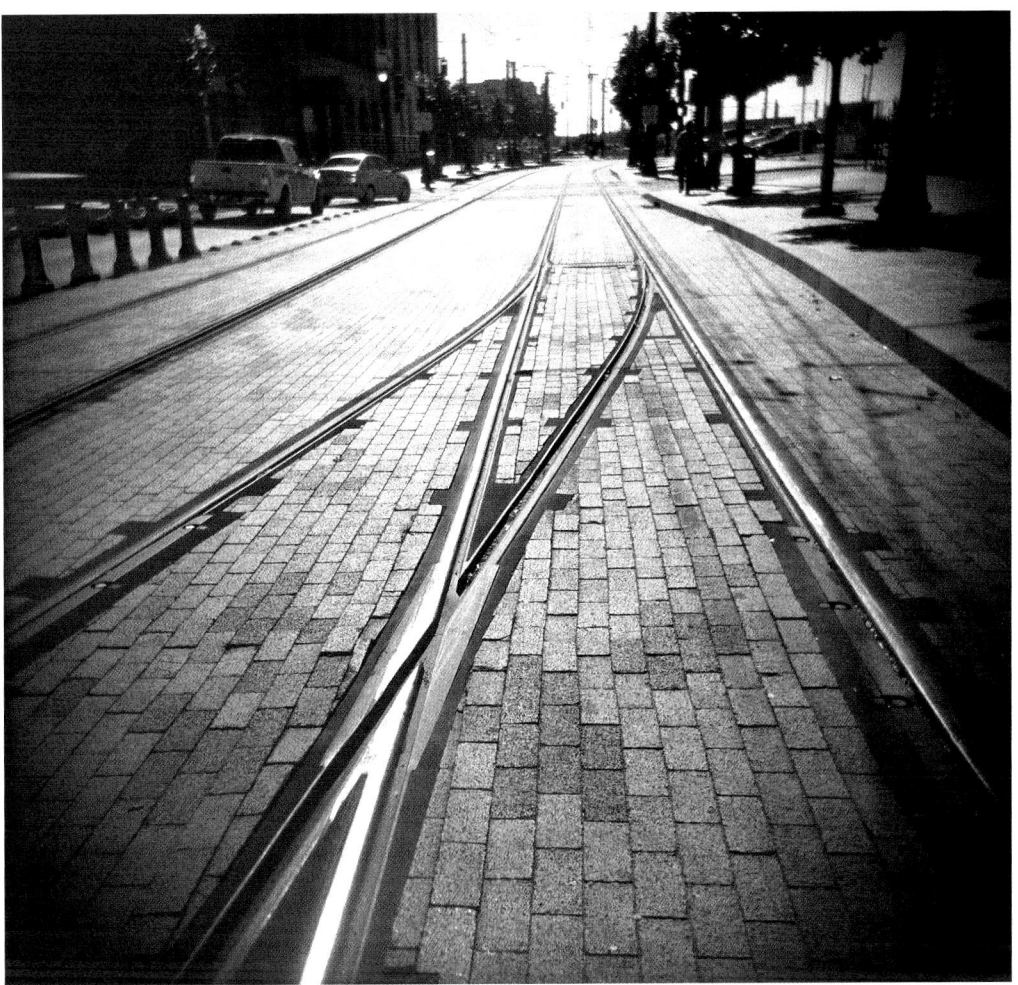

I would be remiss if I didn't mention the Holga. For many strange reasons this is one of my favorite cameras in the history of photography. I love it because it's cheap, surprisingly well made, and easy to use. It also locks you into one aperture, one shutter speed, and one ISO setting. You have to work within some very tight creative parameters.

The Holga is about problem-solving. You'll likely end up modifying it to give you another limiting option or two. In fact, this camera is one I bought from Randy Smith, who runs Holgamods out of his garage. This one enables a cable shutter release, bulb setting, a second aperture, and a tripod socket.

Using the Holga not only makes you understand the fundamentals of exposure but forces you into a small set of possibilities. Boundaries take away options, but they also force creativity. I still recommend the Holga to every beginner student.

Cameras and lenses are tools. Unless you're making photograms, photography is made with some kind of camera and some kind of lens. The tools are required.

If you want to shoot sports, a wide-angle won't work. Or will it? If you're willing to change your approach and vantage point, I would argue it will. That may be a bit extreme, but it's true. It's not ideal, but it's always about problem-solving.

At the time I'm writing this, the photo industry comprises five multibillion dollar companies based in Japan (Sony, Nikon, Canon, Panasonic, and Fujifilm) as well as some smaller ones (Cosina and Nittoh come to mind). There are three major European camera companies (Leica, Hasselblad, and Phase One), and in the last two years China has entered the market (DJI, Laowa, TTArtisan, and others). There is one major imaging software company and one camera company based in the United States (Adobe and GoPro).

Literally billions of dollars go into research and design every year for digital products and software. As smartphones have become standard for the photography needs of most people, product sales have begun to slow down for the dedicated camera companies. This has led to an extremely aggressive marketing push that tries to convince photographers that they need to buy more stuff.

Now I'm not saying these companies don't make great products—they do. Cameras and lenses today provide more value and are of a higher quality than at any point in history. In most cases they are truly outstanding. But

this has created a massively obsessive culture based around these tools that do nothing for photography as an art form. It's more about conformity and getting locked into a product line.

I say this because I know firsthand. I'm interested in lenses so I go online to research. Before I know it, I've gone down a rabbit hole and I'm reading page fifteen of some forum thread watching adults argue over the rendering of "out of focus" areas of two different 50mm f/1.2 lenses. Then I find myself reading countless lens reviews by people who don't understand optics very well. Then I see the accompanying "test shots" of grass, leaves, and a few mediocre portraits of the author's girlfriend showing off the subtle uniqueness of the bokeh. I've spent valuable time that I could have spent doing other things, like taking pictures. It's even more absurd because I already own a decent 50mm f/1.2 lens!

You can find deep discussions over the merits of backside illuminated sensor technology and image processors. One can argue that if you really need a 100-megapixel sensor, the only downside is that it won't let you shoot burst rate speeds of twenty frames per second.

Many of you know I also have a YouTube channel and I've covered all of these things. It's the conversation that's going on all the time in the modern era. And sure, it might be interesting to a degree, but it has nothing to do with making photographs. For example, I love what Sony has done with mirrorless. I've even worked with Sony on multiple occasions. Their cameras are impressive. But let's be honest. The number of people who would require autofocus and shooting speeds of twenty frames per second is ridiculously small, yet Sony will try and convince everyone that it is a necessary feature.

When I was starting to get really serious about photography I didn't have a lot of money. I couldn't afford to buy nice equipment. Out of necessity, I learned to get results with what I had—I didn't wait. The picture was all that mattered. I shot and learned how to develop my own film to keep costs down. I bought my books cheaply at the used bookstore or borrowed them from the library. I learned how to compose. I learned how to light. I was doing a lot of still life work at that time and I remember needing a macro lens. I couldn't afford one so I would do things like turn the lens backwards and hold it in place—it becomes a macro and works great. I remember taping close-up filters to a lens because they were the wrong thread size. I was shooting medium format, but I couldn't afford a Hasselblad; I had a Holga that cost me $15. For 35mm I used Russian Leica knockoffs and they would break. They were loud. With my Kiev 88 I had to learn that shutter slap would blur my images so I needed a workaround. Longer exposure was the answer.

The point is, I learned from my limitations. It was pretty slack, but I have work from that period that I'm still proud of. Sometimes limitations of materials and tools provide the best way to find out what you're really capable of. As a result, I'm very confident today that I can get interesting pictures using anything. You can too.

I'm not saying this is the only way you'll learn. I'm just saying don't be afraid to find solutions within your budget, even if your budget is embarrassingly small. You'll be less embarrassed when you get results you're proud of because you created the solution. If you can afford the best, then go for it. If you can't, use what you've got. Just never think that any camera or lens is going to improve your work in any way. These tools might make things more convenient, but they don't replace thought and reason.

I spent the early part of my career working for a major art museum. I never once heard any visitor in the galleries ask what lens, camera, film, brush, paint, canvas, or any other brand detail a photographer or painter used to create a work of art. In the end, the final piece is all that matters—not the brand of gear you use.

CHAPTER 4

UNDERSTANDING YOUR
OWN WORK

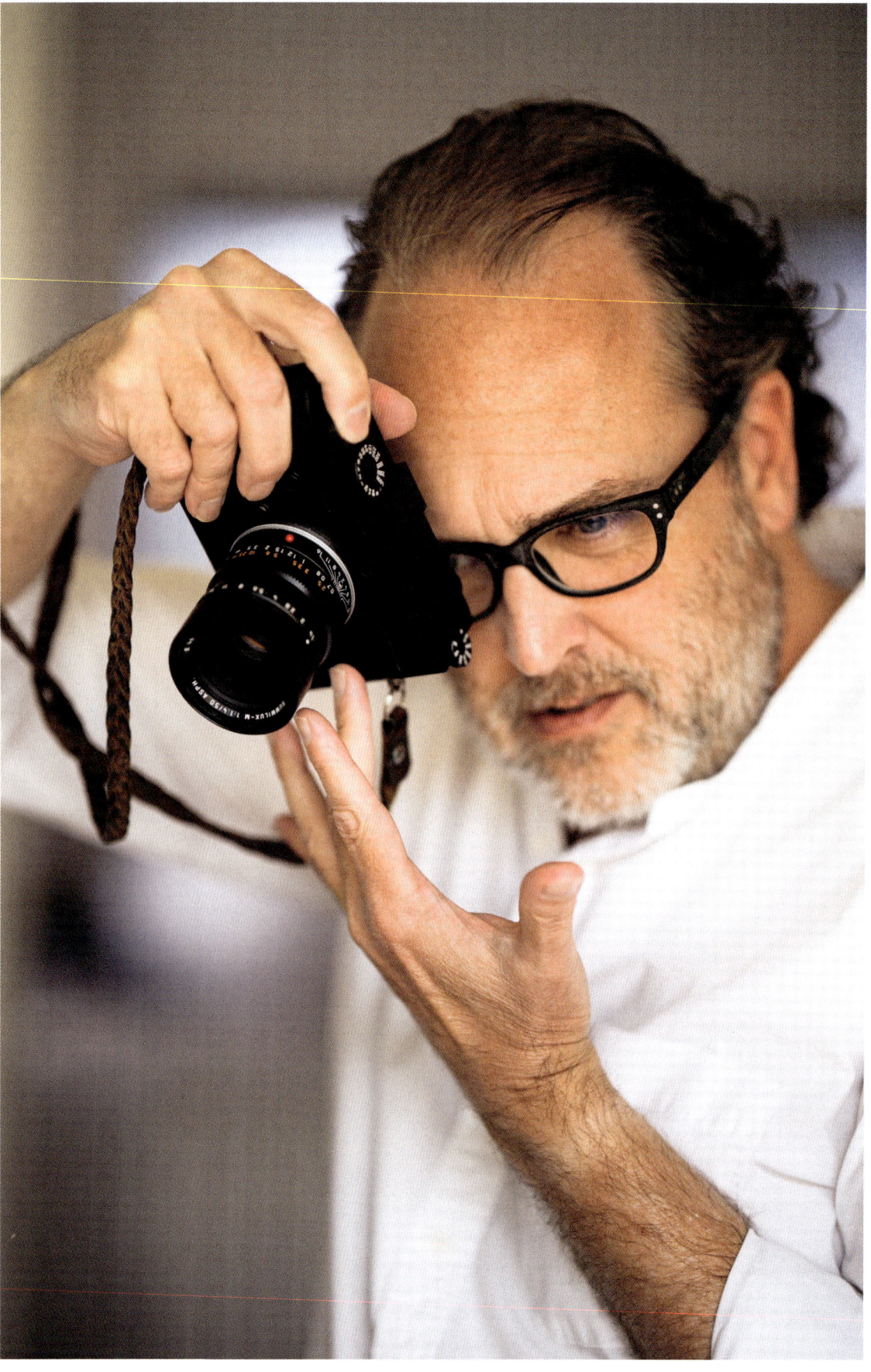

THERE ARE THREE BASIC CONCEPTS you will need to embrace in order to master photography as a creative endeavor.

Photography Is a Practice

The first key to successful learning in any field is the development of a practice. Information, like what you are reading now, is just that—it's only the information. Yes, that is learning, but in order to actually incorporate any of this into your own work requires establishing a practice. This is the key disconnect for most people.

Photography is an iterative process. In other words, there's a lot of repetition required to make certain concepts second nature, just like a spoken language.

You may have noticed there are certain people who are always the exception to formal education. There are many throughout history—the artists with no formal training who are amazingly skilled and talented. Albert Einstein failed his college entrance exam. Jimi Hendrix never learned theory or how to read music. Every field has an unexplained genius that seems to defy the odds of explaining their own talent. But the difference is they understand the language they're working in. They have a practice they're dedicated to. They might not know the formal terms, but they've worked hard at speaking the language.

Unfortunately, this is not something I can give you through this book. I can explain my ideas, concepts, and approach to photography, but to have any impact on your own work, you're going to have to take this information and practice. And practice a lot. This also requires patience.

Looking at Your Own Work

The second key to improving your skills is developing the ability to be objective with your own work. I went for years never really knowing what this meant. I spent an enormous amount of time looking at great photography by the masters I look up to. I would constantly try to discover artists I'd never seen before. I had a clear definition in my head of the language and what the best work is. But I had a major disconnect in that I wasn't objectively looking at my own work.

When I started studying with Ralph Gibson, he brought this to my attention early on. We would look at my photographs and he'd ask me to explain why certain decisions had been made. In many cases they were not decisions at all, just accidents with the camera. This could be the image as a whole, or it could be smaller elements in the image that I had not paid attention to. Ralph finally said to me, "You know how all of this works, but you need to start spending time looking at your own work and asking these things."

He was right. As soon as I started putting the time into looking at my own work, my photographs profoundly changed, and quickly. I stopped wasting my time trying to get things to work that were never going to work. I started pushing new ideas in my head into my own work. I began to make connections between geometrical ideas, framing, and what the photograph was trying to say. I began to see conceptually. Seeing quickly became part of the practice that I'd already been committed to for years. To you this might seem obvious, but it was the missing link for me on a personal level.

The Danger of Subjectivity

Finally, I want to pass to you a word of caution. I often review portfolios or give advice to photographers who come to me. Commonly there is a problem of photographers being too close to their work (I had it too when I was starting out). We remember a mood, a relationship, a time, or a place—things that affect how we view the work we've made. It's the backstory that we know, the nostalgia that defines our relationship with the pictures we make. This is beautiful, but the problem I often see is that the viewer doesn't see anything but the finished photograph. There is no connection the viewer has to the backstory, therefore the picture doesn't successfully communicate. None of the important information was expressed in the photograph.

It's very difficult to remove ourselves emotionally from our own work, but this is an extremely important skill you will have to learn. It helps to have someone to help you "edit" a body of work—someone whose feedback you trust, whether it's something you want to hear or something you don't want to hear.

So now that you understand these three basic concepts, let's begin to understand how we need to approach photography.

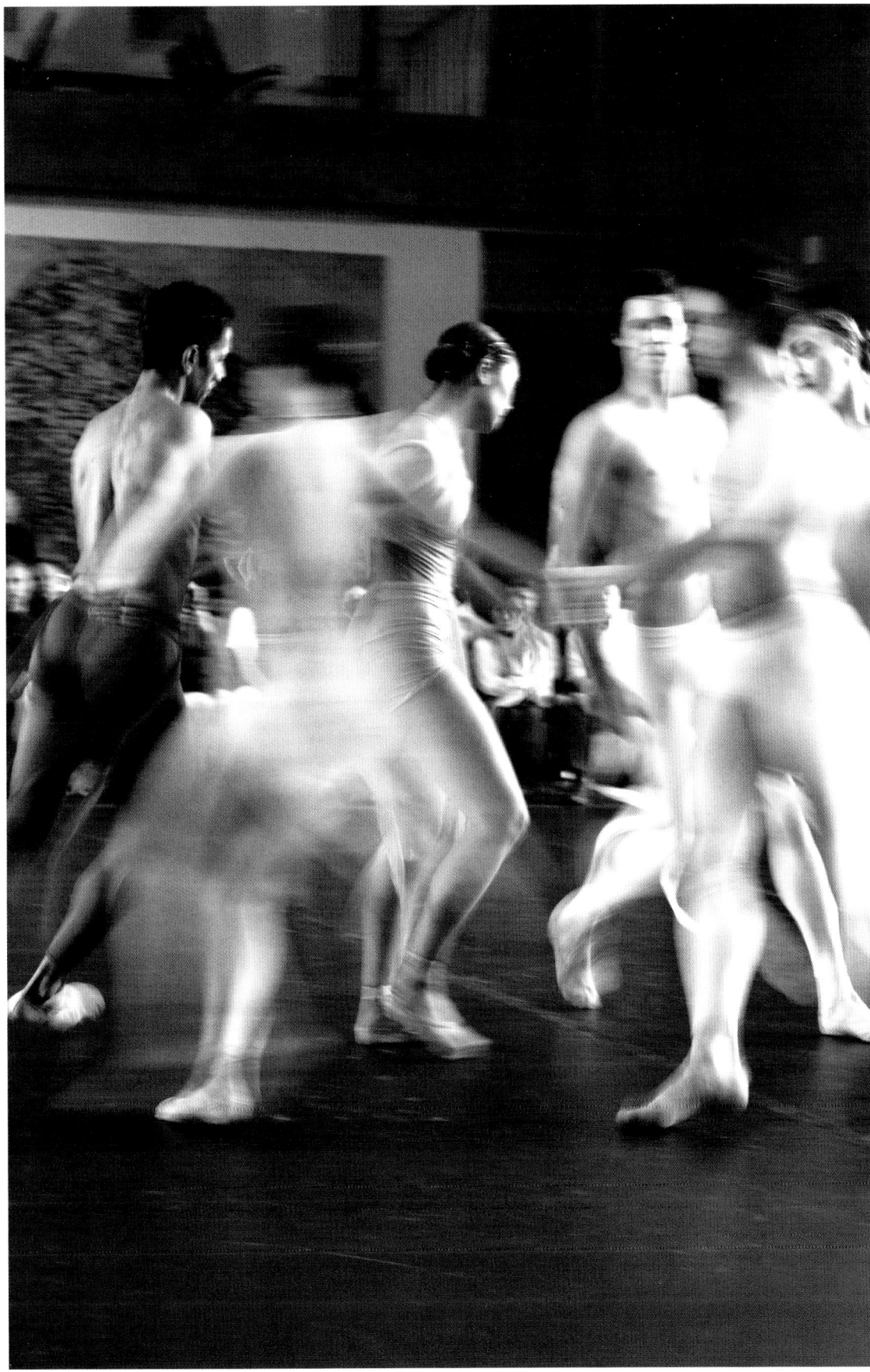

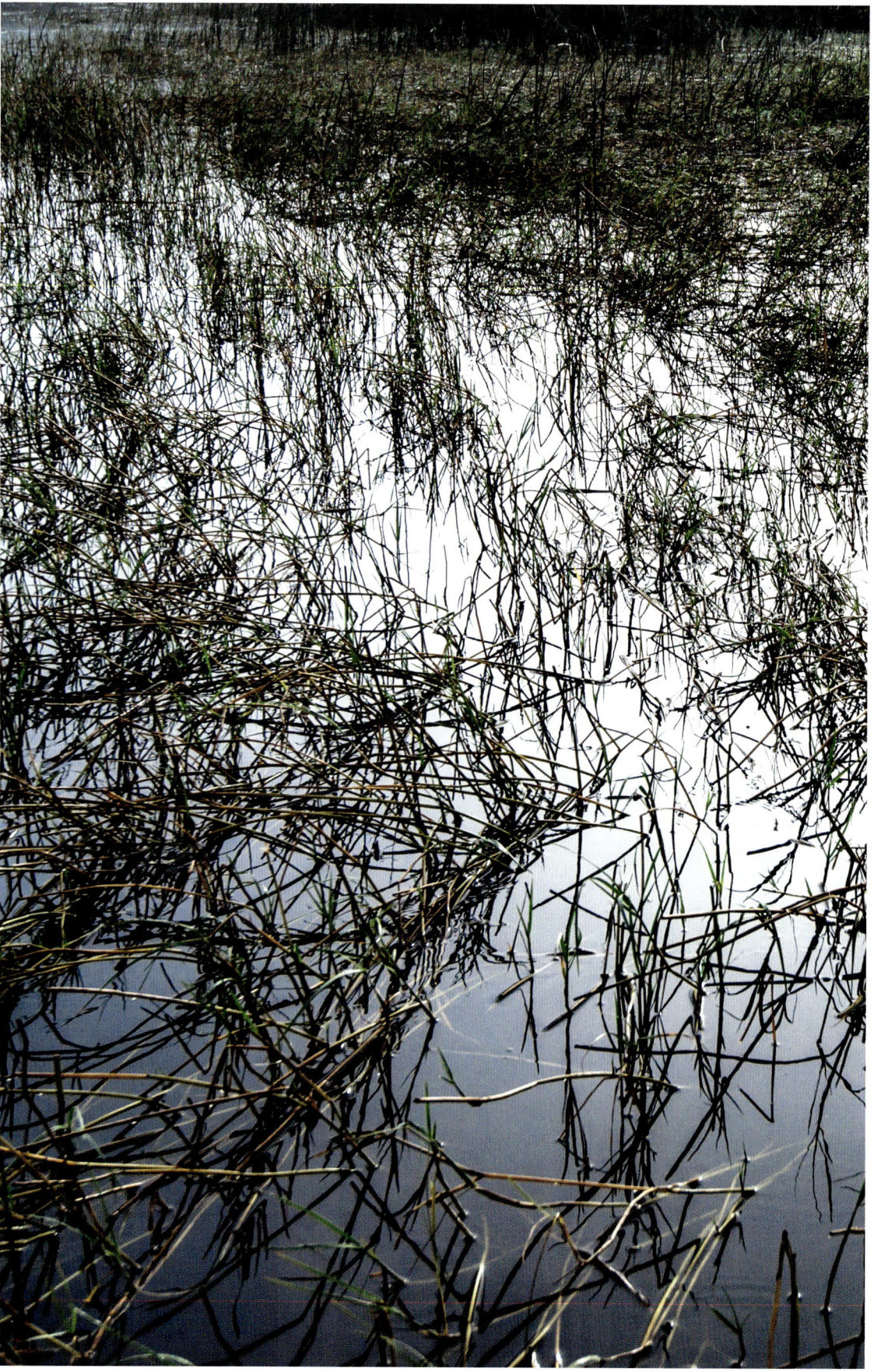

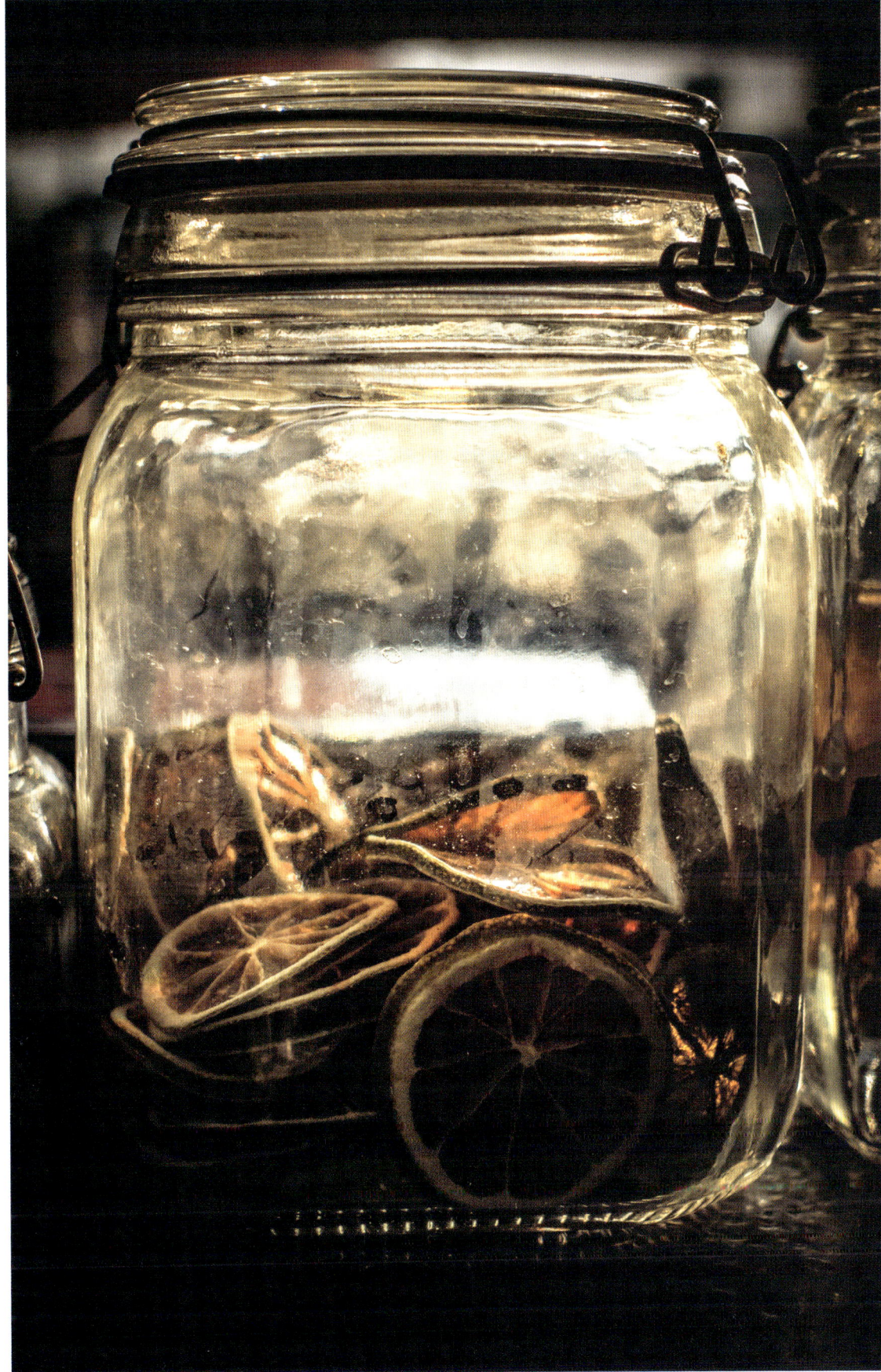

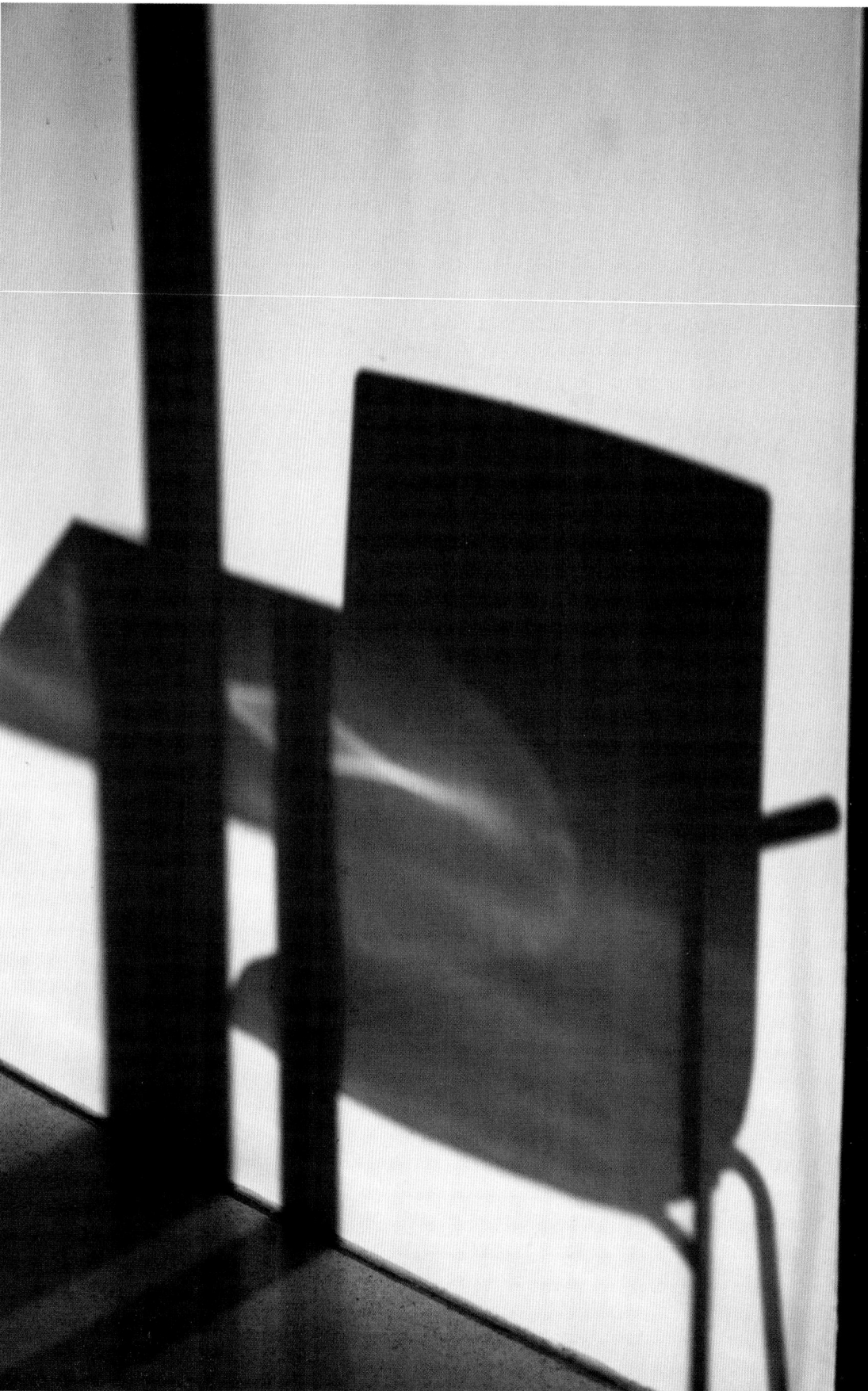

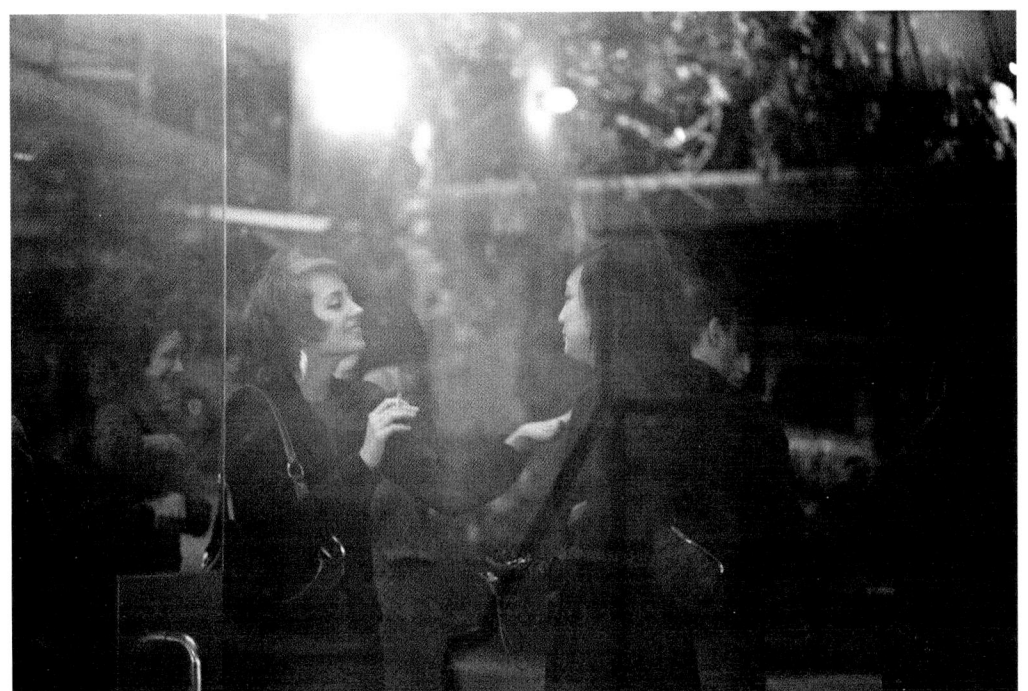

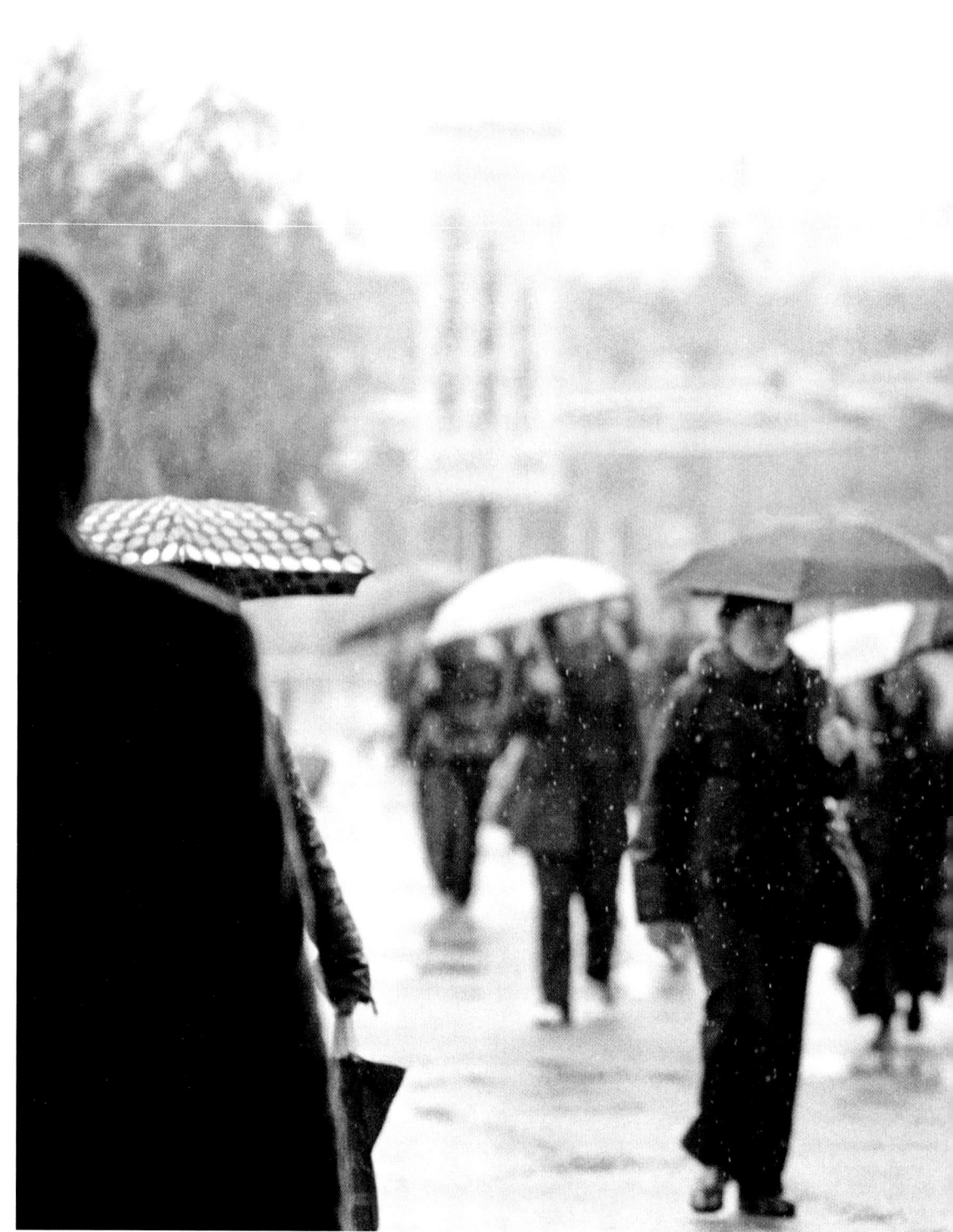

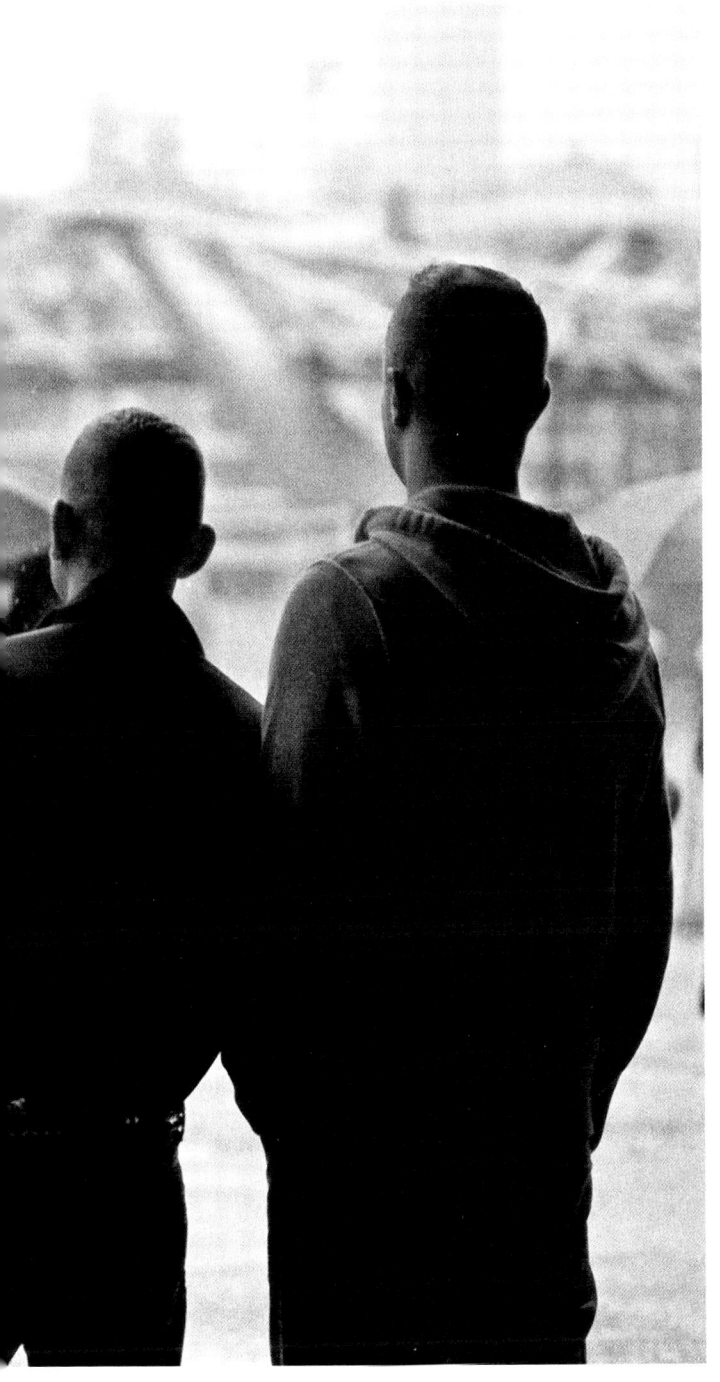

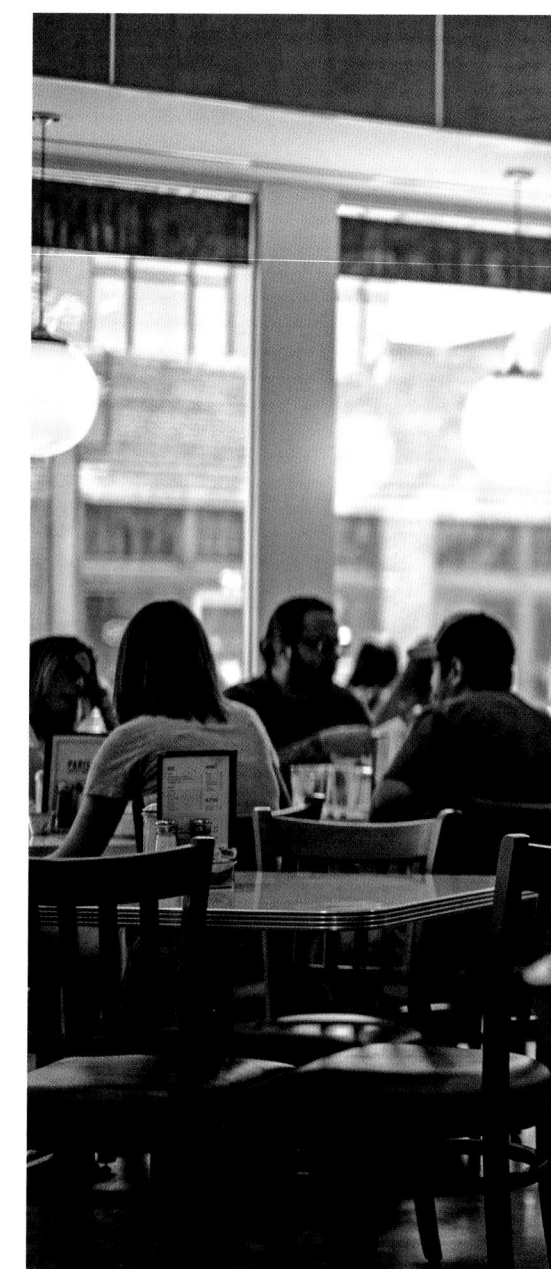

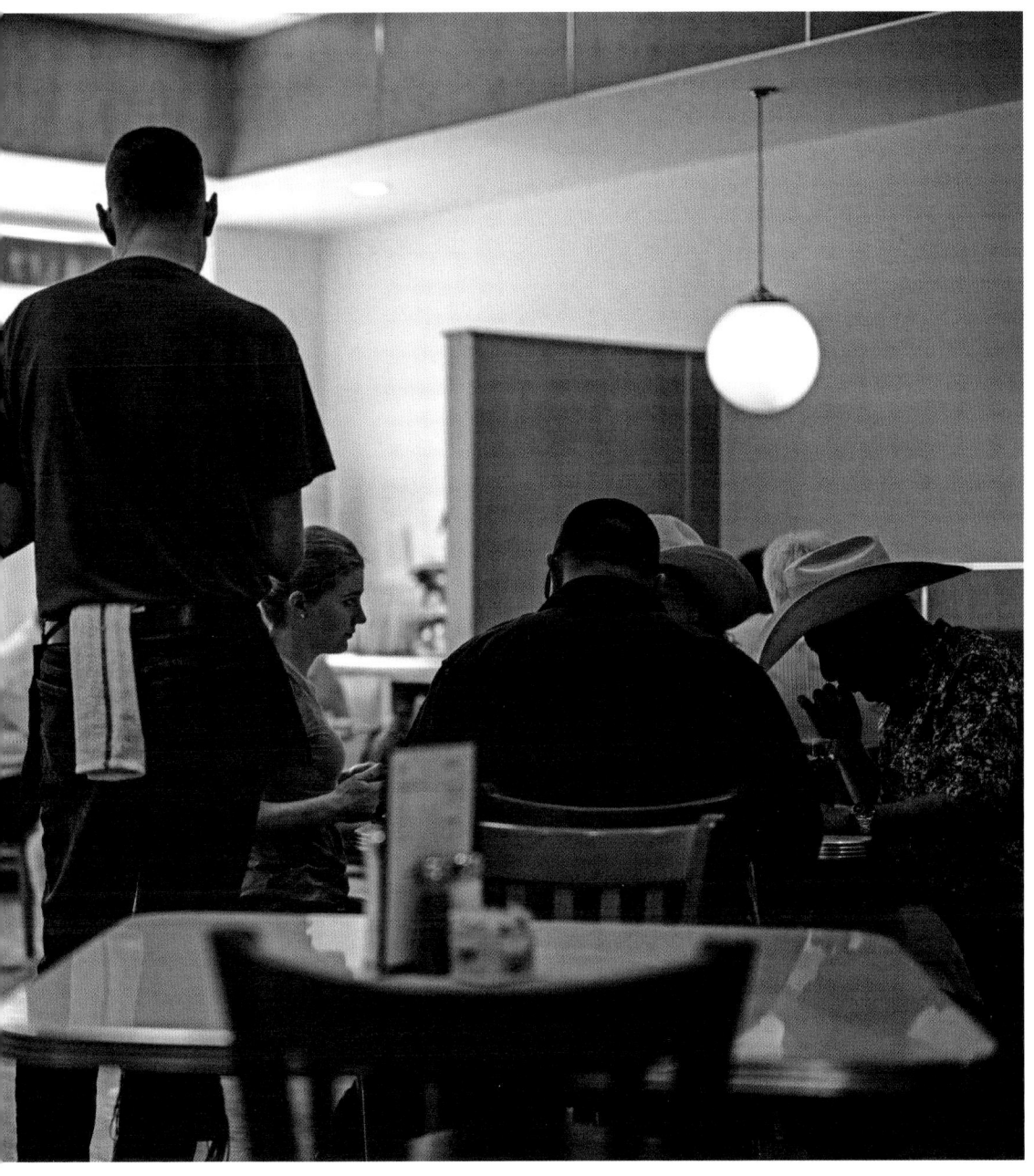

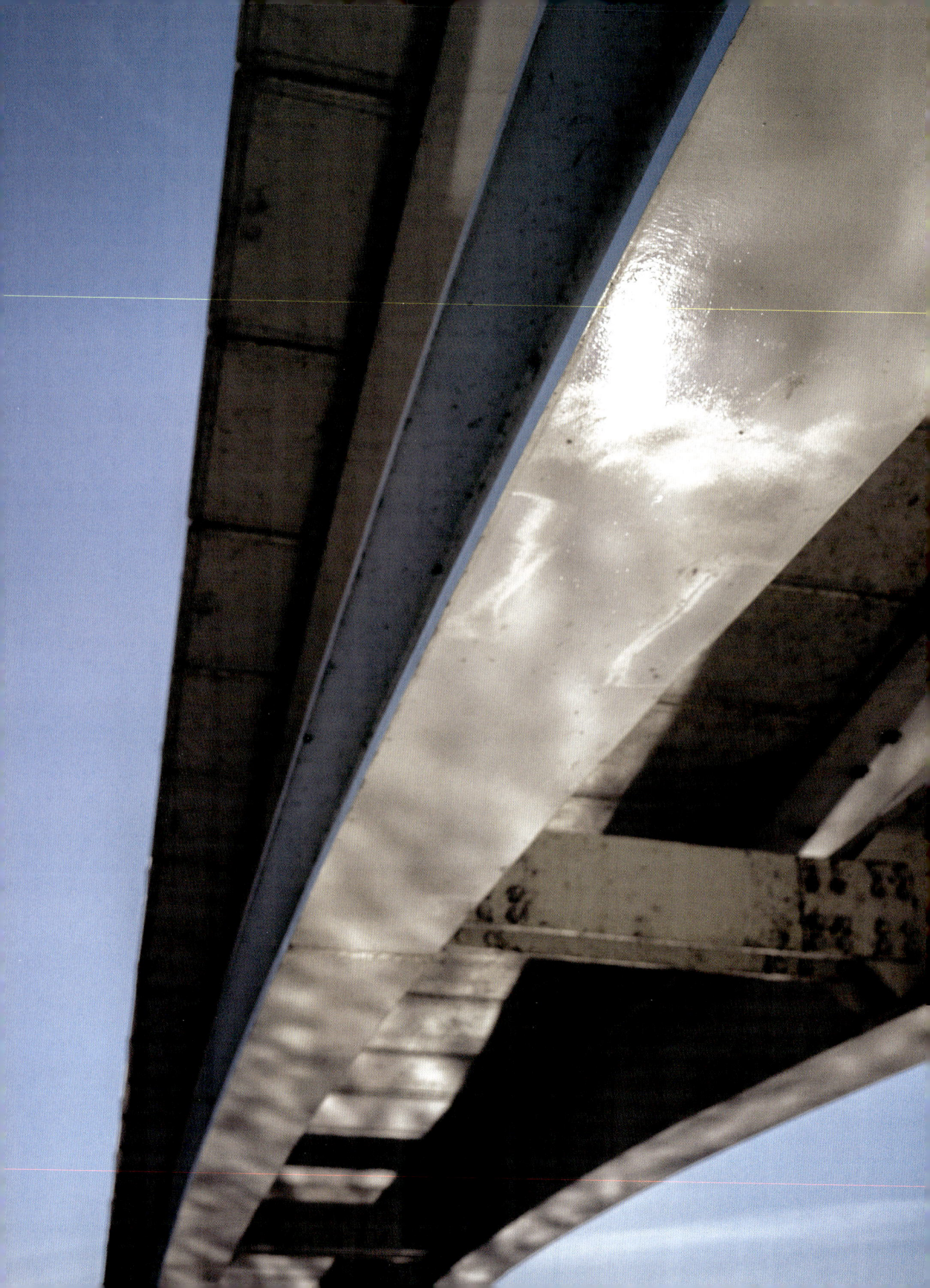

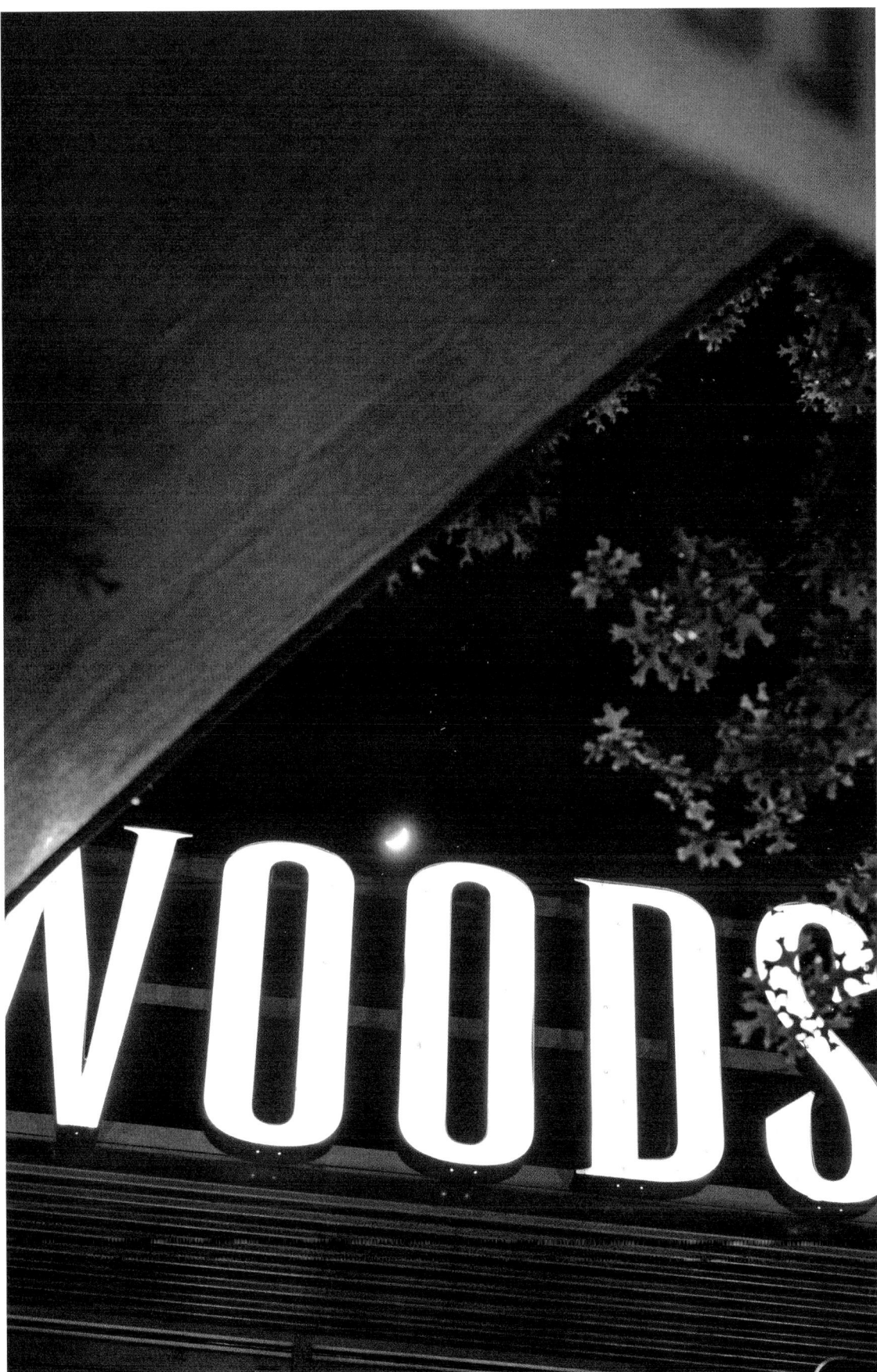

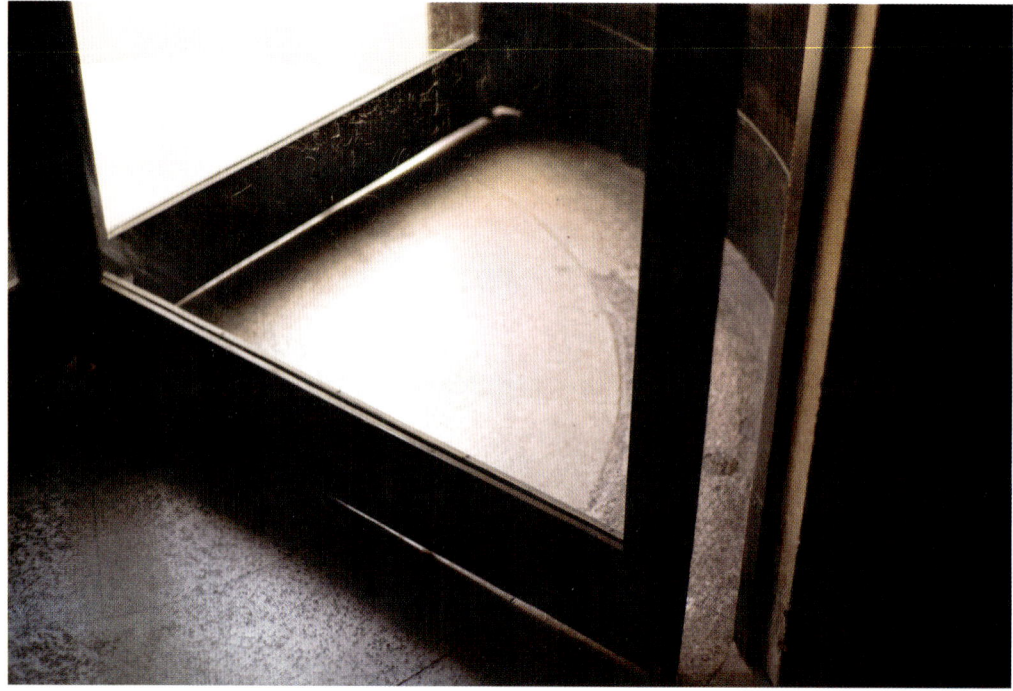

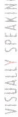

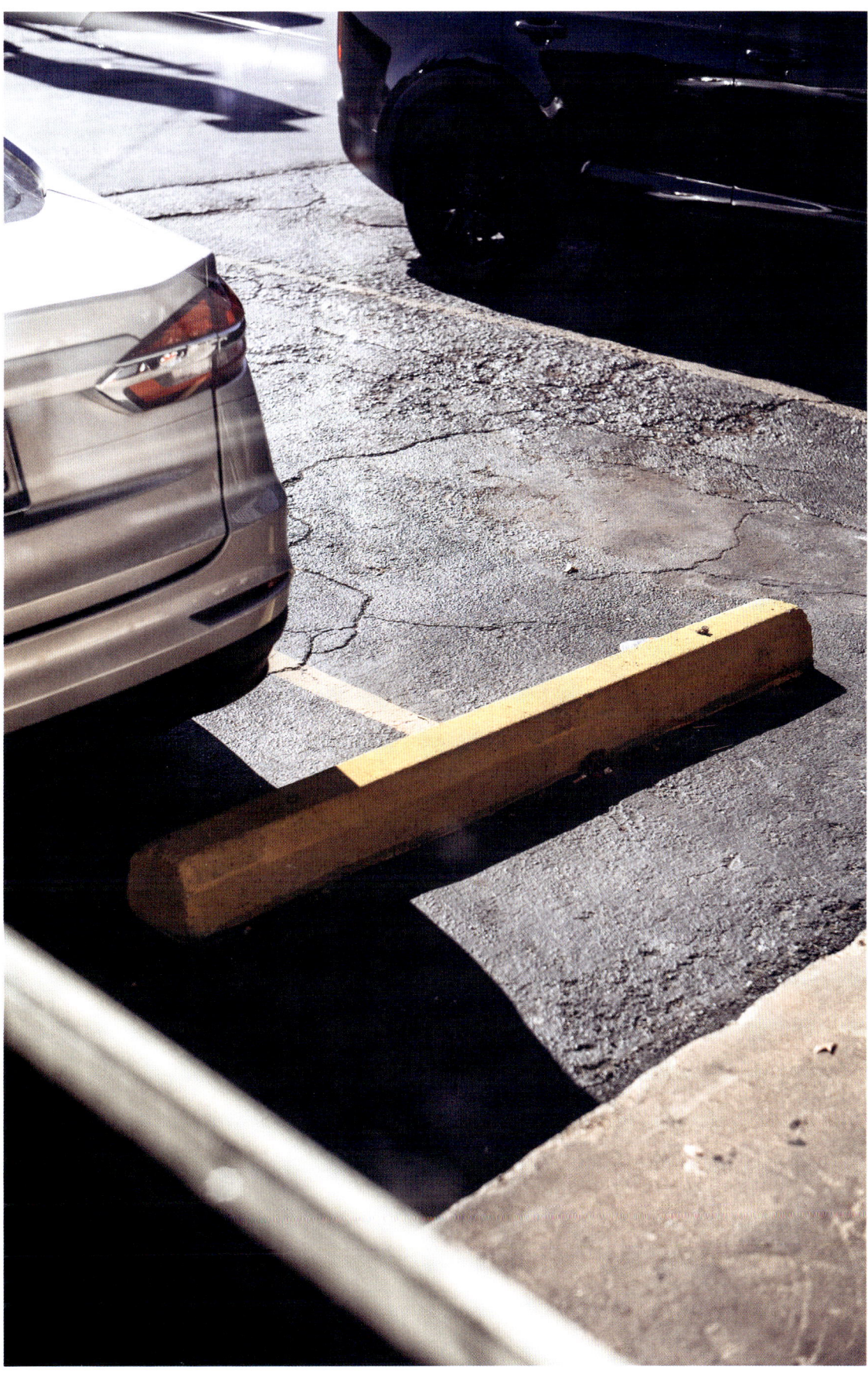

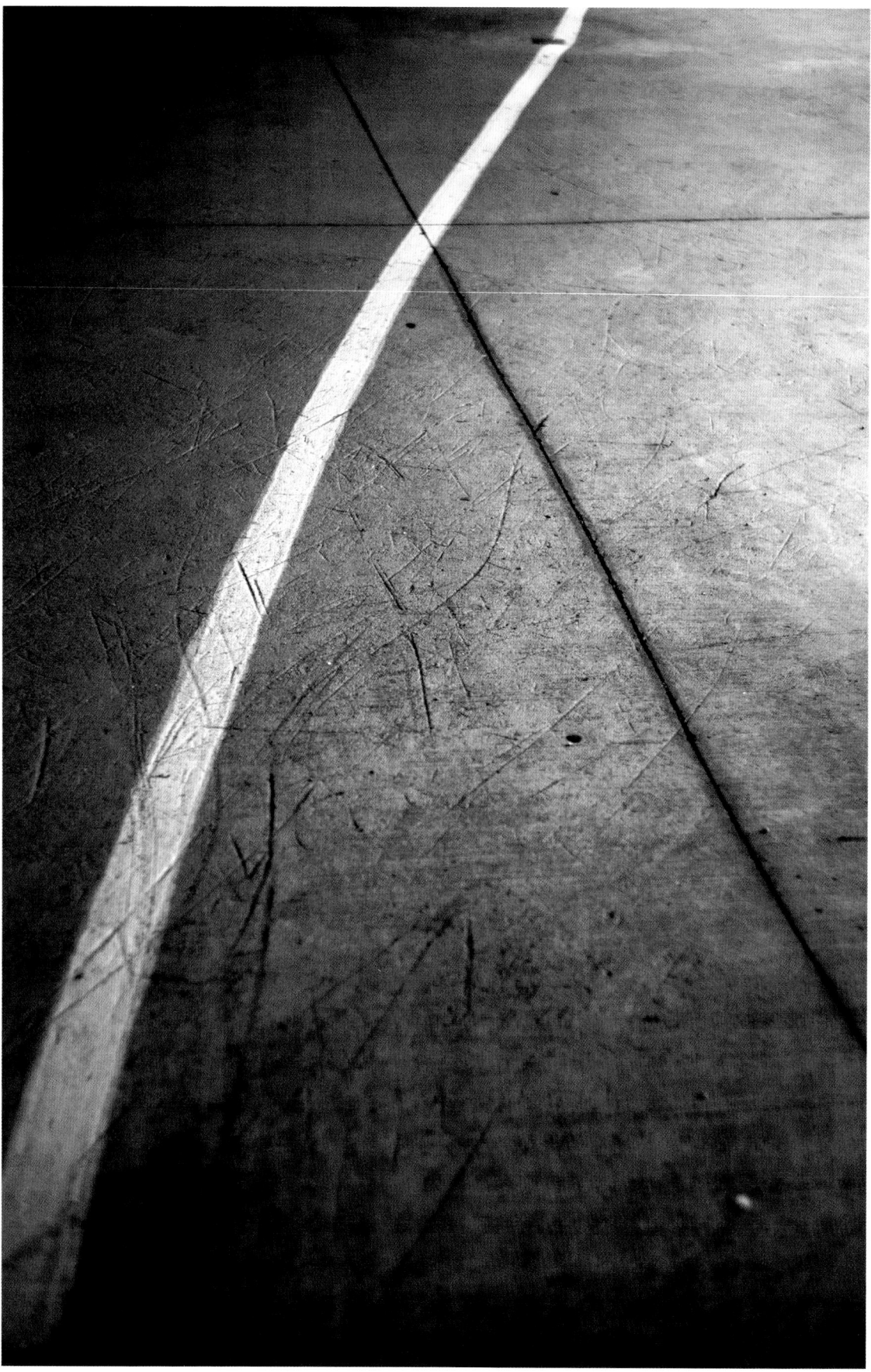

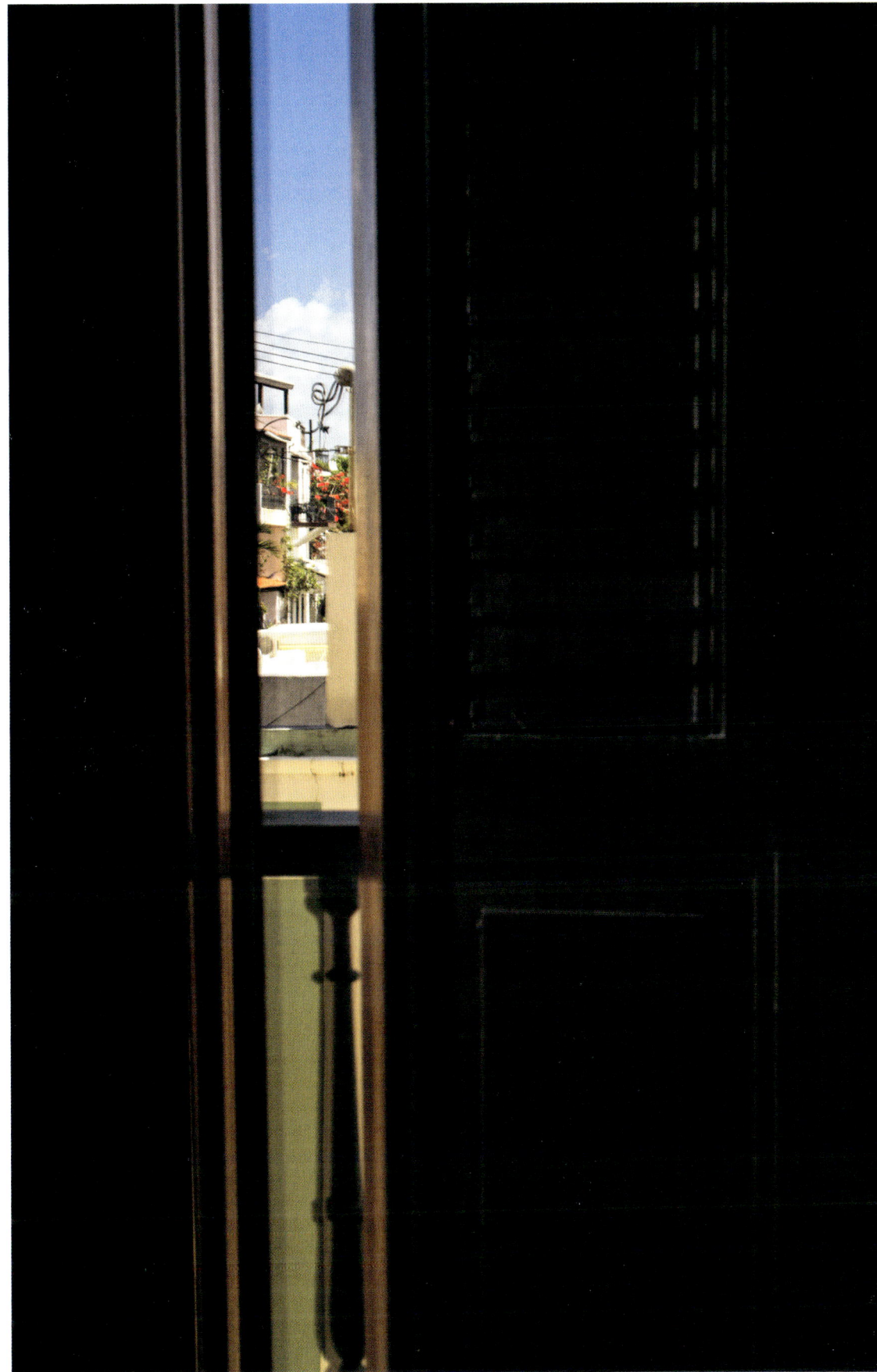

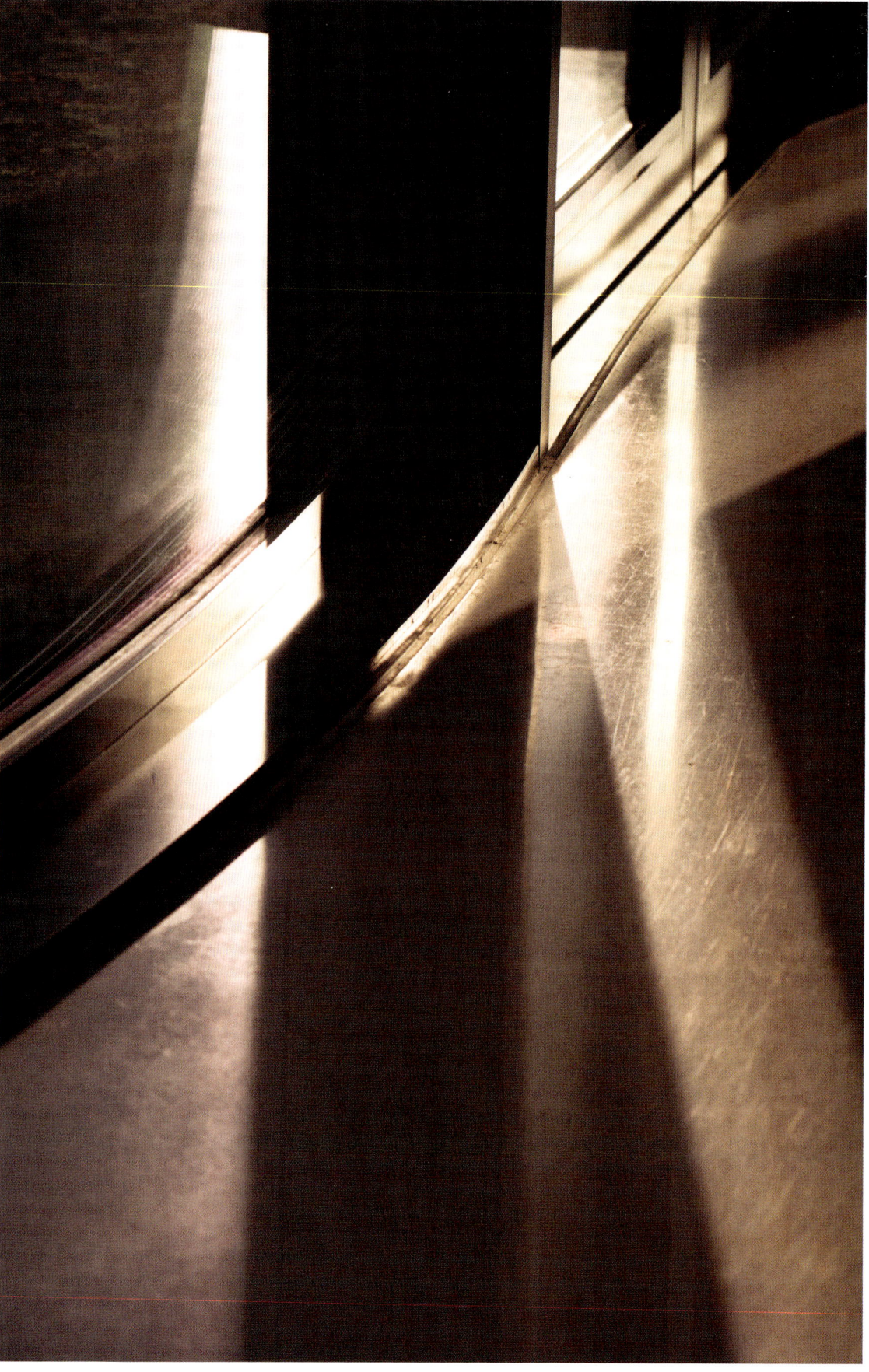

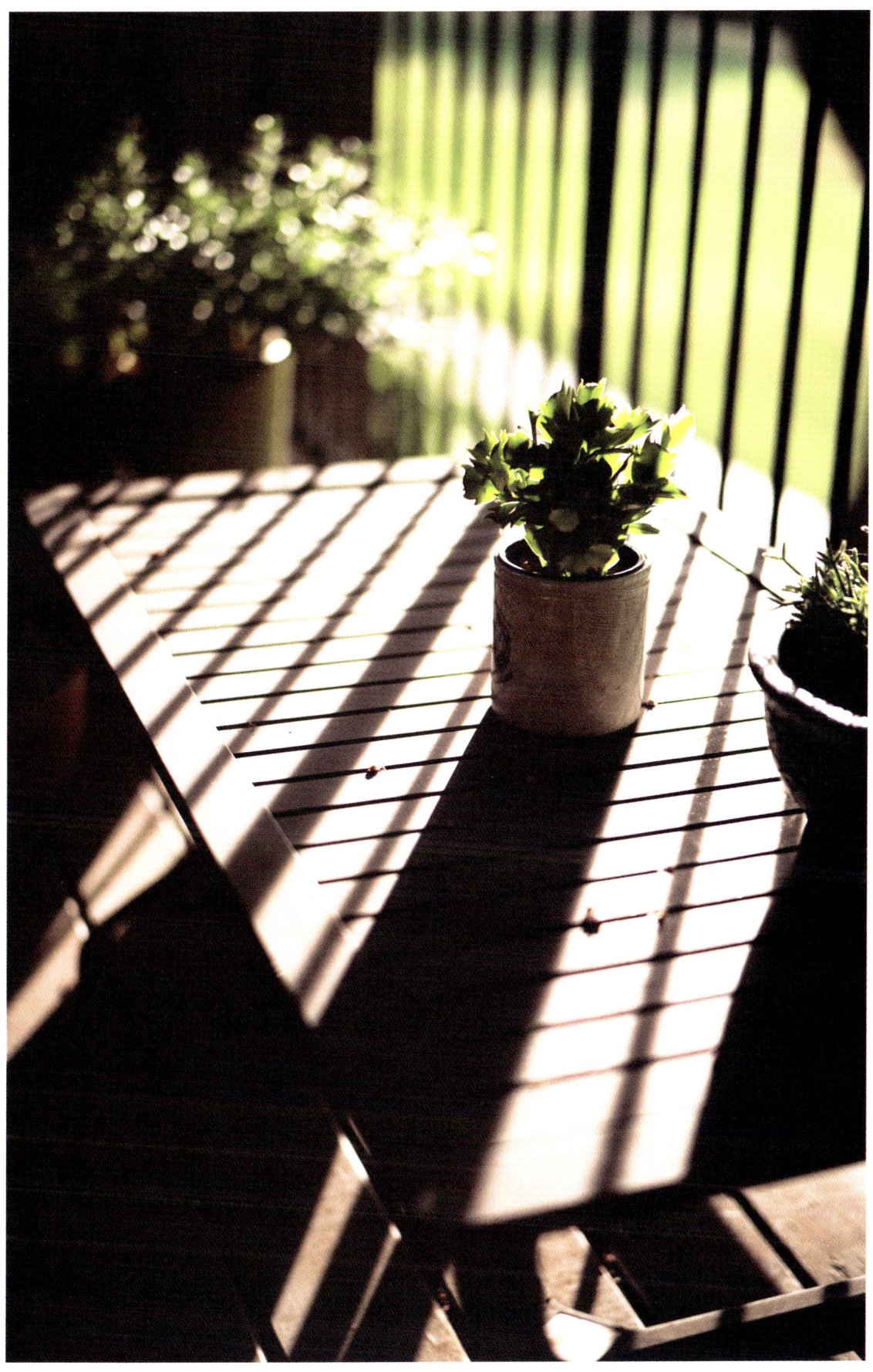

CHAPTER 5

WHAT TO SHOOT

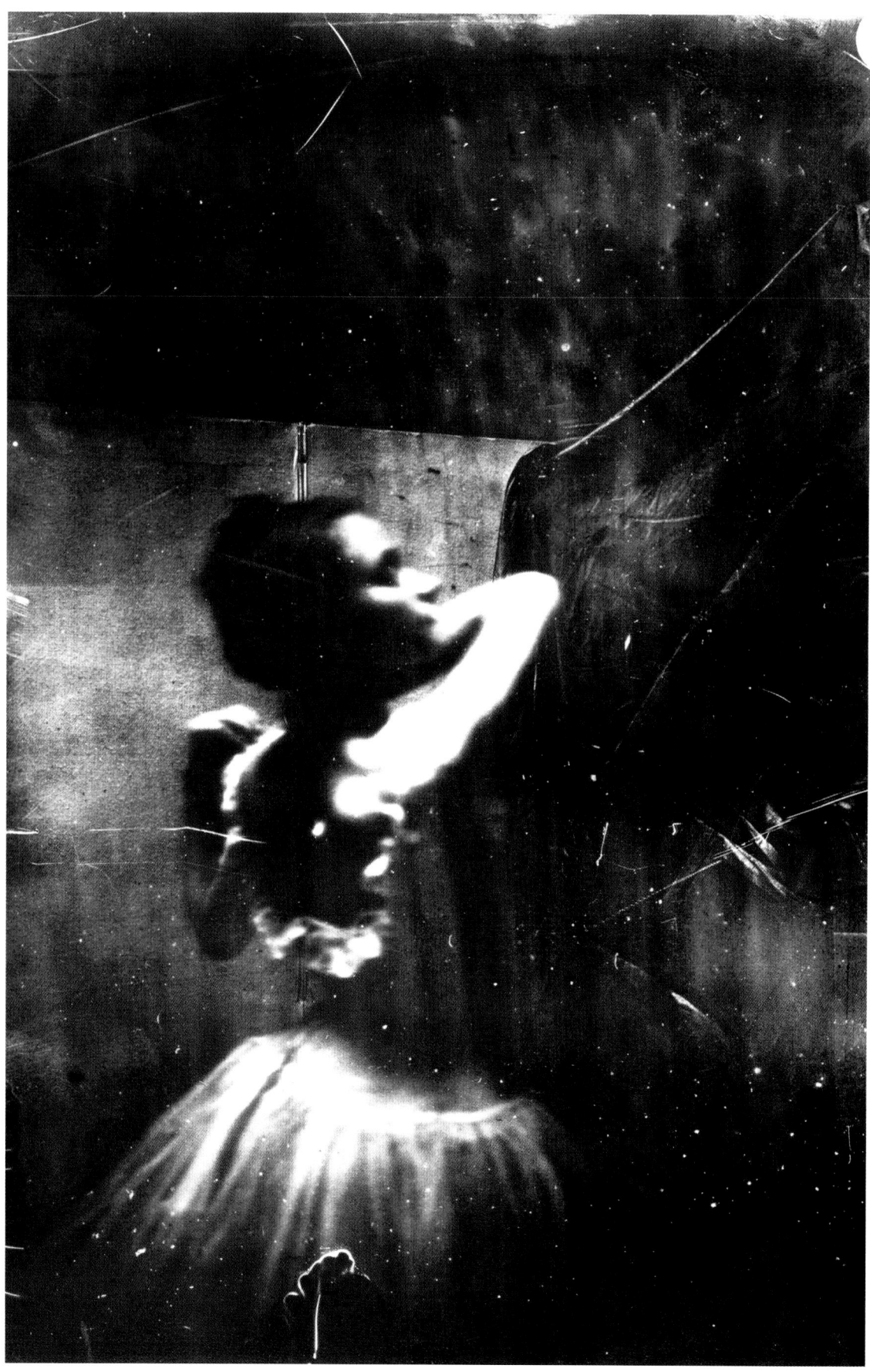

Dancer Adjusting Her Shoulder Strap by Edgar Degas (c. 1895-96); via Wikimedia Commons.

WHAT TO SHOOT? This is the ultimate question. You've got your camera and you have some free time. You're serious about photography and you're ready to set the world on fire. Where do you begin?

This approach is where many photographers get stuck. It's difficult when you have nothing in mind to say with the camera, yet you're going to try and say something anyway by improvising. Sure, it can be done, but trial and error takes way more time than having a clear direction.

So, let's break down what a finished picture actually is.

A finished picture is a presentation. It's an intelligent statement. The final picture needs to say something in a cohesive manner—even if that is something simple. There's nothing wrong with a simple, beautiful picture as long as the intent is clear. History is full of them. One example that comes to mind is a photograph by Edgar Degas. Degas was known as a painter, but he took photographs for reference. Very few photographs actually survive, but the example here is one of my favorites. In fact, I think it is one of the best pictures ever made. It's of a dancer. The surviving sample is weathered with age, which adds to its high contrast, questionably focused ambiance. It is far from technically perfect. Perhaps the image is accidental (especially with the focus) or perhaps completely intentional. This makes no difference. The final result is what's important. It is haunting, mysterious, and fundamentally powerful. It is not a conceptual image with some powerful statement being made. It's simple, beautiful, and perfect.

I share this because of the image's simplicity. Yes, art has the power to be thought provoking. It has the power to make the viewer aware of something or think in a different way. But it can also be a simple statement.

My practice is somewhat unconventional in that I draw from my music training and apply it to a visual practice. As different as aural art and visual art might seem, the formal approaches are actually the same.

When I started as a photographer, I went on a quest to learn the structure behind visual forms. To my surprise, I found that there was very little information and it was very different. Graphic design is a visual language that is formalized to an extent. Traditional painting is also formalized a bit. But photography fascinated me because, as a fairly young art form, it seems extremely immature in having a consistent approach to understanding why and how things work. So I draw heavily from my music training. It's less different than you would think, but that's where I'm coming from.

After two and a half decades of thinking through the similarities, I'm going to share with you what works for me.

That being said, let's look at the visual language as three different forms.

Formal Composition

There is music that is tightly composed, such as a symphony. Every note has a reason to exist. Each note exists in the context of harmony and melody, but every sound produced in the work exists to serve the composition as a whole. For example, think of Beethoven's Fifth Symphony. This is probably the most recognized work in Western music. Beethoven begins the work by establishing a simple motif of four notes. There are three Gs followed by an E flat. They fall in a simple rhythmic pattern of "short short short long." They're then transposed and repeated by three Fs and a D. The motif is now established. and what follows is a complex progression of this simple motif as Beethoven takes the listener through counterpoint and harmonic progressions that weave this simple four-note structure into a major symphonic work. Beethoven uses the motif to leave the listener hanging, as if asking a question. He turns the motif into transition and then uses the motif as resolution. This simple four-note idea is also the basis for the work as a whole, as there are four movements that present themselves over the next forty minutes or so of listening.

So how does this relate to photography? Well, we don't have the element of time, but we do have the space of the work being shown. The idea of a simple motif can be equated to the subject of the picture. In the context of the studio, the photographer can now base an entire composition around a simple subject. And much like Beethoven's command of harmony and counterpoint, a great photographer includes supportive material to the subject that exists for the reason of supporting said subject. Perhaps the subject can evolve over multiple pictures, much like the movements of the Fifth Symphony. How does the language change or progress? What variety is being used so there is a reason to make a statement across multiple pictures?

Consider a larger photographic presentation such as a book or gallery exhibition. Does the relationship to photographs presented across a larger spectrum impact the work you might produce? Does a book or exhibition always have to be a "greatest hits" of pictures that are shown, or can they be viewed as a larger work based on a motif?

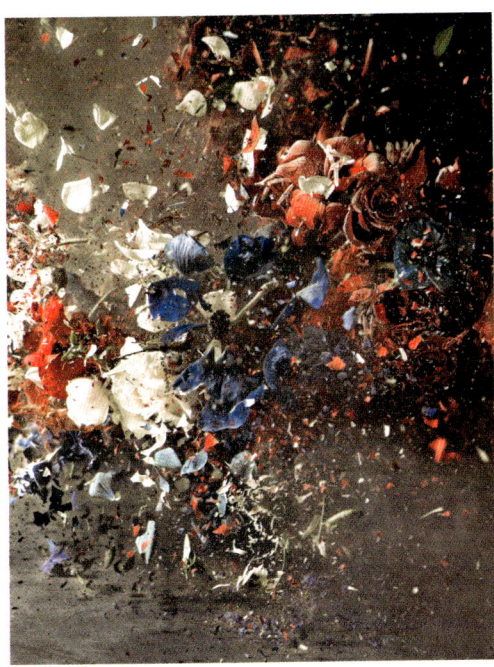

Blow Up 19, 2007 © Ori Gersht. All rights reserved, DACS/Artimage 2023.

Ori Gersht is an Israeli photographer who took the concept of the classic still life and "blew it up." His early works consisted of modern interpretations of pastoral concepts conveying natural landscapes and nature. Long exposure was a common distortive element used to reinterpret his identity from the past masters. But in 2007 his work took a dramatic shift.

Gersht started a series called "Blow Up," which relied on freezing dry floral arrangements with liquid nitrogen. Then, hitting the flowers with air, he photographed the moment of impact. This created an impressive metaphor of violence and conflict visually imposed over the classical still life. The cacophonous result brings to mind the vivid colors of nineteenth century painter Henri Fantin-Latour, transformed into an almost abstract expressionist rendering. Presented as a series, we have a conceptual motif of exploding parts superimposed on the formally quiet genre of the eighteenth century still life. Dark and complex, they are a controlled series of photographs, and the result is powerful. The works center around chaos, but the bold color contrasts make these pictures function cohesively on a structural level. The works embrace an element of chance, though there is considerable control over the final image.

Hiroshi Sugimoto is one of the finest contemporary photographers Japan has produced. His work is highly conceptual, he is very conscious of the history before him, and he works in series at large scale. His seminal seascapes series uses the simple motif of a horizon cut straight through the middle of a horizontal frame. The series comprises over 200 images

Paramount Theater, Newark, 2015 by Hiroshi Sugimoto. Gelatin silver print; image: 47 x 58.75 in. (119.4 x 149.2 cm). Courtesy of the artist and Marian Goodman Gallery © Hiroshi Sugimoto.

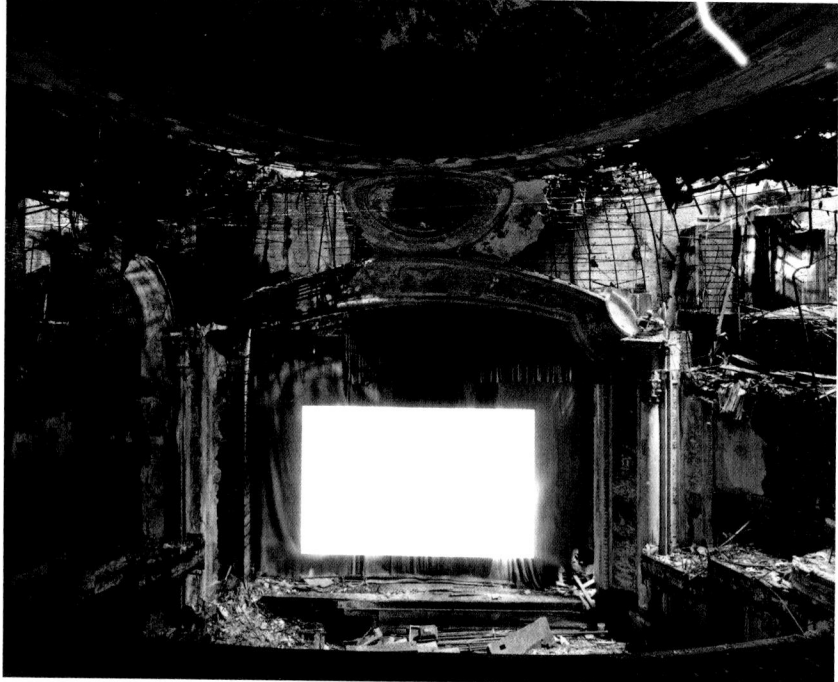

taken around the world in various weather conditions and times of day. What we perceive as a simple motif is presented in what seems like endless possibilities, variations, and developments. There are parallels drawn to Mark Rothko's black paintings and his classic compositional setup.

For another series, Sugimoto creates highly stylized takes on renowned architectural works—all of them strangely out of focus. Here, he's mixing two concepts: classical architectural photography and camera optical physics. When focusing a large-format camera you can find the infinity point of focus, but it is a mathematical distance. You can actually go beyond that focus point so the entire series is a study of the idea of "double infinity." But the result, though somewhat blurry, represents each structure in a distorted but recognizable reality.

Sugimoto has also used the concept of time as a motif. A series of movie theaters in which the exposure time is the length of a screened film shows us a white screen but also a beautiful representation of classic theater design. A series of dioramas in natural history museums of taxidermic animals and photographic backgrounds questions what is real. This same concept is carried over to a series of portraits of wax reproductions of historical figures, including King Henry VIII and his six wives. Are we looking at replicas or the people themselves?

Visual art is not as different from music as one might think. The point is this: with formal composition, the photographer is in control of every element in the picture. Every element is there for a reason. Ideas develop using a formal structure. This is one approach to photography.

Improvisation

Art is also created by means of improvisation. This differs from formal composition in that what's created is a statement made in a moment. It's less about perfection and more about spontaneous creation. It's the excitement that something can exist in form but be radically different each time it is performed. Improvisation is creation affected by the aspects of "the now."

There are many forms of improvisation in music. Jazz in the 1960s embodied this idea in a very profound way. Musicians often used "standard" songs as the basis for the music they would perform. Standards were popular songs of the time, popular music both the musicians and the audiences knew. The structure would consist of the melody, or "head," and the harmonic progression would serve as the framework for improvised soloing. This music offers a balance between structure and spontaneous playing, which is the language jazz musicians spend their careers learning how to use. It's also important to note that jazz as a language evolved over the decades from its earlier forms—like the blues and ragtime—to where it is today. Jazz musicians consider this entire history in the music they produce.

Photography also has a complex history of improvisation, with a notable period in the mid-twentieth century from photojournalism. At the time, people consumed news in a very different way than we do now. The printed pages of magazines were the ideal medium for photography, and they produced some of the most famous practitioners of the art, many of whom are still respected today: Robert Capa and Gerda Taro, David Seymour, and later Henri Cartier-Bresson, W. Eugene Smith, and many others. These photographers gave the public a view of conflicts behind the front lines. This was not photography that could be composed in a studio. It was improvising by reacting to the events as they unfolded. It was photography that communicated a visual language.

Henri Cartier-Bresson is considered by many to be one of the greatest practitioners in the history of the medium. He was very open about his training and approach to what he beautifully branded as the Decisive Moment. He had formal training as a painter and classical forms were an intentional

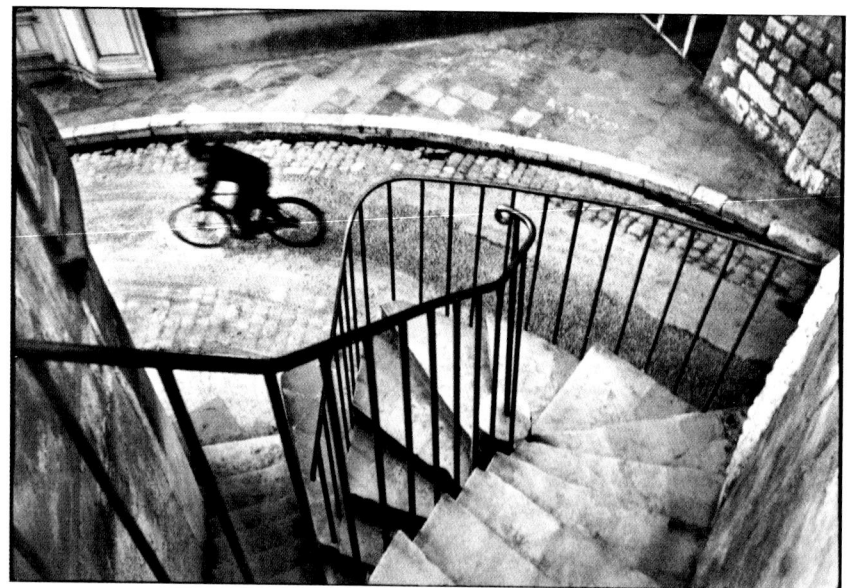

Man Cycling Down the Street by Henri Cartier-Bresson (1932); courtesy of Foundation Henri Cartier-Bresson / Magnum Photos.

influence in where he would position the camera. Timing plays an integral role in Cartier-Bresson's work as well. He attributed this to learning how to hunt. He was extremely intentional in the language that he used, but it was done in the moment.

Cartier-Bresson was an early champion of the 35mm format, which opened up possibilities in photography that did not exist with the previous generation of large-format cameras. Smaller film sizes allowed small cameras that were fast and easy to work in the moment. This change had a profound effect on photography and provided the ideal platform for improvisation—creating in the moment while drawing upon visual intellect and structure. It is, in essence, conversing using a visual language.

Interpretation

Finally, I'd like to consider a third form: the interpretation of an existing work. In music we call this a "cover." When a cover (or reinterpretation) of a song is successful, it offers a different way of hearing something the listener might already be familiar with. But it's not ever an exact copy. It's about saying something new using an existing musical statement.

Nine Inch Nails led a new movement of industrial music into the early 1990s, which combined techno synthesizers with elements of heavy metal. Their song

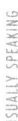

"Hurt" from the 1994 album *The Downward Spiral* was covered by Johnny Cash in 2002. Cash's version was stripped down to guitar and voice and, arguably, had a more profound effect over the original, highly produced version. Though skeptical at first, Nine Inch Nails leader Trent Reznor was incredibly moved by the Cash version, so much that he went on record as saying, "The song is no longer mine."

In the 1980s, classical pianist John Bayless made albums of Beatles songs completely reinterpreted as if they were written by Bach. All of the albums were solo piano in the baroque style; the core ideas of songs such as "Penny Lane," "Eleanor Rigby," "Here Comes the Sun," and many others are presented as choral preludes, suite elements ("Penny Lane" is a gigue), and even fugues. Hearing these made me realize the power of an idea or statement could be independent of the original context in which it was presented. I specifically remember when I was in college studying music—I heard these and they had a profound impact on me. It was as if I could suddenly speak two different languages and at once was able to understand them both. Often you don't recognize the song in the first few notes, but then the themes roll by and you hear something that transcends just a song or a recording. You hear concepts at a higher level, as if the original recording is just one way of expressing something greater. "Is it Bach I'm listening to or the Beatles?" It was neither and both at once. What once was so far apart has more in common than I ever imagined. Incidentally, Bayless is improvising a lot of this work. Bach's interpretation of baroque music is highly structured and is a musical language that Bayless understands at the level where he can improvise it on the spot.

In photography the idea of interpretation tends to be fairly common, particularly with subject matter that is in the public eye. Landscapes and architecture come to mind, as it's quite common for many photographers to reinterpret the same location or landmark. Portraits, particularly of celebrities, are important as well. As a successful portrait can be argued as a collaboration between the subject and the artist, there is a strong desire for artists to want to reinterpret a portrait in their own style.

Interpretation was a very big part of photography in its early days. Pictorialism combined characteristics of symbolism, illustration, and interpretation of both biblical and classical themes. British photographer Julia Margaret Cameron's interpretations of the Madonna provide a good example of this, as well as her interpretations of literary characters and scenes from Shakespeare, Elizabethan poems, Alfred Tennyson, Robert Browning, and many of her contemporaries.

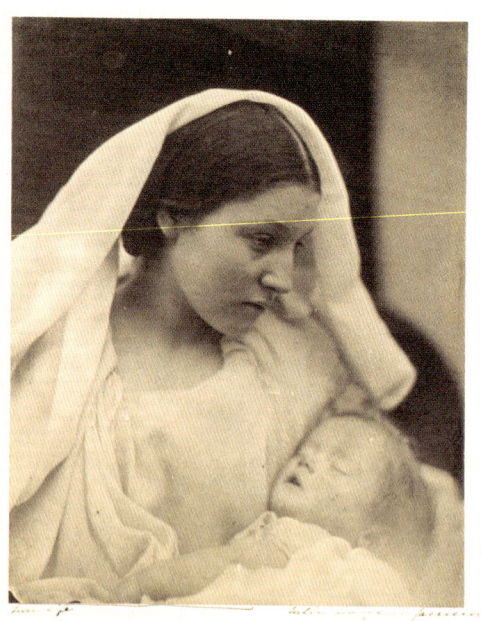

La Madonna Riposata by Julia Margaret Cameron (1864); via The Met Open Access.

American photographer F. Holland Day incorporated classical idealism and symbolism in his work in the late 1890s, which consisted of photographic interpretations of New Testament themes, often posing himself as the role of Christ. This culminated in probably his best-known work, *The Seven Words,* illustrating the Crucifixion.

Interpretive work faded away in photography along with Pictorialism in the early twentieth century. However, there are still interesting examples that have taken on new forms.

A few years ago, I started researching pictures taken of common subjects, such as historical landmarks and popular locations. I ended up identifying seven different pictures of the Brooklyn Bridge interpreted by Alexander Alland, Andreas Feininger, Tom Baril, Walker Evans, J. Jay Hirz, Michael Kenna, and Hiroshi Sugimoto. Although these images

were created over decades, they were curiously all taken from the same vantage point. But each photographer had a different interpretation. Alland is probably the most conservative in capturing the view. Walker Evans changed the center of focus, thus breaking the symmetry. J. Jay Hirz used reflection from a wet surface on the bridge. Tom Baril used a pinhole and long exposure to introduce an element of time in the clouds. Michael Kenna used a Dutch angle—a technique used in cinematography that involves tilting the camera off to the side. Each photographer made this image their own and each image is completely different. Same subject with different aesthetics. But what about interpretation on a more conceptual level?

I met Graciela Iturbide in 2016, when I was filming a series of short films on living photographers. My plan was to portray the "best of the best," and Graciela was at the top of that list. In fact, there are few people more complex and interesting than her. For me, this was the equivalent of traveling to the top of the mountain to meet the monk who will give you the meaning of life. Graciela is not a monk; she's one of the sweetest people I've ever met—and she will give you perspectives on art and humanity that you've never even considered. She's loving, thoughtful, and has more art in her bathroom than I've ever seen in galleries. I'm only half kidding. She had amazing works hanging under the sink when I visited her home that year. If there is one photographer I would hope to learn something from, it is her.

Frida's Bathroom is a project Graciela was commissioned to do in 2005, the fiftieth anniversary of Frida Kahlo's death. Kahlo is

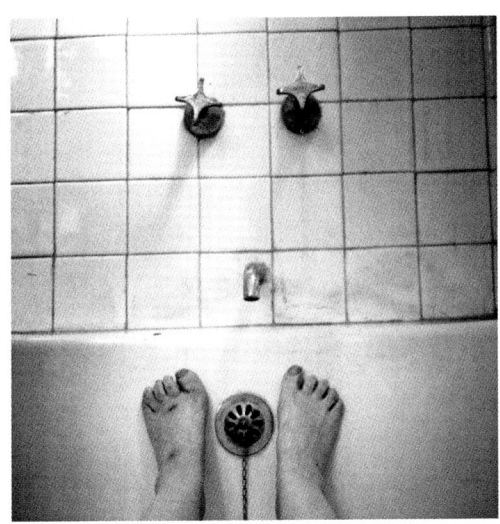

Frida's Bathroom by Graciela Iturbide (Coyoacán, Ciudad de México, 2006); used with permission from the artist.

perhaps the best known artist in Mexico's history. Frida had a rough life physically, to say the least, after being injured while riding a bus in 1925. As the bus driver attempted to overtake an electric streetcar, the streetcar hit the bus, dragging it several feet. An iron handrail impaled Kahlo, causing fractures in her pelvic bone and right leg. Her spine was fractured in three places; her collarbone was broken and shoulder dislocated. Despite becoming a symbol of twentieth century Mexican art, until her death in 1954, Kahlo's life was one of severe pain.

Kahlo lived in Coyoacán, the district of Mexico City long known for its association with the arts. She and her then-husband Diego Rivera (another great Mexican artist) lived in what is known as La Casa Azul (The Blue House). And it is very blue.

The house is the Frida Kahlo Museum today. In 2005, over 300 of Kahlo's personal belongings, which Diego Rivera had stashed away after her death, were found. Graciela was commissioned to photograph a series based on these called *Frida's Bathroom*. The result was an intimate look into the physical struggles Kahlo had endured, but through Graciela's own interpretation. This interpretation pays homage but at the same time shows Graciela's own interpretation of the subject. The result is powerful. It is a dialogue between the two women. It's one of pain and hardship. It's also one of strength and beauty.

Where Is Your Voice?

Unfortunately, I can't tell you exactly where, or how, to find your voice, but I can leave you with some ideas to think about.

I'm going to break this down psychologically into several parts, and hopefully this will provide some inspiration. "What should I shoot?" is a surprisingly common question to not only photographers starting out but also photographers who've had successful careers.

My first reaction, knowing what I know now: "What do you mean you don't know what to shoot? This is photography—it's a complete gift! Be proud of your surroundings, your home! This is what you can show the world and you're too close to the forest to see the trees!"

To some extent, I suppose I've always been jealous of painters. I feel sometimes that if I were creating the entire image I'd be able to do anything I wanted. Photography is about being dealt the elements. What you "want" is how you interpret the picture.

I've also known painters, and there is such a thing as the fear of the blank canvas. Unless you have a vision, you can't move forward with making it a reality. You have to define the result first, then deal with the process.

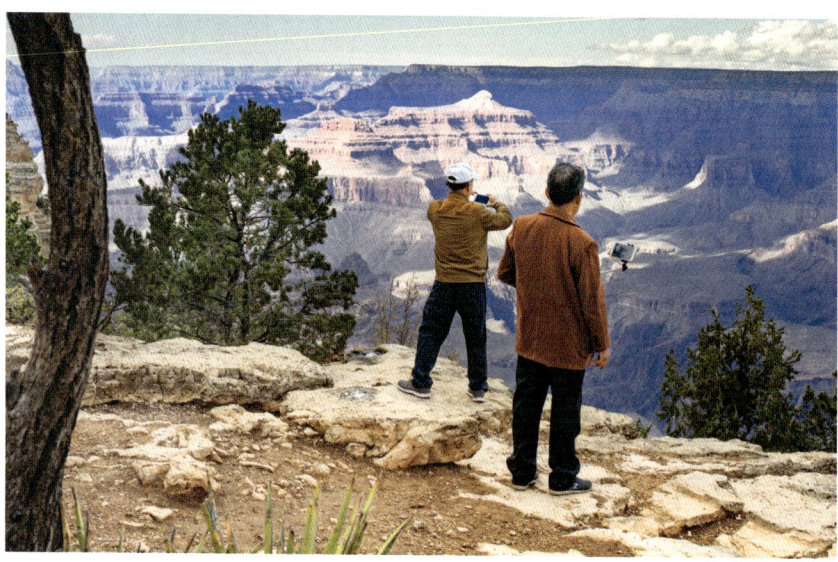

Writer's Block for Photographers

Photographers have a unique problem. If you go out and shoot, you won't ever come back with a "blank canvas." However, you can come back with a bunch of images that just don't meet your expectations. It's worse than the blank canvas in that it can be nothing but "stuff." At least a blank canvas didn't fail yet, right? We've all done it, and even successful photographers continue to do it. It's something you've shot before. Maybe there was nothing interesting, but you shot anyway. Or maybe it's just a lack of vision. This is writer's block for photography.

There's also a psychological element to this. For me at least, if I'm in familiar surroundings, it's often hard to engage with those surroundings because they are too familiar. My home, my neighborhood, my city. I know it and see it every day, so why can't I be inspired with the pictures I'm making?

One thing I can say about this—it is in your head. We assume because we see something all the time that everyone will find it mundane. I know this is not true because I know other photographers who've captured my very surroundings well.

So, the problem here is, if we go back to the idea of visual communication, is it possible we've ignored the obvious, which is that we need something to communicate? Think of it in terms of language. It's easy to photograph nouns (just objects), but perhaps harder to photograph verbs (what they do).

I can take my camera on the street and I can shoot buildings. Not exciting? Ask Eugène Atget, one of the most brilliant documentary photographers of Paris in his day. At first glance, Atget's photographs look like documents—and they were intended to be—but then you find a figure in a window, something on the street. You realize the brilliance is hidden in the details.

The pictures are saying something beyond the subject. This requires thought before action as well as the ability to react in the moment. It's easy to think you're being "busy creating" by just going out to shoot. Consider the result you want to achieve. Be open to the creative suggestions presented. If Atget had waited for action to pass within his photographs, they might have a completely different place in the canon of photography.

In many ways, Atget was a major precursor to what we know today as "street photography"—the ultimate improvisational canvas, the jazz gig for the photographer. One of the challenges is that, today, we see much of this work as great because of the nostalgic qualities. The old cars, lack of logos and advertising on every building, the clothes that people wore—all the greats of the 1960s built iconic photographs of the nostalgia before them. Or did they? Surely nostalgia wasn't nostalgic when it was made. These photographers were just reacting to the moments of their time.

The reality of improvisational photography is this—yes, you can make a photograph of a significant event and you might even be successful with it. But these events are rare, and you need to bridge the gaps between them to keep your skill at a high enough level to react when they do happen.

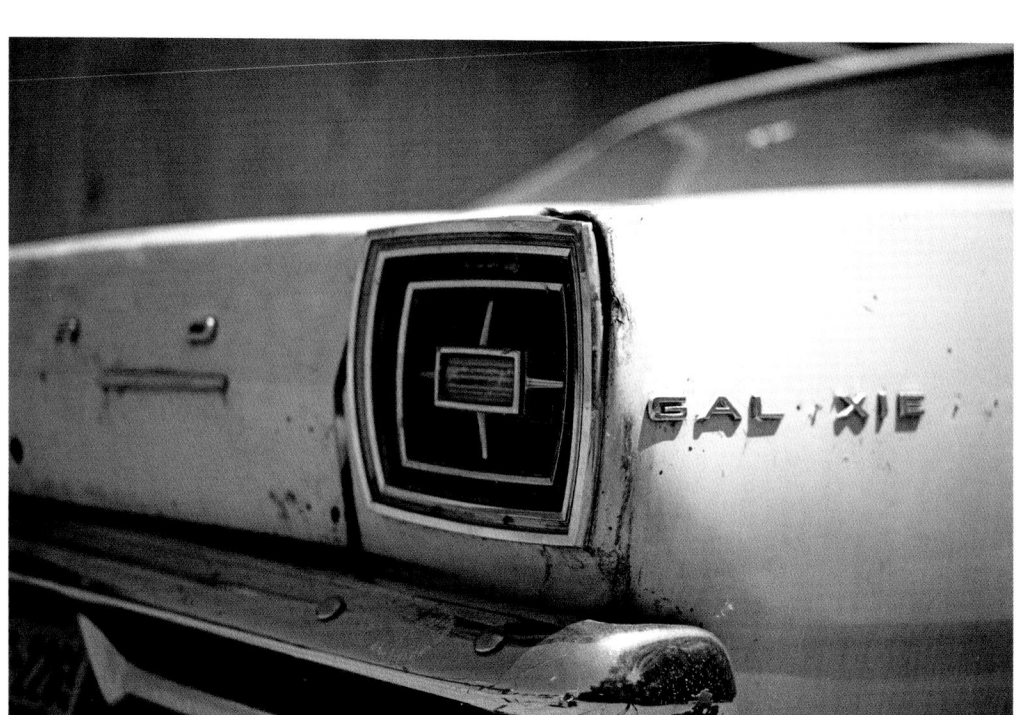

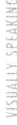
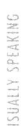

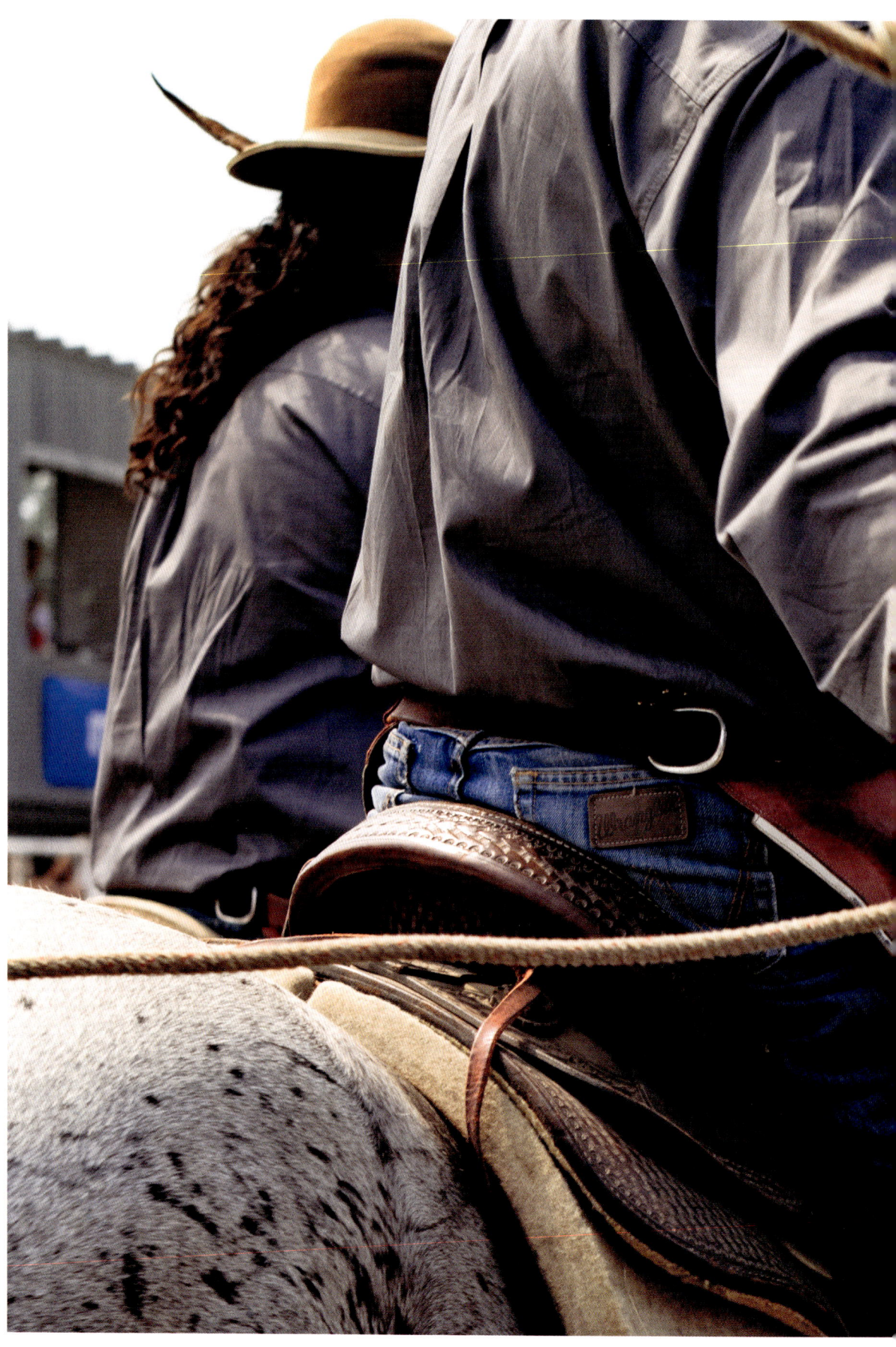

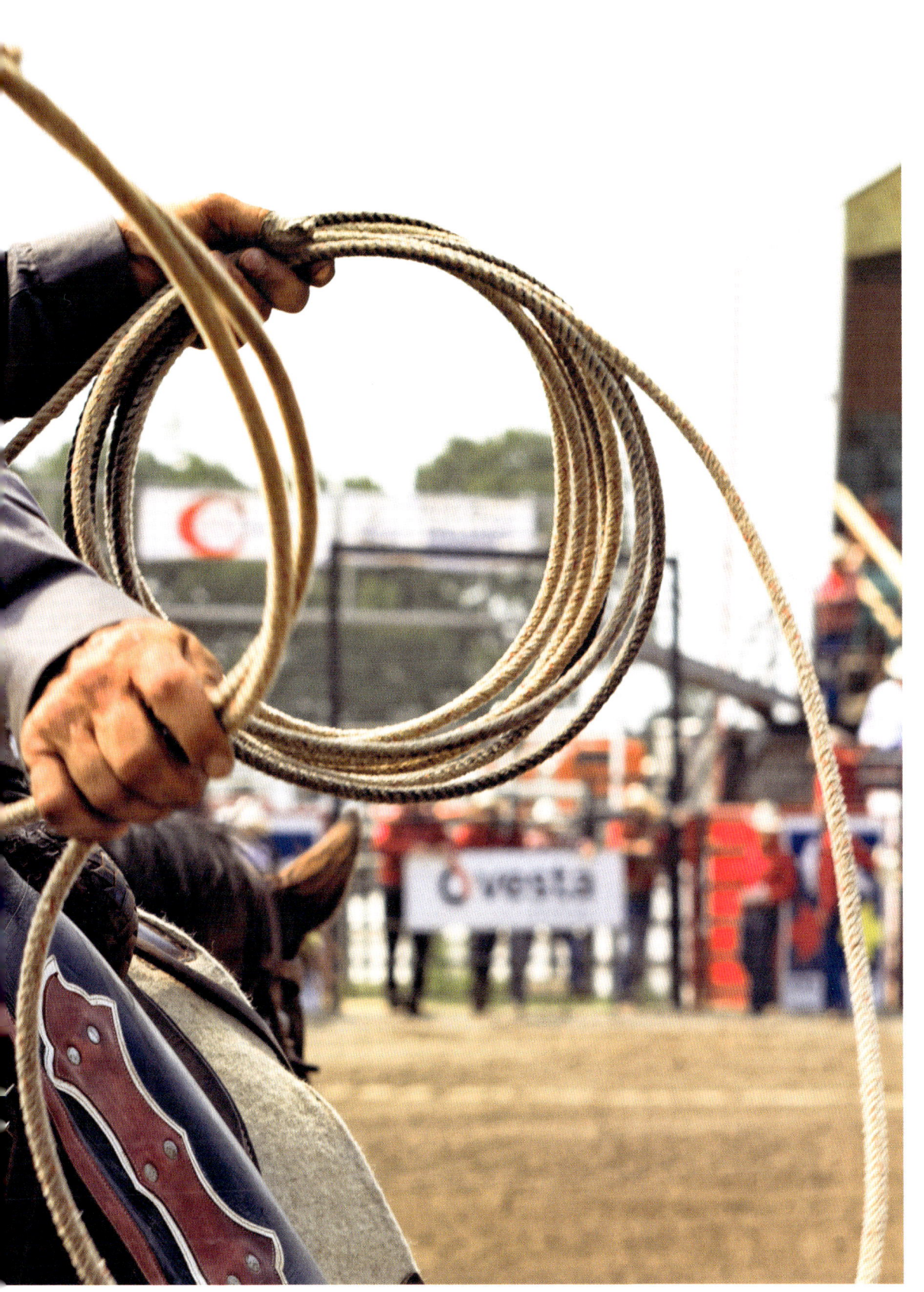

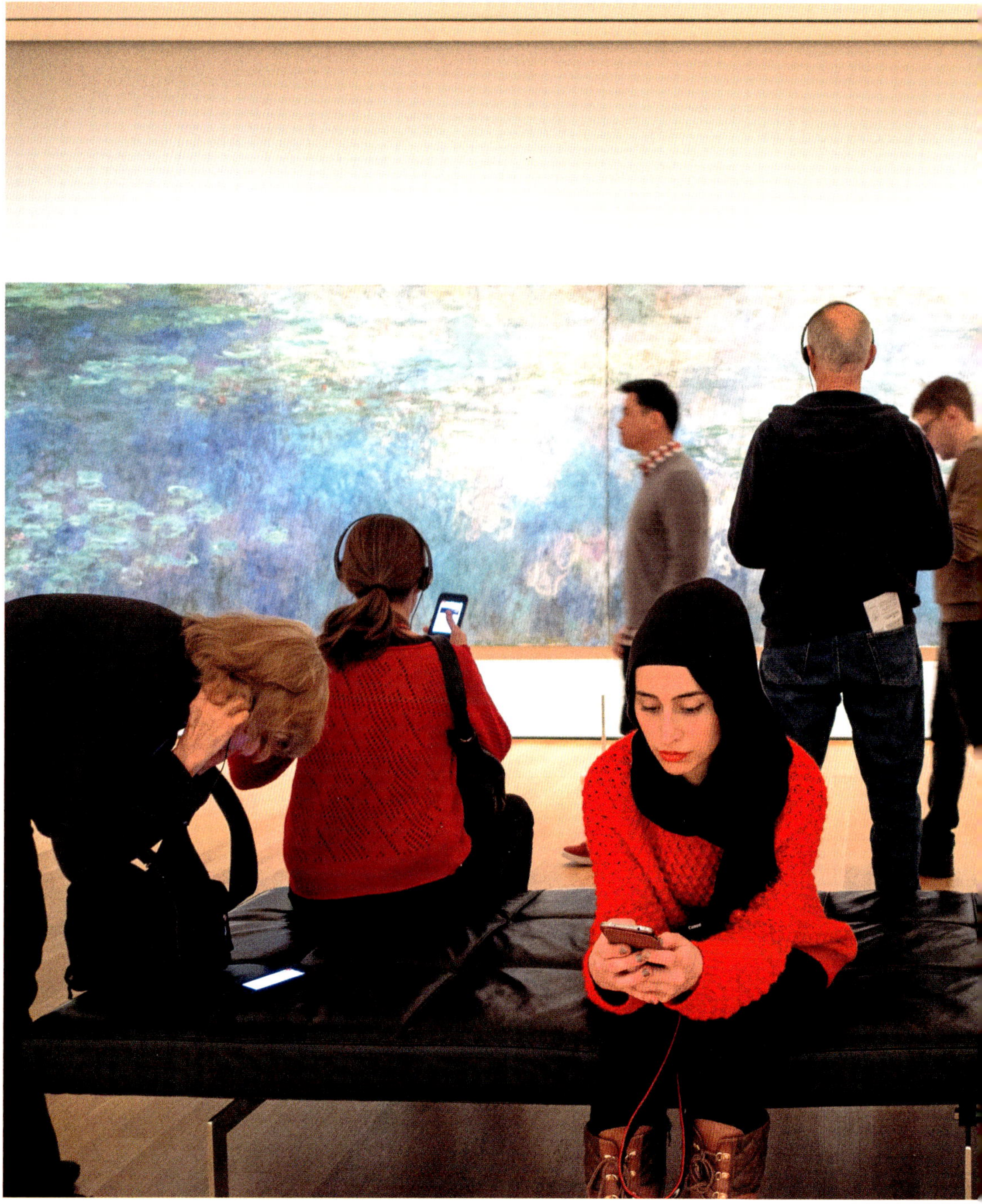

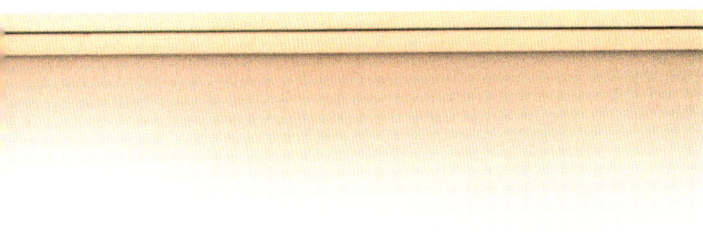
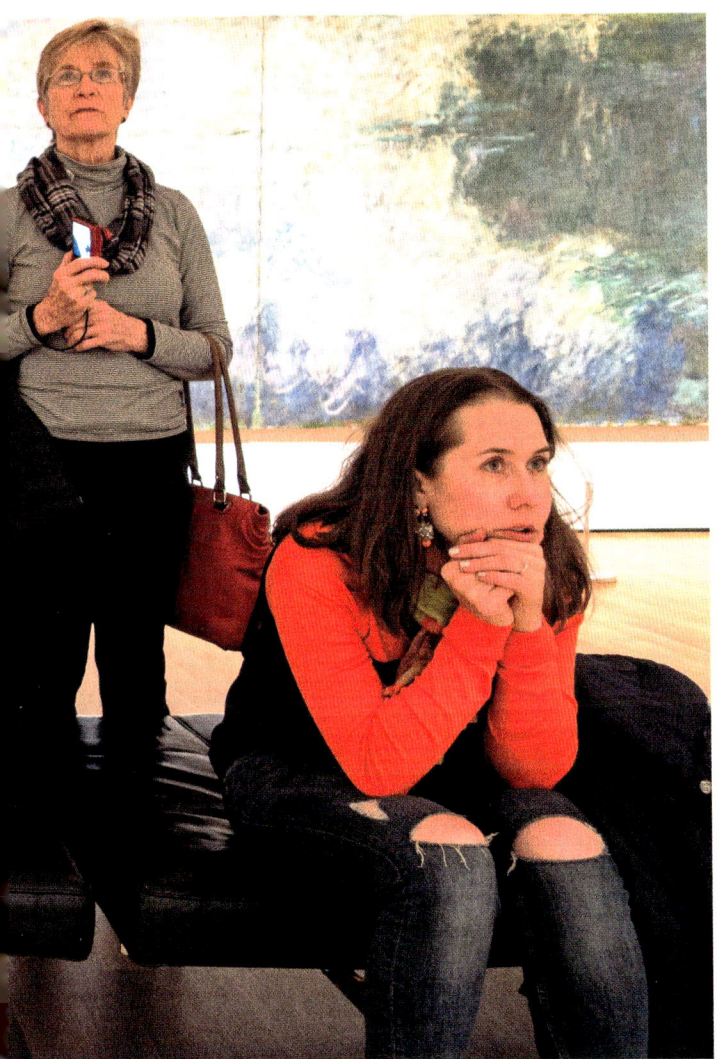

A great photographer should be able to create something in the context of wherever he or she is. Is this correct? I think so. Historic events are few and far between. They're also not likely to come to pass where you happen to be standing with the camera. You can't control that. But does it mean you shouldn't be able to make a great photo? Photography might be less about what the subject is at times and more about what you're doing with what's in front of you. Don't wait to photograph exotic places or events. They matter less than you might think with regard to your own ability to make a statement.

Most photographers don't like photographing in the middle of the day, particularly in the summer. Shadows are high contrast, the light is far from soft—generally the light is not as inspiring as it is in the early morning or early evening. The conditions are not perfect for good pictures, we say.

This is nothing more than an excuse. There is soft light and hard light. Light and shadow work together to create a sense of hard or soft geometry. What does that say to the viewer? Look at the elements you have. An informed photographer can work with any element before the camera. The time of day is just what you are dealt. It is never a reason to not take a photograph.

You have to start somewhere. Not every idea hits you like a bolt of lightning. Writer Steven Pressfield talks about this extensively. His point is that it's easier to rewrite than it is to write cold. In photography, are you developing a visual language in subject matter or abstraction that leads you to the next picture you take? Perhaps one image doesn't work well,

but it leads to a second idea. Reacting to the second idea takes you to the third. Sometimes it takes a lot of these experiments before you land on something that *really* works. But you can't get there if you haven't done many experiments, hundreds of them. I'm exaggerating perhaps, but it does require patience. Perhaps I'm not exaggerating. Quality requires trial and error at times.

There's a saying that "one thing leads to another," and really this describes the journey of anything great. It could be business. It could be personal. It definitely is the artistic path.

We forget this because, when we look at the work of great photographers who inspire us, we only see the good stuff. The bad shots, moments of insecurity, the stuff that doesn't work—we never see these images.

All this is to say photography is a mission. It's messy at times, but you have to keep trying.

Remember, the nouns are important. But more important are the verbs. What is the action? What are you photographing? Action works best when it's crystal clear.

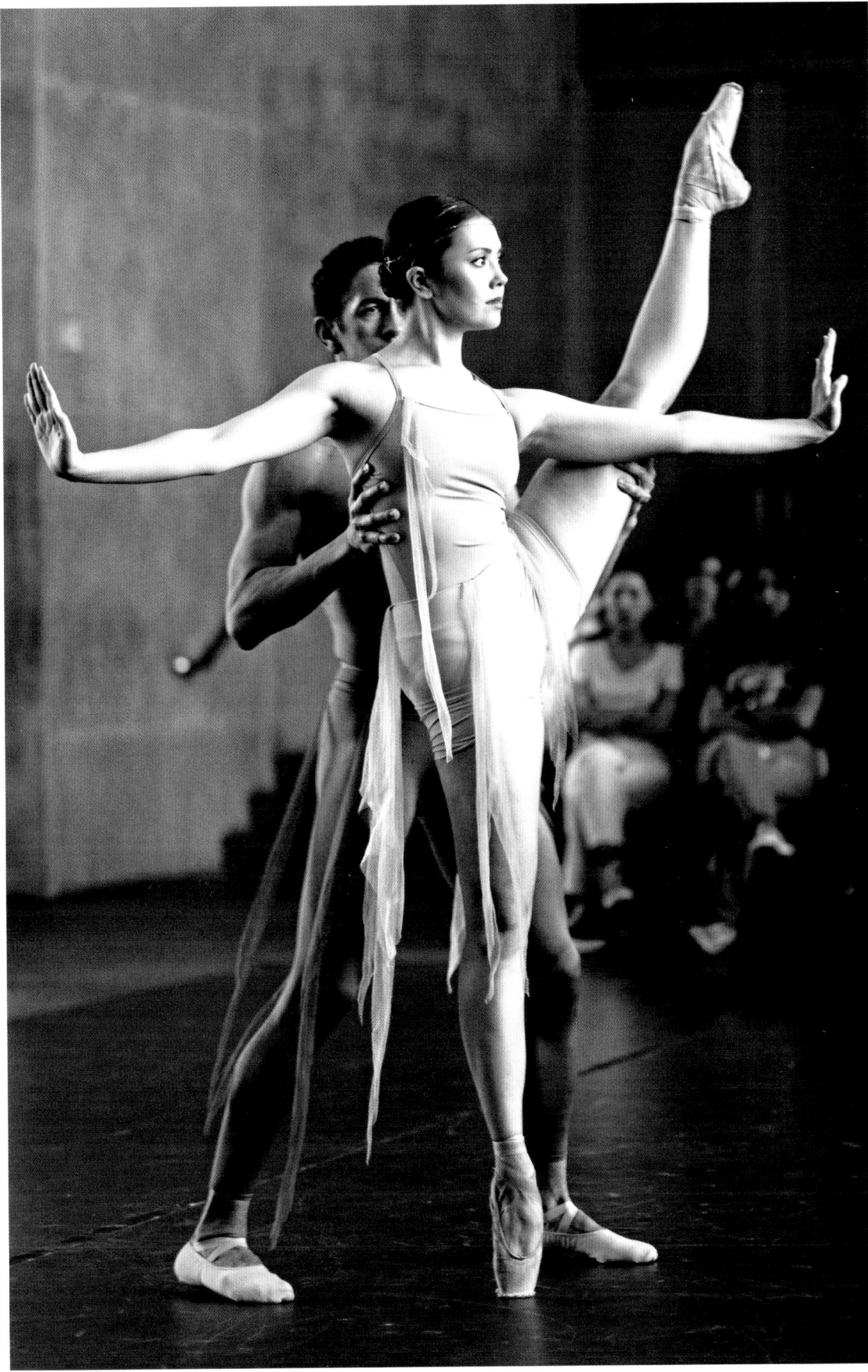

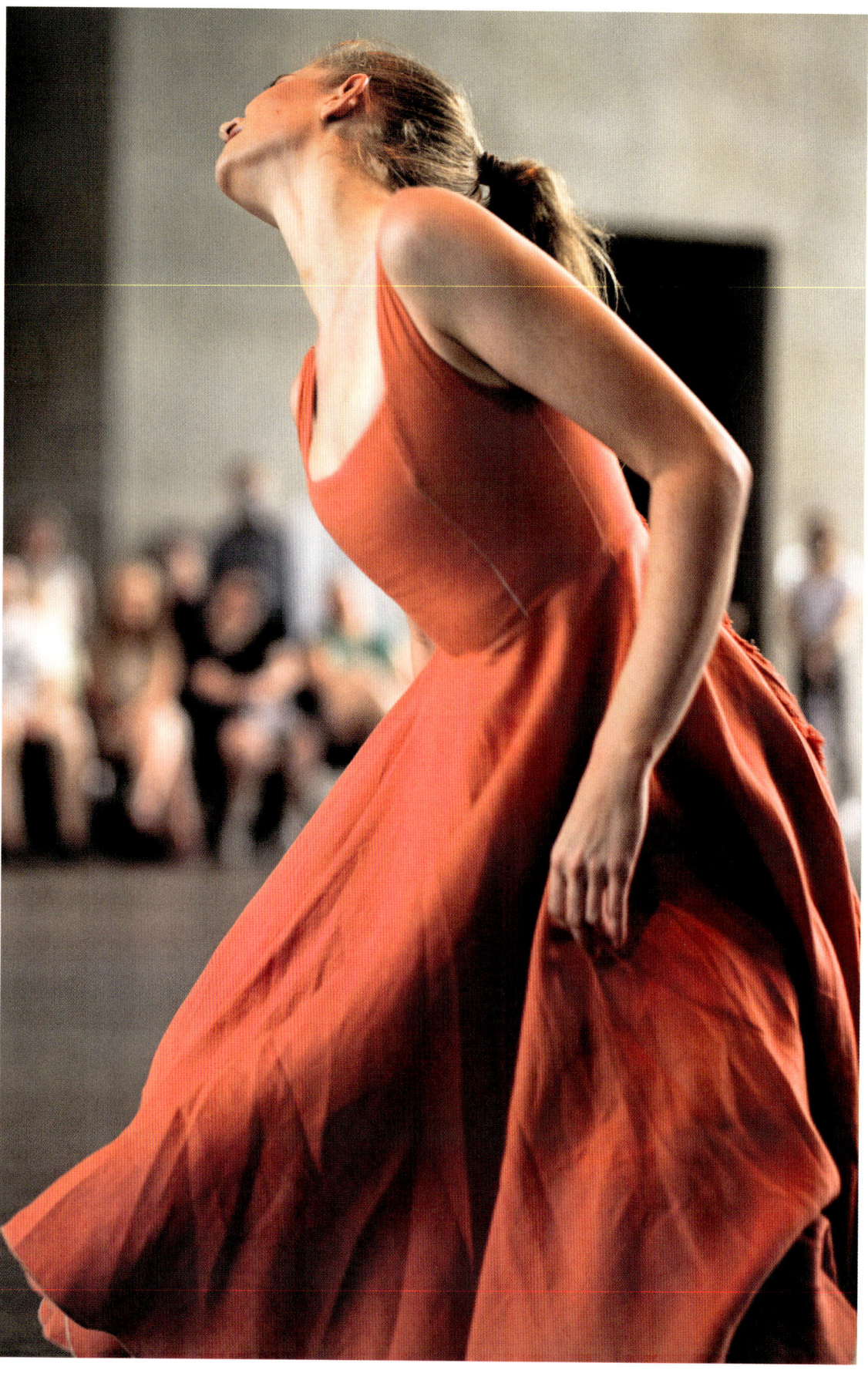

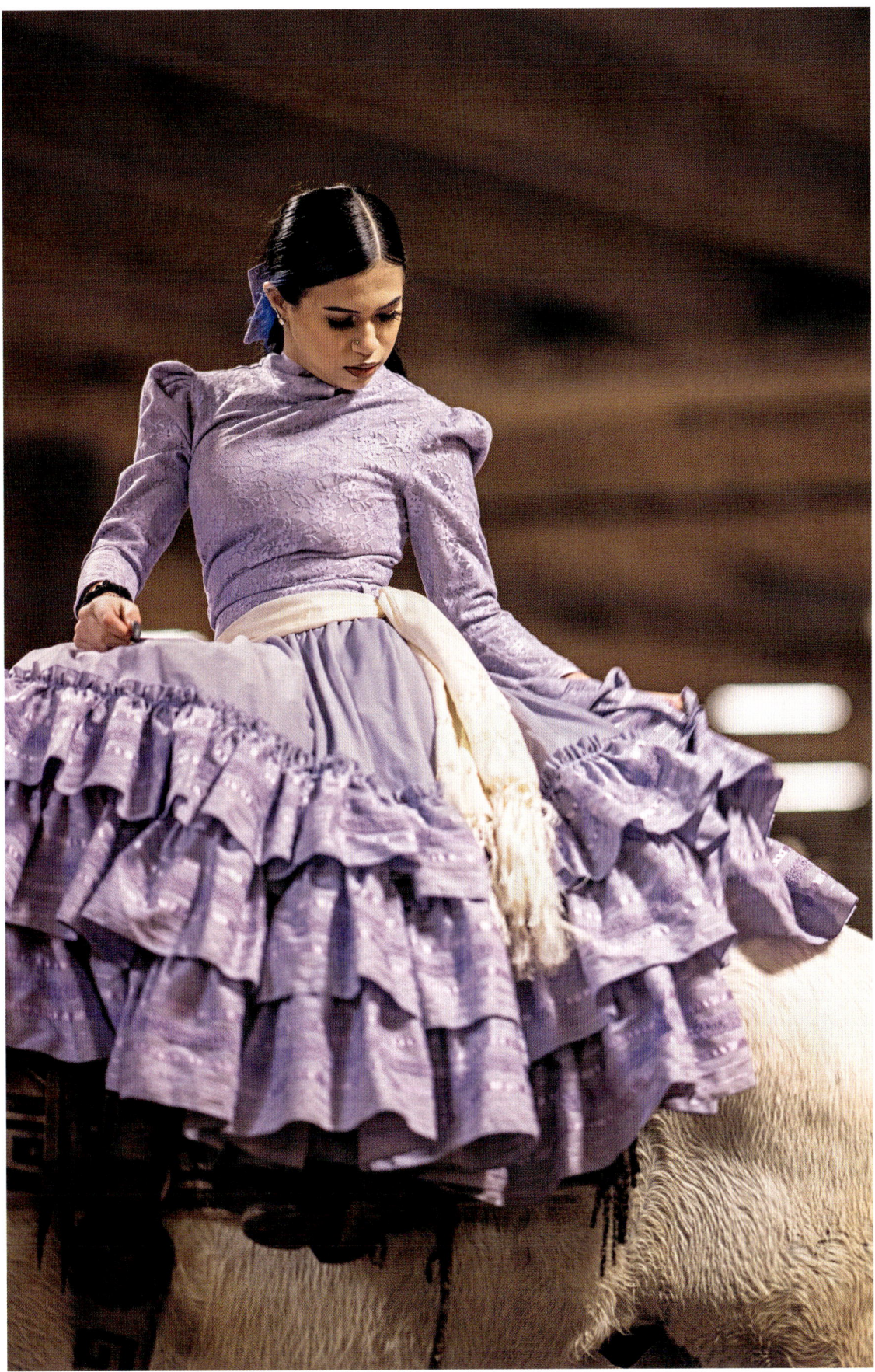

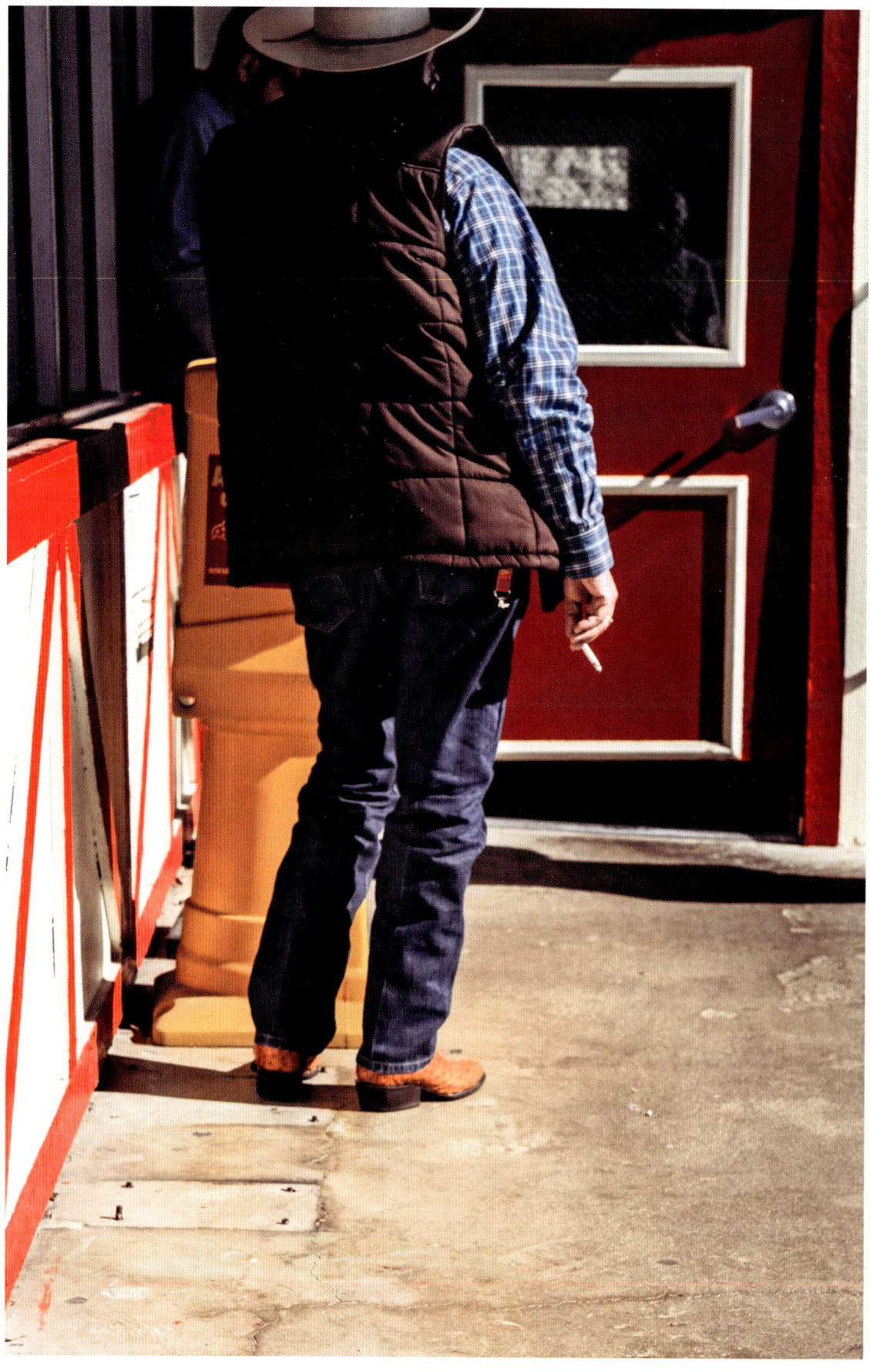

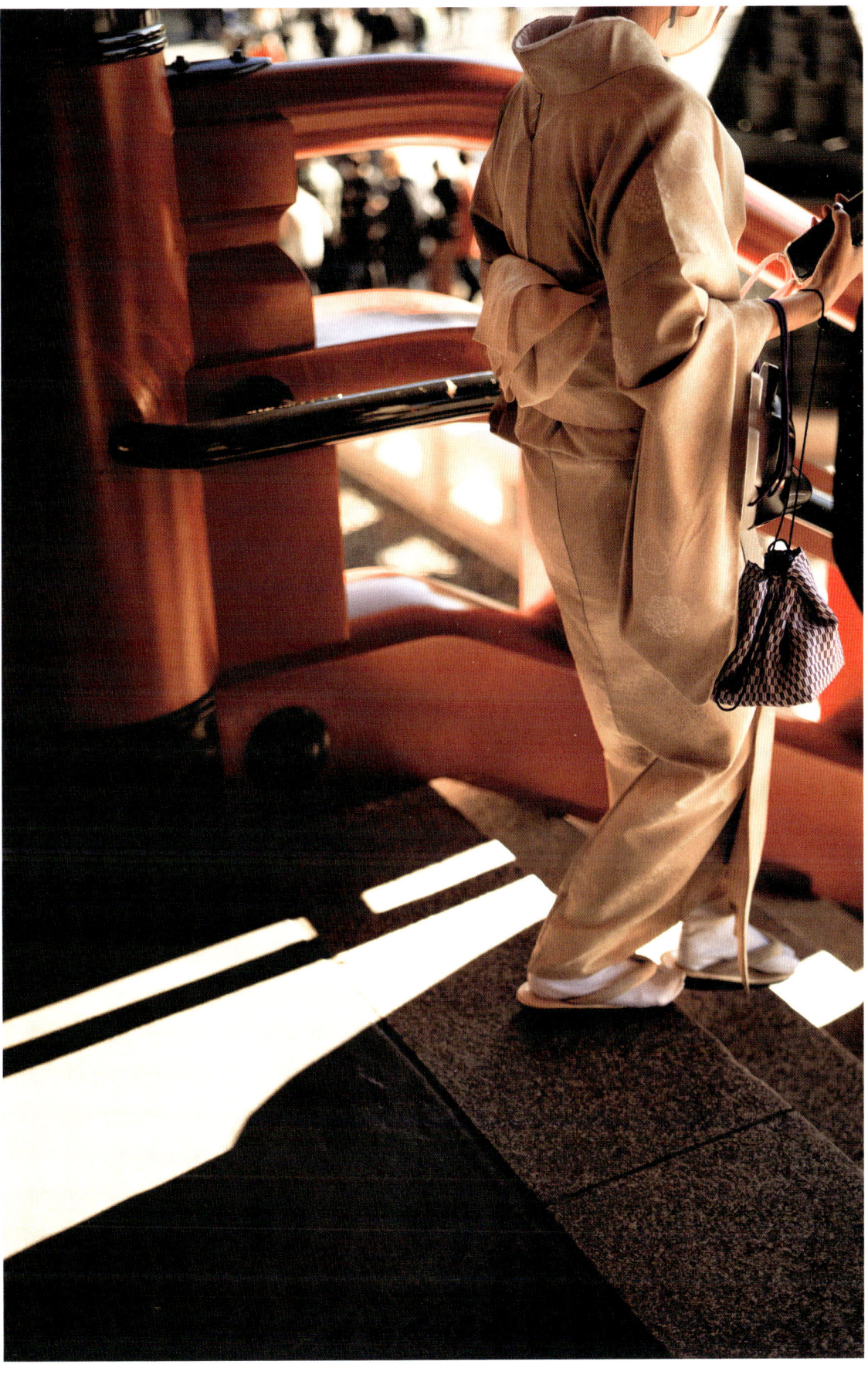

CHAPTER 6

THE FIGURE/GROUND
RELATIONSHIP

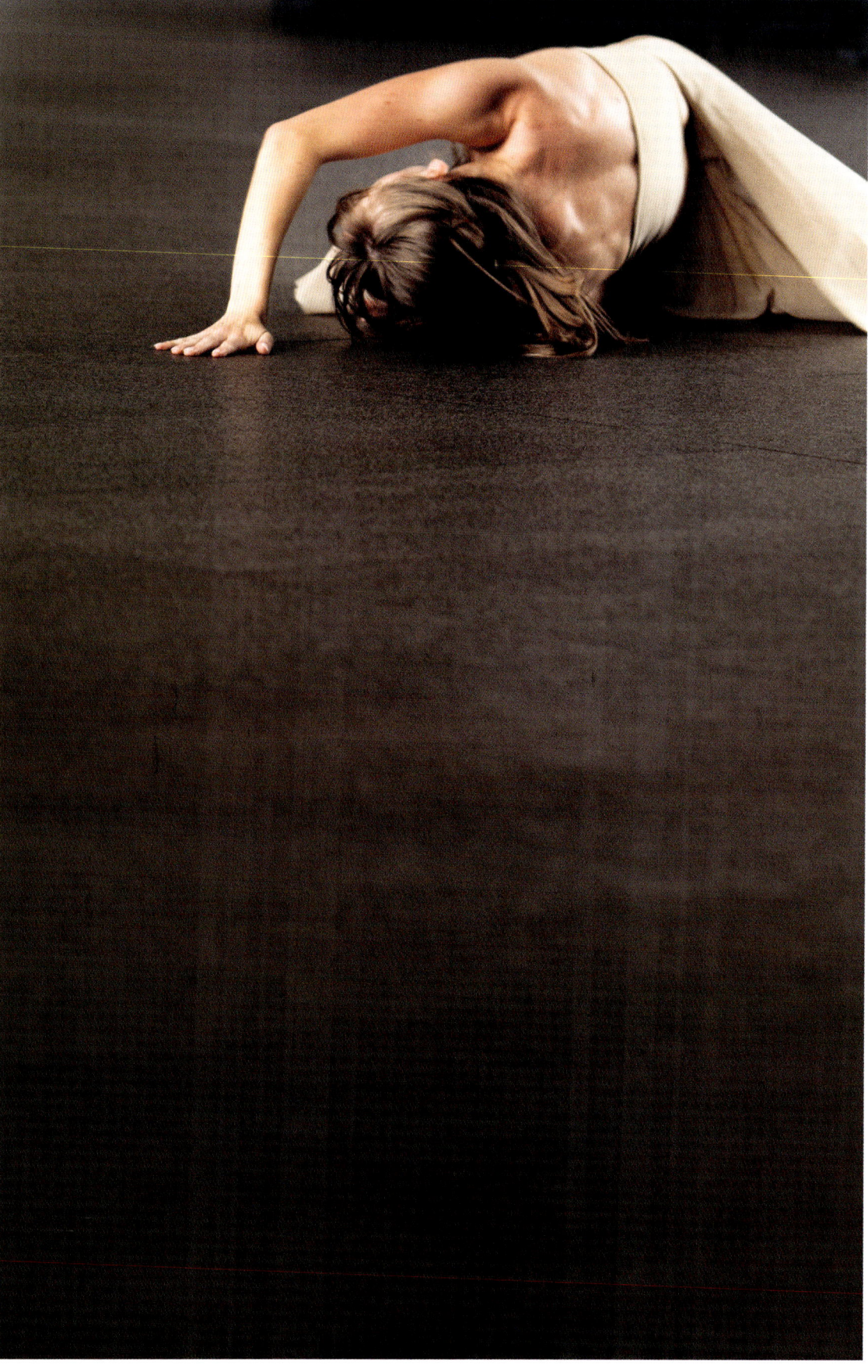

PHOTOGRAPHY IS A TWO-DIMENSIONAL representation of a three-dimensional reality. Think about it. When we create images, they are displayed on flat surfaces, whether it's a screen or a framed print. The third dimension is a lie—it does not exist. The dimension of depth is a conclusion in our minds through hints of perspective, proportion, shadow, focus, and other visual phenomena. We certainly don't have to think about creating depth; it will occur naturally through the lens optics, but understanding the visual components that create this illusion will give you the ability to control the perception of depth. In the end this will give you a more creative visual impact.

But before we get to that, we have to first understand the control we have with the two dimensions that are real. We traditionally refer to this as the figure/ground relationship. Quite simply the ground is the surface you're creating on. You can think of it as the screen or the paper, perhaps both; but more importantly, it exists with an aspect ratio, which we will explore in this chapter.

The figure refers to any object individually or as a group that lives on this ground that we have defined. Most often your image has many figures on it that make up your image—not just the subject of your image. For example, you might be creating a portrait and the figure is most certainly your subject. But there will most likely be other "figures" in the image. These might include physical objects, shadows, patterns, and other details that are part of the background. Do these elements support the subject or sit close and distract? Perhaps they have geometric qualities to them that can give you a sense of balance, or even tension, in the image. These elements might seem inconsequential, but I argue they're just as important as the subject itself.

In the early twentieth century, the Staatliches Bauhaus was a school in Germany that taught various disciplines and combined formal art training with commercial design. It became famous for combining an approach to design that brought together the ideals of form and function. Architecture, interior design, painting, and typography were disciplines that combined for a short fourteen-year period, leading up to political turmoil. Nonetheless, the Bauhaus formalized concepts and principles in a radical and new way for the time. Students learned theory but also practical application.

When we think about the figure/ground relationships, we're literally arranging what's visible in the image onto the surface we've predefined. As simple as that sounds, you have an incredible amount of control in the overall image. You can also have unintended results, say, something in the background is too prominent and distracts from the subject. The success of any image is dependent on the sensibility and experience of the photographer to essentially orchestrate the image.

Aspect Ratio

Photography, unlike painting or other forms of visual art, works mostly with various standards of a square or rectangular ground. Of course, we can crop to our own tastes through editing the image, but we pretty much tend to work with four 45-degree corners. You can, of course, work in unconventional shapes or even a circle. This is something more commonly found in the art of older cultures. But for our purposes here, I'm going to be talking about the modern, conventional choices in photography.

The most common aspect ratio found in photography is the rectangle with a 3:2 ratio. The dominance of 35mm photography over most of the twentieth century is the reason why this is so common. The ratio came about with the first 35mm camera, designed by Oskar Barnack. Barnack began designing the camera in 1913 and it was released as the very first Leica at the Leipzig Fair in 1925. There were, of course, other ratios in early 35mm cameras, but this is the one that stuck.

Barnack's solution was the result of his idea of using 35mm cinema film, which had an aspect ratio of 4:3. To maximize the quality of the image produced, he turned the film sideways and widened the frame to a 6:4, or 3:2, ratio.

It is often said that Barnack also used the reasoning that a 3:2 ratio produced what is referred to as the "Golden Rectangle." A Golden Rectangle is a plane that can be divided into a square with a leftover rectangle. The leftover rectangle has the same dimensions as the original. This ratio occurs in other mathematical concepts, as well, including the limitation of the ratios of consecutive terms in the Fibonacci sequence. This makes a great tale, but Barnack was using a 3:2—the Golden Rectangle is approximately 3.2:2; many get this confused.

Either way, Barnack, along with optics designer Max Berek, invented a masterpiece with the 35mm camera. The 3:2 ratio stuck. In fact, it's the same ratio that carried over to digital cameras today that we call "Full Frame" and the reduced-in-size APS-C format. At the time I'm writing this, we're at 100 years of consistency in one-aspect ratio. That is fairly impressive when you consider the incredible range of work that has been created in these confines.

Victor Hasselblad used the square. There were probably several reasons why, ranging from images on a roll of film to cropping possibilities in post. This was an amazing achievement as well, though secondary to what Barnack had done.

There are other common formats over the span of photography as well. 11:14, 5:7, and 8:10 were all common in large-format photography. Hasselblad popularized both the square format of 1:1 as well as the super wide 65:24 X-Pan format. Medium-format film cameras were also made in both 3:4 and 6:7 ratios. Modern digital medium-format sensors are 4:3; so are Micro Four Thirds and even smartphones. The list goes on.

I'm making a point of telling you all of this because it is important in composition. While the 3:2 is historically the most common, the aspect ratio does change the composition and

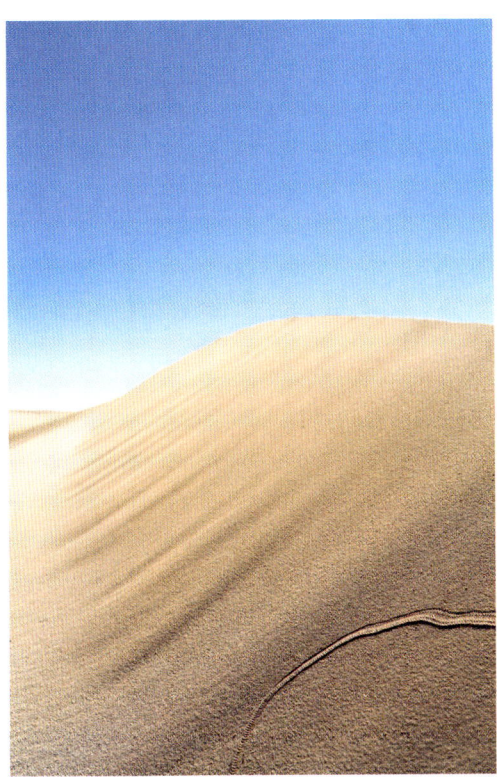

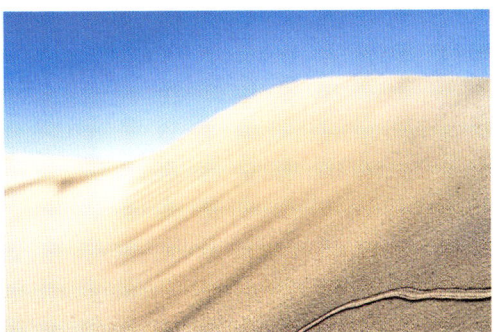

therefore the way that you compose. It affects the way you approach making an image. Finding your voice as an artist is dependent on being deliberate in your choices. Yes, it's always possible to crop, but cropping is not the result of intention. Cropping is a rescue solution. That doesn't mean it's wrong, but in understanding a visual language, we want to get as much right at the point of capture. This visualization in the moment will give you way more consistency.

Portrait vs. Landscape

With the major exception being the square 1:1 format, there are two conventional choices you have for composing on the ground: vertical (portrait) orientation and horizontal (landscape) orientation. Admittedly, for most of my creative life, I didn't put much thought into this. I would respond subconsciously in the moment, depending on what I was going to photograph. Eventually it was Ralph Gibson who changed my thinking on this and got me to start making deliberate decisions on the selection of orientation.

If we consider the physical makeup of the human head, we use two eyes. These give us a field of view that is essentially a landscape orientation—this is how we view the world. Coincidentally, this is also how the world is represented in the moving picture, which, until the smartphone, was standard as a horizontal landscape picture.

Early photography followed the same, with early landscapes being horizontal. Vertical was chosen for portraits most likely to maximize the subject on the ground and to naturally eliminate negative space or elements of the composition that didn't support the subject.

This is still somewhat the status quo, but one thing Ralph inspired in me was to consider the potential in thinking outside the conventional. Ralph largely prefers working in vertical format, as it creates a sense of tension and fills the standard page of a book well. He will move to landscape if he wants a more cinematic feel.

I would go further and argue that it can be very effective to break from the standard conventions to perhaps inspire new creative solutions in your own work. For example, if you shoot a portrait in a horizontal orientation, how would you compose with the negative space? Can that support the portrait somehow? What other techniques can you use to bring emphasis to the subject?

I would argue the same is true shooting a landscape image with a vertical format. The first thing that comes to mind is you'll be cutting away information on the sides. How does this represent the landscape being photographed? How do you suggest what's not in the image by using the subjects, the space, and other elements that do appear in the image?

These are two fairly generic examples, and there are great photographers who have done exactly what I'm describing. But this is my point. Orientation is deliberate and is one part of the whole when making a photograph. Consider this when you're studying the work of other photographers (and even include painters as well). Learn from what others have done and consider this in your own work.

Figure/Ground Relationships

So far in this chapter I've outlined the ingredients of a picture. But ingredients alone don't make for a compelling meal. What makes a composition work is how all of these things relate to one another on the ground we have defined.

I like to teach an exercise—a quite effective way of learning how to understand tension and symmetry in the context of the figure/ground relationship—that I first learned years ago when studying graphic design. All you need is a dark piece of paper (the "ground") and then some shapes cut from a lighter piece of paper (the "figures").

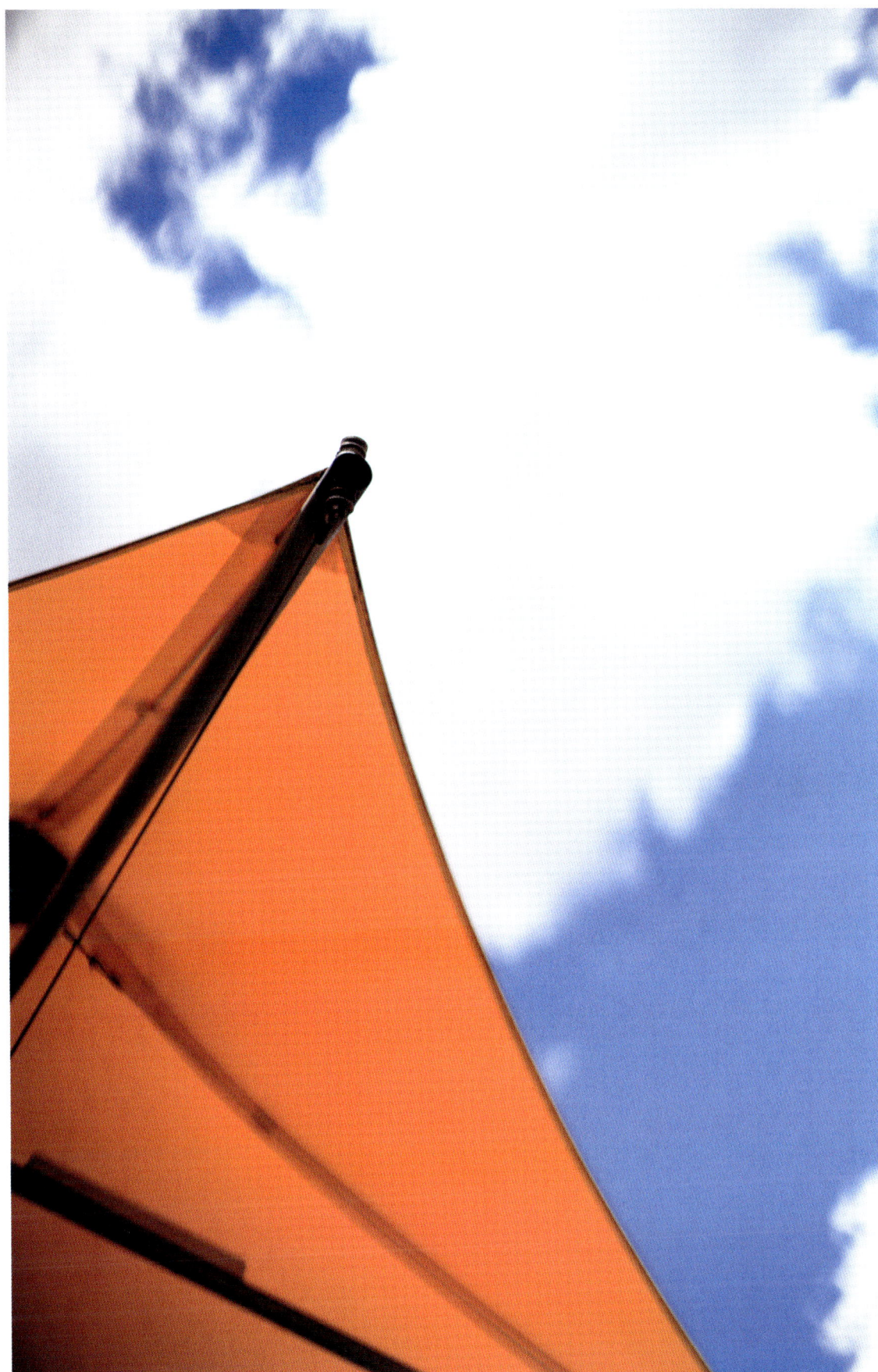

Take one figure and place it on the ground. This gives us ultimate minimalism in that we only have the basic components
of the image. If you want to suggest symmetry, you have one
choice—it's the center of the image.

Now here's the interesting thing: there are actually two centers
you could choose. There's what we call the "geometric" center
and there's what we call the "visual" center. Geometric center
is the exact middle of the ground, or the point where two lines
would cross if drawn diagonally from corner to corner. Visual
center is just above and slightly to the right of the geometrical center. This is sometimes referred to as "museum height."
Even though this is geometrically incorrect, it's the natural
place of visual focus to the human eye.

It's important to understand these two distinctions because
they have different impacts. They represent tension vs. symmetry. They represent the mathematical vs. the human. If I
place something in the middle of the frame, there is no surprise. If I move it off-center, I can create tension or interest.
Why is it no longer in the center?

With the exercise we're doing here it might be difficult to support the idea of visual center, but when the image becomes
more complex, you'll see that it does have a slightly more natural feel to it, as illustrated in the examples to the right.

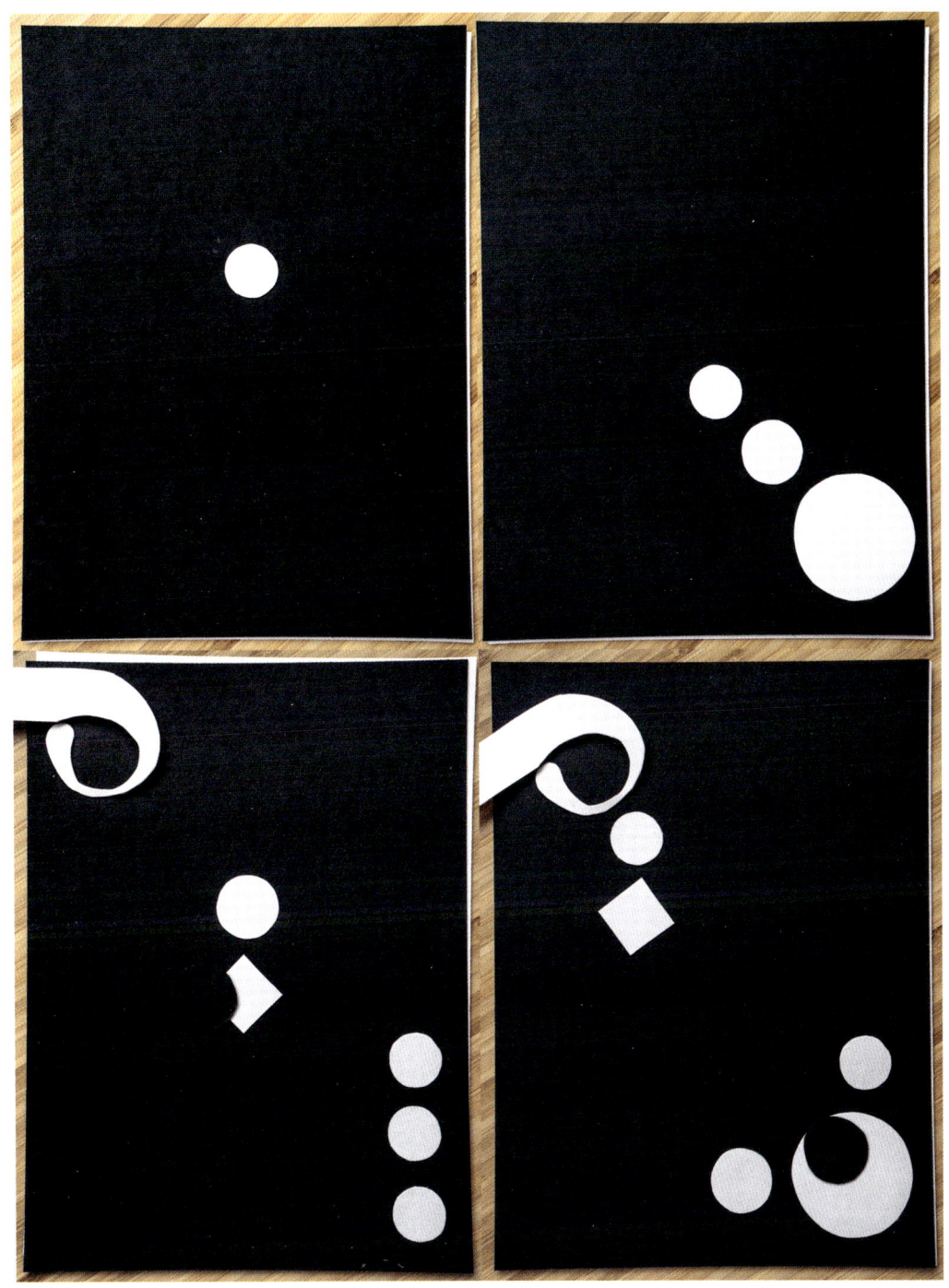

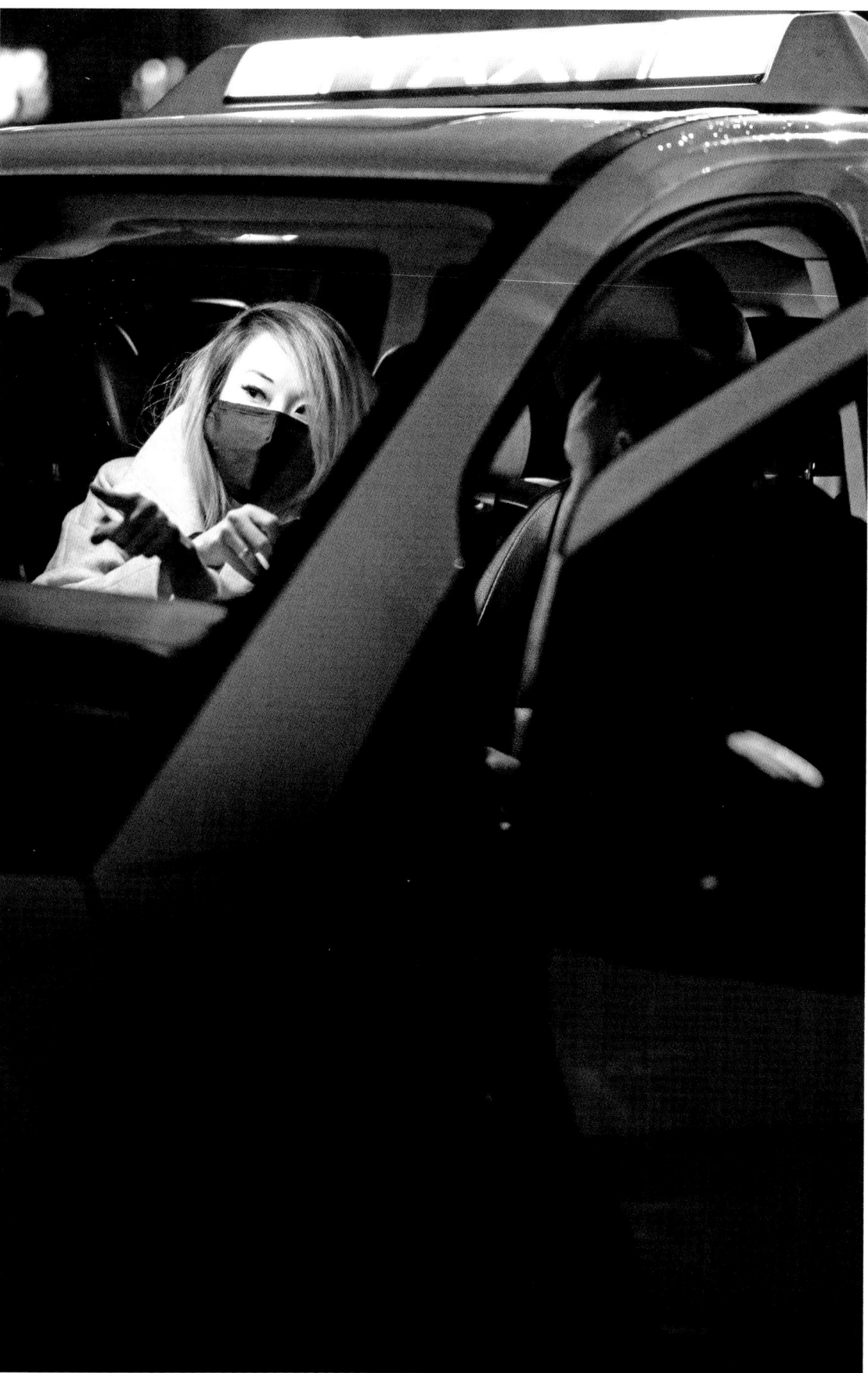

Balance and Proximity

Visual balance is a way of creating a visual resolution. As I explained with the idea of visual center, this resolution is based on human perception, not always mathematical reality. This is an important concept to internalize. When I started studying visual theory, I expected to be told where to place visual elements due to governing mathematical reasoning. While there are certainly theories to tell you what to do, there are no rules strictly requiring placement. In art the human reaction is always the most important reason for any composition.

Proximity helps you achieve visual balance. The "Principle of Proximity" is a design concept. The human brain organizes images and design elements into logical groupings. The Principle of Proximity suggests that related objects can be grouped to emphasize their relationship. Perhaps more importantly, this suggests unrelated objects should not be grouped together.

Emphasis

Emphasis is about contrast—you can't have a point of interest without components of less interest. This is achieved in one of three ways. You can work with scale: the interest will fall on the larger element in the composition. You can also use space: negative space can emphasize an element even though it is not the largest in the composition. You can also work with light: brighter points in an image always bring more emphasis than darker points.

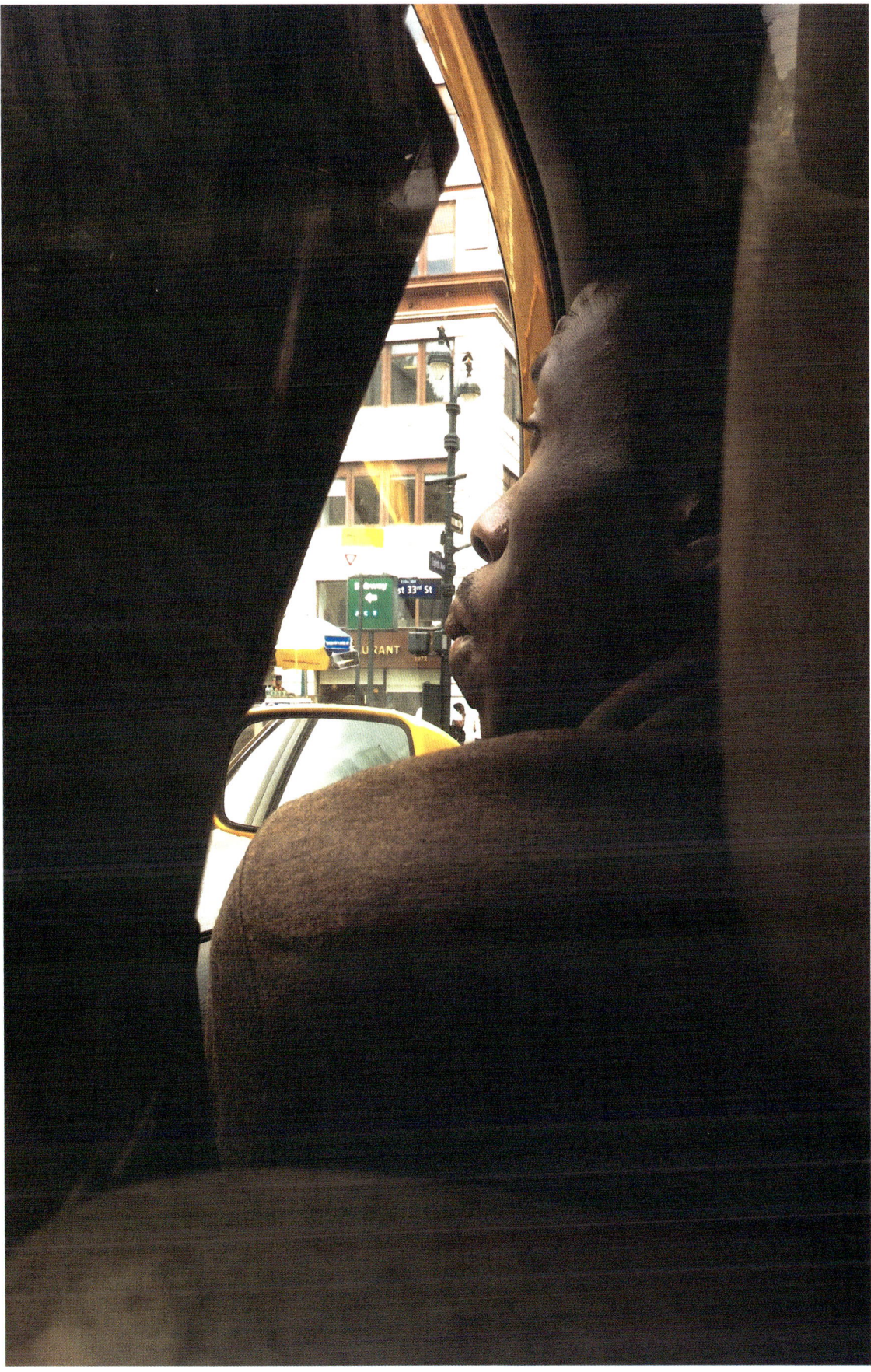

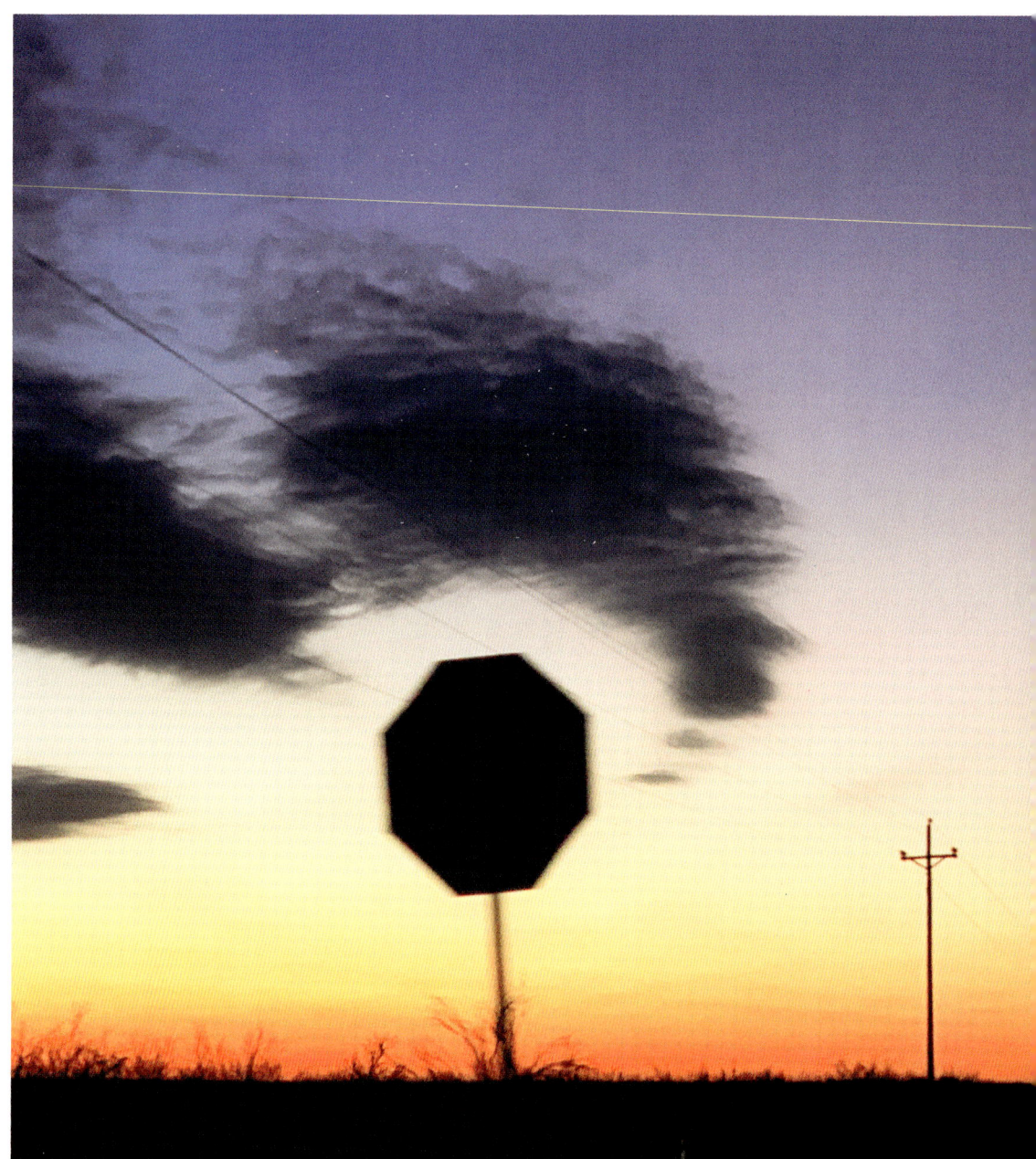

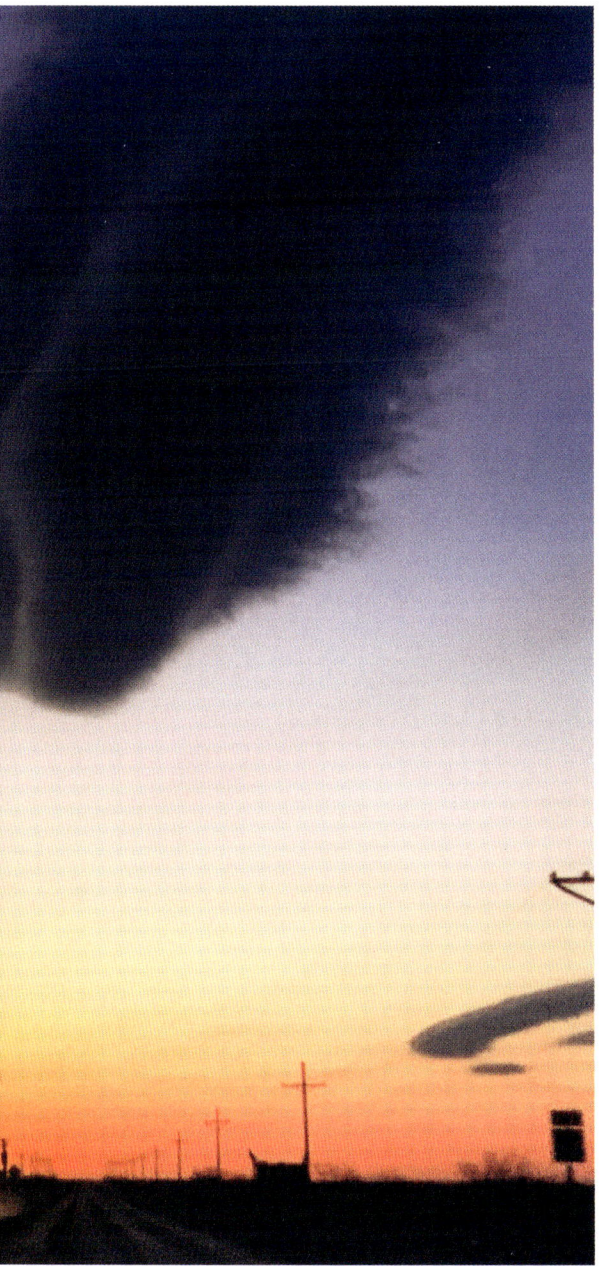

Hierarchy

Hierarchy refers to the order of importance of various elements in the composition. If you have an understanding of how to emphasize specific parts, the ordering of their importance is the next step toward communicating the idea of the overall composition. Typically, three elements are all that are possible in any photograph. So what is the order of importance for those elements? This will lead you to the technique of showing the hierarchy that you define as the artist.

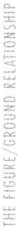

Perspective

Perspective has a dramatic effect on the composition as a whole. It can also affect the previous examples of emphasis and hierarchy. This is a technique originating from motion picture composition. Consider the camera angle. If it is at eye level, this yields a result that is somewhat expected. Changing the point of view from the camera has a dramatic effect on the end result. Interpreting the image from a very low angle near the ground enhances the dramatic effect, as everything in the image appears to tower over the viewer. However, using a high angle changes the perspective of everything in the image. The result can have a feeling of oversight or control from the viewer's perspective. These are subtle changes that have a dramatic impact on the picture as a whole.

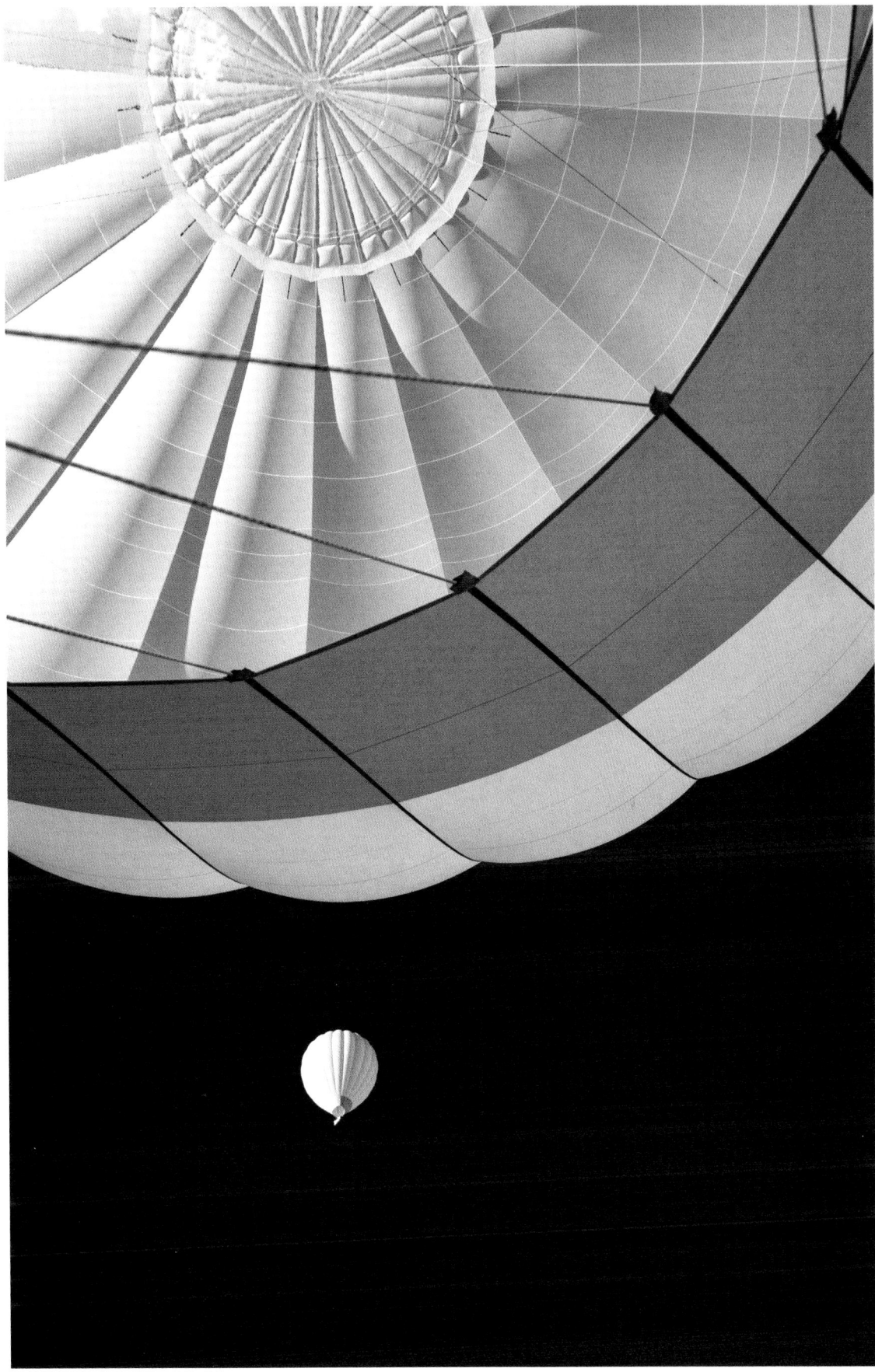

Scale

The closer we are to an object, the larger it appears. The further away we get from an object, the smaller it will appear. Seeing objects next to one another is going to create the perception of scale, particularly if it becomes dramatic. For example, we know through experience that buildings are taller than humans. If our subject is a human and the building on the side appears smaller, then we conclude that it is further away.

This can also be manipulated for a dramatic effect. This is done a lot in surrealistic contexts where objects are intentionally placed "out of scale." For example, a hand holding an airplane, or a figure standing on a giant fork. These are scales that don't exist. This use of the technique can be effective when using metaphor or creating abstract emphasis.

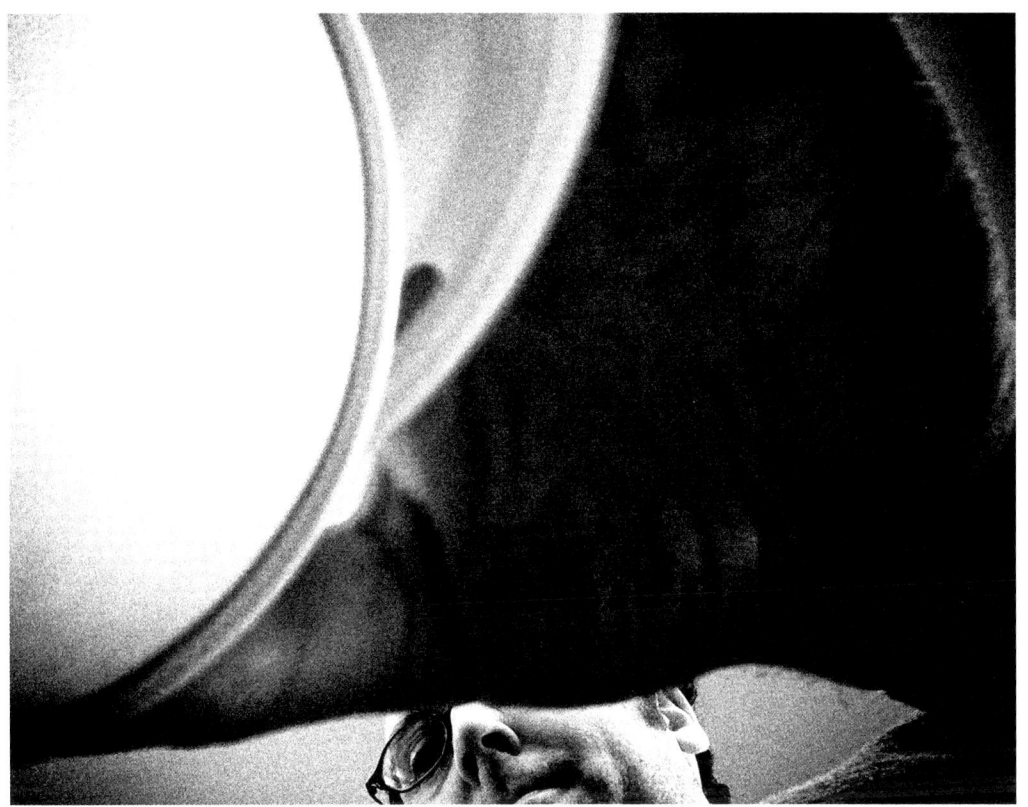

THE FIGURE/GROUND RELATIONSHIP

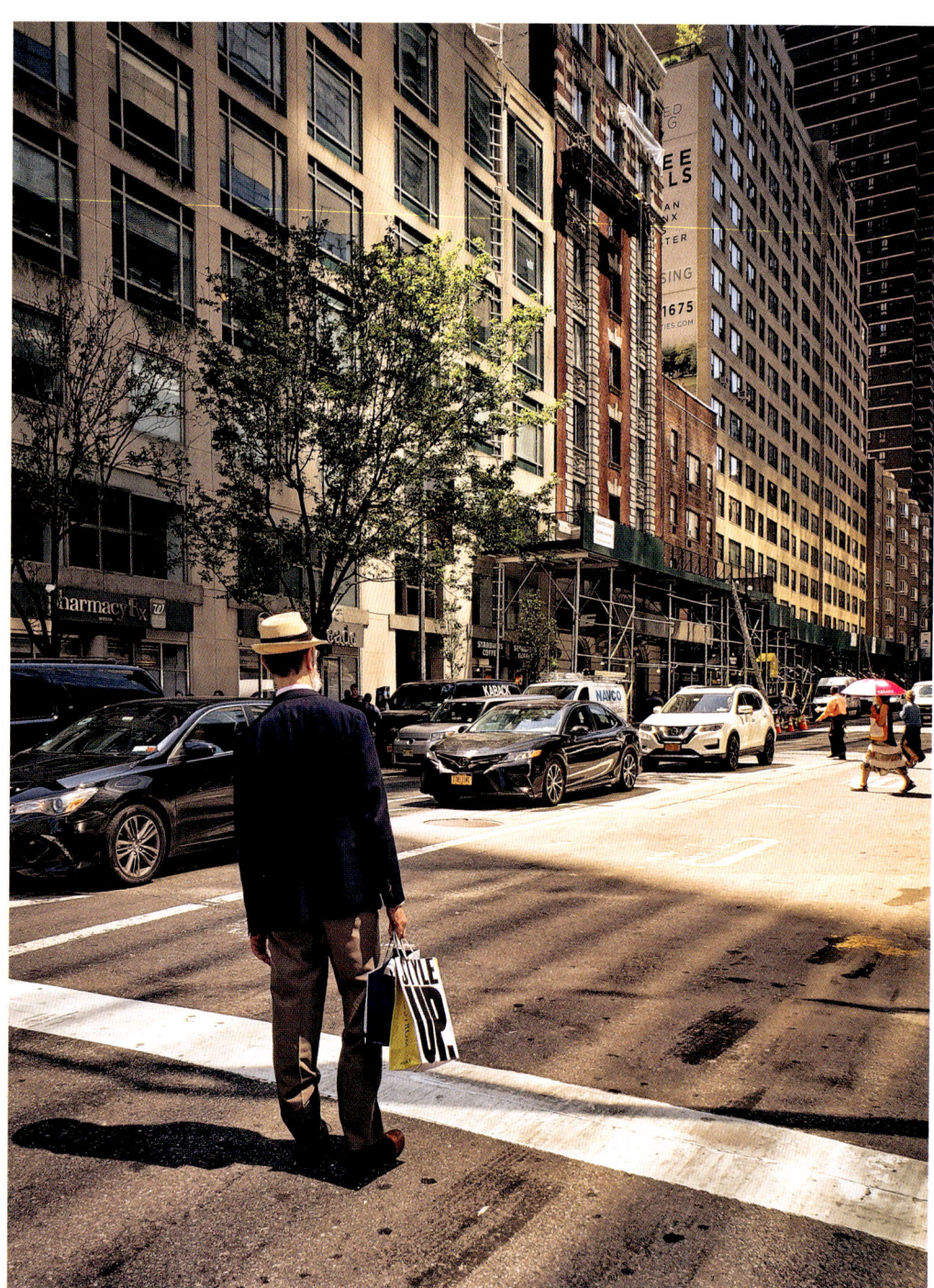

Depth

Depth is arguably the magic of any two-dimensional work of art. As I stated earlier, it doesn't exist. Therefore, depth is concluded in the mind of the viewer based on visual indications in the image. These visual indications include contrast, light falloff, perspective, and scale. If you're familiar with the work of M.C. Escher, you've seen that depth can be manipulated and questioned in two-dimensional art.

Depth is probably the most powerful concept in photography for how it can be used to create interest or surprise. We can use it to support our subject. We can use it to create complexity, or reduce it to create simplicity. Ironically, it's probably the least considered visual element in most photography. Because the camera will create some kind of illusion of depth automatically, it becomes easy for photographers to consider it less.

CHAPTER 7

FIGURE/GROUND RELATIONSHIPS are the essence of any visual composition. Another way of looking at these is through the relationship of positive and negative space.

Positive space is an area of the image with detail of importance. This could be an area that is the subject of the photograph itself, or it could contain supporting detail to the subject. Positive space is where the attention of the viewer is directed and typically has a higher energy of visual weight.

Negative space is the opposite of positive space. Negative space is lower in detail if not just pure shadow or highlight. Negative space is void of any subject or other compositional element. This suggests a lower energy to the overall picture.

Now, it is important to distinguish between negative space and dead content. Dead content is usually composition that does nothing to serve the overall picture and should be cropped out. Negative space is different in that it usually contains very little detail, but the idea is to use it to support the subject.

To use negative space to your advantage, you must consider the balance of the image. If positive space is higher energy and negative is lower, then we generally need a greater ratio of negative to positive. There is no specific ratio, as it depends on the composition. But, in general, I think the proper ratio is two-thirds negative space to one-third positive space; in other words, our golden ratio from the previous chapter. This is only my rule of thumb. You should always use your own intention of what looks balanced. Truly "negative" space usually takes up a large proportion to create this balance. It's a game of proportional contrast. Contrasting visual energy requires a proportional shift in scale to make it functional.

Another note is that negative space should be just that. If you have objects, shape, or a higher degree of detail this idea won't work. However, low energy texture and consistency of detail, throughout the negative portions of the image are fine. The idea is not to distract from the positive space in the image.

In the end, the negative space draws the eye to the subject and visually supports it.

CHAPTER 8

THE EDGE OF A PHOTOGRAPH

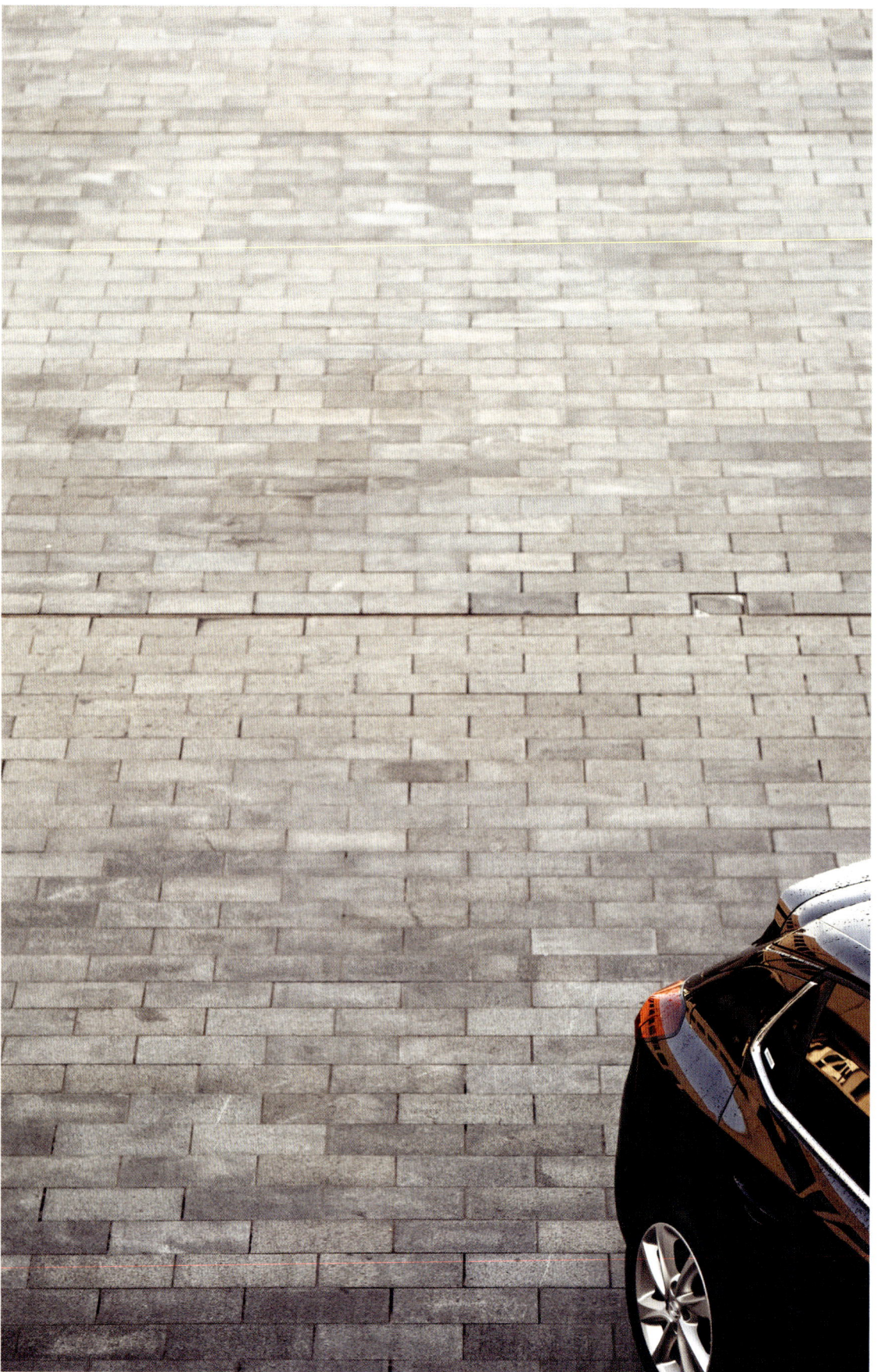

IF WE CONSIDER ANY VISUAL COMPOSITION, the borders of the ground are what define it. This differs from the way our eyes see the world. Human eyes are designed as binocular optical systems. In other words, our two eyes form one image that our brain perceives. There are two things I find fascinating about this. First, we don't have perceived edges to our field of vision either on the sides or the top and bottom of our field of view. We can perceive that we see more side to side than top to bottom, but there's no "frame." Second, our brains constantly adjust how we perceive this field of view depending on where our attention is. It's working like a zoom lens, though technically the optics in our eyes are only prime lenses.

For example, as I type this I'm looking at a screen and sometimes a keyboard. My attention is focused in, and I'm not paying conscious attention to my peripheral vision. If I look up from what I'm doing, I might immediately perceive the entire room. My cat is telling me she needs food (though she's at least an hour early). My cat is ten feet away, but that's where my attention and perceived vision goes. I might walk outside to see what the weather is doing, and I take in a wider angle of perception and notice the mail has arrived and my car needs to be moved out of the sun. And there's the neighbor so I wave.

Our eyes and brain work together in a very complex way. Now what's interesting is that visual composition is not this at all. We can create a picture by controlling the elements in a scene. We can decide what to show. We can decide what not to show. We decide what to emphasize. We might lead the viewer's eye to a specific part of the image.

Now, back to the borders of your composition. Because they define the image area, everything within those boundaries is your composition. We don't expect the viewer's brain to tune out unwanted information. Therefore anything inside those borders is important.

Photographs can live or die at the edges of a composition. These are very sensitive areas. There is a natural emphasis that happens in these areas that gives considerable weight to the subject. This relates to the negative/positive space relationship. This can be used to a very effective visual advantage with intention.

This can also be a horrible disadvantage when you have elements near the edges of a composition that are non-essential. Because there is more weight near the frame, any element will get more emphasis. This is particularly a problem in photography because we have more limited control over the scene than a painter does. Photography is a subtractive process and inevitably something might enter the frame at the moment you activate the shutter. Or sometimes our brain is focused on the subject and we just don't pay attention to the borders at the time of image capture. The only solution at this point is cropping, which is easy enough, but you'd be surprised at how many photographers don't pay attention to this and leave things in on the final composition.

This is a good point to discuss cropping, as it's an age-old argument between the purists who only crop in camera and the others who are fine with taking care of it in post. There are many famous photographers who crop from the original file or negative. There are also great photographers who are consistently amazing at cropping in camera.

So, is one better than the other?

Honestly, the argument can be made that photography is all about cropping. Photography is a subtractive process of defining the image within a scene. We don't paint on a blank canvas, and everything we physically show exists in front of the camera.

Basically, every photographer is always cropping. There is no getting away from it. I personally feel that the final image is of most importance. Any photographer should be willing to sacrifice all for the final image. That is visual communication. If this means cropping in post, you should absolutely crop to serve the picture. Now how much you crop starts to cloud things. It can be done at the cost of resolution—especially if you're using a smaller format or lower megapixel count.

In the beginning, everyone is learning. As you are learning, you're going to be cropping a lot in post-production. But you should really try to learn from any cropping necessities and start getting it right in camera when you're framing a shot. If you need a longer lens, then get one. If you need to get closer when you're shooting, then stop being lazy and move closer. Think about the crop as you're shooting. I've always tried to keep post-production to a minimum. It's just more efficient to get it right at the time of capture. You have to practice this, which takes time to master. But this skill will save more time in the long run. You will become more of a photographer and less of someone simply using a camera.

CHAPTER 9

BLACK AND WHITE

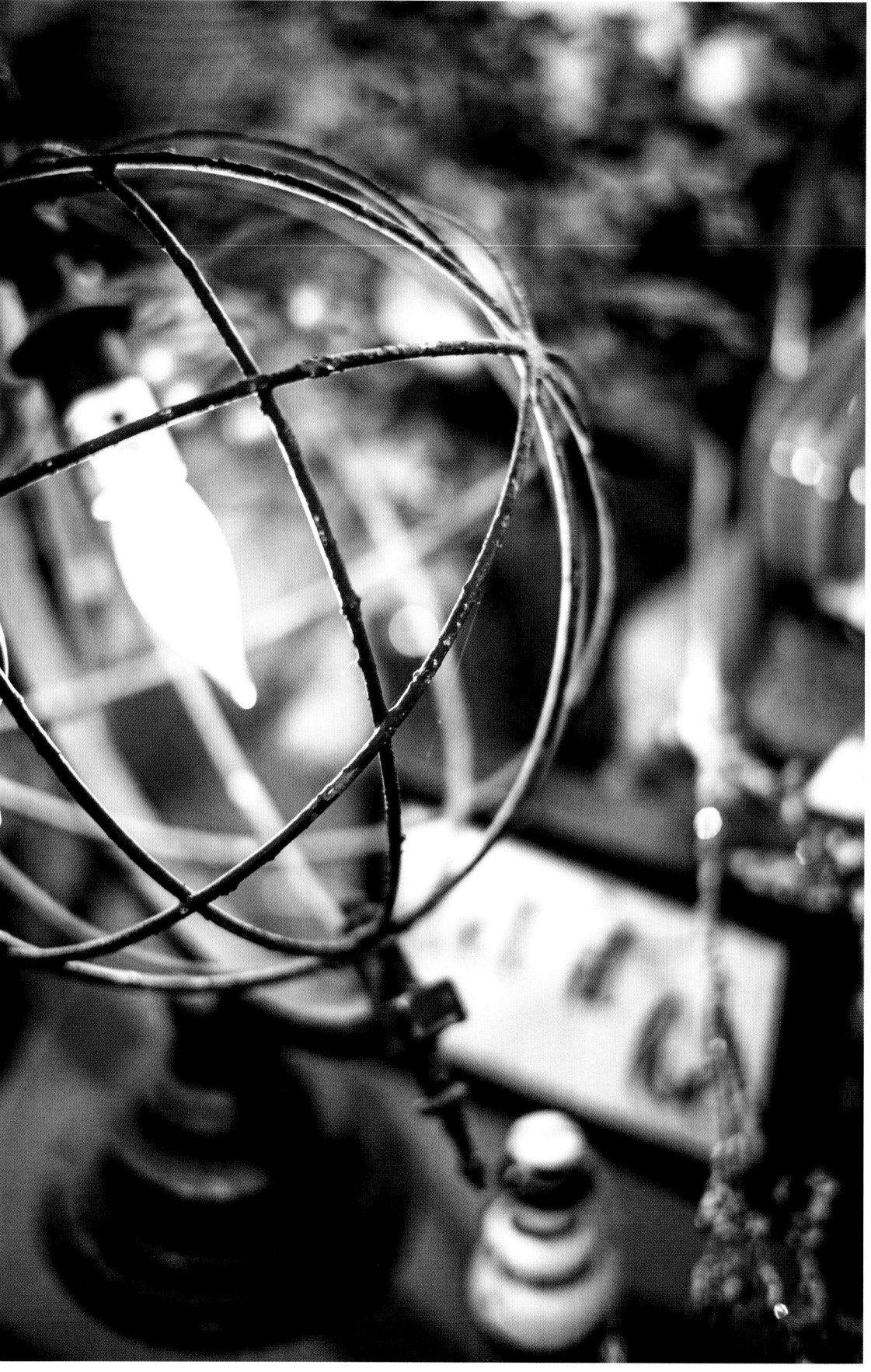

IN THE EARLY 2000s I was working a lot in black and white. This was during the dawn of the digital revolution. Nikon and Canon were producing DSLR cameras that were somewhat affordable and the photography world was changing rapidly. However I wasn't quite ready to embrace digital as a medium. I was a big practitioner of Ansel Adams and the Zone System. I experimented heavily on how to manipulate chemical temperatures and development times to control the overall look I wanted in a black and white photograph.

And since I was a complete nerd, I shot all my "family shots" on 35mm in black and white. But I would scan everything I did—at the time, that was me "going digital."

One day, I gave my sister a set of images framed for her birthday. My three-year-old nephew said to her, "Mom, how come Uncle T always takes pictures of gray people?"

Then it dawned on me. My nephew was young, but his somewhat limited life experience had shown him that all still photographs were in color. I realized that a whole generation would see color as the default medium in contrast to much earlier generations that might not have ever seen a color photograph.

Originally all photography was monochrome. Technically it still is. Digital cameras use filters over a sensor to split the image signal into color fields. Software brings this together in a form the eye sees. But even in the early years of photography, color wasn't conceived until the 1860s, and it was another 100 years before color film was readily available in every drug store.

Writing this chapter, I'm realizing that this topic merits an entire book. So, for our purposes here, I'm going to specifically talk about black and white in the context of visual communication.

Consider for a moment the concept of "reality." Photographs are certainly not that. Even as much as photojournalism strives to deliver some kind of "truth" through an image, I believe it is never possible.

Photographs represent a frozen moment in time. There is no obvious past or future—they show only the moment of a now. This becomes interesting as every image we see is from the past, even if only the few seconds between taking an image and then seeing it on the back screen of a digital camera. Now we can imply the past and future, but those are never the reality of a photograph.

Photographs are two-dimensional. They consist of height and width and are printed on a flat surface. The third dimension of depth is implied. It doesn't really exist. As photographers we can effectively enhance the perception of depth with techniques of angle, compositional depth, light, and even focus, but the reality is, these are only conceptual techniques. The element of depth is a lie.

The point I'm getting to here is that photography is its own reality. If we consider frozen time as one step removed from what is real, then consider depth as an illusion as abstract a second step from reality. Removing color information from an image is now a third step.

Earlier we talked about the idea of abstraction Visuals are a balance between elements that are representational and the abstract. Both evoke meanings for the viewer because our brains are wired to make associations. Color information comes with associations of its own, so its removal is another level of abstraction.

Effective use of monochrome in photography comes down to several basic concepts.

When we reduce an image down to the essence of light using only monochrome, the image is defined by shapes and textures. These have to fall on the continuum of the gray scale somewhere, and you must understand that there is a point when texture becomes too dark or too light and loses its definition.

We are talking about dynamic range. If you're familiar with Ansel Adams's Zone System, you know that it's completely dependent on this concept of texture. Adams, along with Fred Archer, created the Zone System in the late 1930s when both were teaching at ArtCenter in Los Angeles. The Zone System was a formal method for developing a negative that would print easily on standard contrast paper in the darkroom. It was an important concept, as it was based on technical sensitometry. A photographer could get predictable, consistent results without the typical trial and error.

Adams's idea was that if you understood how to control development times and temperatures of the chemicals, you could achieve the exact results you "previsualized" behind the camera. It's an intense practice of being able to achieve anything you want through spot metering and understanding how to expand or contract development.

While this process is designed for black and white film, there arc concepts here that apply to digital photography today. The time I spent learning this process had one of the most important impacts on my work as a photographer today: I learned how to understand and control dynamic range, and I learned how important it is to understand the limitations of the equipment you are using.

Perhaps more importantly, the photographer is always smarter than the exposure meter in a camera. The human brain knows the important elements of a scene and how they should be rendered—a computer cannot make these interpretive decisions.

Adams divided the grayscale spectrum into eleven zones, each one stop of light apart. They were labeled evenly across this spectrum with Zone 0 being pure black and Zone X being pure white. The photographer understands that skin tones should fall on Zones V to VII, depending on how dark or light they are. Snow is defined by fine details so it cannot be on Zone X; it must be rendered around Zone VIII or IX. Darker elements also lose definition if they go too dark, so placing them below Zone III results in a loss of texture.

The Zone System defines a dynamic range of Zones II through IX (eight stops) and a textural range of Zones III through VIII (six stops). The combination of using a spot meter, calculating the differences, and either expanding or contracting development times will give you the results you're looking for.

Now, with digital photography, it might seem like this is a dated technique that doesn't apply. Our cameras can capture a greater dynamic range. We're not using chemicals to control contrast. However, the basic concepts are still there.

When is an image too dark? Are you losing important texture to clipped highlights? Is the image well-balanced? These are important considerations photographers must understand. They can be different camera to camera. I would argue it's more complex now than it was in Adams's time.

But this understanding is part of the language. I don't believe it requires spot metering and math today, but it does require the photographer to understand what is important in an image and how to protect highlights and shadows to preserve detail.

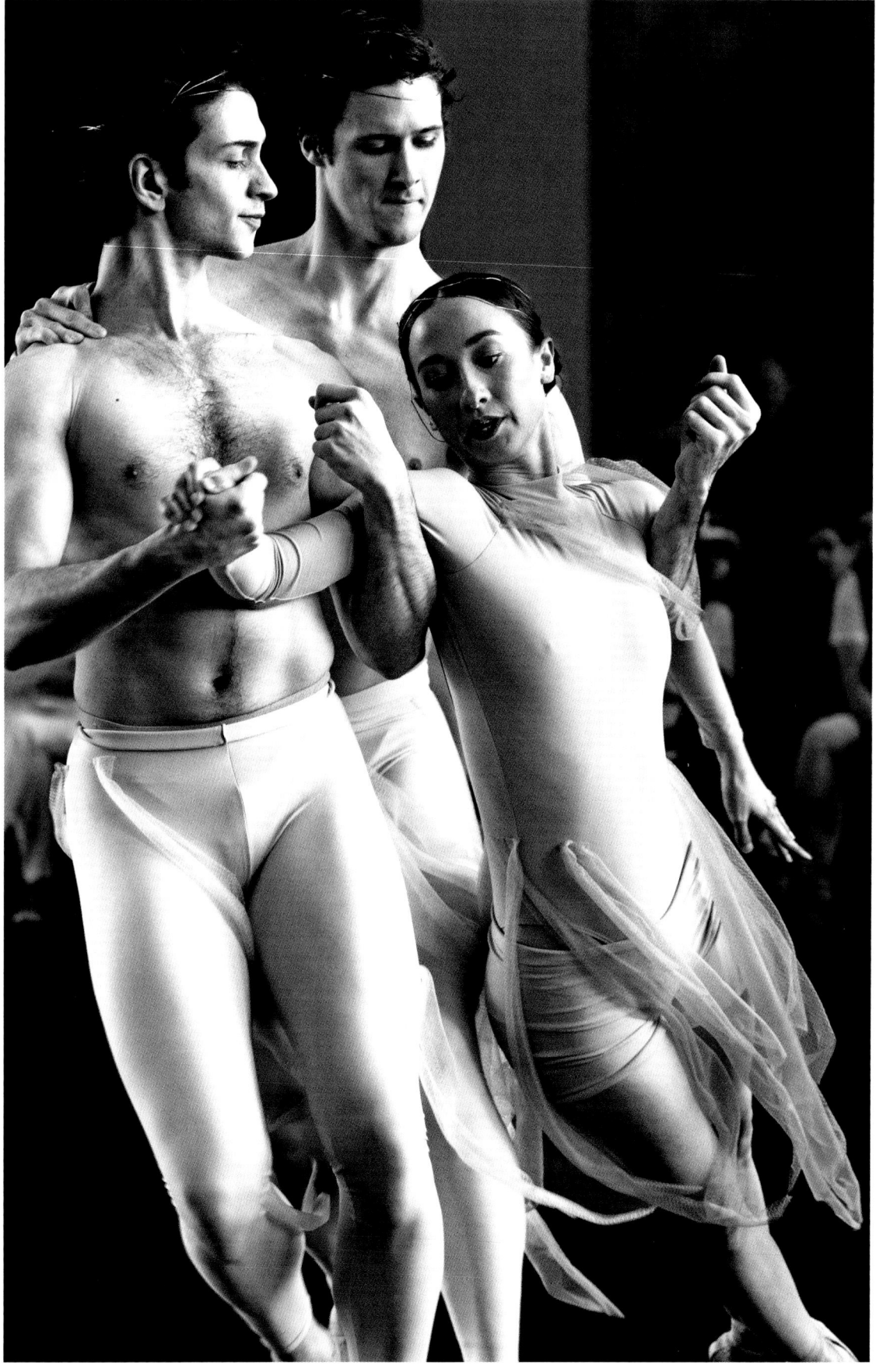

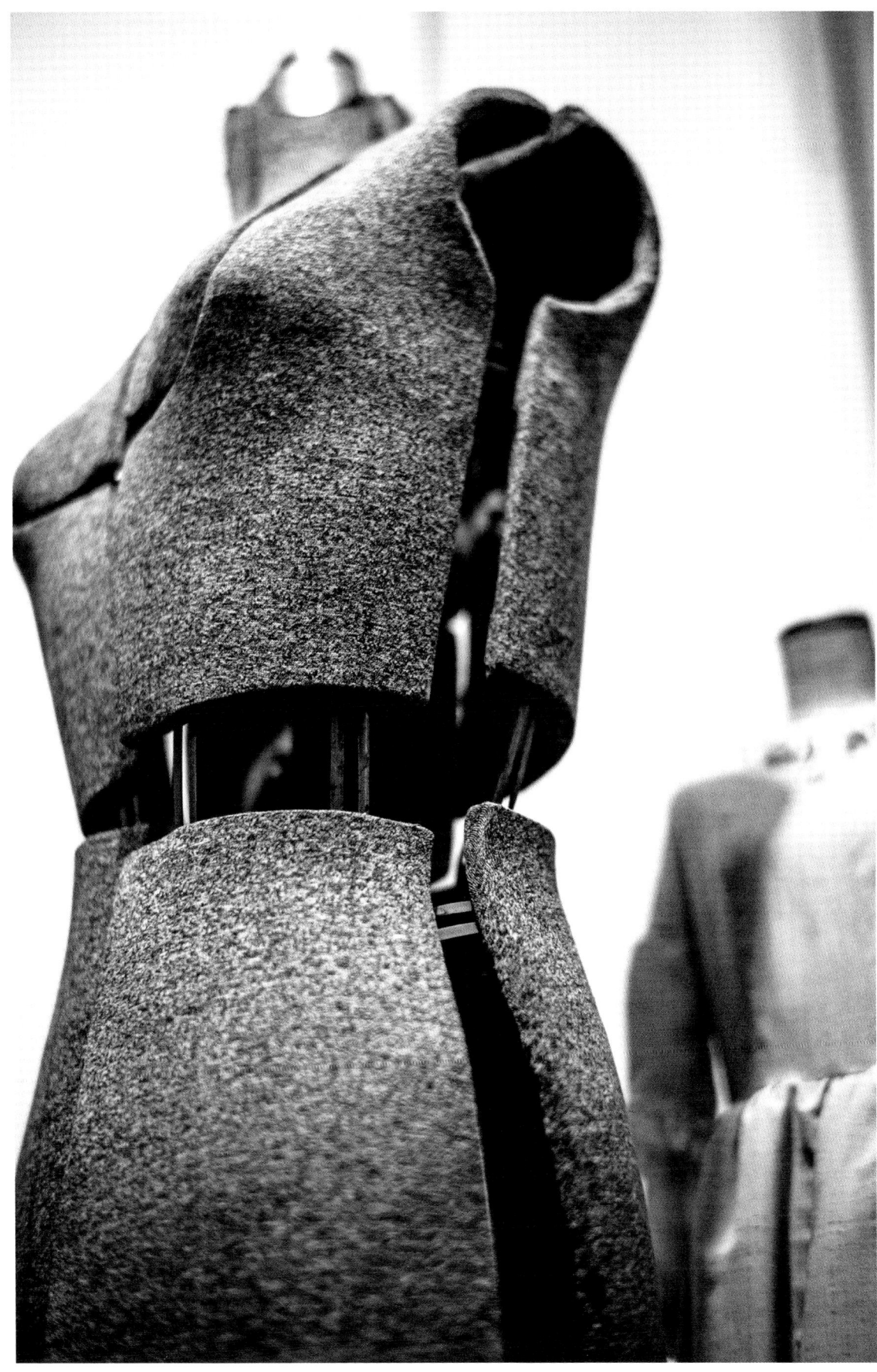

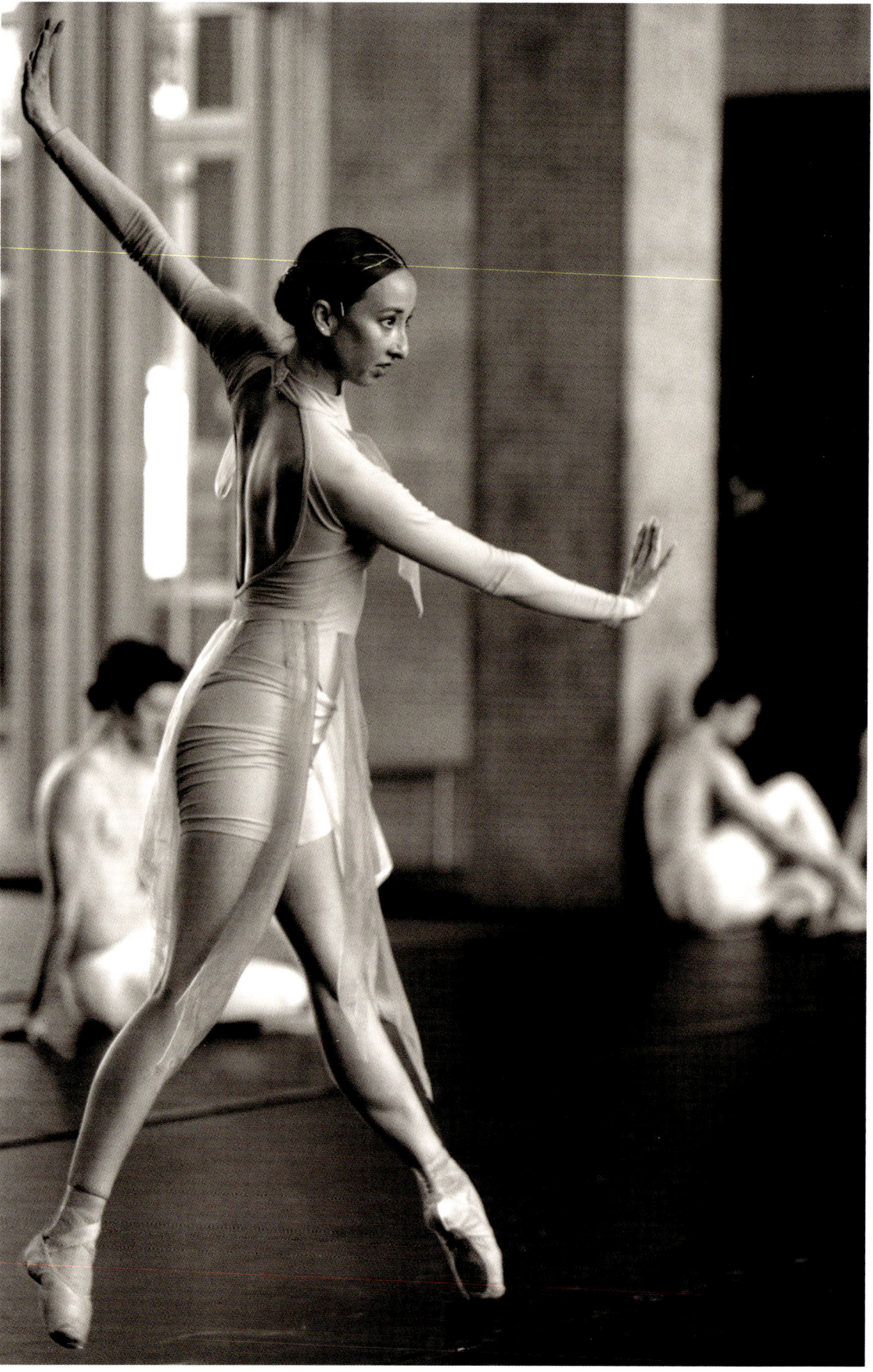

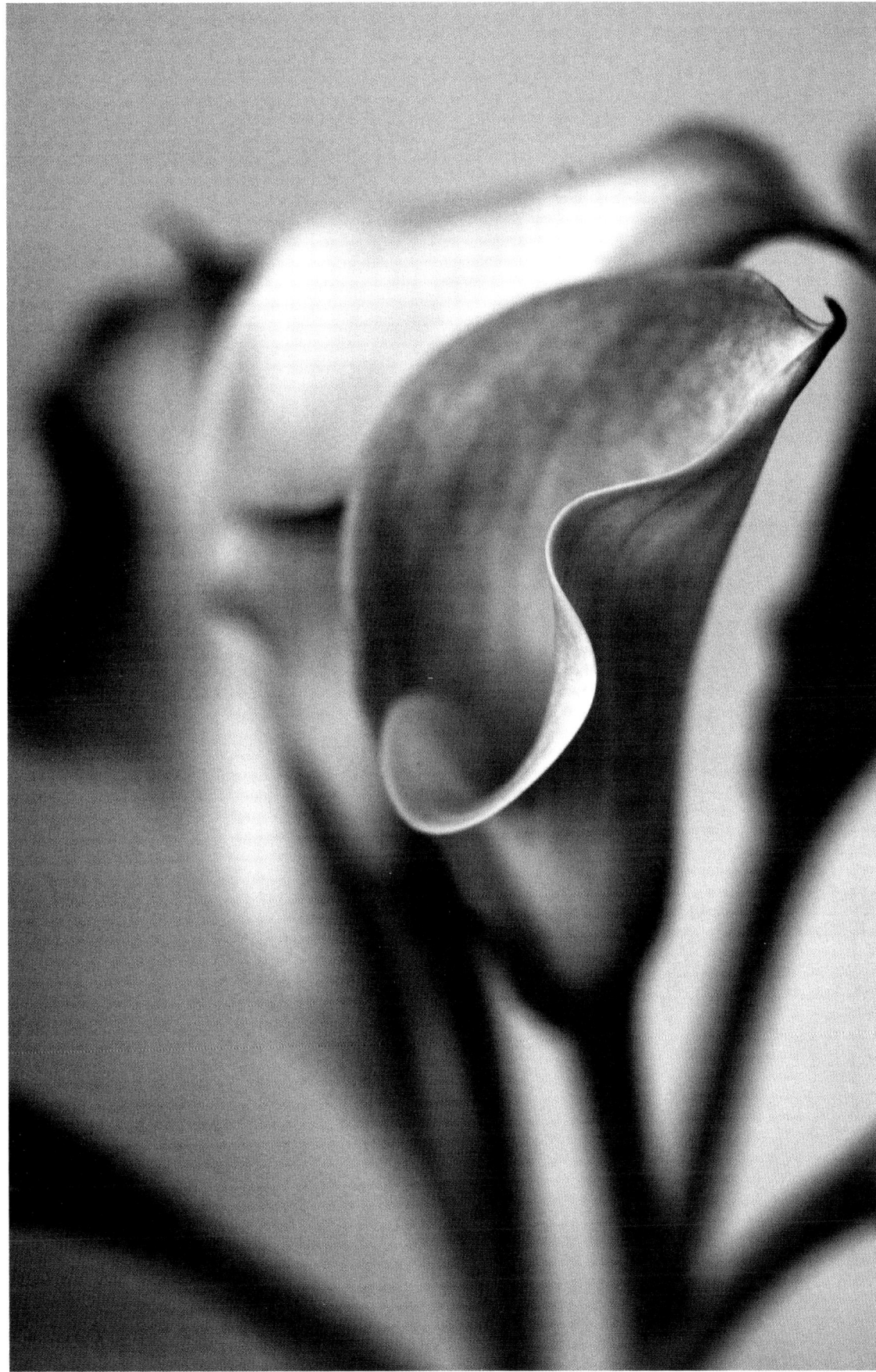

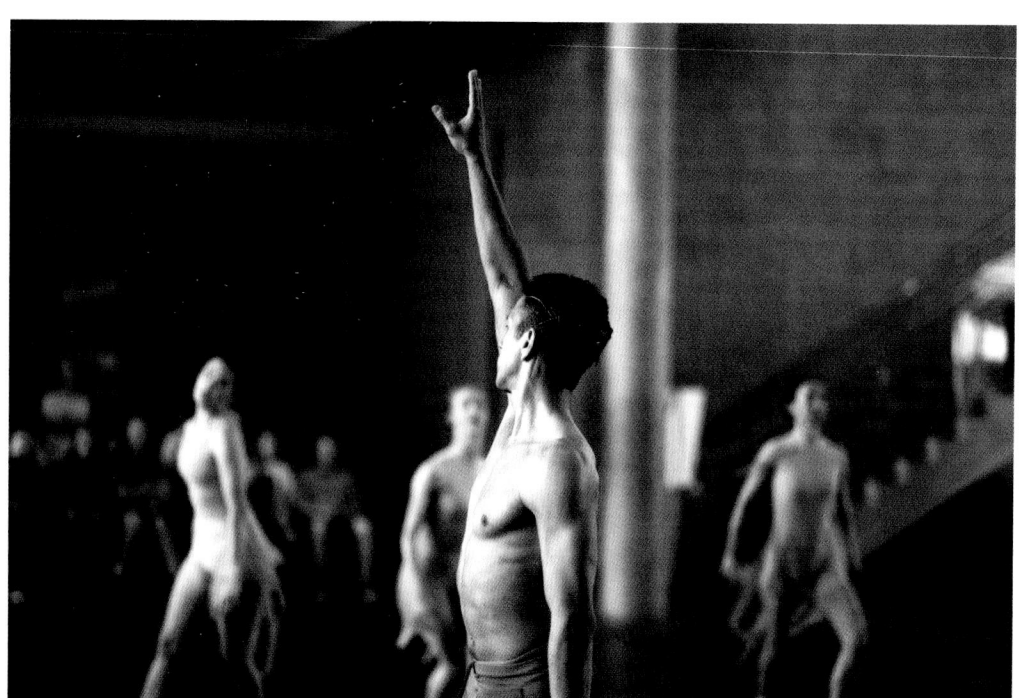

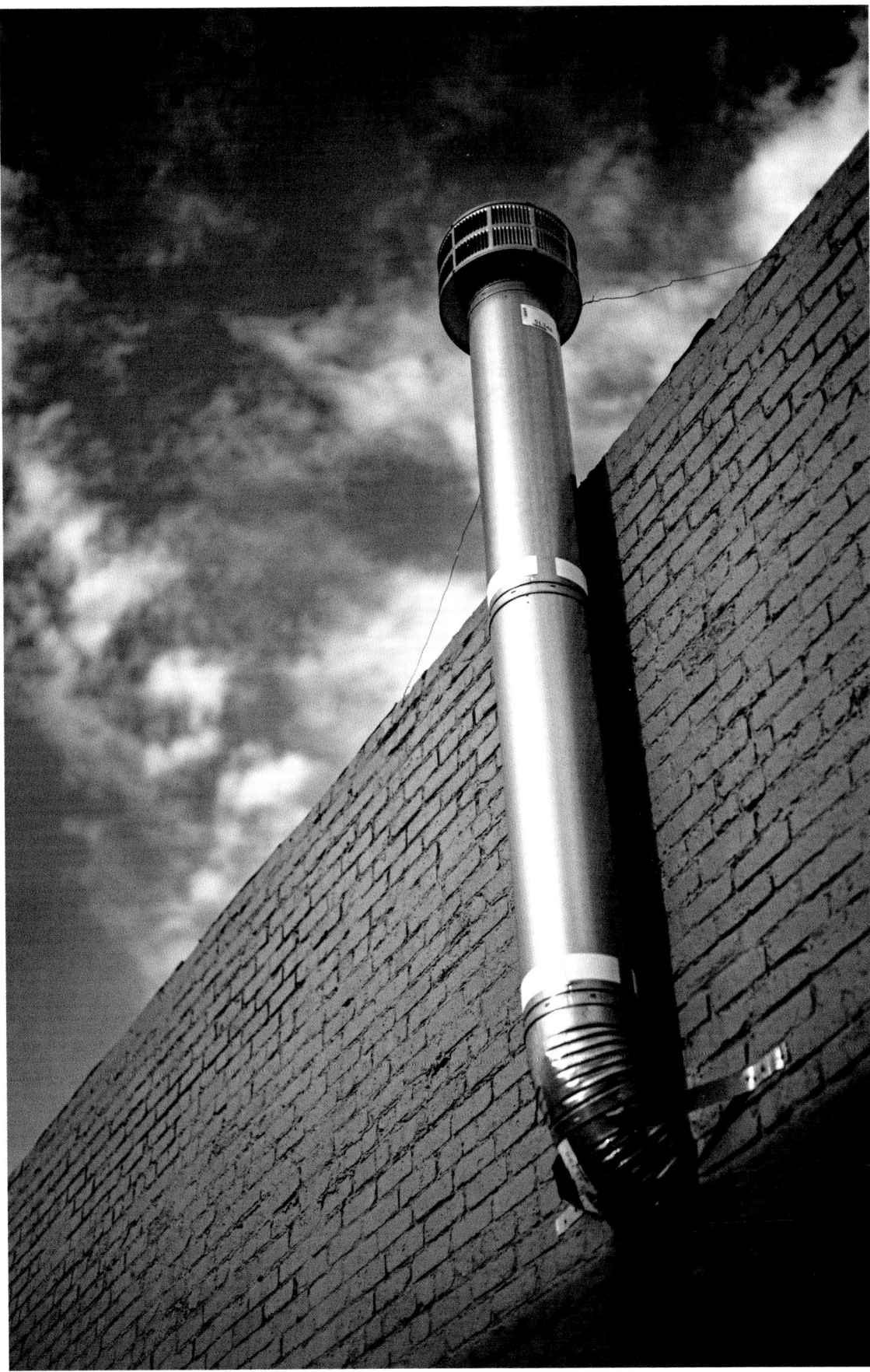

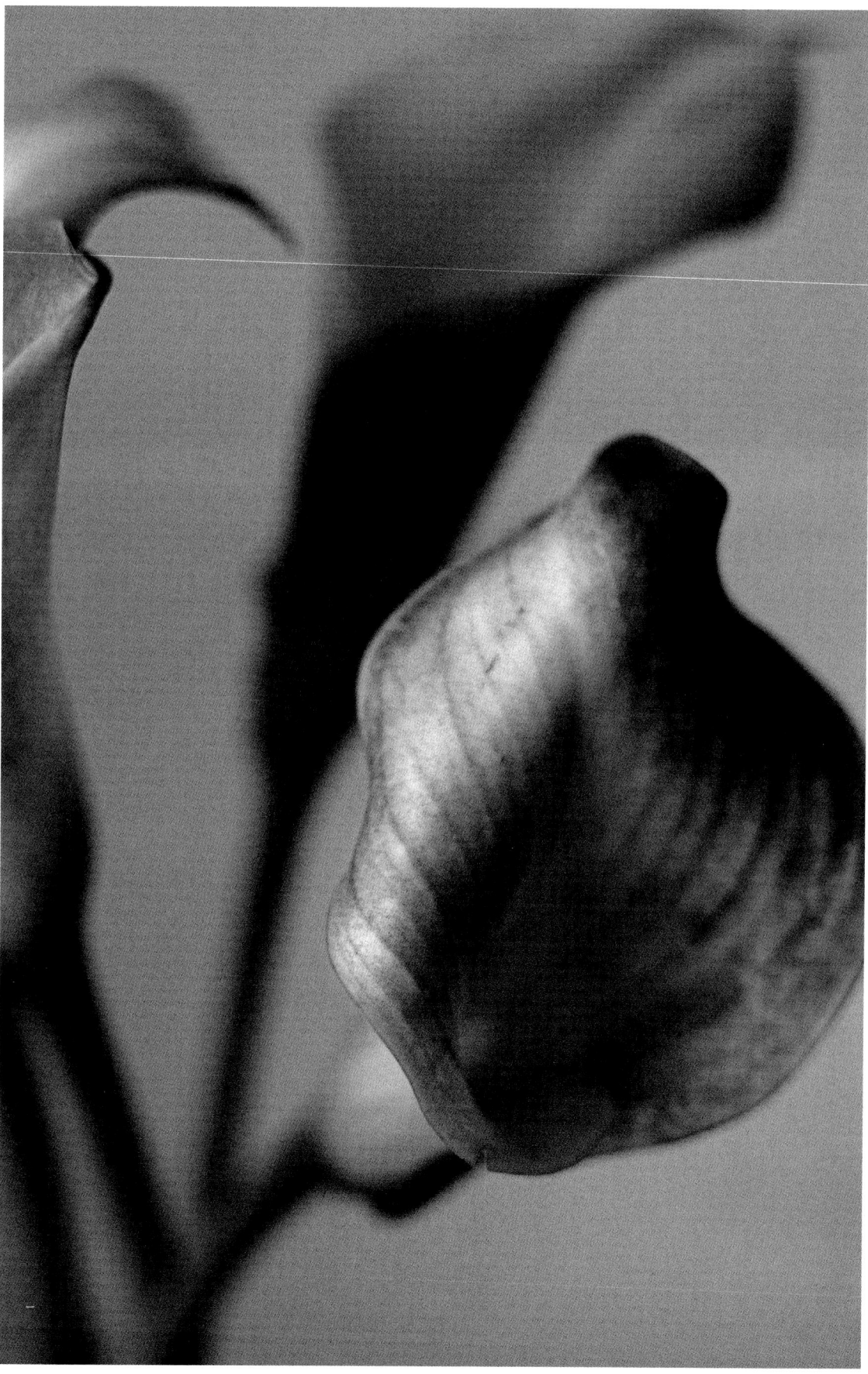

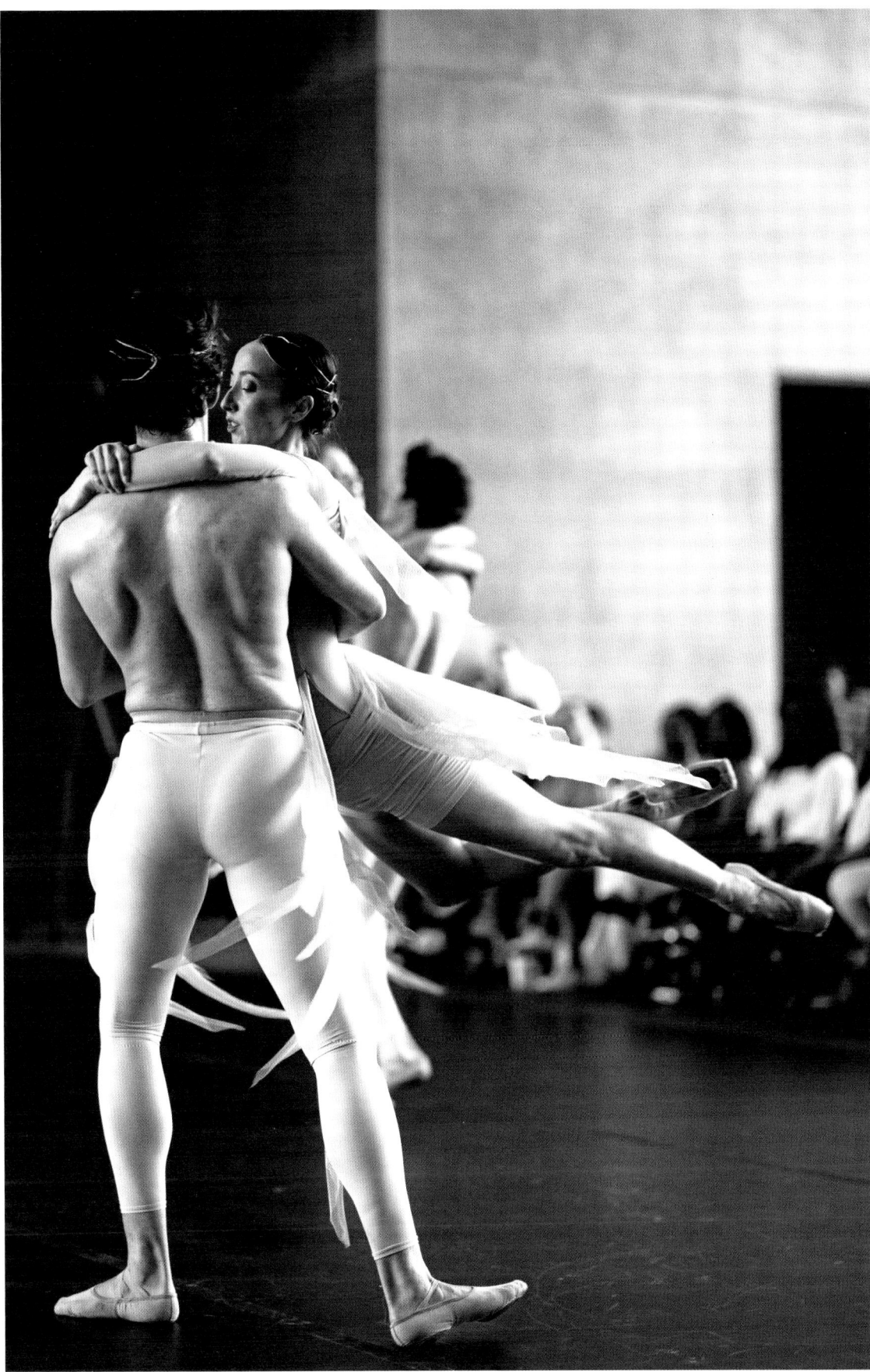

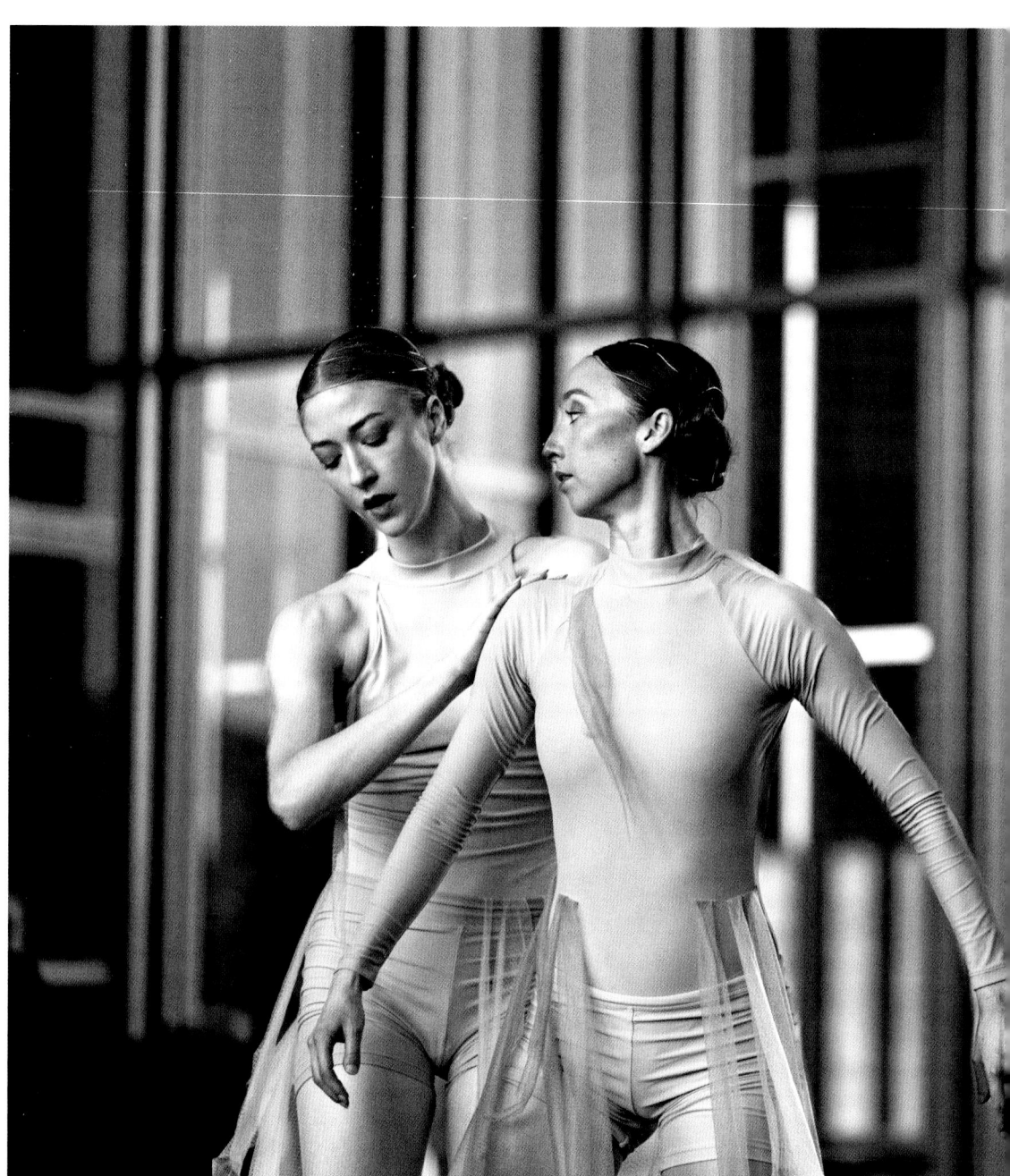

John Blakemore is a British photographer who is a major practitioner of the Zone System. And what he does with it opened up doors in my understanding of monochrome technique that I had never considered for creative options.

Blakemore takes the limitations the Zone System tries to avoid and turns them around into opportunities for high- or low-key photography. If we understand that detail is lost by Zone IX, what if we push the limits right to that edge? What if our photograph then only is made up of three or four zones? Is that an unbalanced photograph? Do shadows have to be black? This type of questioning of the subject had a big impact on the way I started to think about a black and white picture. I once spent an entire summer on a series of studies using flowers and other organic objects, creating still life photos that tested my new found thinking of the Zone System.

I live in Texas and the summers can be brutally hot. Years ago, I had a loft in an old textile mill that had been converted to apart-

ments. It was great for natural light but not so great if you wanted ultimate control of the light. Summer came and I started working after dark. I'd work most of the night on these studies. I talked about this time in my life back in Chapter 3, but I want to make the point again here that I didn't have fancy cameras back then. I didn't own fancy lights either. I used lamps and work lights I had purchased cheaply at the hardware store. For diffusion, I used sheets and fabrics. I would bounce light off the ceiling or a large sheet of poster board if it was too harsh. I really wish I'd photographed my various "setups" to show you, but at the time I was embarrassed that my equipment was so cheap.

But what I did that summer was one of the most impactful things I've ever done for my own skill set. In three months, I put in an enormous number of hours studying and learning how light and detail rendered in black and white. It had nothing to do with the cheap cameras and lenses. It had nothing to do with the horrible lights. It had to do with me understanding how to communicate

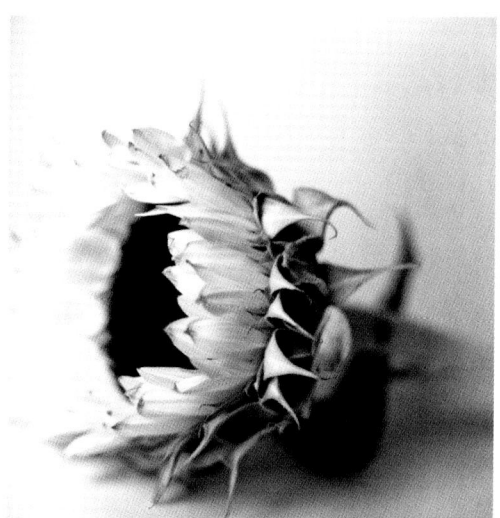

in black and white—nothing else. I learned a lot and improved a lot in a very compressed amount of time.

Monochrome, to me, is the essence of photography, since it represents light on its own. I've always been of the school that if an image doesn't work in black and white then it's not going to be very strong in color. There are a few exceptions to this in the history of photography, but on the whole that statement is true.

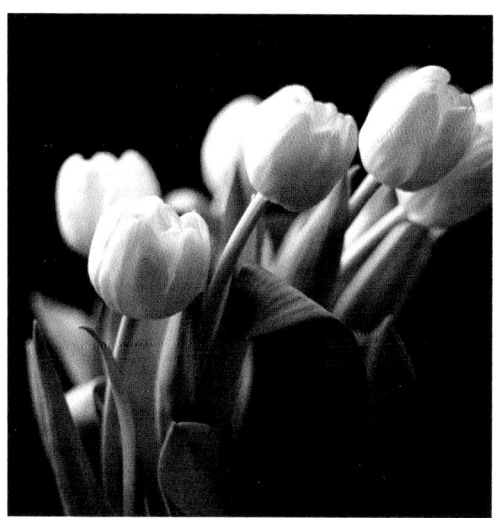

One of my favorite things about black and white is the ability to create minimalism using contrast. The look of my work has largely changed over the years as I've come to love embracing pure whites and pure blacks in an image. I love to shoot in high contrast lighting, even at night. Remember, when you clip highlights or your shadows get too dark, you lose detail. This is actually a technique that I enjoy making part of the image. As long as the essential parts of your subject are conveyed, letting parts of the image go to a pure white or black can actually be a technique to mask information that is not essential, leaving you with a cleaner composition.

Monochrome has always existed as the base form of photography. It is simply the difference between light and shadow. But having spent many years working with it, I can tell you it gives the basis for everything we're seeing in a photograph. Monochrome photography gives you the foundation that extends into color.

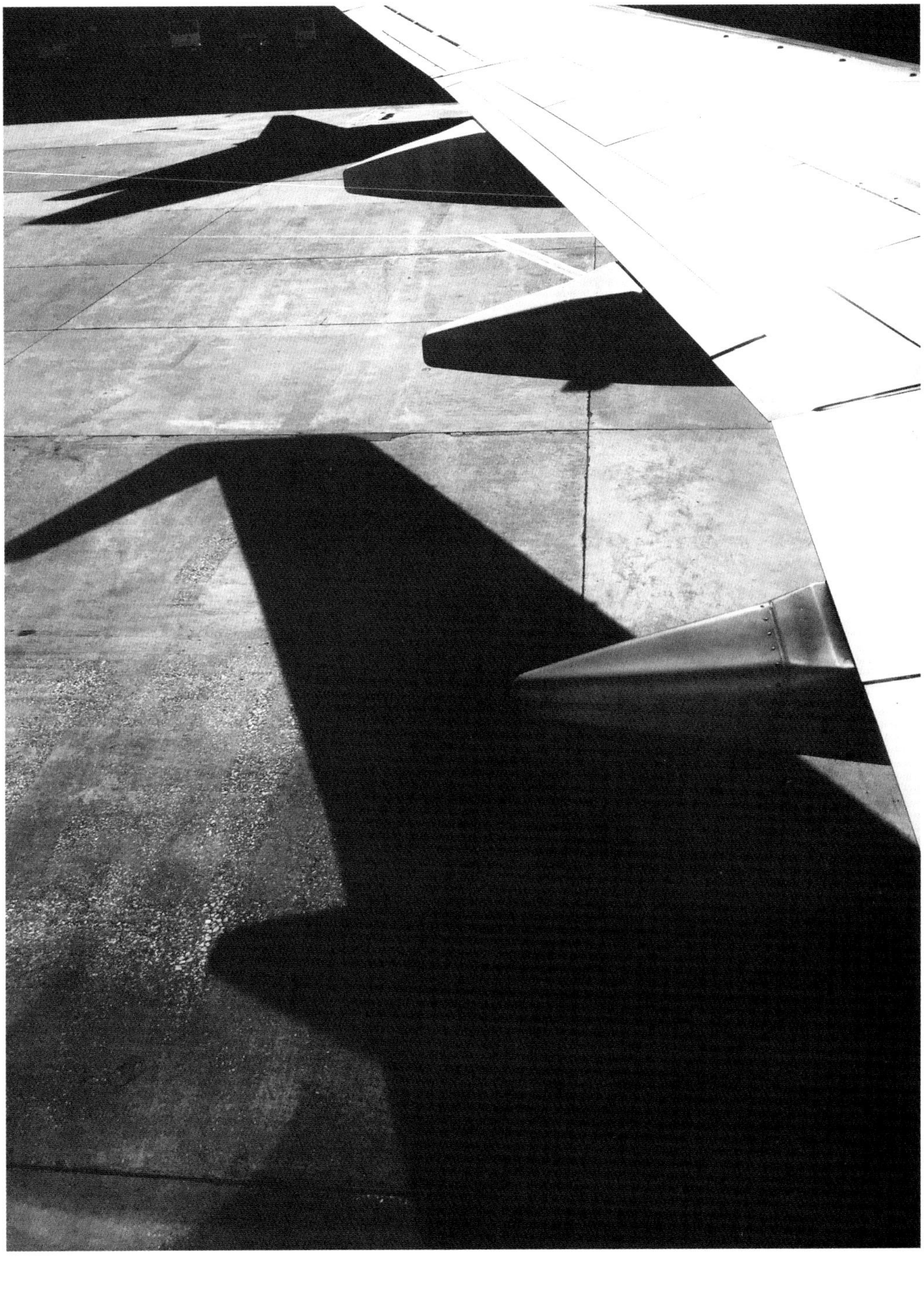

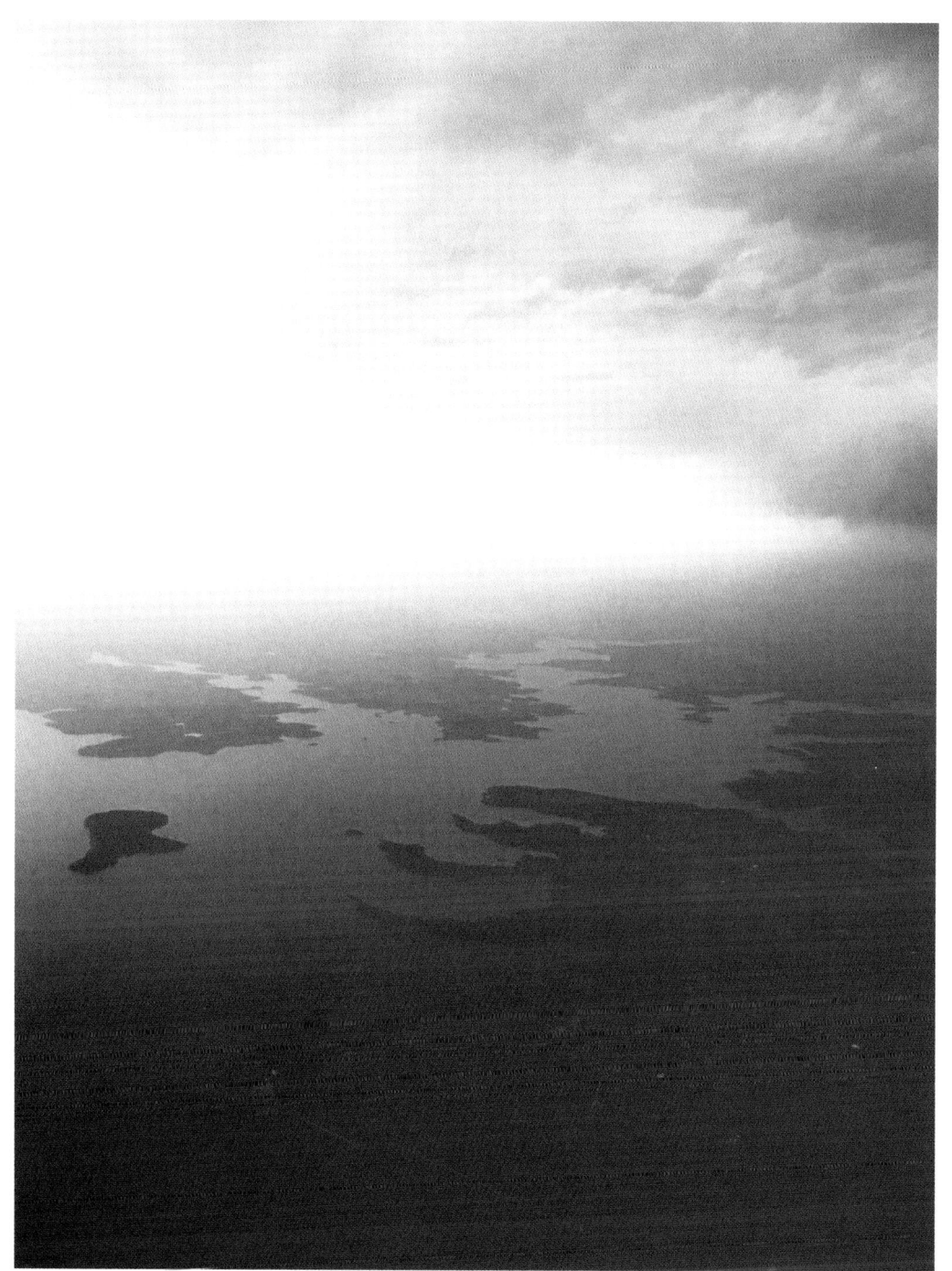

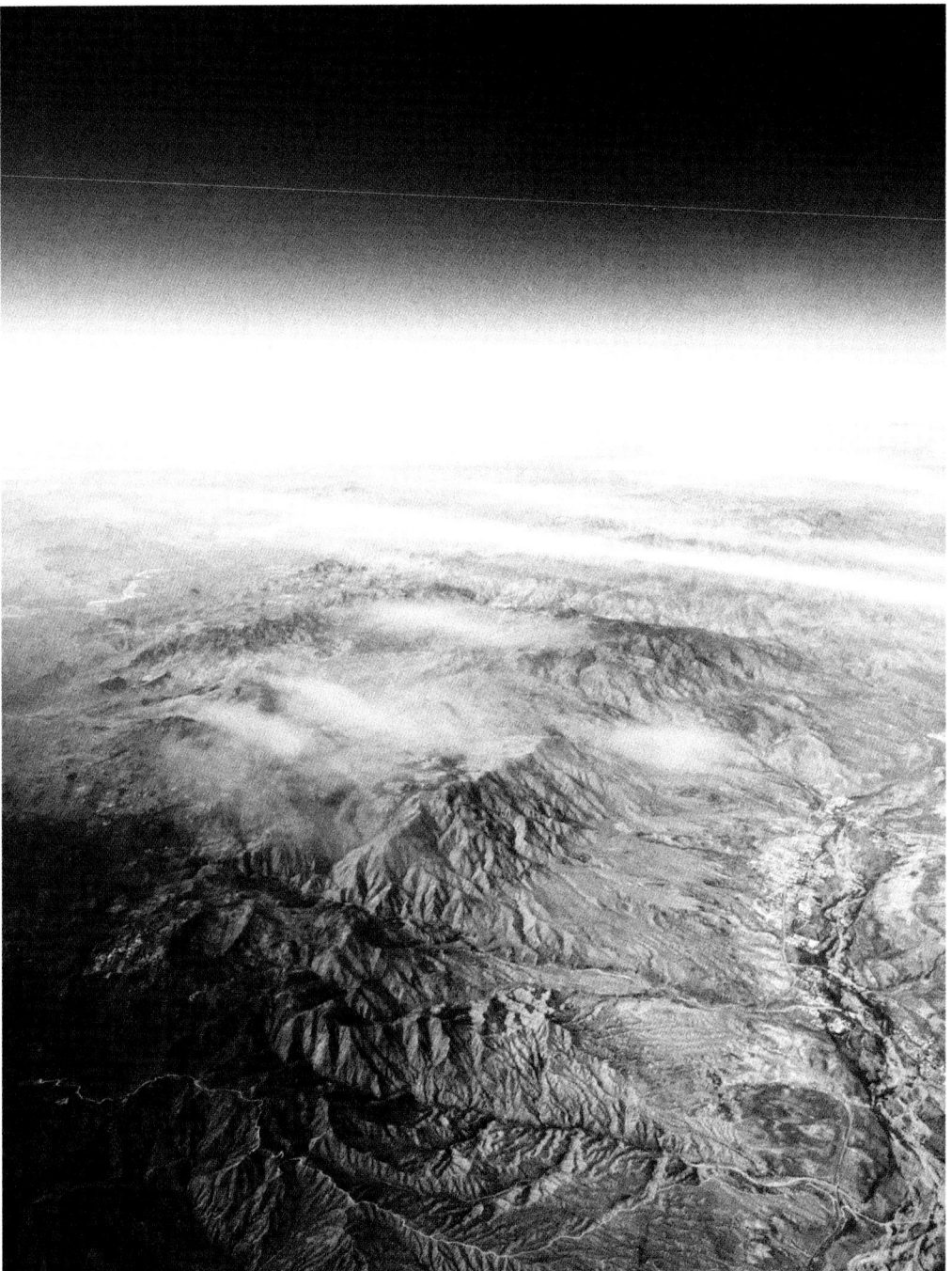

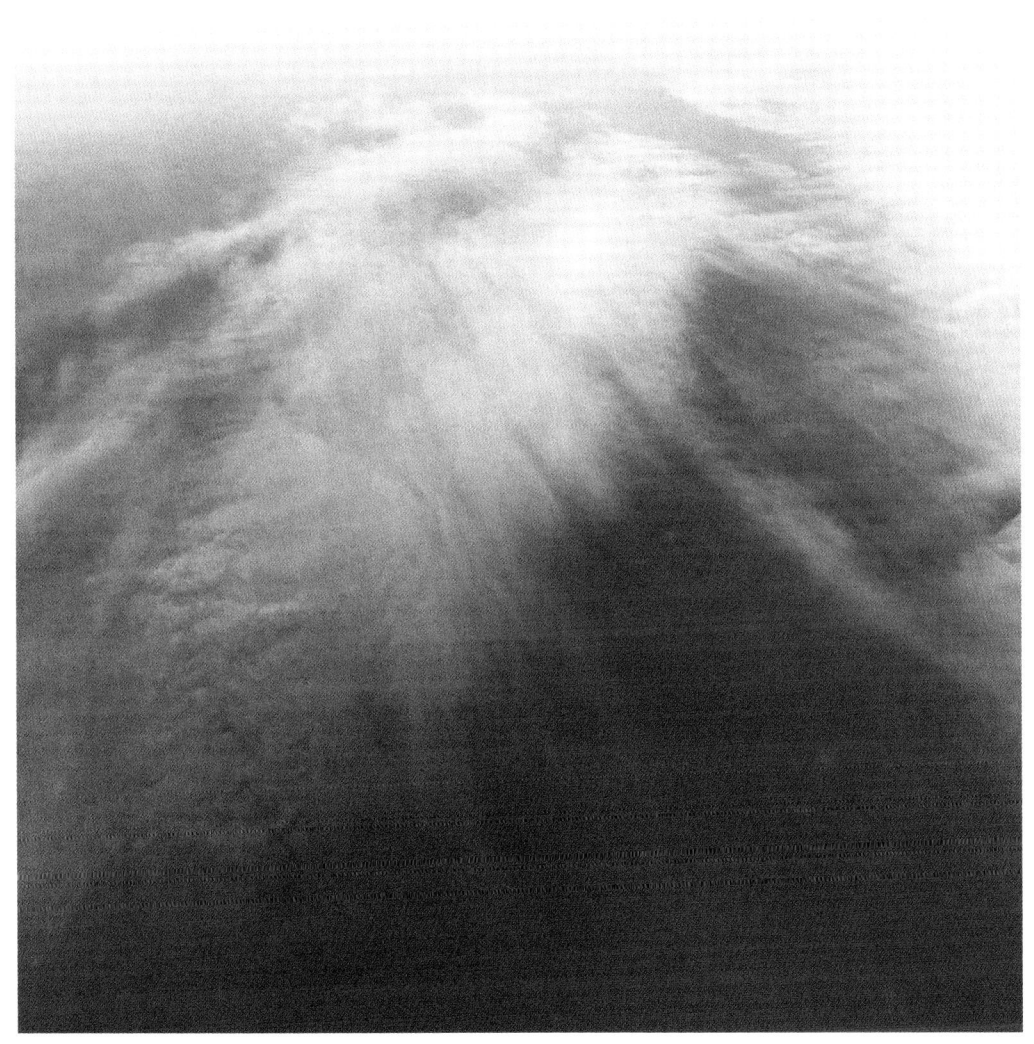

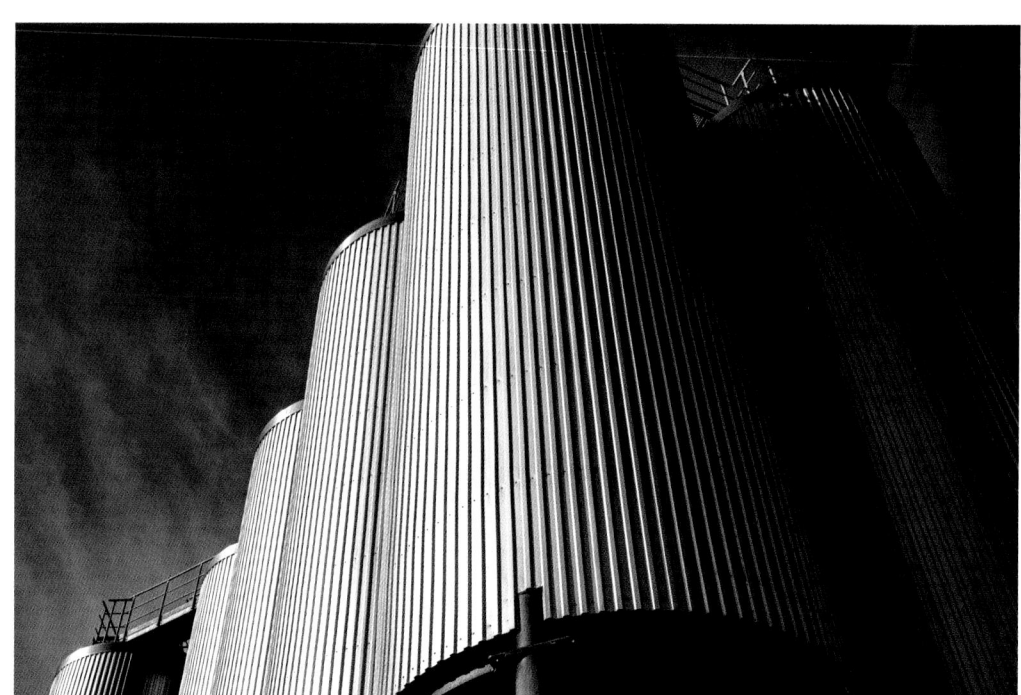

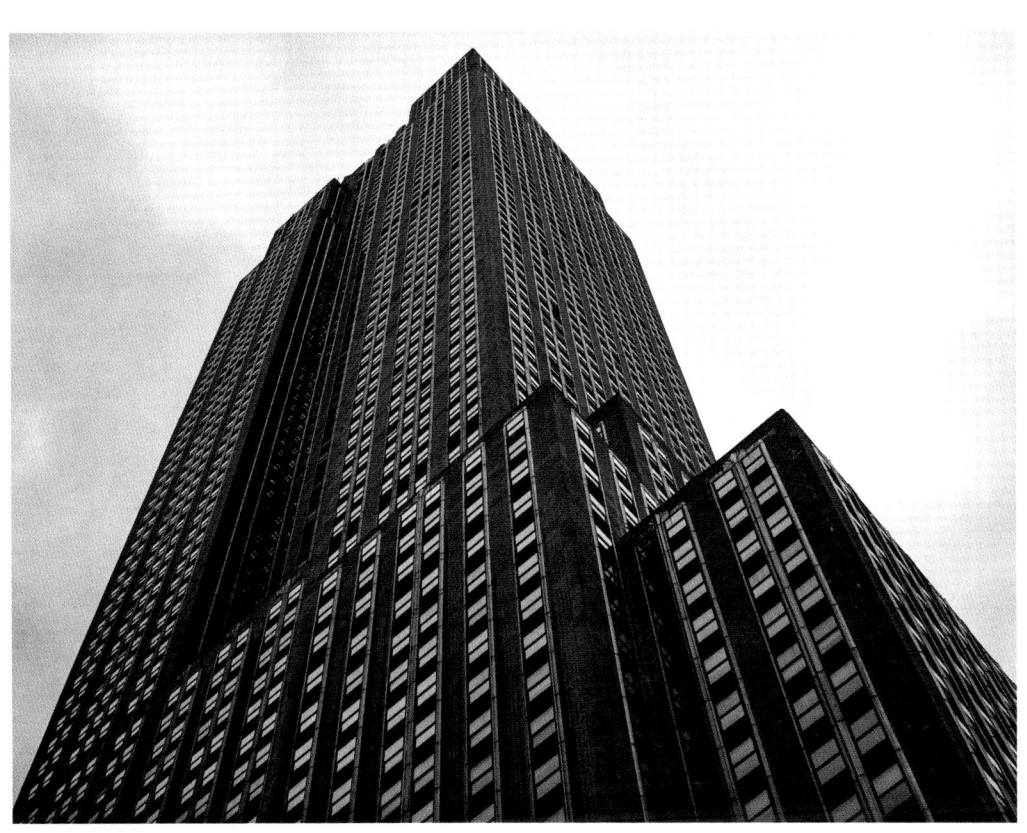

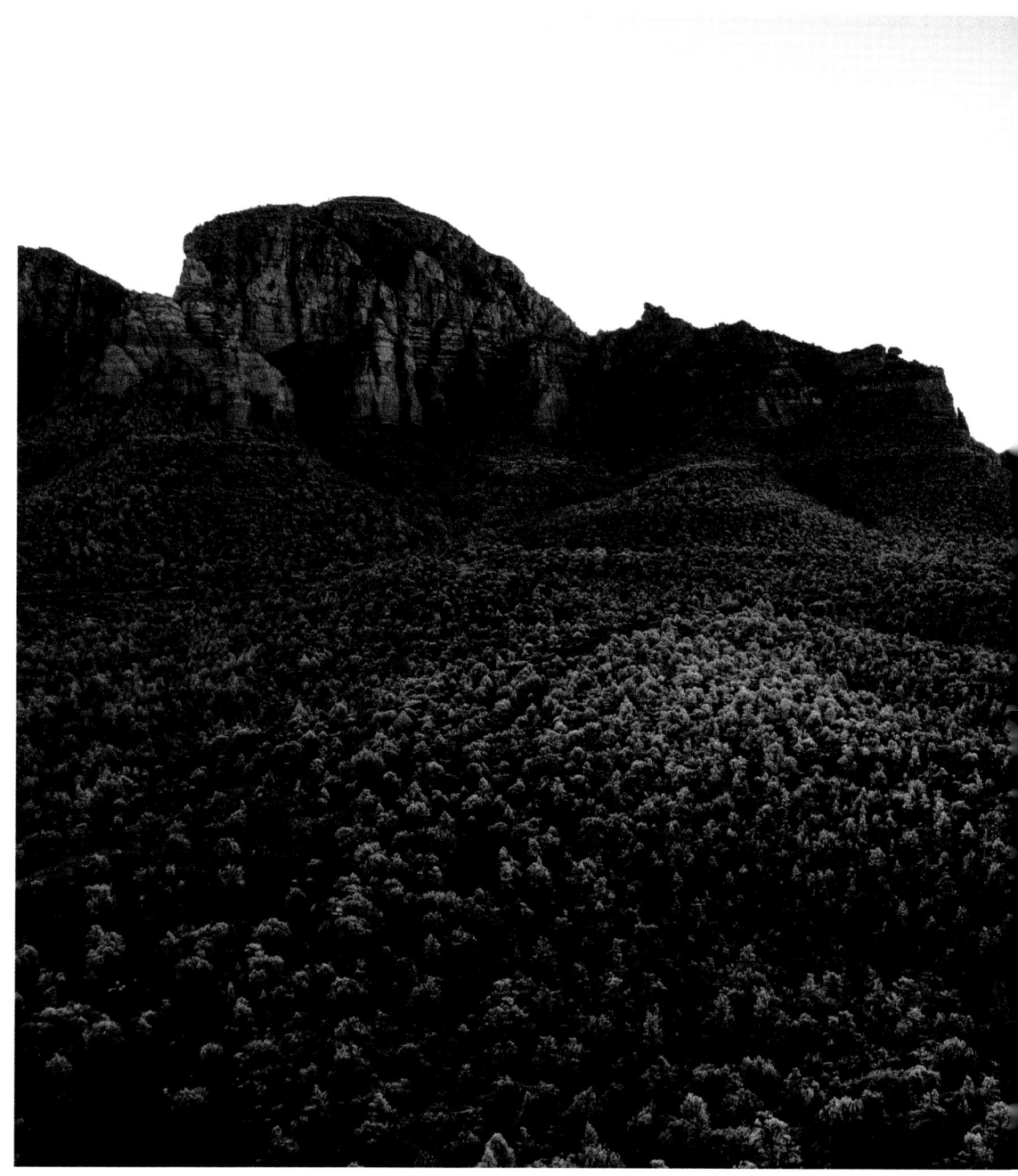

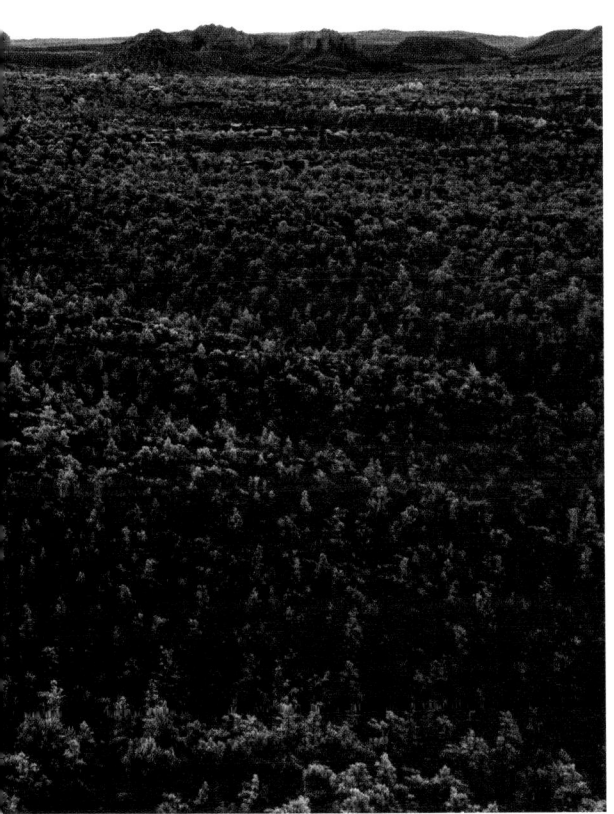

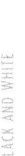

CHAPTER 10

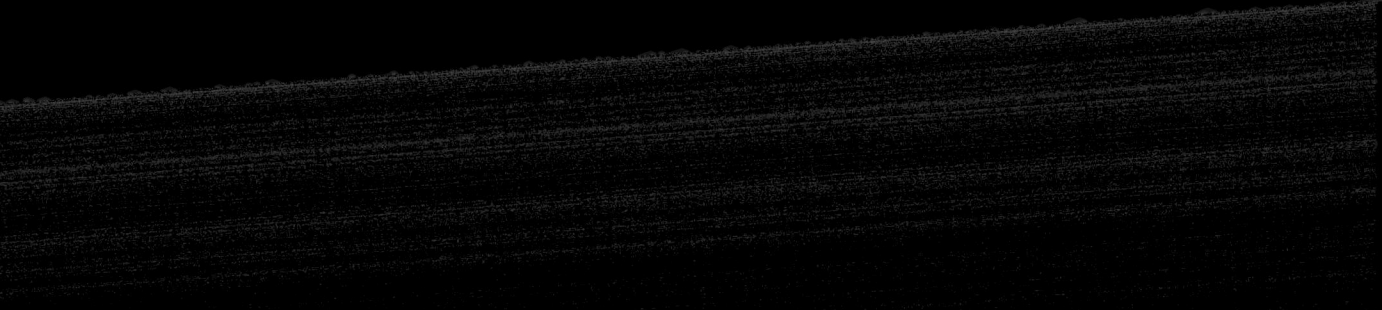

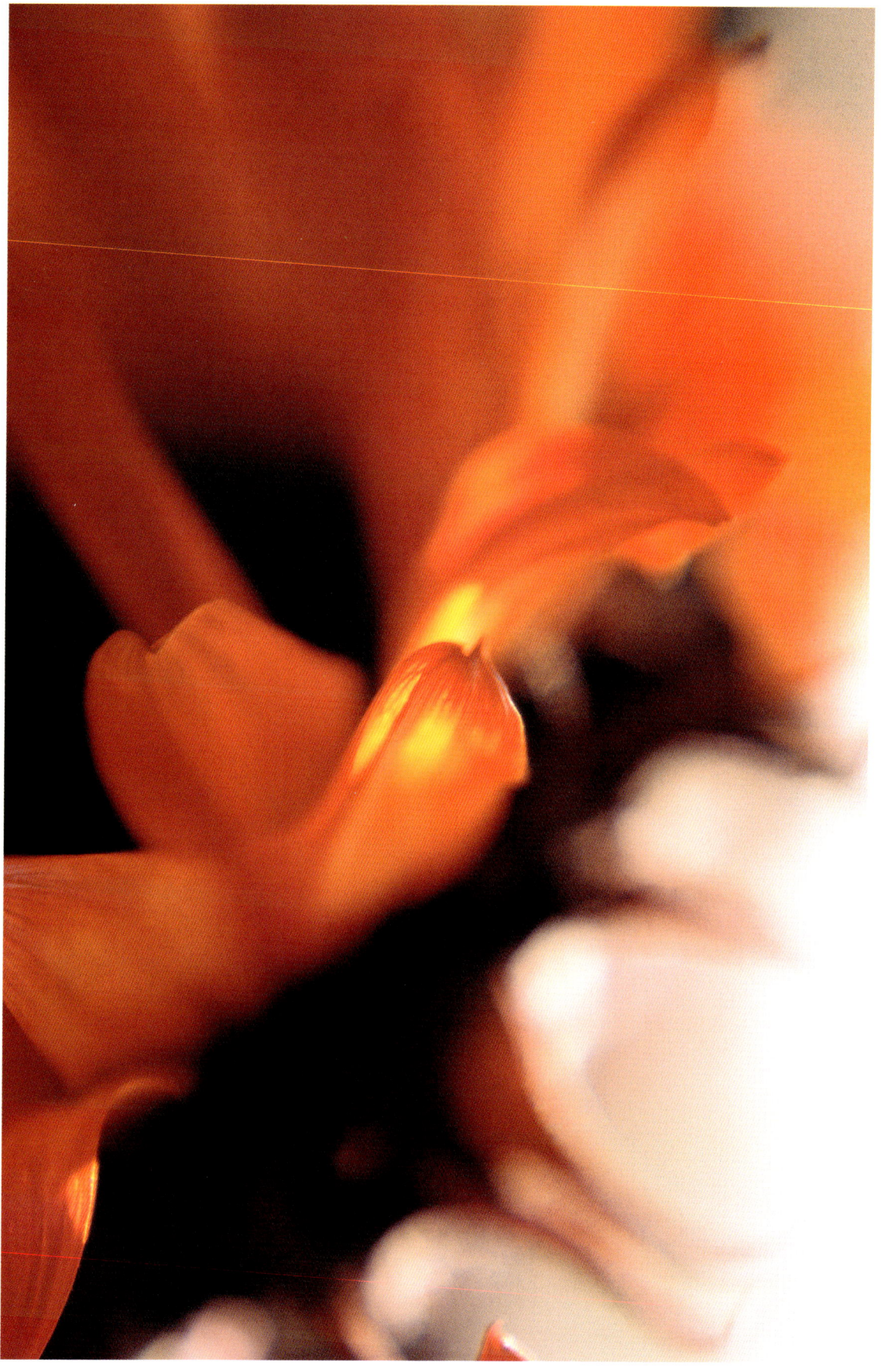

IN MODERN PHOTOGRAPHY, color has become the default form that images take. We don't really think about it. In digital photography you have to deliberately create a black and white image from a color image source.

Ironically, digital sensors are monochrome and a filter is used over the sensor to divide the signal into channels that are combined by the processor to emulate a color image. It's not a native process.

You can find native monochrome cameras or have a color camera modified, but it's an extremely niche product, and most photographers find it easier to convert from a color image.

Early photography was all monochrome. The earliest attempts at color soon followed in the 1860s, but it took many years before formats appeared that would be consistent on the consumer level. In fact, it wasn't until the 1970s that you could easily find inexpensive color film at any store.

It's also important to recognize color photography in context with printing. For decades, magazines, books, and newspapers defaulted to black and white because the process was more affordable. What the public saw in news periodical publications was usually black and white, so most photographers that had high visibility were shooting black and white. This slowly began to change until, arguably, the 1970s, when color was much more the norm than the exception.

But no matter what the format, all color photography is derived from some type of process that attempts to replicate color as our eyes see it. Some are additive, some subtractive, but all are a method to arrive at a perceived color. Therefore, all color photography is interpreted. This is what gives each process a "look" that we associate with a digital process or film type.

Often this look is from a certain era. Autochromes have a look we associate with the turn to the twentieth century. Kodachrome has several eras of looks that we associate with the 1940s, 1950s, and even the 1960s. Digital is interpretive as well, and there might come a time when there's a certain look to what we are accustomed to seeing today.

About four years ago, I started working extensively on this idea. If photography is its own form of reality (as discussed in the previous chapter), then color is no different. In my personal experience, as someone who started when there were no digital cameras, there is an aspect of nostalgia that speaks to me in the form of color.

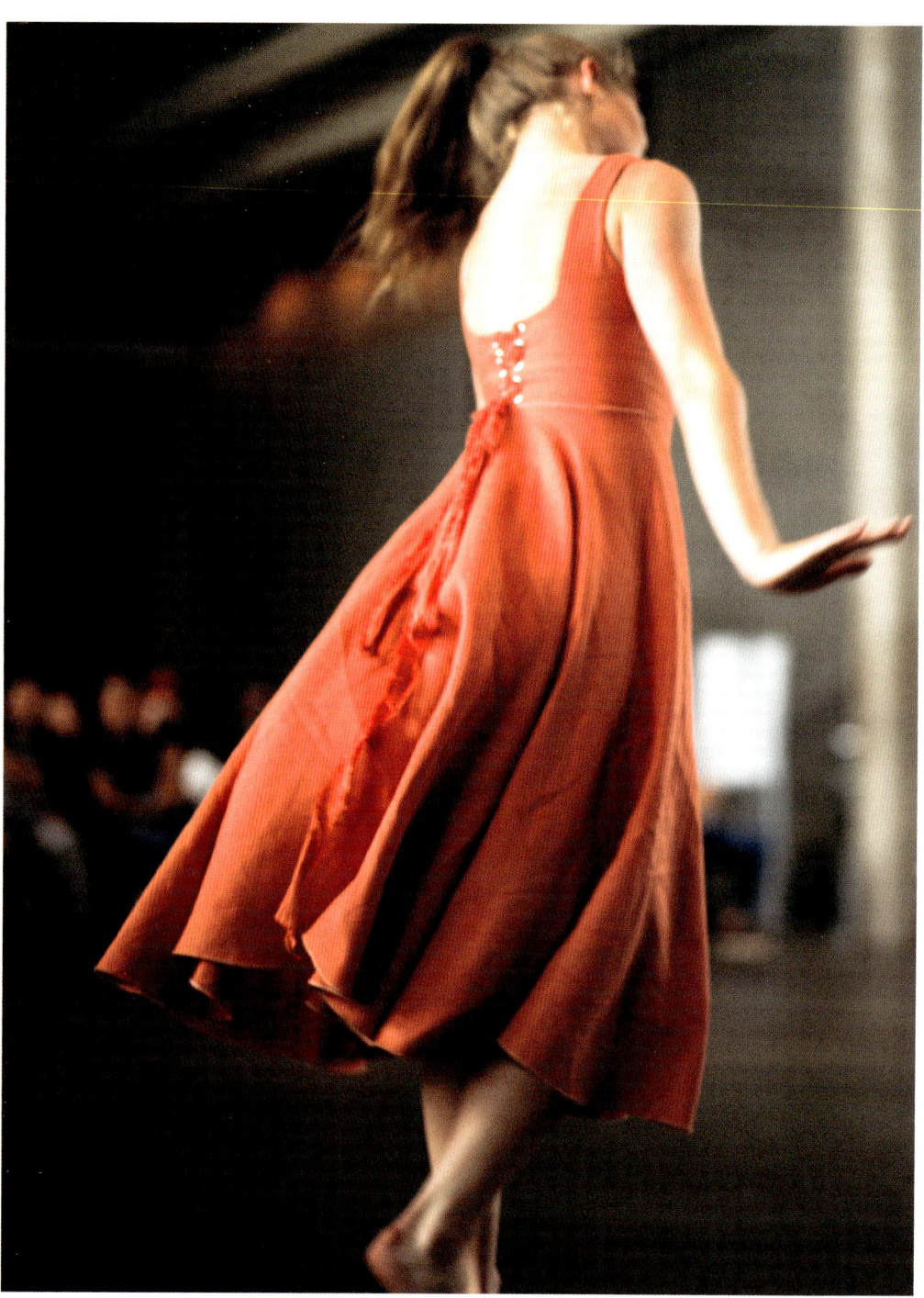

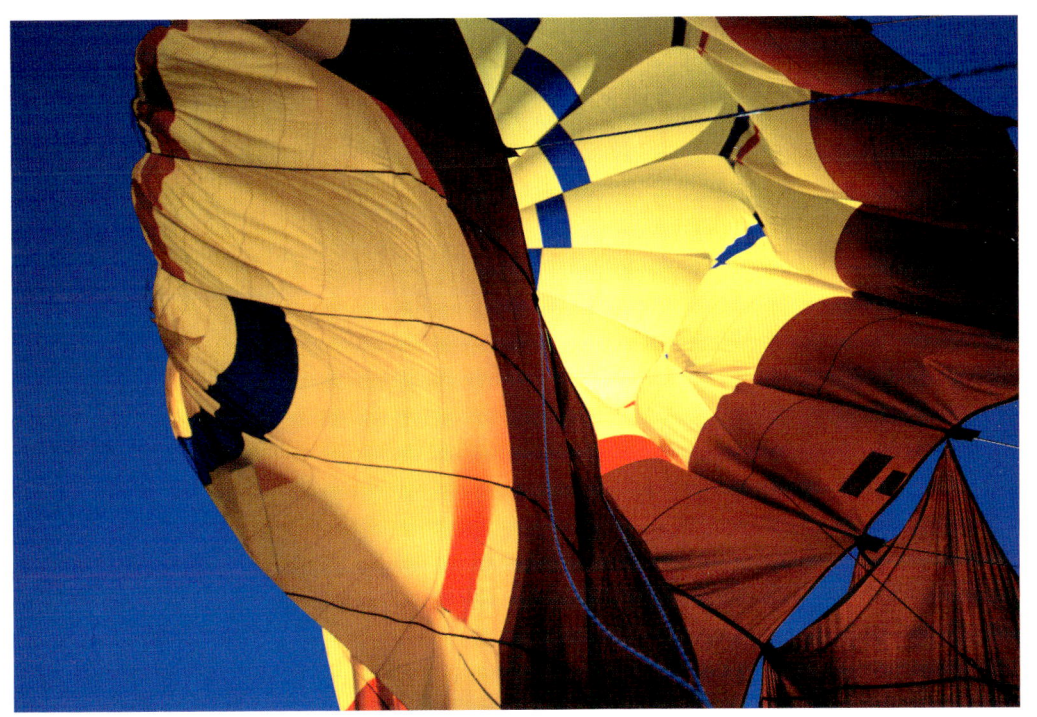

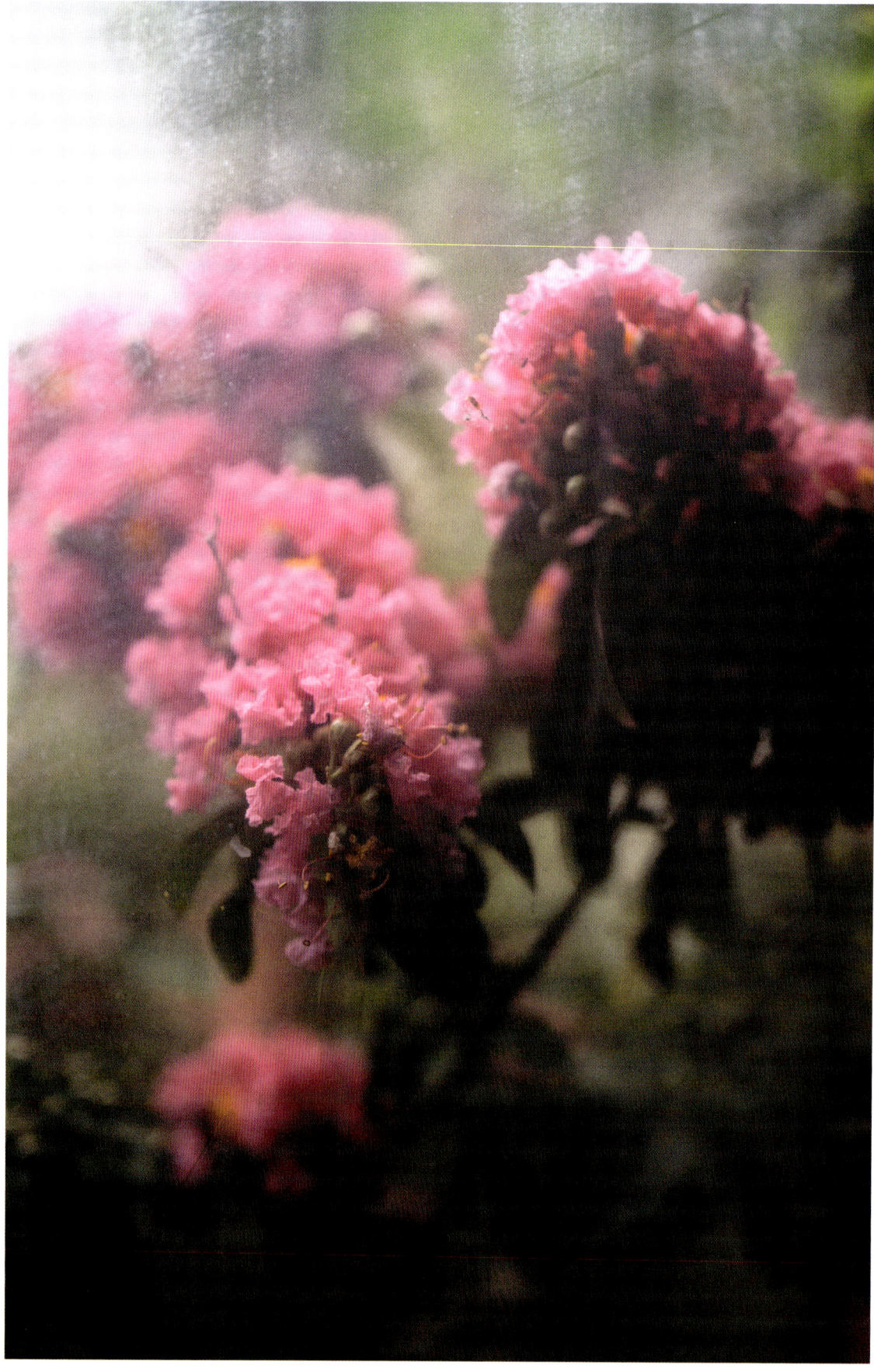

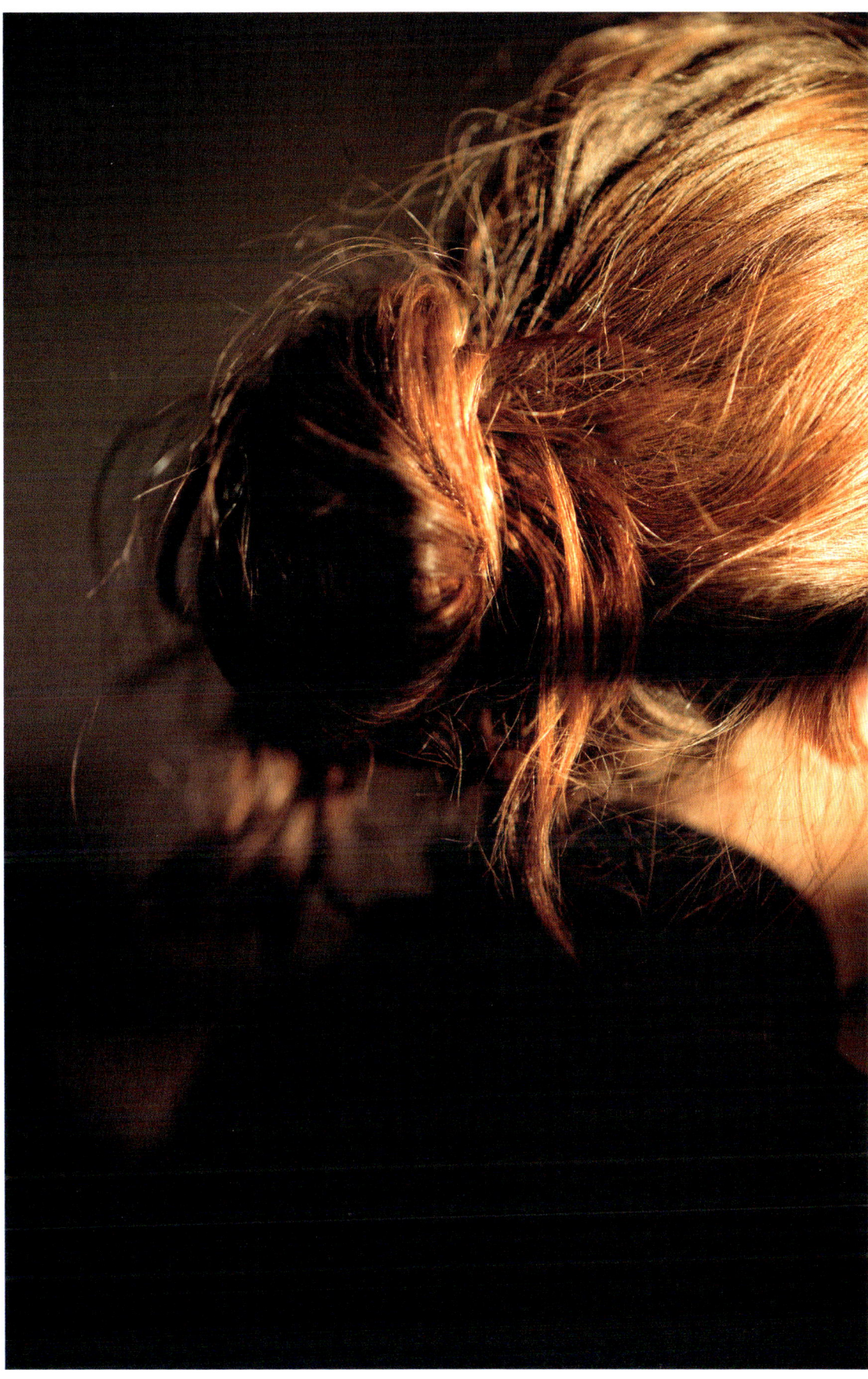

When I started shooting, Kodachrome was more or less the standard for transparency film, but Fujifilm was also a decent and common option. Film types were often contextual for me—certain types were best for certain applications. I would use Fujifilm Velvia for landscapes but never portraits. Portraits looked best with Fujifilm Asita or even Provia. If I needed more dynamic range, it was time to use C41 films.

Now, in the digital age, there is a sameness. There is a monotony in everything more or less having the same look all the time. Digital cameras have a well-balanced color look. Things are constantly evolving to emulate the idea of reality more than the last technology.

A few years ago, I was scanning some old images I had on slides. This included the last few rolls of Kodachrome I had used right before the deadline when Dwayne's Photo in Kansas City announced it would be shutting off the last machine. I remember shooting those rolls over a few days—portraits of friends, whatever I could find—and then racing to FedEx so I could overnight the film before the deadline. I also had images on Velvia, Provia, and other film stocks, and I found myself really missing that way of working with color. Yes, you can still buy and use film, but it's gotten prohibitively expensive to use on a day-to-day basis.

Not too long ago I was "scanning" some old transparencies using a high-resolution mirrorless camera, a 1:1 macro lens, and a film holder that allows me to digitize my old slides much faster than the flatbed scanner. As I started looking at the results, I thought to myself: "Too bad the camera doesn't natively

shoot with these colors." Then it dawned on me that it does. The digital camera is neutral enough in its color rendering that the final image looked like Kodachrome, Provia, Velvia—whatever it was I was digitizing.

So why can't we elect to use these looks with digital cameras? Sure there were "film" presets that you could buy that would get you close, but since I'm a little off centered mentally, I needed to understand why Provia looks the way it looks. I wanted to know why Kodachrome looks the way it looks in the 1940s or 1970s. So, I've spent two years working on my own set of film simulations that I could have as picture profiles in Lightroom or Capture One. Something I could adapt to future software as well. I created emulations for both Kodak and Fujifilm stocks and I learned a lot on the way.

The first thing I did was try to match colors. This seemed like the obvious starting place. The color red from a digital camera needed to match the red off my Provia images. This made more of a mess than anything else. Then I realized that it comes down to contrasts, and this is important.

When your eye identifies something as red, perhaps a shirt or a blouse, your mind is simplifying this and you see it as the color red. The truth is there are thousands of micro shades of red. Each fold in the blouse casts a shadow, the shoulder closer to light. Skin tones have even more variations because everyone's skin is different. Just trying to "match" a given color resulted in random results that looked nothing like the film colors. But if you consider contrast, this changes completely. Slide film has a very tight dynamic range. Modern digital cameras capture a lot more dynamic range than slide film. Once you have the localized contrast matched, then matching the colors becomes easy.

Another variation I found was that film is dependent on the person developing it to get it right. Or if it's a machine process, it still has to be set up and calibrated correctly. This means there are variations that can happen on any film stock. Sometimes Kodachrome would have a red or magenta cast to it if not set up properly. Film used past its expiration date also introduces problems in consistency. This can be used to artistic effect, as can be seen in the work of William Eggleston and Saul Leiter. They developed entire looks around expired film stock.

This also started to bother me—that's something we've lost. People today don't experiment with color in the same way. Modern technology allows us to capture more color information in a very neutral way. This has resulted in a lot less experimentation, mainly because we don't really have any control over how a digital camera captures raw data. I was very happy to be experimenting by borrowing from an older technology. Ironically, modern technology was allowing me to do this in post-production.

But something interesting hit me when I was working on my film simulation project. Once I started testing my "film looks," I realized that they really amplified any images where the exposure was too bright or too dark. Film has a way of "rolling off" the highlights as they are being clipped, and I worked this into my profiles. But then the amazing thing I discovered is that the digital file contained way more

information. Since I was feeding this into a picture profile, I could adjust the sliders and bring the raw image into the look I wanted. You could never do this with film—it's fixed once you've taken the image.

This opened up an entire world to me for color. I could have the looks of classic film stocks with all the convenience of digital imaging. I can rescue shadow detail. I can bring back highlights. I can dial in contrast or flatten an image if it's too contrasty. I created my own process, which was no longer trying to replace film. I was bringing the various film stock looks into the digital space. Color appeared more natural to the way I think of color photography, which is largely influenced by the analog era.

This project took over two years and I'm still expanding on it today. Yes, it felt like a complete rabbit hole and a waste of time in places along the way. I would get stuck and wasn't sure how to get out. I'd question why I was doing it. But I tell you this because these kinds of neurotic deep-dives are important. This is deep learning for humans. My profiles are available for anyone to use now. Perhaps someone will take this idea and expand on it even further with their own work. They've been extremely popular, so I know there is a desire for this type of color interpretation.

But it's also important to understand that this is one type of interpretation. It might not be right for every situation and it might not be right for every photographer.

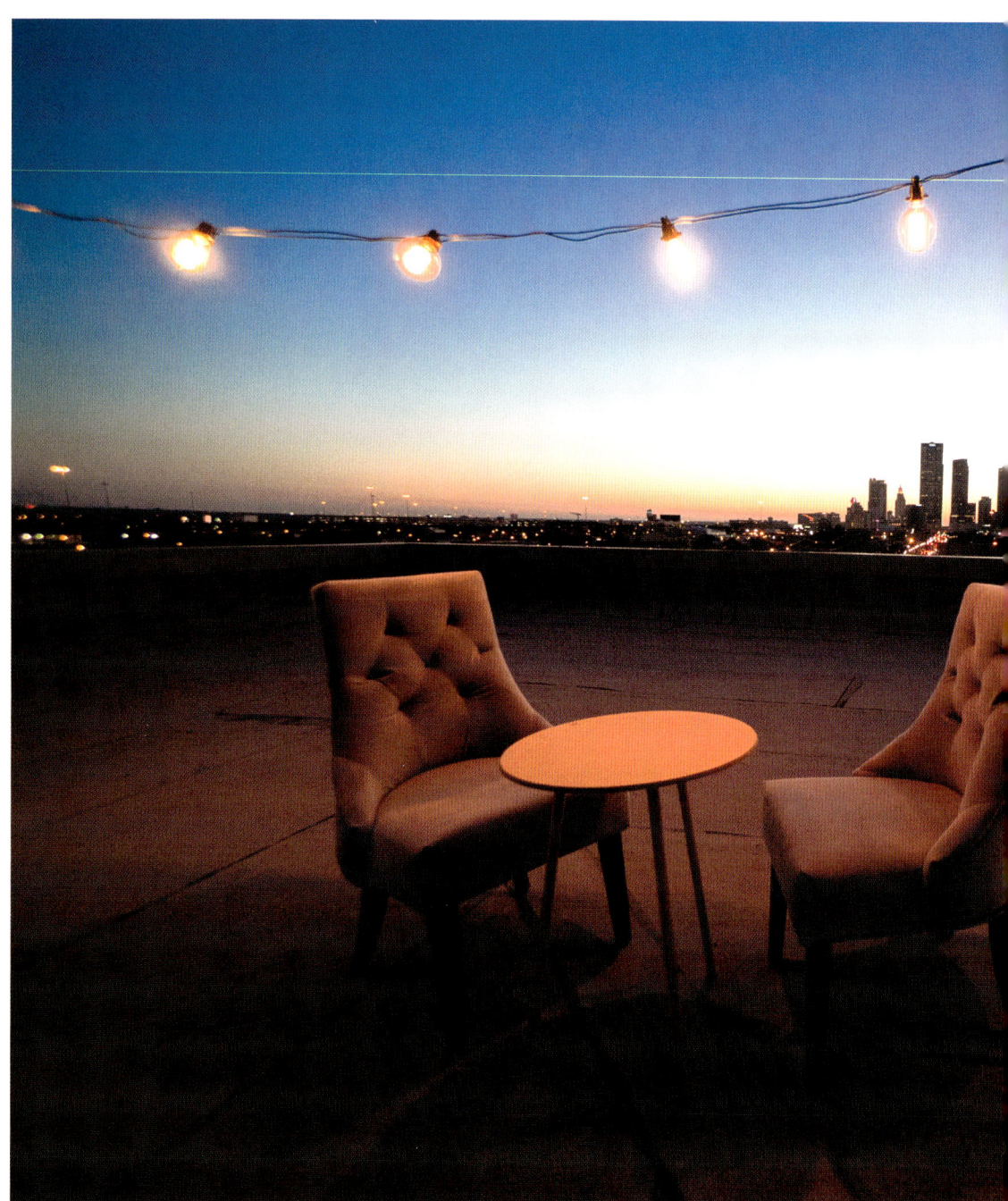

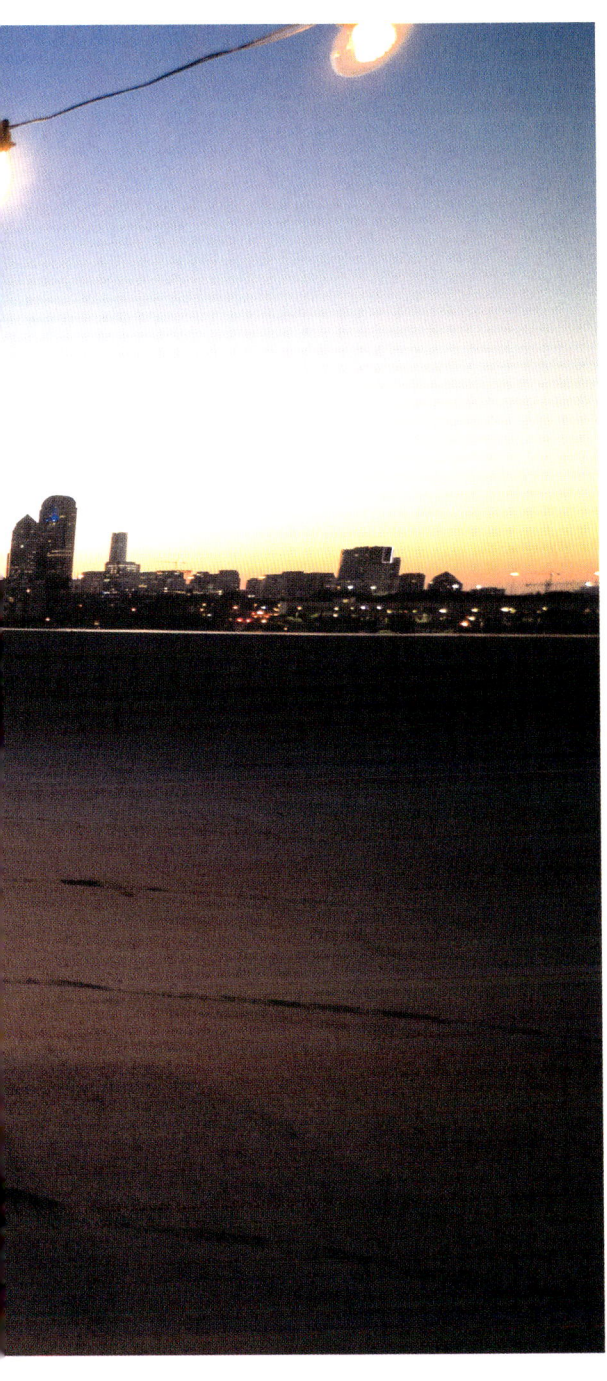

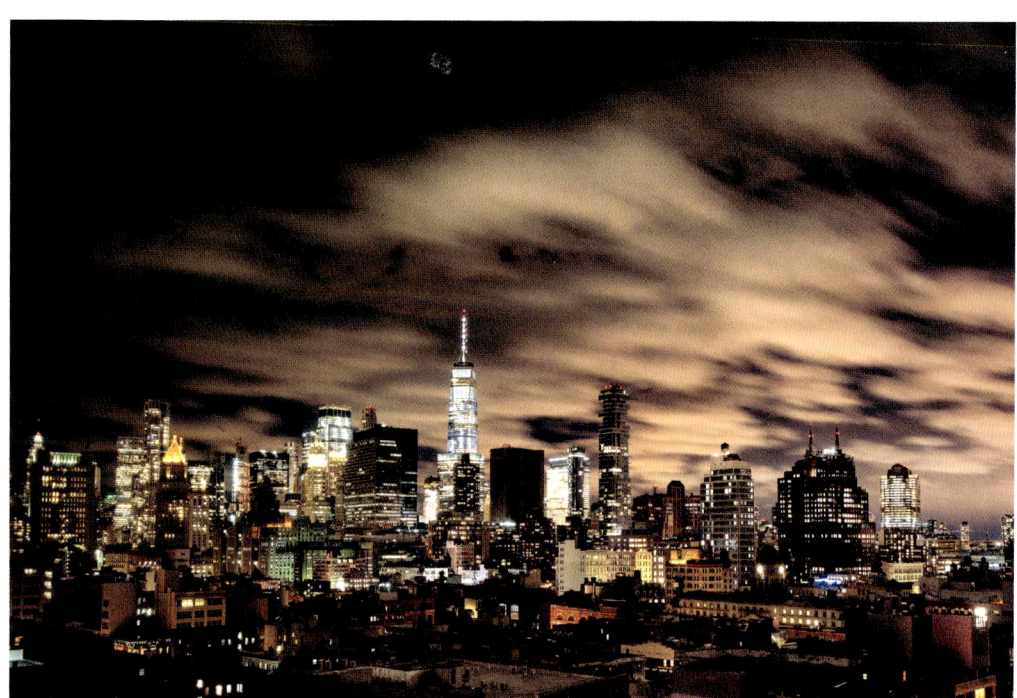

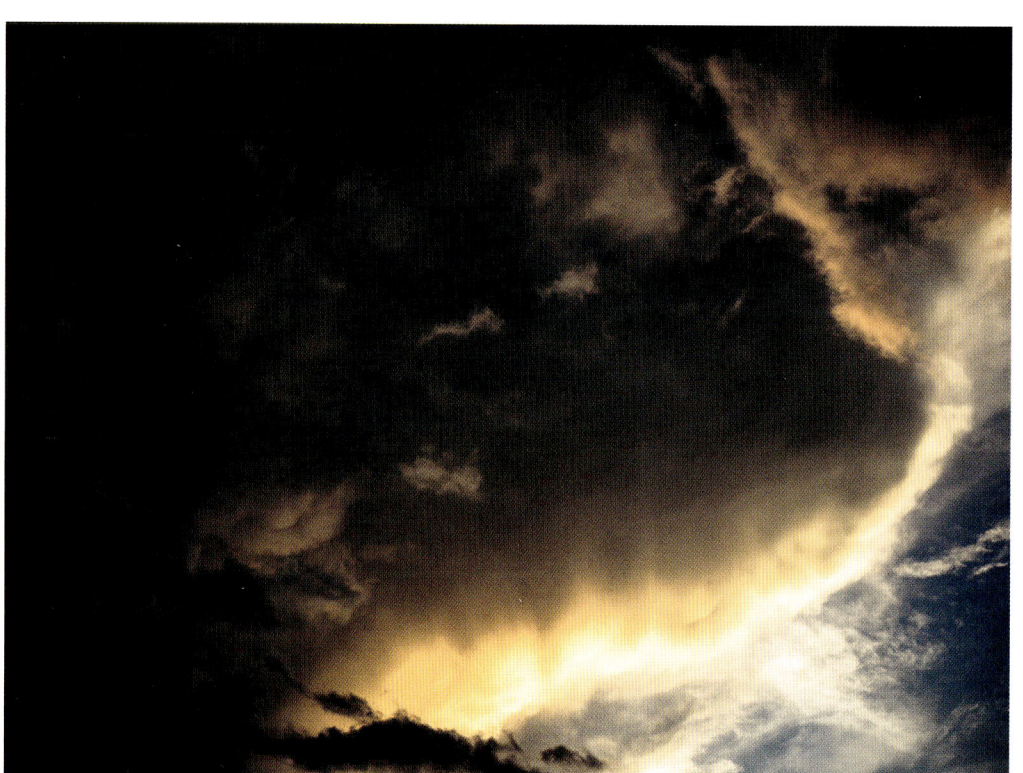

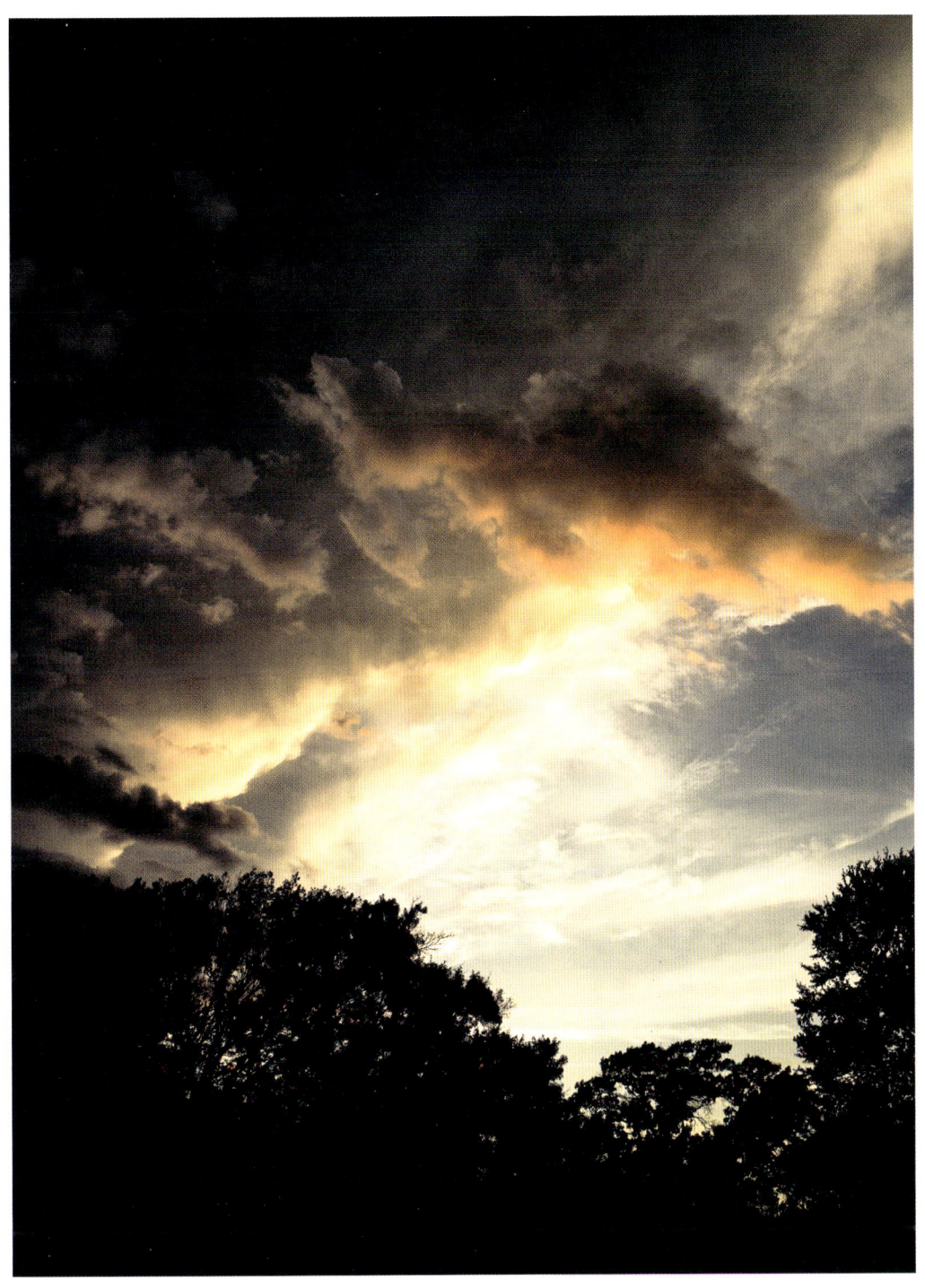

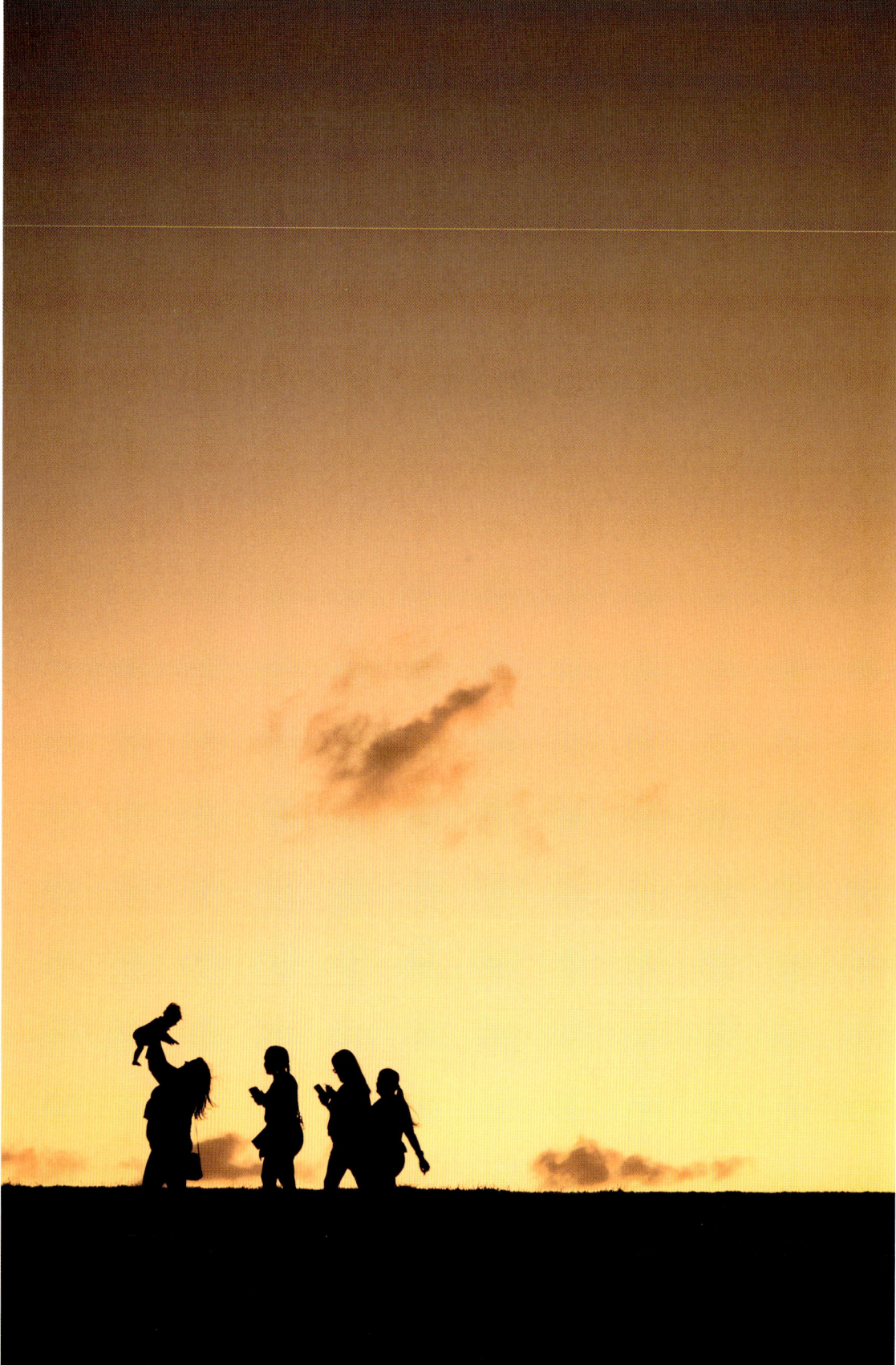

Color in Photography

Thinking of color as it's taught in traditional art education is difficult to apply to photography for a number of reasons. For one, we don't have the level of intentionally selecting color like a painter or designer has. We can make color choices in certain situations, but not to the level of other media. Yes, the idea of Photoshop voids my argument, but I'm a firm believer of preserving at least a degree of intent from the point of capture. Falsely interpreting color is retouching, not photography. Retouching implies the photographer couldn't finish the job.

We also don't mix paint. We can control color appearance in post-production, like I have explained above in the perception of film looks. But we're not working with paint on a palette. It's a digital approach and much different. But there are things we can control that have an effect on the final picture.

Color Relationships

Typically, color is shown on some type of color wheel as established by Isaac Newton. This is a way of presenting color hues and how they relate to one another. Color models are designed around their three primary colors. The color wheel traditionally taught in color theory is based on the RYB (Red Yellow Blue) color model. But there is also the RGB (Red Green Blue) color model, which is used in more modern applications.

Complementary colors are pairs that exist opposite from each other on the wheel. When combined, they cancel each other out to pro-

duce a grayscale value. When placed next to each other, they represent the greatest contrast value for the pair.

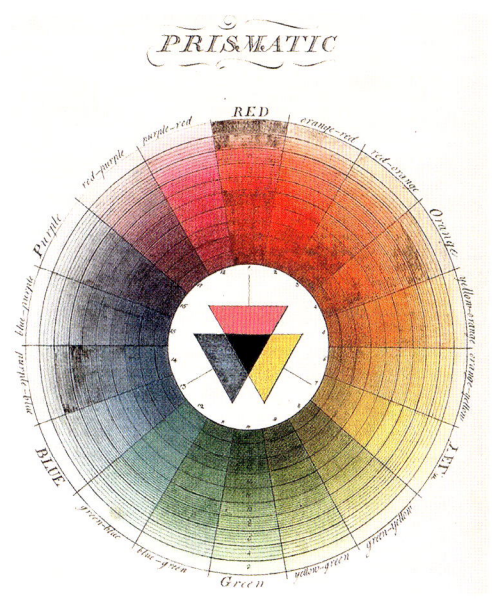

In the RYB color model, these pairs are red/green, yellow/purple, and blue/orange.

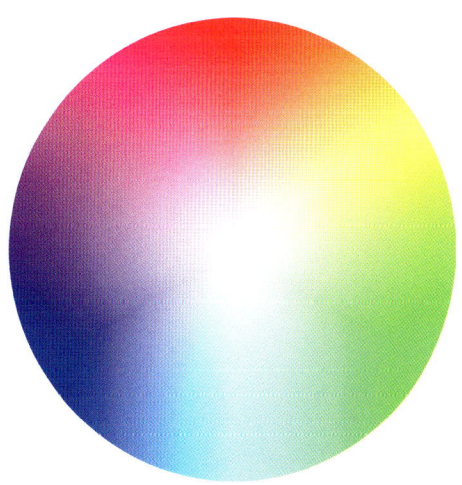

In the RGB color model, the complementary colors are red/cyan, green/magenta, and blue/yellow.

For example, if you have a blue subject on a blue background, it has the lowest color contrast and makes it possible something is less likely to stand out. Changing the background to another color will increase the emphasis, and using a complementary color like yellow or orange is going to give you the most contrast. Other options will be more subtle and might be the best area for exploring possibilities. This leads us to analogous colors.

Analogous colors are colors next to each other on a color wheel—for example, blue, purple, and red. These color combinations aren't as intense a contrast and usually work very well together. But perhaps you want something that stays very low energy and keeps a subtle interpretation. You might consider a monochromatic color scheme.

Monochromatic colors are different shades of the same color. For example, you might have a composition that is only various shades of blue. This is a minimal approach and, though it expresses the lowest energy in terms of color, it has a nice effect. Or think of a minimalist approach to an entire composition of blues with a small yellow subject. This combines these techniques and will really make the small object stand out despite its size.

So what we have are three ways of viewing contrast with color. Complementary colors are the highest energy and contrast; analogous colors are medium energy, medium contrast; and monochromatic colors are low energy, low contrast. If we start thinking about color in these categories, then we can make decisions about how to control the energy contrast and mood of a photograph.

This actually makes for an interesting exercise. Start with a series of images of monochromatic color schemes. Then limit yourself to analogous colors. Complementary colors are going to have the most contrast and might be difficult to approach an entire image with, but complementary colors can have an interesting impact when contrasted with scale. For example, if you have a small subject on a large background, monochromatic colors might cause the subject to lose emphasis. But if you use complementary colors, it can stand out in spite of the scale difference.

HSL

To this point I've only discussed color hues in a relative sense. But hues can vary as well, particularly when you consider different shades of the same color.

HSL is an abbreviation for "Hue, Saturation, and Lightness." These are the three ways to define how a color is rendered in a visual space. We have sliders in imaging software that allow control over these three concepts to define color. Hue refers to the color; saturation is the intensity of the color; and lightness is where it falls on the spectrum of light to dark.

In a photograph, colors and light will change depending on variables such as shadow or distance from a light source. Typically, there will be variation in light as well as saturation. So when we control these we can do so on a local level (e.g., controlling only the reds in an image) or on a more global level, which brings us to ambient colors.

Ambient Colors

One of the great things about digital photography is the control we have over the look of the final picture. We've talked about controlling HSL sliders on a local level, but most imaging software allows you to do this on a more global level.

We can divide light into three basic areas: highlights, midtones, and shadows. Controlling these three regions independently allows you to control the overall mood and feeling of an image. For example, a common technique is to add warmth to the highlights. We can do this by moving the hue toward yellow or orange and adjusting the saturation and lightness. This will only affect the highlights of the image and adds a warmer ambience to the image as a whole. We might also apply this concept to cooling down the shadow detail. The intent is not to change or modify existing colors, but to shape the scene's overall ambient lighting.

A Word of Caution

Color is a big topic and I've only scratched the surface here. It's also a very subjective topic and quickly starts moving into areas of mood, emotional effects, and even color psychology. These ideas are way beyond the scope of this book and quite frankly are too open-ended and speculative. I will leave it up to you to decide what colors you like in your pictures. But please decide what you like to work with.

I've taken the approach here to address thinking about color at the moment of composition. There is obviously an entire approach to editing color that is beyond the scope of this book. However, just like compositional elements, cropping ideas, and the edges, lighting, and exposure, I feel the same about color. Learning how to get this right at the moment of capture makes for a more natural result and saves a ton of time in post-production.

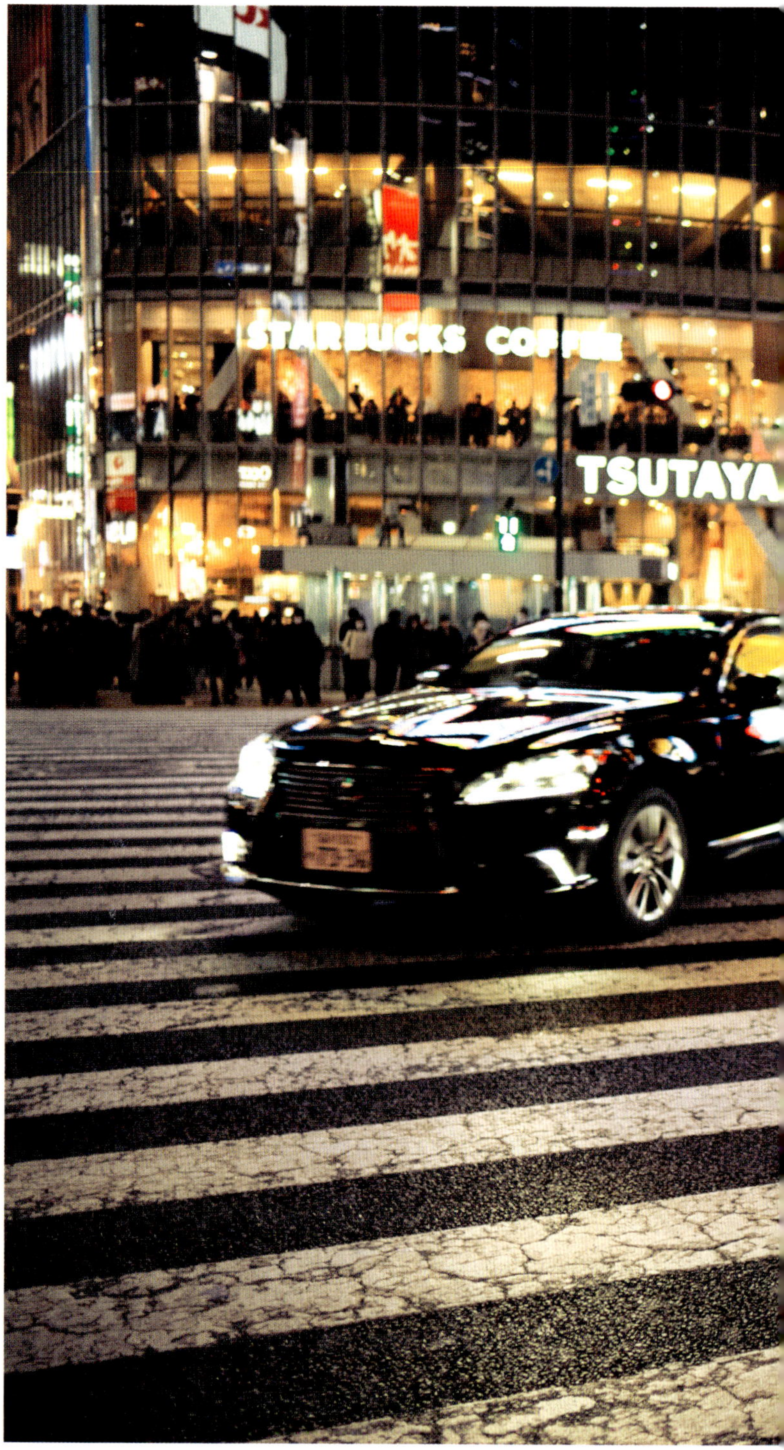

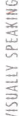

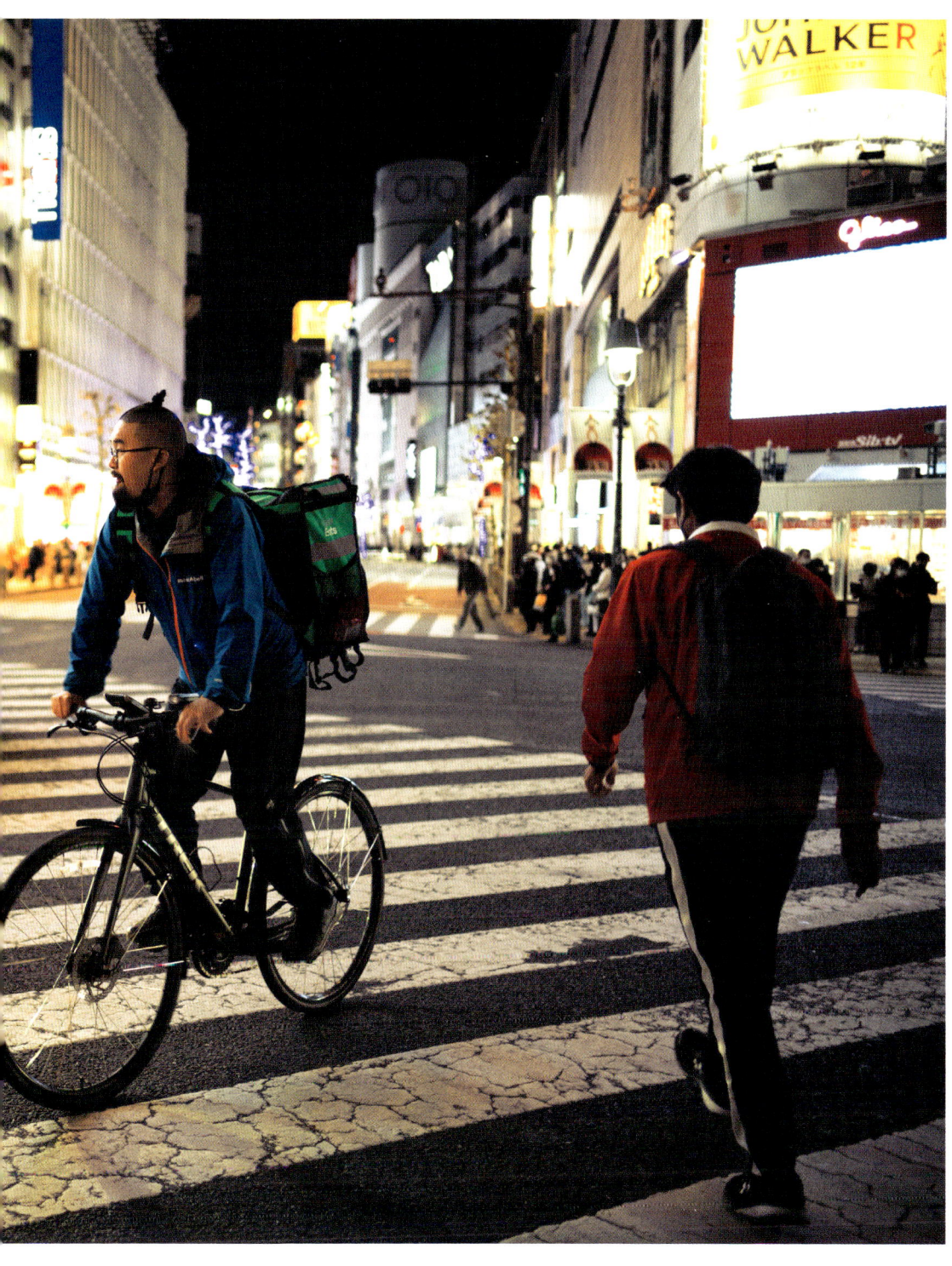

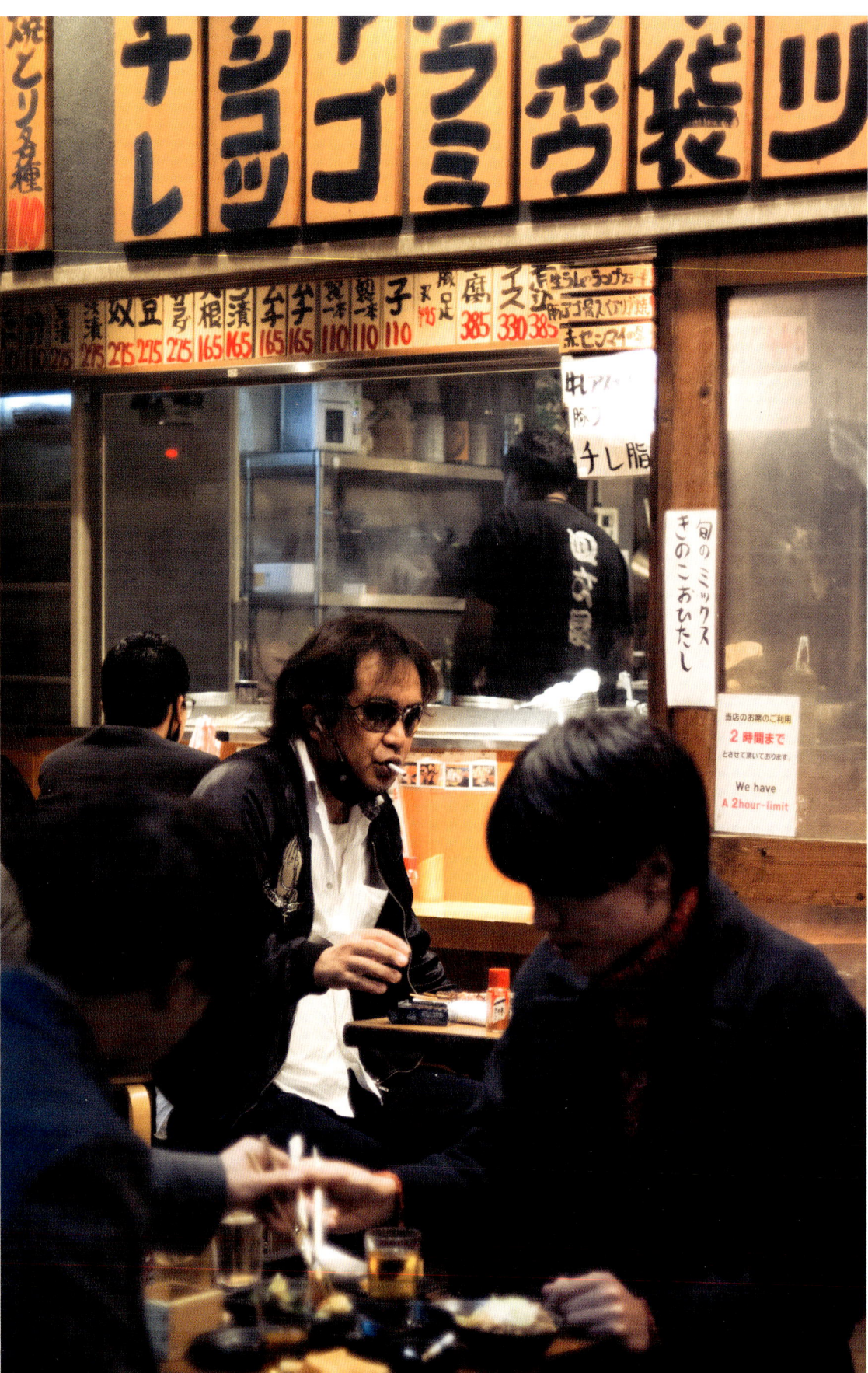

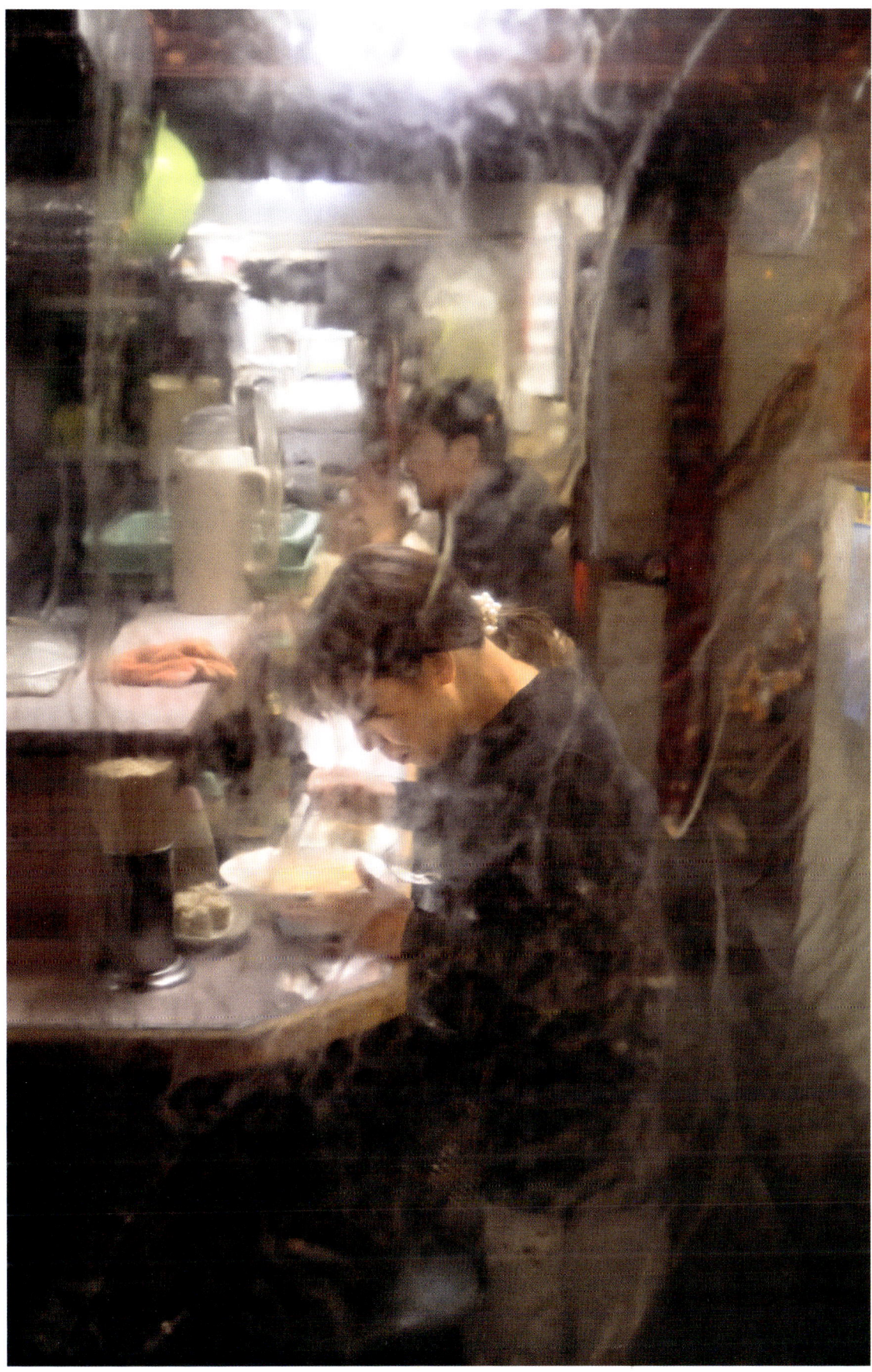

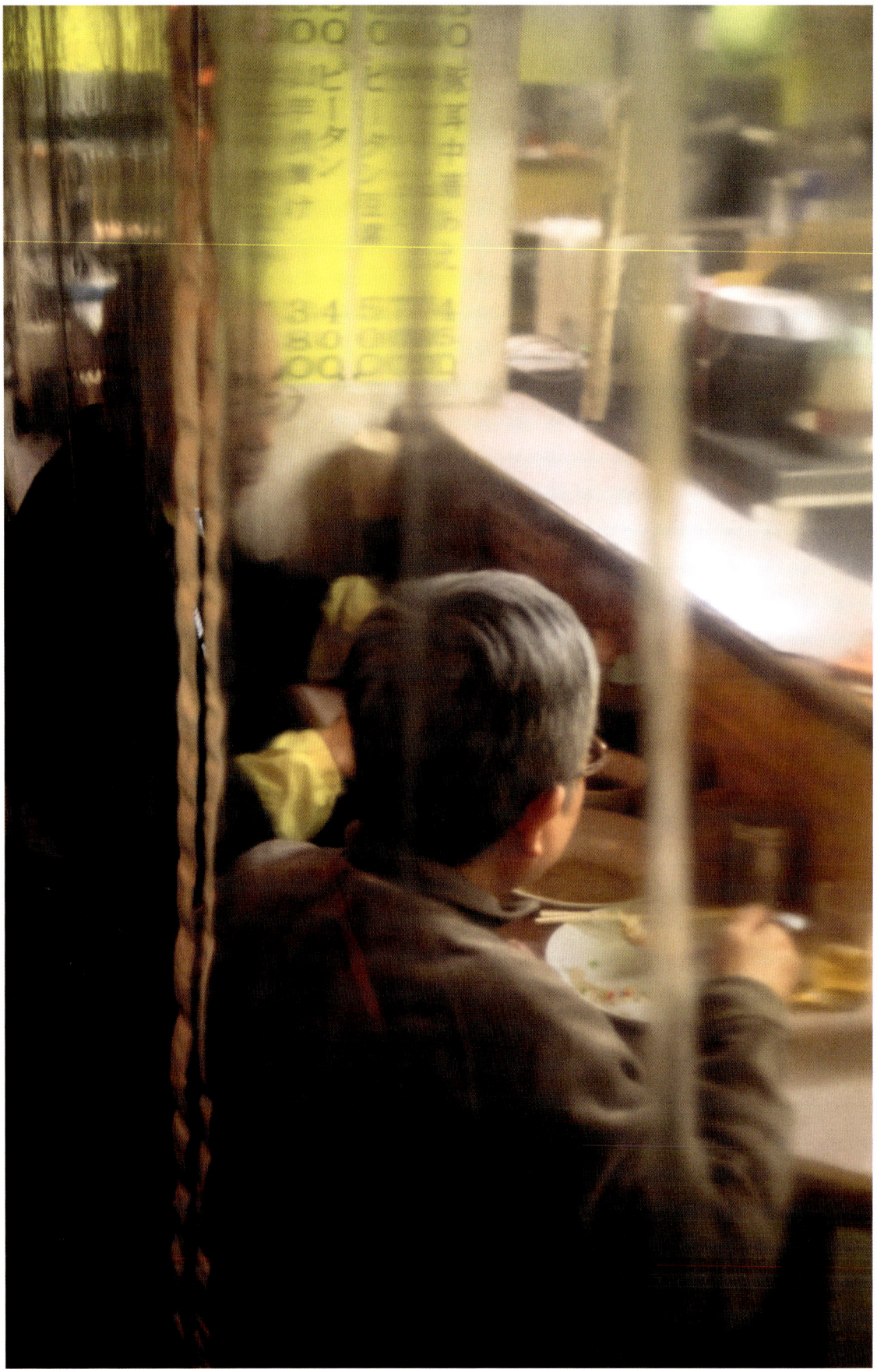

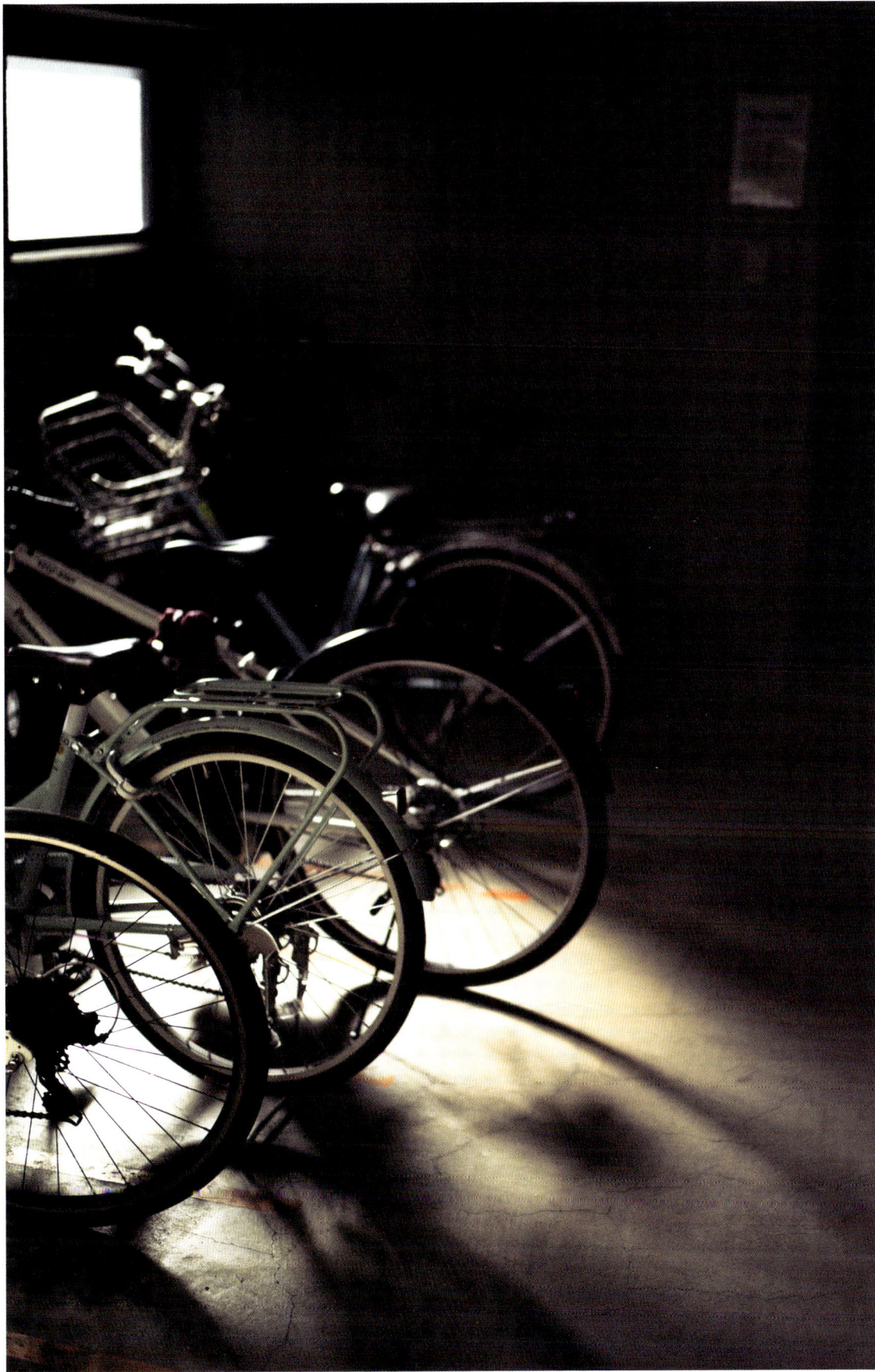

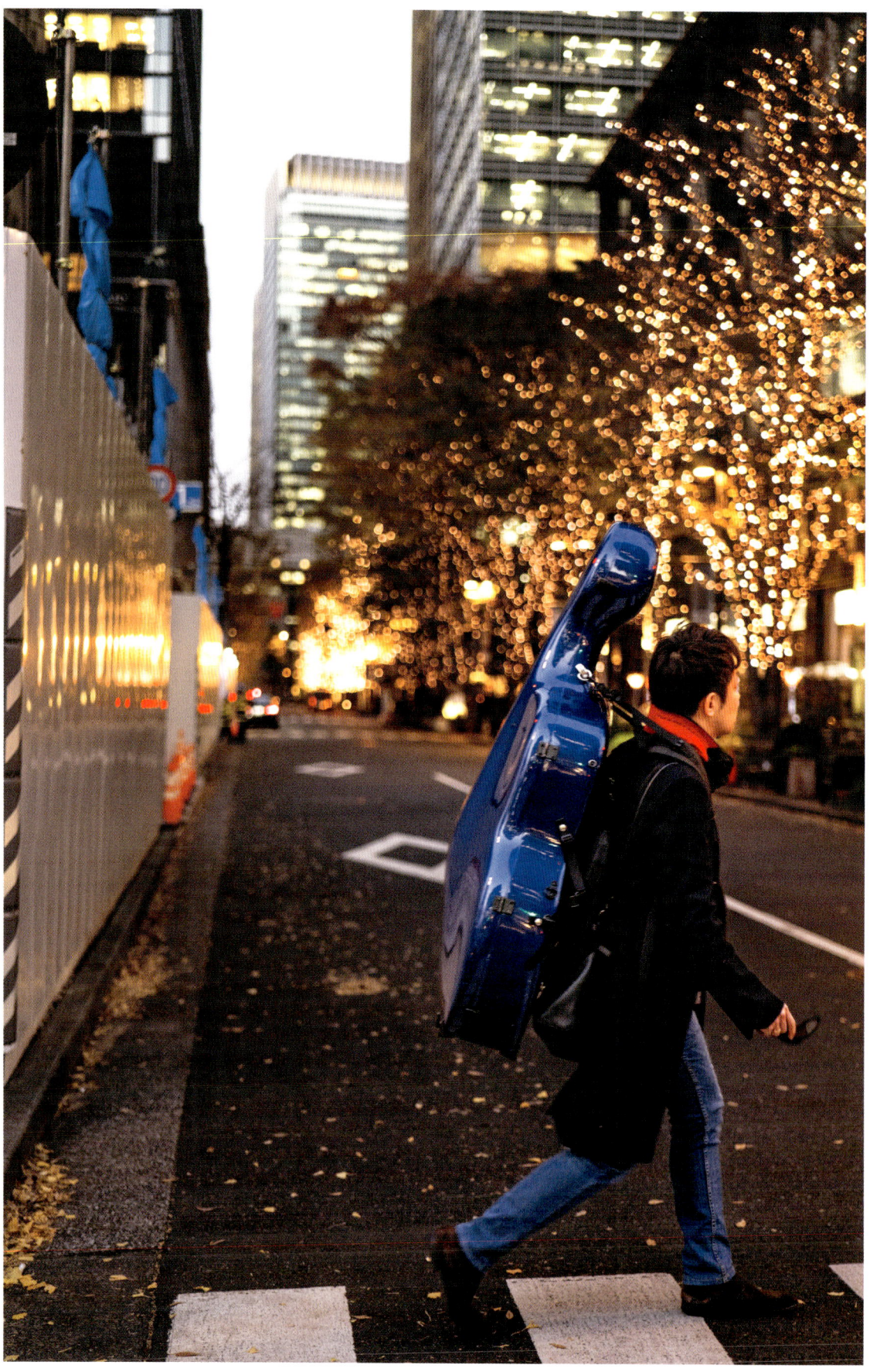

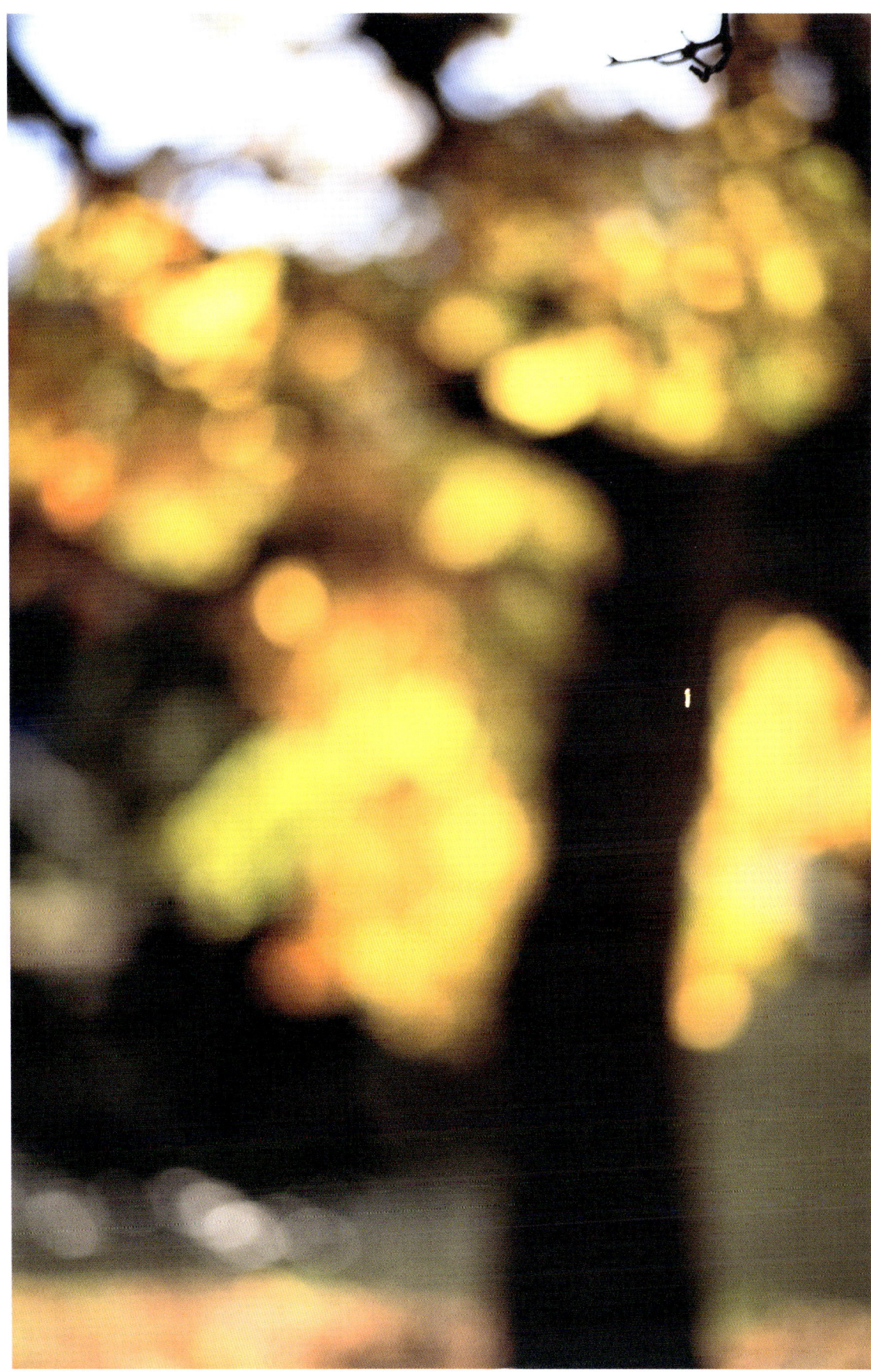

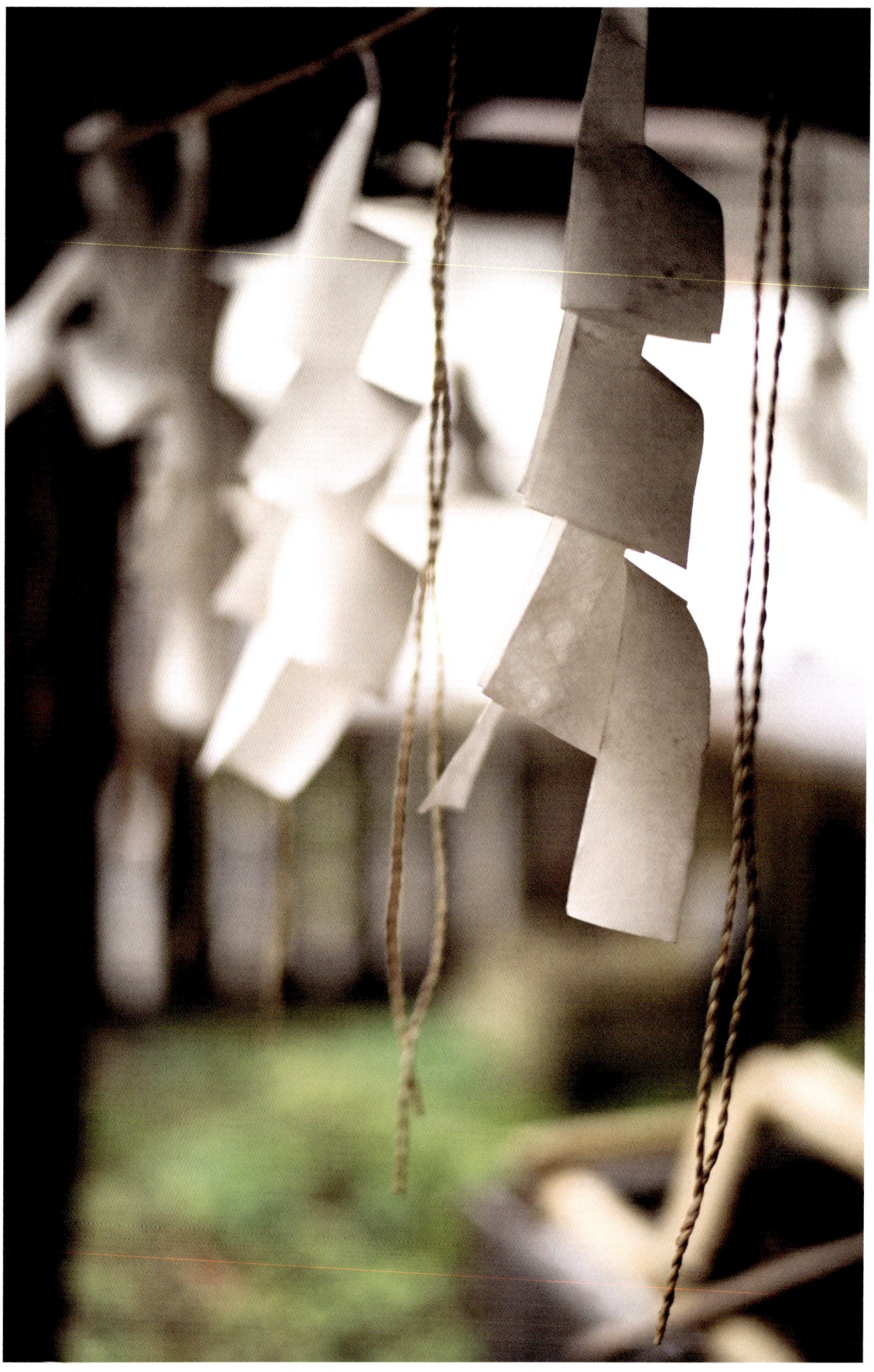

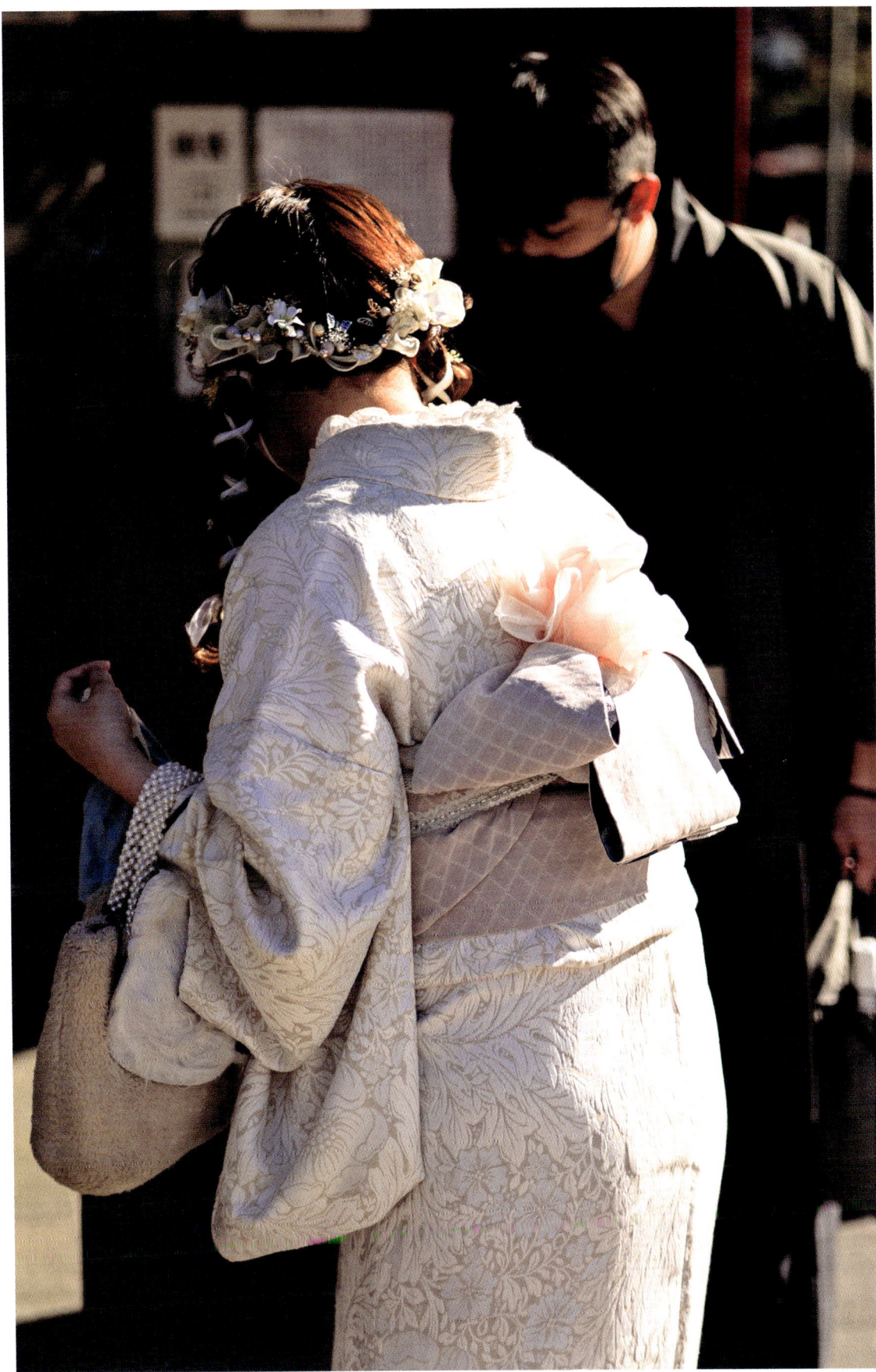

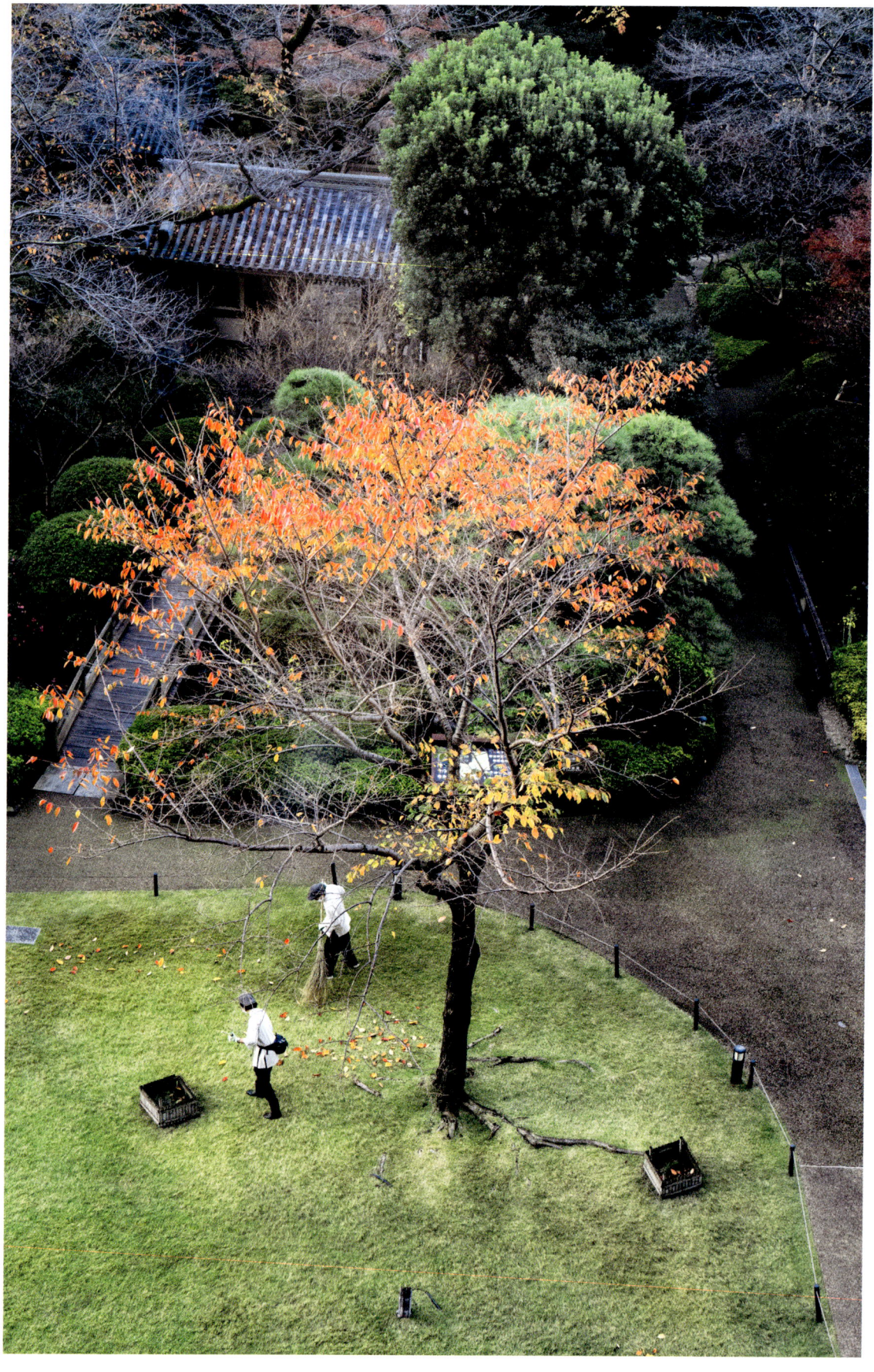

CHAPTER 11

FOCUS

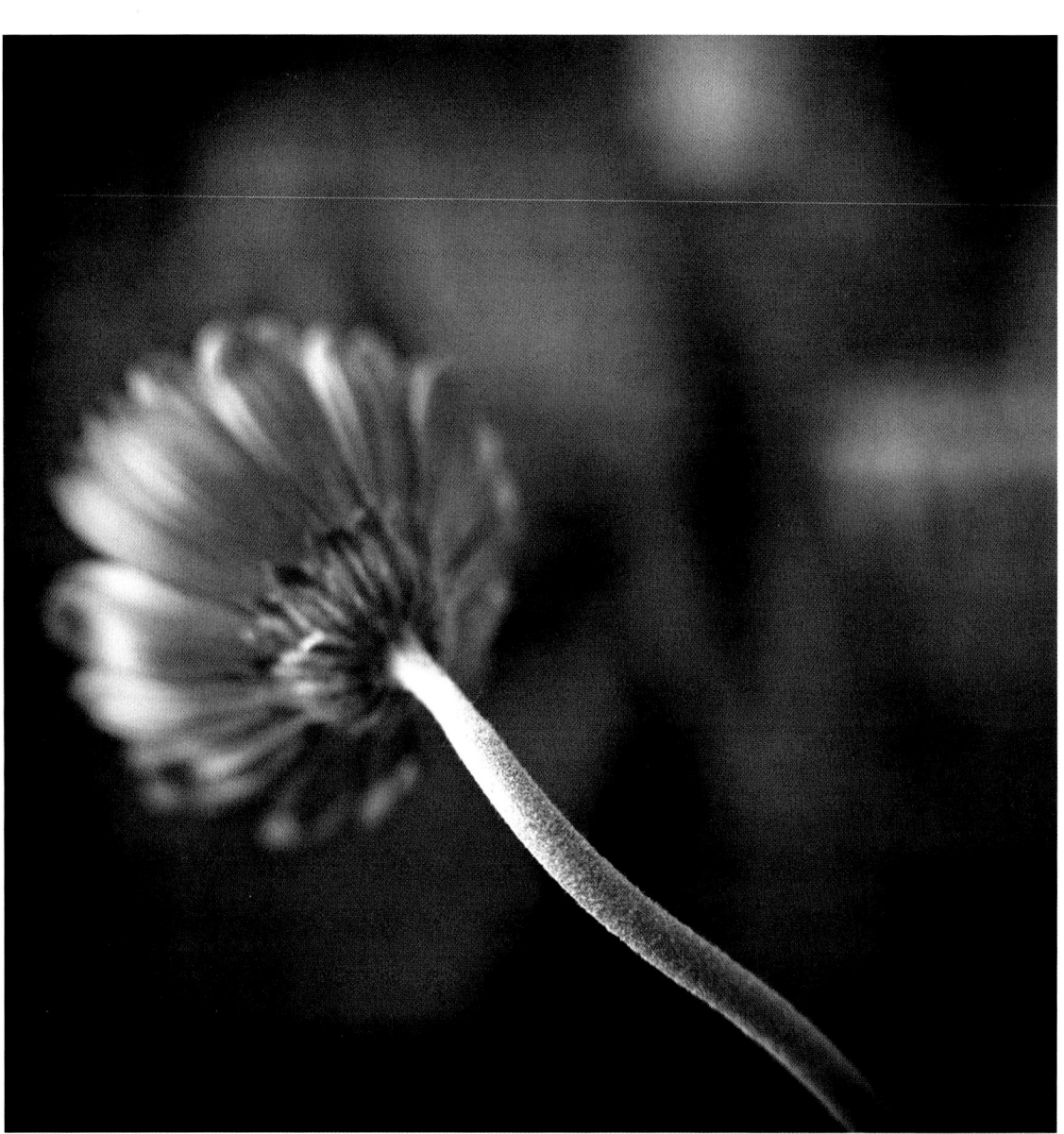

FOCUS USED TO BE the first thing one learned when beginning to explore photography. Autofocus has changed that considerably. Autofocus is so good on cameras now that most photographers don't even bother to learn about focus, much less consider it something that is an option in a visual composition. I'm not attempting to belittle modern technology, but I am stressing the importance to you as a photographer that this is maybe one of the most important aspects of photography. Whether you rely on a camera to focus the lens for you or not, it is extremely important to understand that it is the photographer who decides where the point of focus is in an image and why.

The idea of focus is somewhat unique to photography. Our eyes actually focus, but it's an involuntary action that our brain carries out for us. It happens so rapidly that we interpret everything we see as "in focus," unless of course you have issues with your vision. I'm nearsighted and I have an astigmatism in my left eye, so without glasses, life is usually fairly blurry. But for our purposes here, let's assume we have perfect vision, or at least remembered our glasses.

No matter the time period, it is rare to see areas in a painting out of focus. Yes, there are exceptions, but painting historically has intended to mimic the way our brain interprets focus. We perceive everything as being in focus.

But photography relies on optics that don't have the brain to quickly focus. Therefore we introduce depth of field. Within a three-dimensional space, an optic is influenced by the aperture the lens is using. This is essentially the "iris" in the lens that determines how much light is allowed to pass through. The larger the aperture, the shallower the field of focus is. This is also influenced by distance. If you're focusing on an object close to the camera and you're using a large aperture, the background will be out of focus—it appears blurry.

Consider this from a bird's eye view and you could measure the area that is actually in focus. That object one meter from the camera that you're focusing on is sitting in a field that is probably only a few centimeters deep. Anything in this area will be in focus.

Chances are you've run into problems if you're photographing two or more people and they're not lined up in this field of focus. If you're using a large aperture, chances are only one of the subjects will be in focus. You need to stop down the lens, or make the aperture smaller, to increase this depth of field to get both people in focus at the same time.

This is an optical phenomenon and exists because we're directing light onto a flat film surface or a digital sensor. But it gives you some creative advantages as a photographer.

When I started, I didn't really give this much thought. I understood the concept and just considered an image to be in focus or not. It made the most sense that if there was a person in my image, I needed to focus on their eyes. Otherwise, the point of focus was on the closest prominent object or subject in the scene.

Technically that rule is a pretty safe one to go by, but it doesn't create a lot of creative possibilities. Ironically two different painters made me realize how important focus is in photography and how you can create some very creative solutions if you consider its purpose.

Gerhard Richter is a contemporary artist from Germany. Unlike most artists, Richter works in many different styles, spanning from abstract to photorealism. He's one of the most important artists of the contemporary era. Richter has consistently worked in the opposite of anything that's popular and as a result has developed a true identity for his work that is somewhat hard to classify. He's really more like four artists combined in one, as his talent seems limitless. Known best for his paintings, he also has incorporated photography and glass sculpture into his output. For me, Germany has produced some of the contemporary era's most incredible artists, and Richter is at the top of my list.

In the 1960s, when abstract expressionism was in vogue, Richter went the opposite direction with photography-inspired painting techniques that he absolutely mastered.

I remember the first time I saw some of his photo paintings. I thought they were some of the more interesting photographs I had ever seen. I didn't even realize they were paintings.

In the early 2000s I worked for the Dallas Museum of Art in Dallas, Texas, as a multimedia producer. I made digital resources and videos for both in-gallery experiences and the museum's various websites. I also built the first museum "smartphone tour." I was exposed to a wide range of art and culture that I had not experienced.

During my first week on the job, I had gone "off campus" for lunch one day. As I returned, I went through a door that led to a long concourse and walked by the first gallery on the right. There in the doorway was a giant portrait of Mao Zedong. It was several feet tall, monochrome, and completely out of focus. Yet it was clearly the chairman of the Chinese Communist Party. I went closer and read the label, which explained that it was a work by Gerhard Richter and that it wasn't a photograph at all. Richter had painted the subject as if it were out of focus. I had never seen that in painting before. I had seen paintings that looked like photographs, but they were always sharp. This guy was painting the effect of a lens as it renders out of focus. Yet I could still tell who the picture depicted. The painting gives you the essential information and hides anything else. This blew my mind. Could I perhaps do that with a camera?

I then started researching Gerhard Richter and found an entire universe of work, but was particularly fascinated by these photo paintings. There's one of Queen Elizabeth II that is also out of focus, but it also emulates the "dot matrix" from a magazine or newsprint, as if it were blown up from a thumbnail image.

Then I found his photo paintings from the 1980s, which look precisely like photographs. There are a few photo paintings of candles, but what really grabbed me is the famous portrait of his daughter, Betty, that he painted in 1988 (which is also called *Betty*). Richter was literally painting out of focus. Not only is the technique incredible but the pose is sublime. Betty is sitting on the floor with her weight forward on her left shoulder, but she is turned away and we only see the back of her head. Her red patterned shirt is contrasted by the muted green background. It's an incredible study of light as well, the way her blonde hair is lit—everything about this is just fabulous. It would be an incredible photograph, but it's not a photograph.

The focus is on her left shoulder (if this had been taken with a lens). It's not a super shallow depth of field (but moderately shallow). This painting started making me think about photography. How do I render something like this? A portrait of the back of someone's head? This painting led me to so many questions about photography. To this day, this picture burns in my mind because it crosses media, defies the expected, and is a picture with this amazingly lush beauty.

Over the years I've often thought of this picture. I realize that it was entirely controlled and rendered by the artist. It's not real. It has the illusion of being real. It's the type of image that I want to create with my camera.

In Richter's own words: "Picturing things, taking a view, is what makes us human; art is making sense and giving shape to that sense. It is like the religious search for God."

Please read that twice and pause for a minute.

Leonardo da Vinci is another major source of inspiration for me, and he certainly never took a photograph. He is one of the great legends when you consider the range and skill level of what he contributed to not only the visual medium but challenging the way human beings think. The word "polymath" comes up a lot to describe him. I really hate that term, as it's usually ego-driven, but I have to say that if there is anyone deserving of that label, Leonardo da Vinci is the one.

Back to my museum career . . . In 2011, the museum hired a new director, Maxwell Anderson. It was an interesting and exciting time, to say the least. Max was extremely well connected in the art world, and you never knew what was going to be presented when you walked into work.

One day he called me to his office. It was very secret and also very weird. Max told me about a group of art dealers that claimed to have discovered a lost Leonardo da Vinci painting. Only about twenty or so da Vinci paintings exist today, and because attribution can be hard to prove, the authenticity of many of these paintings is debated.

Salvator Mundi (Savior of the World) is an iconic image that was rendered by many Renaissance artists. This was not uncommon at that time, as there was no printing press and copying was a somewhat common practice for certain iconic pictures. For example, there are many copies of the *Mona Lisa*. This painting of Salvator Mundi was special in that UV testing was done and revealed that the hand position of Christ had been changed by the artist. The consensus of scholars was that that would never have been done in a copy, thus giving some evidence that this was indeed a da Vinci original.

At the time, the museum was to make a bid based on what it could fundraise for the acquisition. In order to do that, Max had arranged a loan from the owners to display this work for potential donors to view. So for the next year, under maximum security, this painting lived in the basement of the museum with scheduled visits from special guests you'd never expect to see on the way to the elevator.

But first Max organized a symposium of da Vinci experts, mostly curators from around the world. I was asked to film this symposium and interview various people on the work in question. The most interesting to me was Dianne Modestini. Dianne is the conservator who restored *Salvador Mundi*, which was in pretty rough shape when it was found. She literally repainted large sections of this as if da Vinci himself had done them. There aren't many people on the planet who can do this. Her level of talent is staggering, to say the least.

I tell you this story because I talked to her extensively about da Vinci and the technique used in his paintings. Da Vinci was particularly terrible at selecting wood to paint on, but his skill was on levels of brilliance above anything else being done at that time. In many ways he defined the Renaissance in his level of performance and innovation.

One of his techniques that I find particularly impressive is his use of the sfumato. This word means "smoke" in Italian and refers to the soft edges rendered in the application of paint. Earlier artists had always rendered high contrast with hard edges. Da Vinci painted the edges soft and more realistic than I had previously seen. This technique is only a small sliver of his talent, but it was the one that, to me, related to photography. Da Vinci did not paint the depth of field like Richter would centuries later, but he softened certain parts of paintings in a way that drew an enormous amount of interest to the viewer. In *Salvator Mundi*, the sharpest point of contrast is on Christ's hands. The lifted right hand and the left hand with the globe. Was da Vinci building on an aesthetic idea, or is he balancing the emphasis between Christ's face and hands?

This led me to think of photography. Lenses are physical tools designed by optical engineers. The design goals of any lens are established to balance optical performance with budgets, retail pricing, and available materials. They serve commercial purposes. But lenses are always a balance of distortions and corrections. This gives us an entire history of renderings at our disposal to use in our image making as artists. As with da Vinci's sfumato technique, does every point of focus have to be of high contrast and sharp? Soft rendering is as valid a technique as any other, but in photography our quest for sharpness and resolution stems from science, in particular, physics. Why does this quest dictate the art we produce?

The globe in *Salvator Mundi* is of particular interest to me. There are two major problems with lenses designed before the 1970s.

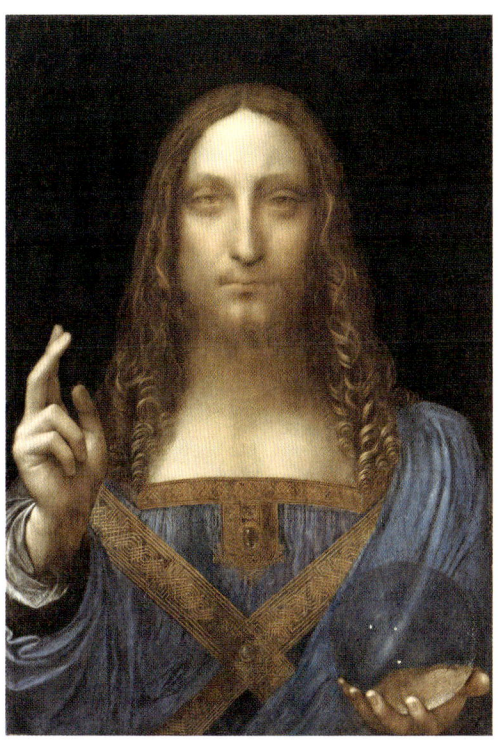

Salvator Mundi by Leonardo Da Vinci (c. 1499-1510); via Wikimedia Commons.

Before multi-coating, there was a limit to how many surfaces light could pass through before losing significant momentum (the limit was commonly six surfaces, or three elements). Second, the techniques in producing lens elements were crude by today's standards. Often 1960s lenses exhibit spherical shapes in the bokeh areas of light points, which look exactly like this globe. Of course, this is a stretch—the globe is in the foreground and clearly not bokeh. But I can't help but think that da Vinci's knowledge of optics during his time inspired the rendering here. If nothing else, it's a curious observation.

Between the history of lenses and where we place the focus, I think this is a highly over-looked area of photography that has barely been explored. It is important to ask ourselves these questions as artists. We must advance the medium as we strive to stand out as individuals. The industry tells us to do things a certain way. Follow that lead and we're assured to all be producing the same type of work. That is not interesting to me and shouldn't be interesting for you either.

Sometimes it takes a past master to make you consider your options in a modern world. There were some great lenses made in the 1960s, and every other decade as well.

Learn how to focus a lens. It's not hard. Then decide where you want to place the point of focus in the composition, even if it is not the conventional location. Make things sharp when you feel they should be. Don't be afraid to make them blurry, as long as it serves a purpose and still communicates the core idea that you want to convey.

FOCAL LENGTH

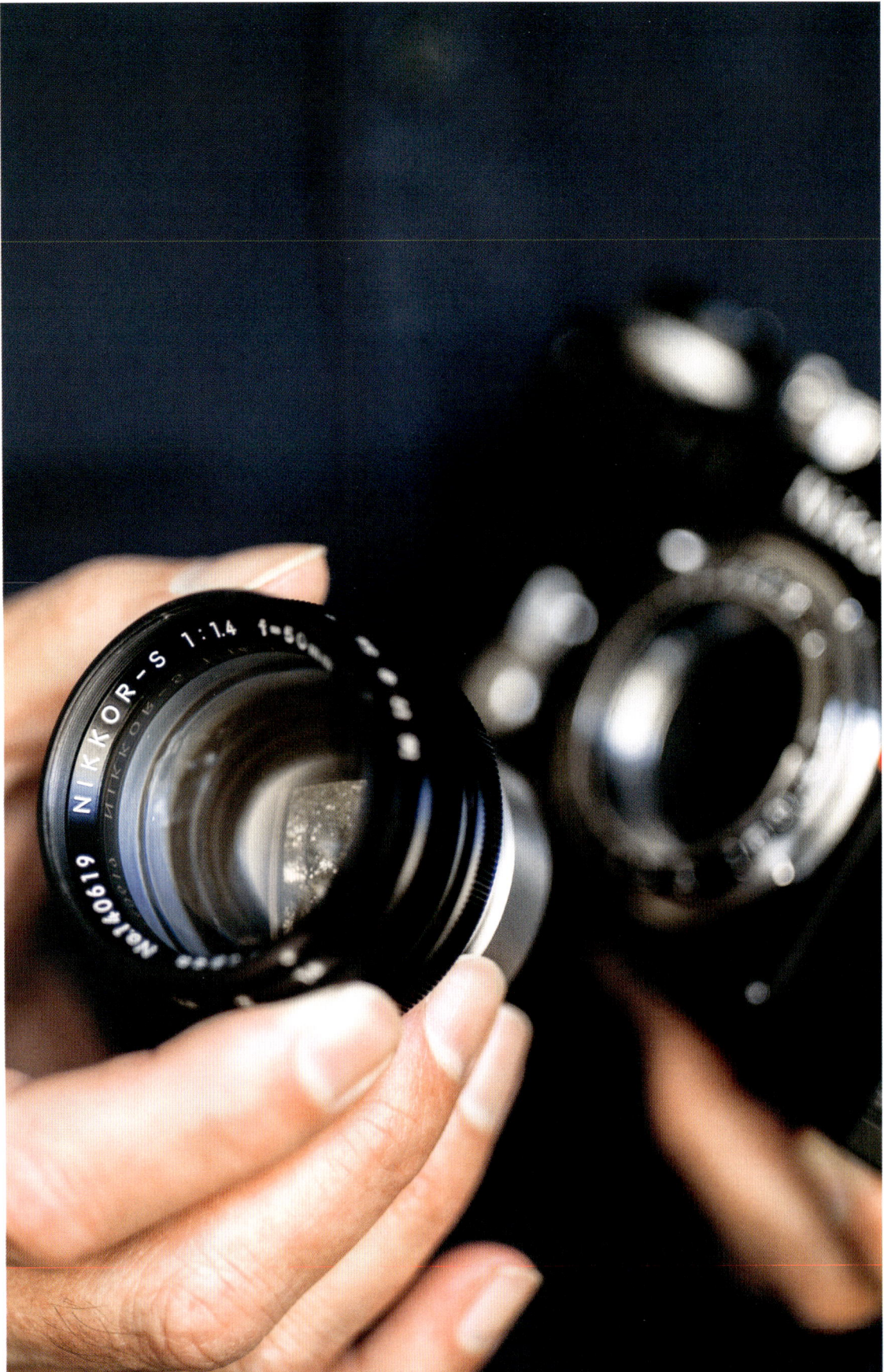

FOCAL LENGTH IS A MUCH OVERLOOKED yet governing aspect of the types of images we create. Focal length is a measurement of an optical system's convergence or divergence of light to the sensor or film. We see this as a wide or narrow field of view. In the application of photography, we measure a lens's focal length in millimeters. When you set a rectilinear lens to infinity, the focal length is the distance between the lens's rear nodal point and the focal plane. The shorter the distance, the wider the field of view.

The first photographic lenses were all a fixed focal length, so to change the field of view, you would need a different lens. We refer to these as "prime" lenses. "Zoom" lenses came along much later, and I would argue it took many years before they captured the same image quality one could get using prime lenses.

Prime lenses tend to come in standard focal lengths, for the most part. A lot of this is due to the earliest 35mm cameras being dependent on a rangefinder to focus, and the frame-lines for different lenses were limited. Leica rangefinders are still made this way today.

In the early days of 35mm, the "standard" photography focal lengths were 28mm, 35mm, 50mm, 90mm, and 135mm (wide to telephoto). Later, with the advent of the SLR system and composing directly through the lens, more focal lengths were introduced. Today there are many.

For the sake of simplicity, I'm going to be discussing the early five focal lengths in the context of the 35mm or full-frame system. APS-C, Micro Four Thirds, and medium-format digital cameras have crop factors that change the corresponding field of view.

In the context of photography, smaller numbers equal a greater field of view. The 28mm is considered a wide-angle. At the other end we've got the 135mm telephoto. Visually, if we move through this range, two things happen. Most obviously, the field of view narrows as we move up. The 28mm is wide, 50mm is considered standard, and 135mm is a telephoto. But slightly less obvious is that the perception of this field of view changes between two types of distortions, pincushion on the wide end and a barrel type on the telephoto end. Even with the modern correction optics that almost perfectly straighten out lines and alleviate optical aberrations, this distortion is still perceived by the nature of the focal length.

If the camera moves closer or further back to match the same field of view using two different focal lengths, the resulting images still look very different because of their optical signature.

Each prime lens has a unique look. This is essential information for the photographer in order to choose the right lens for the right application.

Choosing a Focal Length

First off, I must stress that as a photographer you have to understand the tools and why you would use one over another. If we have an understanding of the optical footprint, then we will know what various focal lengths will do when called upon.

Another good exercise is guessing the focal length when looking at photographs for study. You would be surprised how easy it is to start noticing this right away. Particularly with photography shot up through the 1960s, before zoom lenses, you'll be able to guess the exact focal length, as it will likely be one of the five lenses I mentioned in the last section. Even with zoom lenses you can guess in the ballpark. The exact number isn't important but the look of the field of view is. Elements of the optics, such as compression or pin cushion, usually give it away, but take it a step further: Why did the photographer use that lens? Does it make a difference on the impact of the picture?

The concept of "practice" is something that I come back to a lot in this book, and for good reason. Learning requires experience and there's no way to really shortcut this. I've outlined the family of lenses above that are traditional to Leica, since it in many ways is the system everything else springs from. But there are other focal lengths as well. My recommendation is to start with what you have and keep things simple. The goal is to make decisions, not create more options.

One way I teach focal lengths is by using the metaphor of musical instrument families. For example, look at the string family. Our different variants cover a wide range of notes, with a double bass on the bottom, followed by the cello, the viola, and the violin. A string player can play any of these instruments, but the technique changes enough so most musicians end up specializing in one.

Another comparison is to the saxophone. I'm a huge jazz fan, and I'm particularly fond of John Coltrane's music. His playing range was wide, from ballads to bebop and avant-garde music. And he did most of it on the tenor saxophone. (Yes, he could play soprano sax as well, with a high degree of skill.) I have no doubt that Coltrane could also play alto and baritone, and probably clarinet. Why? Because the technique is very similar across all of these instruments. But he specialized because each has a distinctive sound and fingerprint.

Coltrane chose what worked well for his voice and for his own expression. You can make the same argument for Charlie Parker and the alto sax or Gerry Mulligan and the baritone.

To me this is very similar to the focal lengths of prime lenses. Garry Winogrand shot almost exclusively with the 28mm and found his voice within that field of view. Henri Cartier-Bresson—arguably one of the most significant and well-known photographers in the history of the medium—made an entire career with a 50mm lens.

Do you have to specialize? Absolutely not. There are many examples of photographers who use a variety of focal lengths. But my point here is that you should have an understanding of what each has to offer. Your choices are based on those visual understandings. In larger series works, varying the focal lengths has the effect of using different saxophones. Varying the fields of view will give you more interest and variety over larger works.

My advice is to practice with one prime lens at a time. Put a 28mm lens on your camera for a week and only shoot with that. Understand its strengths and weaknesses in a compositional sense. Work with it and find out what it does. Take a different focal length the next week—say a 135mm—and really learn it. Practice is the only way to understand what it is you are photographing with.

And finally, can you visualize focal length without your camera? This is an interesting exercise. Pick something from the room you're in at the moment and mentally frame up a composition. Consider where you are currently standing. Do you know what focal length you would need to get everything you want in the composition? Test yourself. Put the lens you think you need on the camera and see if you're right. Do this repeatedly and you'll start to understand intuitively what you want without thinking about it. Remember, the idea is to speak visually and not think about it.

The Perfect Focal Length?

For my work, the right focal length comes down to form vs. function. In other words, I'm from the school of one camera and one lens. I shoot about 90 percent of my work with a 50mm because I know that will work for the way I see. Perhaps I also love the challenge because it's not the perfect focal length for every image, but I can make it work with my vision about 90 percent of the time. Nine out of ten shots isn't bad. I'm fine with that.

I can't tell you what focal length is the best for your style and the subjects you shoot. That is something every photographer has to decide. If you don't know the answer, start with the 50mm. After you've shot on that for a month, see if it's starting to work for you. If it's not, then try another focal length for a month and see if it meets your needs in a better way.

I will admit I used to be a bit of a gear head and loved the possibilities of shooting with anything. Before a trip, I'd pack a bag full of prime lenses. Then I would try and put some zoom lenses in the bag as well. Any space left in my other bag? Stuff it full with film or any other tool that might come in handy, whether I needed it or not! I loved the idea of being prepared for any situation I might find myself in. I saw it as a photography version of the boy scouts.

But as I got older, I realized there were two problems with this. First of all, I had too many options. I'd spend more time thinking about what I was going to use than enjoying the trip. Secondly, I'd carry around too much stuff when I finally did get out to shoot. I spent more time changing lenses, fumbling around with lens caps, and digging around in the bag than actually photographing. I'd also find bizarre ways to convince myself that I always had the wrong lens at the right moment and that was why my work wasn't making sense. The image wasn't great? Well, I obviously didn't have the correct lens!

But then I started to consider one of my personal heroes, the great Henri Cartier-Bresson. He used one lens for almost his entire career—the 50mm. That man made so many iconic images with that simple setup. He traveled light and focused all of his attention into those Decisive Moments.

Ralph Gibson once told me that if I wanted to start getting a better understanding of my own work, I needed to commit to using only the 50mm lens and a rangefinder. Why the 50mm? Ralph made the interesting point that not everyone prefers the 50mm, but one can't deny the fact that there are more iconic photographs made with the 50mm in the history of photography than anything else.

I took those words to heart and realized that Cartier-Bresson used the same tools. Simplicity is important. All of a sudden, I was photographing more. I wasn't wasting time and energy selecting camera and lens combinations. I was putting my own eye and the act of photography in front of me and leaving the gear at home. The rangefinder allows you to see what's in the frame as well as what you're leaving out. This is an efficient and beautiful way to compose because you're not viewing through the lens. Imposing these kinds of limitations on yourself is quite a liberating experience; you just have to decide to do it.

Of course, you can get very macro with this concept as well—I'll be the first to admit I have. I started realizing that there are many different 50mm lenses. Any system usually offers f/1.4 and f/1.8 versions and some systems even more. Then you look at out-of-production lenses; the list can go on. On a side note, for a separate project, I started building a spreadsheet listing every 50mm lens ever made for 35mm format and that can currently be adapted to a modern mirrorless camera. The project is nowhere near completion and I have over 500 lenses listed.

My point here is, yes, there are different flavors of 50mm lenses. Remember we're eliminating options, and this book is about the visual language of photography. Don't get lost in the micro. The viewer will never care what lens you used and, unless they're another nerd photographer, they'll never judge the quality of the bokeh, or even care. This is the ultimate fool's errand. If you take this advice to heart, it will save you a lot of money and you'll make incredible images on whatever you've chosen to use.

Now, as I've waxed 50mm, I realize this lens isn't perfect for every situation, and I do own and use other lenses. But for me, I found my voice in the 50mm so that's where I tend to live. Sometimes I'll "travel" to other focal lengths when needed, but I always return home.

If you're just starting out, try the 50mm. If you already shoot something specific, you might already have a sense of what is required. If you shoot sports or wildlife, start with something longer, like a 200mm. If you shoot architecture, start with a 20mm.

When you're starting out, avoid zoom lenses. The idea is to understand the field of view to the point where you know where you need to stand in relation to the subject. Learn to predict your results this is how you learn to previsualize. Zoom lenses are convenient, but you won't grasp this concept shooting only a zoom. You should experiment and decide what works best for your own visual aesthetic. Live there.

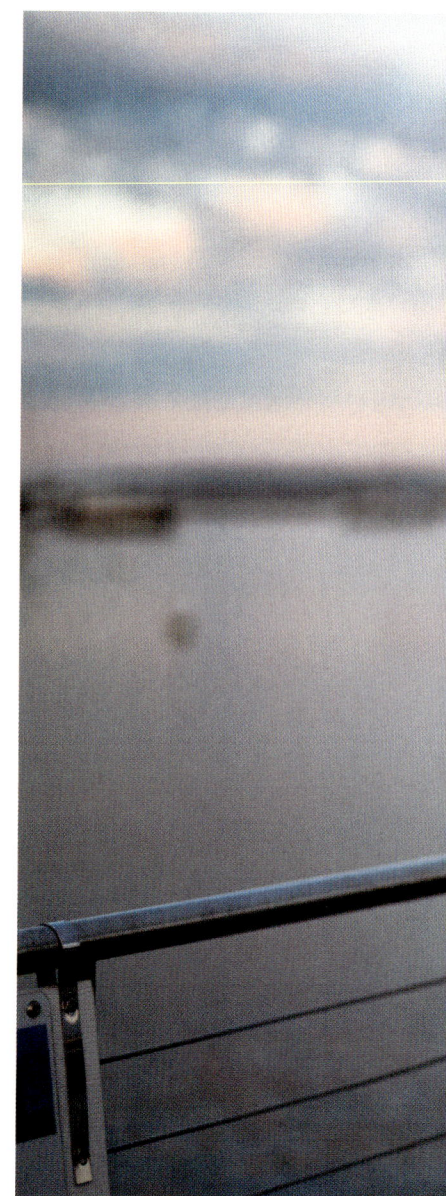

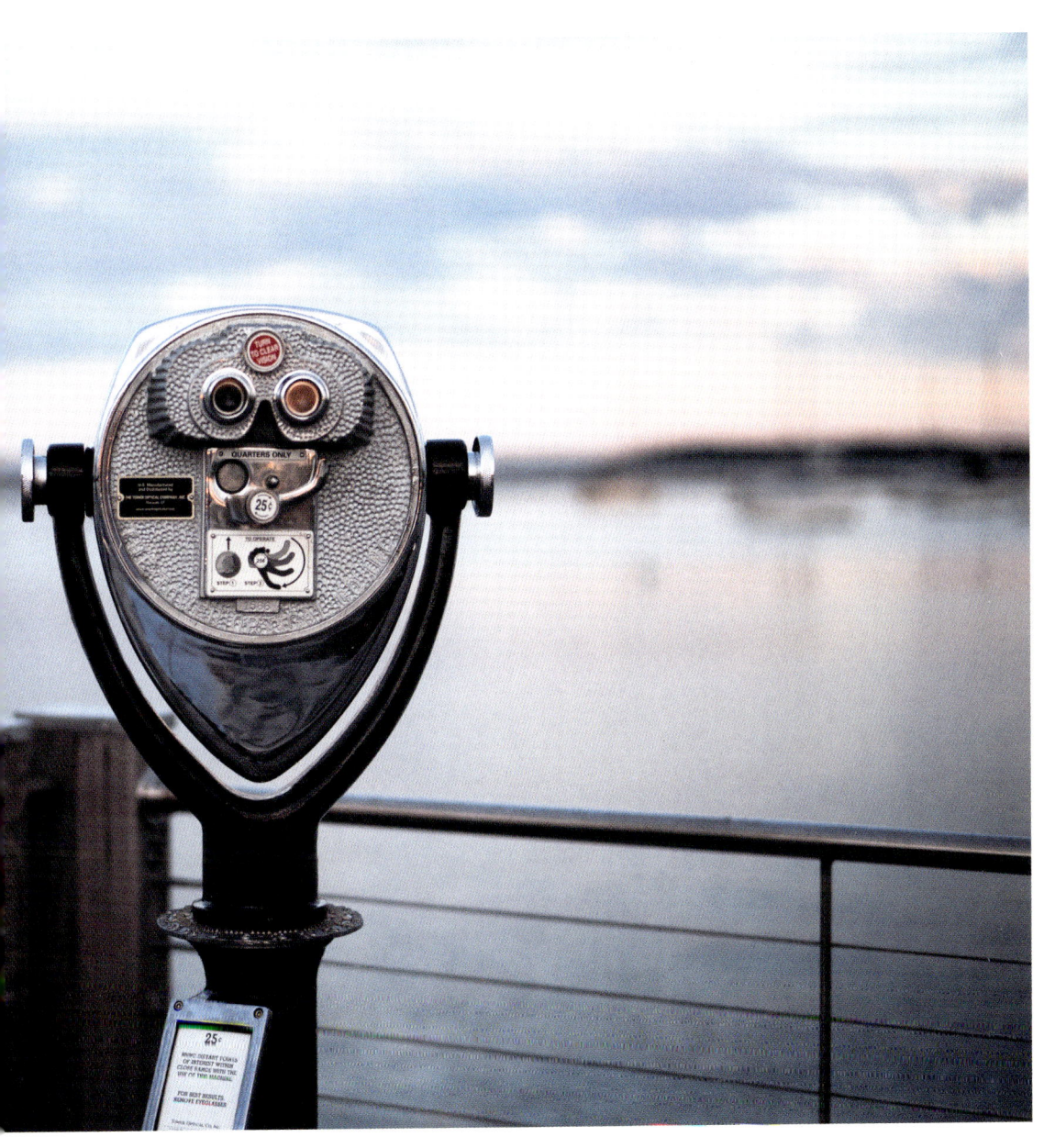

CHAPTER 13

VISUAL ELEMENTS

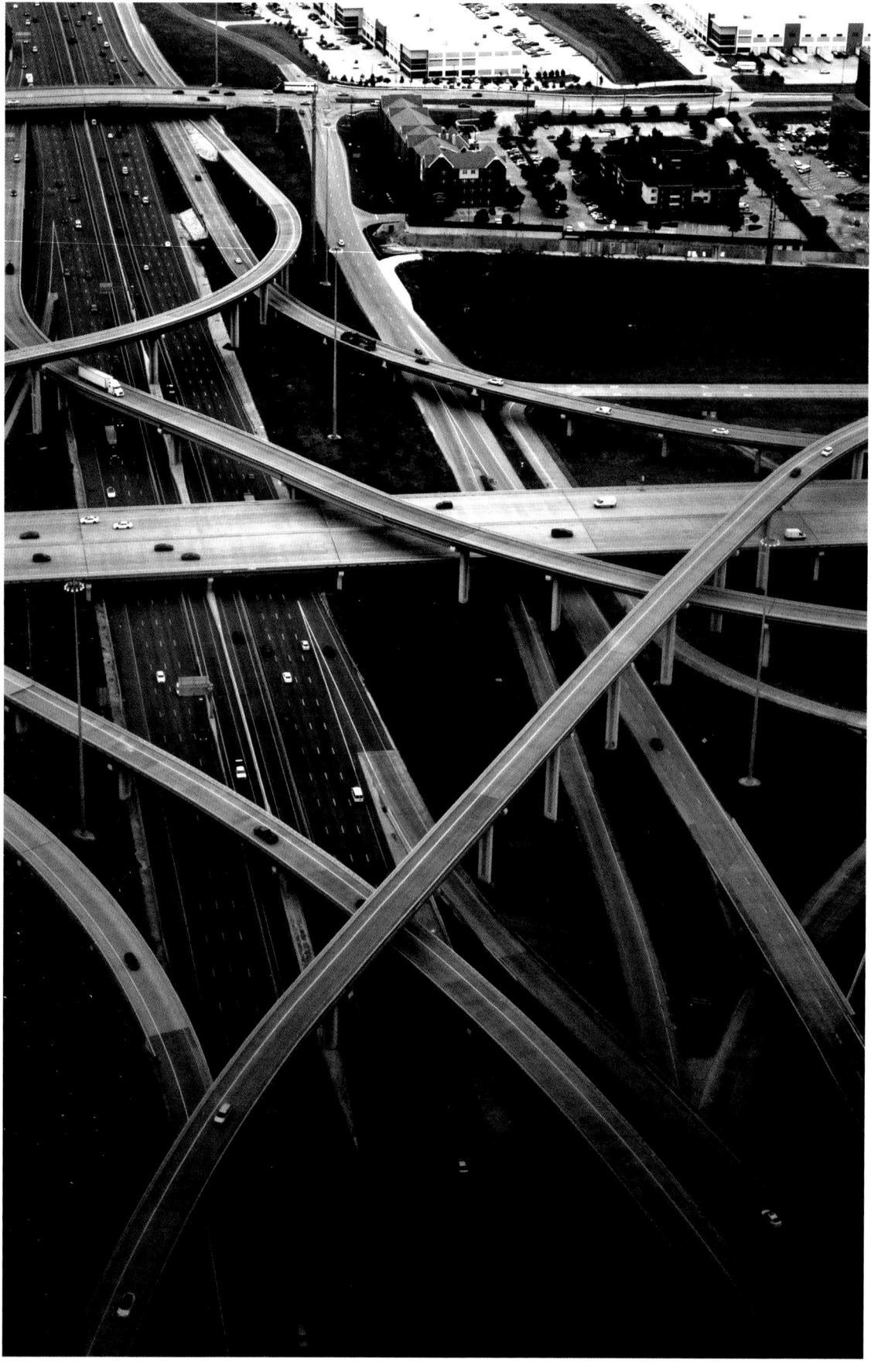

VISUAL COMMUNICATION can be broken down into several basic elements. There are five that I feel are most important to photography: line, shape, focus, texture, and light. These visual elements are essentially building blocks for composition.

Line

In a composition you can have actual lines or implied lines. Let's start with lines that are visible. They can be thin or thick, curvy or straight, and so on. They can connect two points. They can define the edges of a form.

The function of a line is most often to lead the eye of the viewer through your composition to a point of interest. Lines can be horizontal and vertical, but more often than not, it's the diagonal lines that create the strongest impact.

Lines that are not physically present or seen are called implied lines. There are a couple of ways to do this.

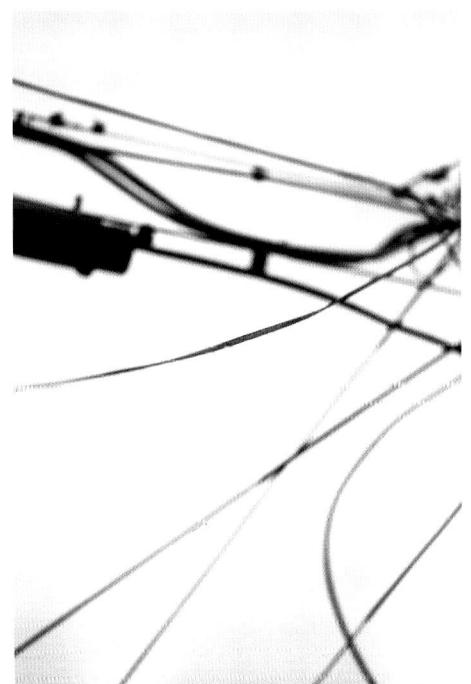

One way is to include a visible yet incomplete line in the composition. If placed correctly the partial line can seem to extend or continue beyond what has been physically established.

Another way is to use the concept of gesture for an implied line. This includes sight lines (where a subject is looking) as well as any figurative movement done with the hands or body. This is particularly effective in Greek sculpture, where the eyes can imply a direction away from the figure. In photography sight lines can lead toward a point of emphasis and even suggest geometry when combined in a single composition.

Shape

Shape is essentially the antithesis of line. Whereas lines draw the viewer's eye in a direction, shapes are generally stationary elements in the composition.

Shapes can be geometric, figurative, or abstract. They can be recognizable objects. Shapes can also be symbolic or metaphorical, especially when they are abstracted.

Focus and Bokeh

As we've stated previously, photography is unique as an art form in that it uses a lens to render the picture. Focus and depth of field also distinguish the medium from other art forms. Focus is one of the building blocks that I refer to as an aesthetic element. It is essential because it plays an important role in creating the third dimension in images. Lines and shapes remain pretty flat on their own in a composition. Focus and depth of field transform them from two-dimensional elements to something more interesting and three-dimensional.

Areas and objects in an image that are out of focus become abstract. It's important to consider that they are still a major part of the composition. Everything in a composition should exist to support the image.

In the last few decades, with the rise of digital photography, the idea of bokeh has become an obsession for both photographers and camera manufacturers alike. The term comes from the Japanese word "boke," which means "blur" or "haze." It was coined by photography magazines in the late 1990s and caught on over the years as

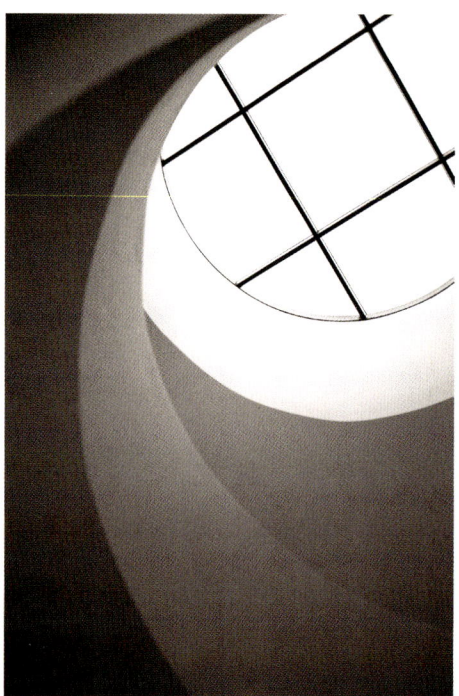

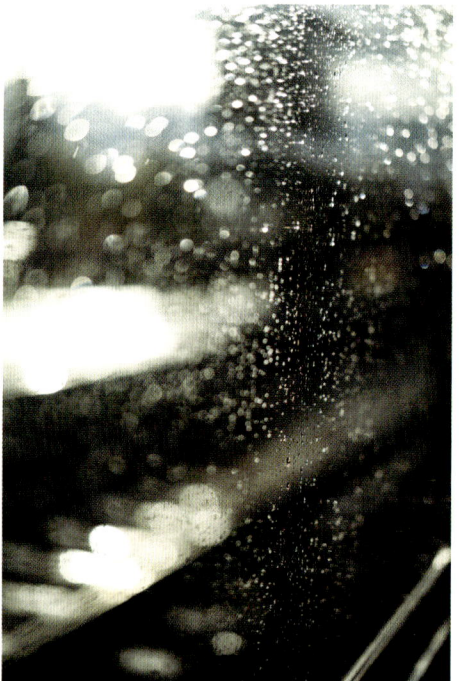

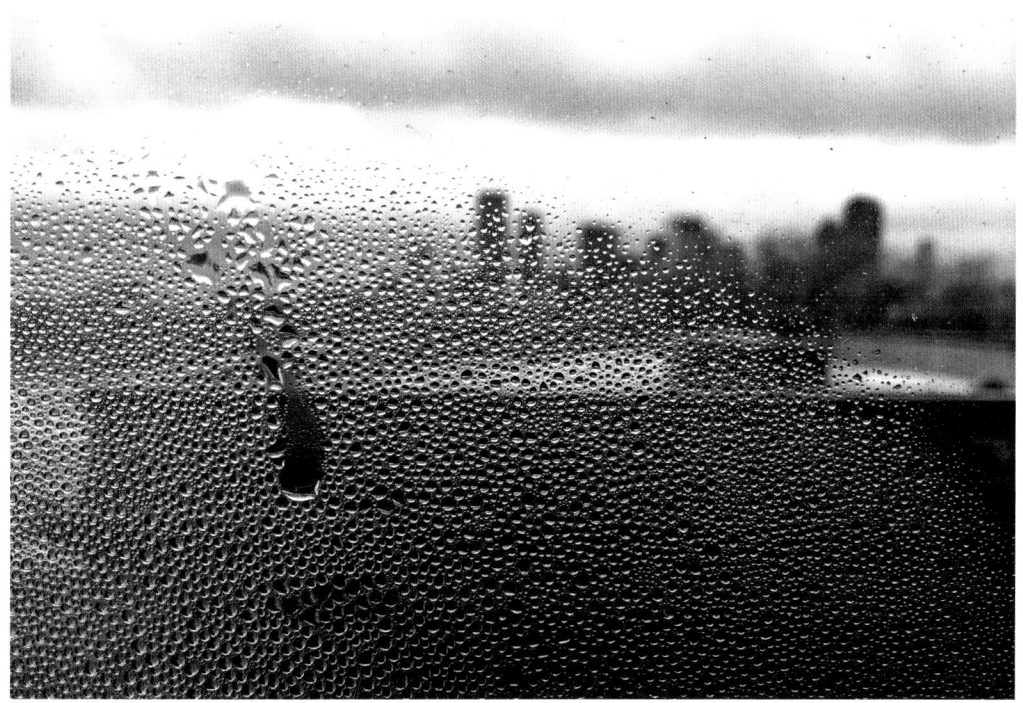

a bit of an obsession with amateur photographers. I've even seen technical bokeh analysis on photography blogs with a breakdown of "bokeh types" and "transition zones."

Use bokeh with caution as you compose images. While it can create a nice separation between your subject and the background, the problem is that this is all that bokeh really does. I feel that there are too many photographers today who use bokeh as a compositional crutch. Much of this work ends up looking the same. There's little visual interest created in the subject and the overall visual statement is lacking.

Texture

In a two-dimensional composition, texture plays a very important role in how objects appear "real." Without texture, things feel flat and removed from reality. We see texture in everything that has a surface. The texture of skin is extremely important in portraits. Without texture, snow would appear as large, flat areas of white. Texture is also what defines an object that is still visible in a shadow.

We talked a lot about texture in Chapter 9 when I discussed black and white photography. Remember that texture is very dependent on exposure. If an object is not exposed correctly, the micro-contrast starts to change what we perceive as texture, and we lose the feeling of reality.

Light

Like focus and texture, I consider light to be an aesthetic element. Photographs cannot exist without light. Light comes from a source—the sun, a lamp, fire, and, of course, flash devices. No matter what the source, we see the visual impact as light is cast on an object or subject. The subject is brightest at its closest distance to the light source and darkest at its furthest distance from the source. This gives us depth in an image. It is important to be conscious of how depth renders upon all objects and areas in the image. You never want to lose important information in shadow areas.

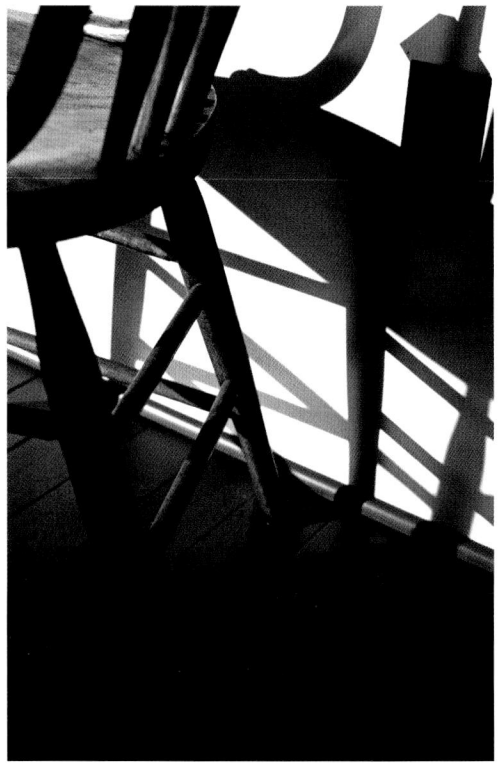

Images become particularly challenging when the light source is behind the subject. If you've ever tried to shoot a portrait against a beautiful sunset, you know what I'm talking about. This is typically referred to as "backlighting." Because of the limited dynamic range of the camera, anything in front of the light will appear as a silhouette. In this case, artificial light such as using a flash can bring the dark subject up to balance it out.

W. Eugene Smith was once asked if he used available light. His response was, "Of course, I use any light that's available." As funny as that sounds, his response perfectly and simply reflects the job of the photographer. Sometimes images are about problem-solving. You work within the limits of what is available. This includes natural light as well as artificial. Understanding light sources is essential to photography.

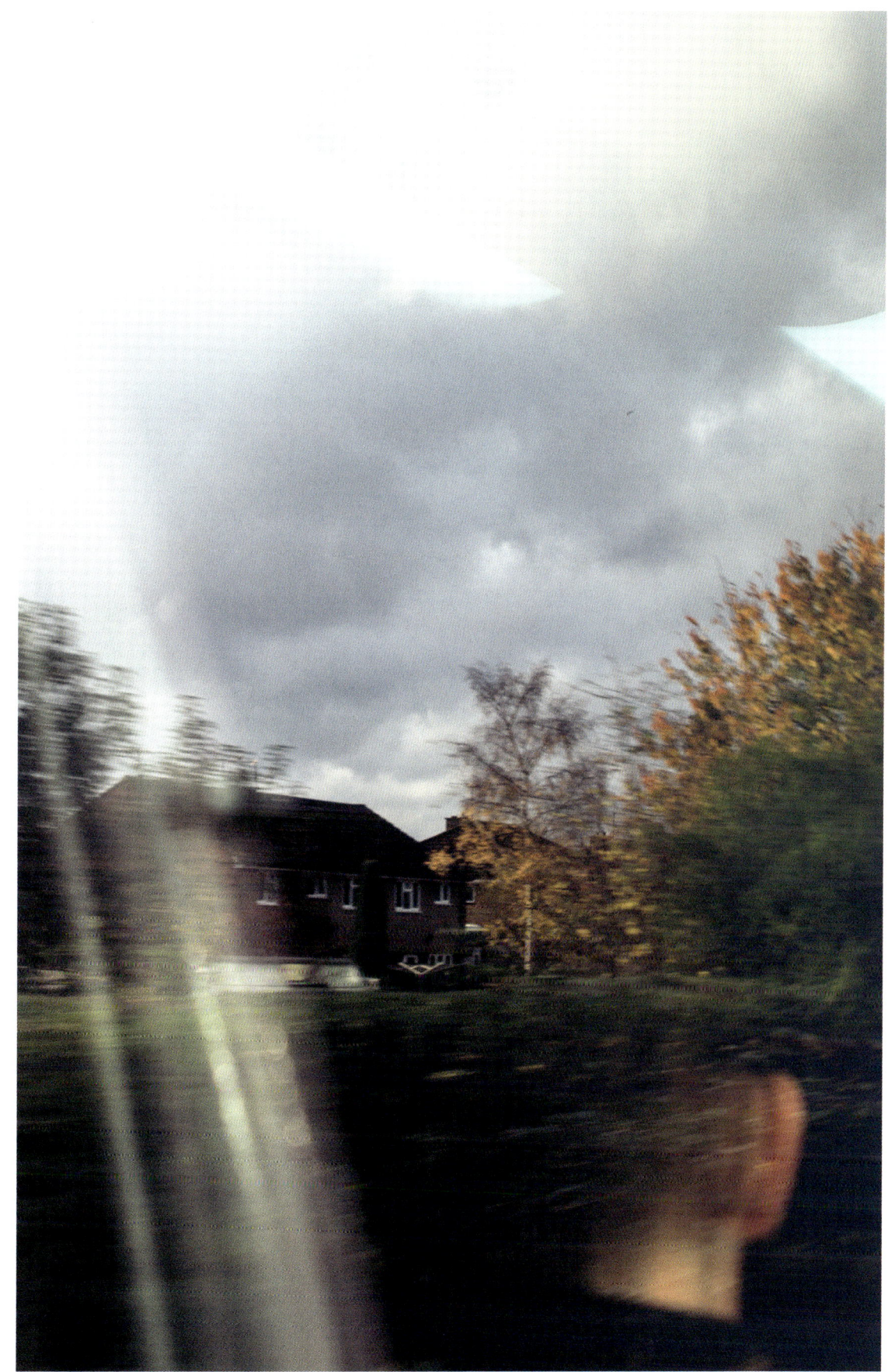

CHAPTER 14

SYNTAX

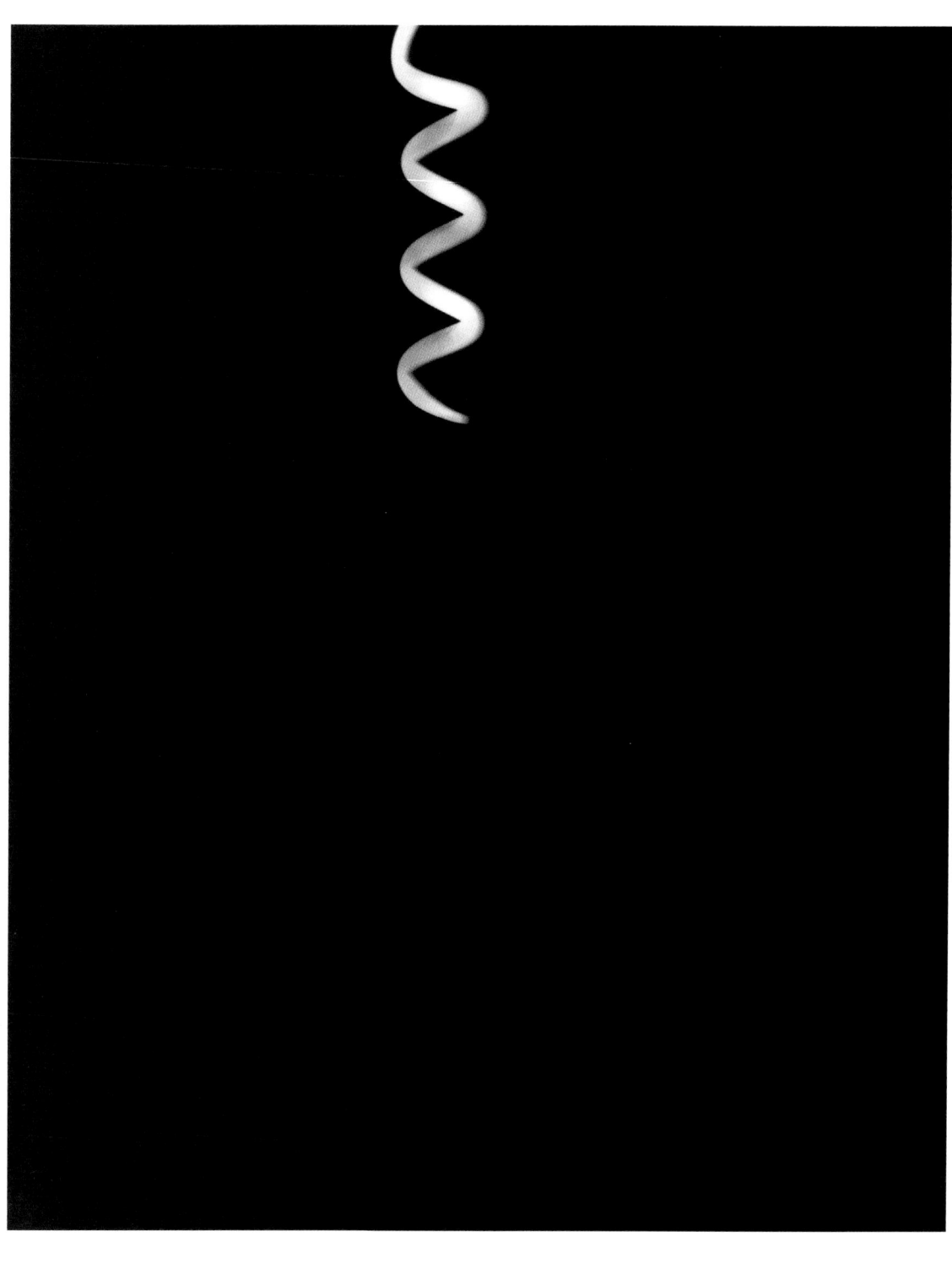

SPOKEN LANGUAGES consist of words. These words all have meaning, but they require syntax to start communicating ideas. Syntax is the arrangement of words and phrases to create well-formed sentences in a language.

Visual composition also requires intentional arrangement and form. The visual elements discussed in the last chapter are only so effective on their own. For example, I can lift up a camera in the air and press the shutter. I will have a composition of whatever was in front of the lens. There may be some lines and a shape, and certainly a light source somewhere, but there was no intention. The composition was simply made by chance, without consideration for the subject matter and visual elements or the relationships between them.

When we approach composition with intention, we'll be on a path to communicate more effectively. Think of syntax as the framework for the statements you want to make with a picture. It is the structure for bringing out creative ideas and the freedom of visual expression.

A lot of my own thinking about photography is drawn from other art forms. Originally this was done from necessity—I've mentioned that my formal training was in music. I'm going to be using a lot of musical connections in this chapter as a means of understanding syntax visually. These connections, I believe, give us even more creative options and ways of thinking about visual composition than what I've learned in art or design classes.

This is an unconventional approach, but one thing I have learned in life is that the best inspiration often comes from the least likely sources. I encourage you to experiment with each of the following music-inspired frameworks. There are no right or wrong answers. Try them on to see what suits your personality and supports your effort to communicate visually.

Monophony

Monophony is a musical term used to describe when only one note is played at a time. The earliest known musical forms are generally monophonic. Early synthesizers did not have the technology to support two notes being played at once. Gregorian chant consists of melodies sung in unison with no accompaniment.

In the visual world I think of this as the single statement. It quickly becomes minimalist. What is the least amount of statement you can have and still consider it a photograph?

When you buy a box of printing paper, you have a stack of white sheets. Think of one sheet for a moment as the canvas. As soon as I have one thing on this canvas—it could be a simple line, a small figure, a shape—I have now made a visual statement. This is how painting works—I've added something to the canvas.

Let's try to translate this scenario to photography. Remember that photography is a subtractive process. You will need a white backdrop that should be lit evenly to eliminate shadow gradients. This serves as your blank canvas. Then you have to find something to photograph that constitutes that "one mark"—abstract or otherwise.

This is a very complex starting point for a photographer. But it's an incredibly thoughtful way to approach photography. We begin by subtracting everything possible from the scene or composition. In fact, every time I lift the camera to my eye, I'm in this mode of thinking. How can I possibly move what I'm seeing to the level of monophony? What is the one important visual I want to draw attention to? What is the minimal statement?

The accompanying image here is a photogram I made years ago of a corkscrew. I didn't even use a camera. I created the composition in the dark with a piece of silver gelatin paper and exposed it with a flashlight. To me, it is a statement. There's an implication of the rest of the corkscrew you clearly can't see. Direction is

implied. The corkscrew is close to the edge, therefore it has a certain emphasis. There is no texture or detail—only a silhouette. It has a nice gradient due to uneven light, but otherwise it's about as simple as one can get with a photograph.

The irony is, the photographer has to work hard to get something this minimal, yet this barest root of photography is our starting point. I highly recommend you experiment with this idea of monophony. Once you understand it, you can begin to build on the idea.

When you're working with a purely monophonic image, the entire composition is simply defined by the relationship of your subject to the image frame.

Placing an object in the center of the composition creates the least interest but the most balance. I would consider the following questions. Which is more important to you: balance or interest? Does having the subject near the edge create interest? What is the ratio of size of the subject to the canvas? In my example there is a lot of negative space—the canvas is way larger than the subject. What if I'd picked a different subject to take up more space? How would that change the relationship?

Polyphony

In music, polyphony is the introduction of more than one note or melody being played at the same time. Polyphony includes but is not limited to counterpoint and harmony. In visual art, think of this as the introduction of

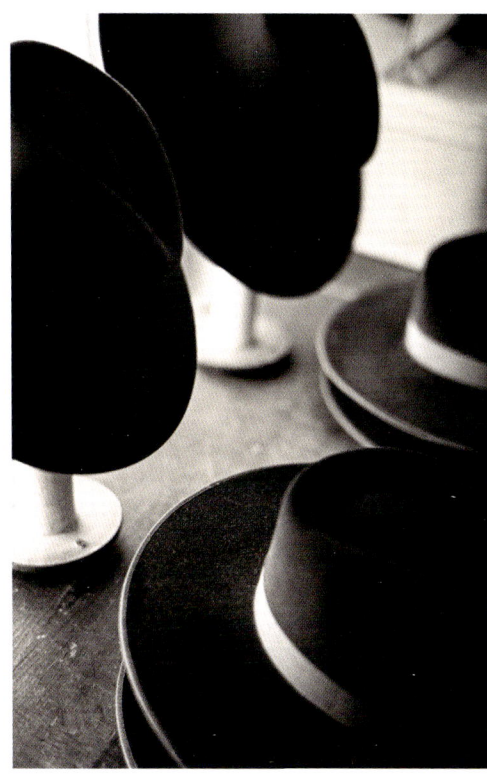

to control the multiplicity of people, logos, advertisements, or other attention-prone objects from being in the composition. There's something to be said for persistence in this context. This could mean waiting for the right moment or trying to find the right angle.

Motif

In music, compositions are often written around the idea of a motif. A motif is defined as a few notes that make a simple melodic statement. It is the seed of an idea that can be expanded on a much larger scale. Consider the idea of motifs in the visual world. A motif might be a subject, a gesture, a shape, or a color scheme. Anything that can be expanded on a larger scale. Two or more images in a sequence or series are required to fully explore this concept.

multiple visual elements into the composition. It becomes more complex. The relationships among and between the elements are extremely important. Do they support each other or create tension? Tension can be effective. What are you trying to communicate artistically as the photographer? Remember that everything you choose to include in a photograph is there for a reason. I think we've all seen photographs with the unintended misplaced tree branch in the background that looks like it's growing out of someone's head. This is an obvious example, but any visual element that doesn't support the composition should be avoided.

The polyphony framework seems particularly challenging for modern street photography. When working on the street, it's very difficult

Alfred Stieglitz made heavy use of motifs throughout most of his career. Most notable is a large body of photographic studies with Georgia O'Keeffe. Some are figure studies, some feature only her hands. But the simple idea of gesture is used to drive a much larger portfolio that is well known today.

Equivalents was a large-scale project Stieglitz began in 1925. For nine years he photographed over 220 images of clouds. These images are essentially studies in abstraction, as the majority of these photographs contain no reference to a horizon or other objects. They are all images of clouds against the sky. This motif might seem basic by today's standards, but in the late 1920s these images were fairly groundbreaking. At this

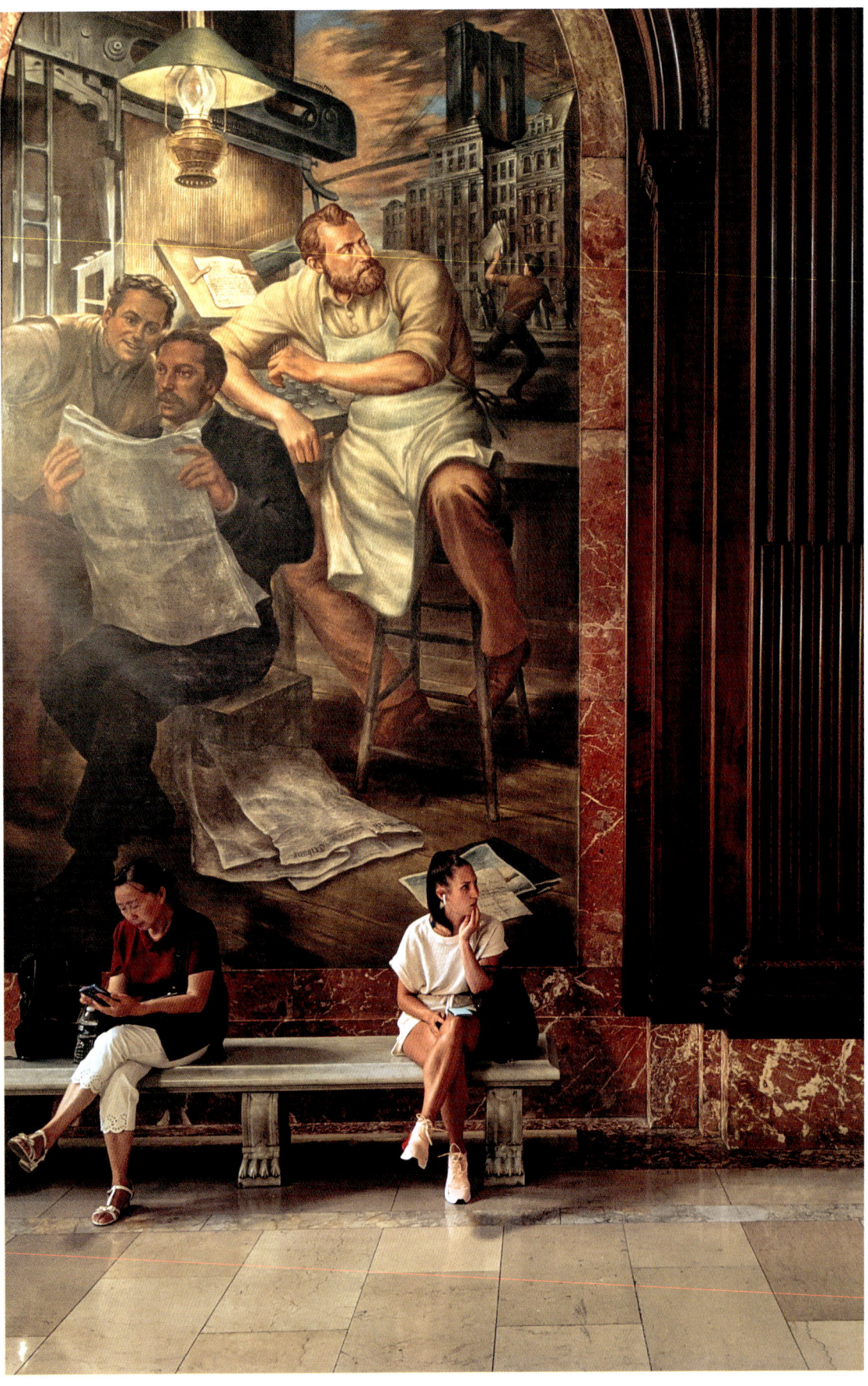

time photographic emulsions were largely orthochromatic. This emulsion type is more sensitive to light on the blue end of the spectrum, so photographing clouds was nearly impossible. Blue skies would render white, making it difficult to create contrast with clouds. Inspired by new possibilities, Stieglitz's work combined technology with the abstract approach to the subject, garnering praise from critics at the time as aligning with modernist painting. Ansel Adams noted that this body of work had a profound effect on his own direction as a photographer.

These motif examples by Stieglitz are based on literal subjects in the images. But it's also important to note that an explored motif can be conceptual as well. Robert Frank influenced an entire generation of photographers with his seminal book *The Americans* in 1958. Frank was born and raised in Zurich and certainly had an impression of American culture that was very different from the "nuclear family" ideal of the 1950s. His photographs for *The Americans* explored ideas about racism and class differences. These images were raw and divorced from the photojournalism of the time. Frank created tension because of his distinct interpretation of mid-century America. This tension serves as the motif for the images that make up *The Americans*. It's not something that's physically seen; it is a conceptual motif.

Initially inspired by Robert Frank, William Eggleston went on to develop a very unique visual voice in the 1960s. At a time when color photography was not considered serious in the art world, Eggleston developed a complex, conceptual style using color transparency film and dye-transfer process. He sometimes selected ordinary objects as the subject for his photographs. A tricycle, some old tires, condiments on a dinner table, and "No Parking" signs may not seem worthy of attention to most photographers. Eggleston also includes people in select images, but usually in a way that is unconventional to portraiture. Sometimes his photographs seem to be about nothing at all—simply a place with no obvious function or landmark. But the motifs of color and nostalgia serve to bring consistency to the body of work as a whole.

CHAPTER 15

VISUAL BALANCE

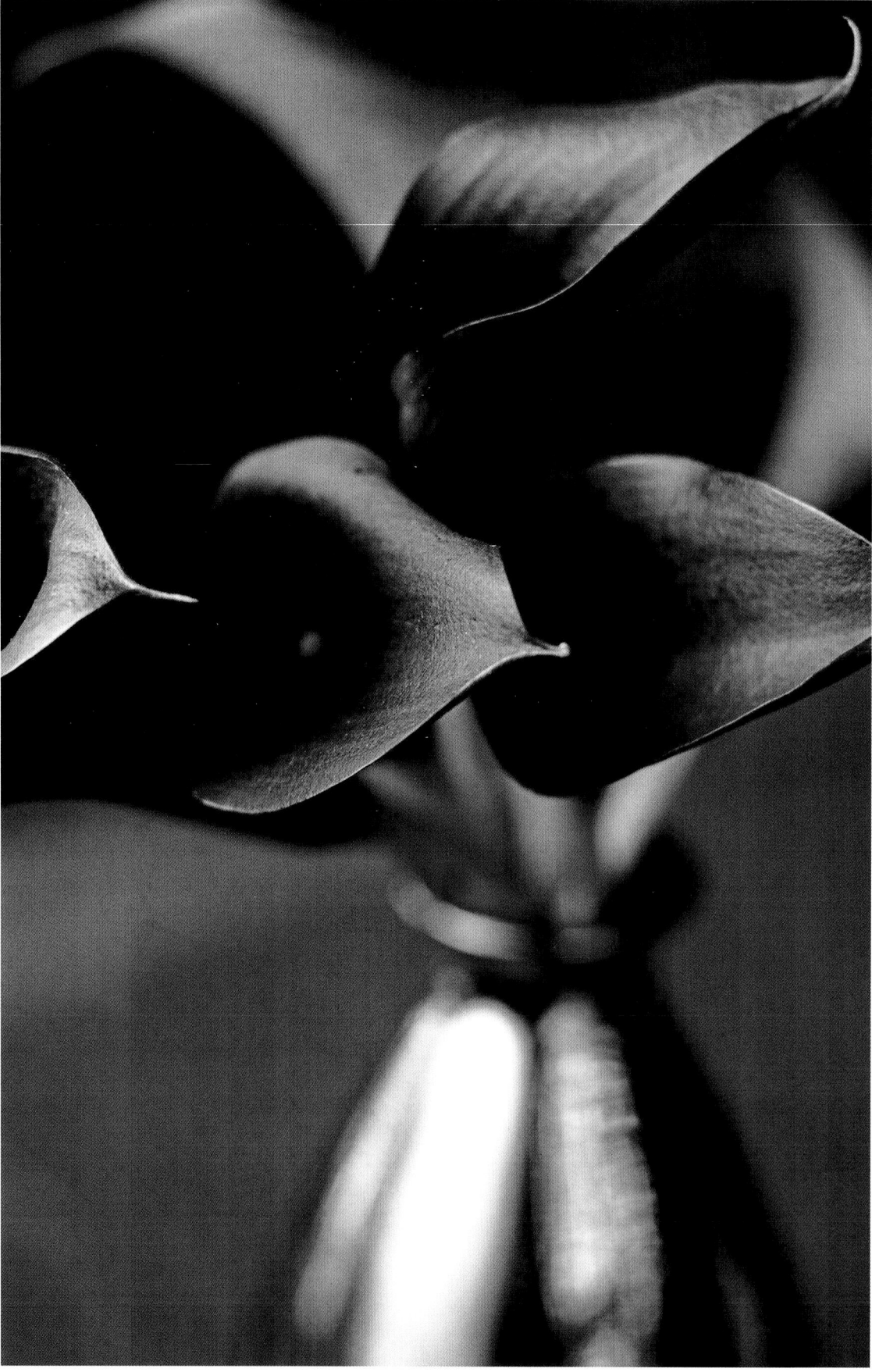

COMPOSITION IS THE arrangement of visual elements. This is dependent on the idea of balance. All of the elements have a certain visual weight. Let's consider an object and space within a composition. The larger the object's proportion, the greater the visual weight. Negative space also has visual weight, but considerably less than a physical object. Balancing an object against space requires a greater proportion of space, as you can see in this example.

In visual composition, balance comes in several forms. This chapter highlights symmetry and asymmetry and also discusses several formulas and rules that relate to visual balance.

Symmetrical Balance

The most obvious way to achieve balance is by using symmetry. Placing the subject in the center of a composition creates equal parts of the composition on either side. While this can work, it doesn't create a lot of interest. If we move the subject off center, it's important to consider how this impacts the visual balance of the composition. This will break the symmetrical balance, but can be very effective.

Asymmetrical Balance

In an asymmetrically balanced composition, visual elements are juxtaposed to create a slight tension and break pure symmetry. The key to achieving asymmetrical balance is that it is still in balance. Think of it like a seesaw. Perfectly matched weight on both sides will create symmetry. Motion and force will move

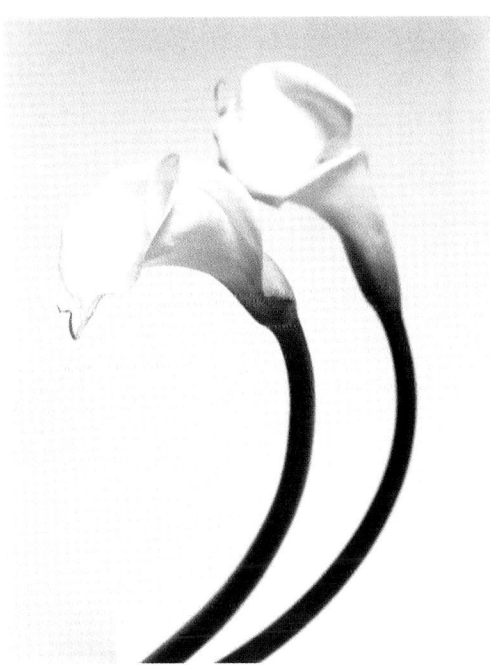

the seesaw, even though it is still in balance. Visual composition works in the same way. The side with greater emphasis needs to be balanced with some type of interest on the other side.

Phi and the Golden Rectangle

Most photography is conventionally conceived on some type of rectangular ground. Square grounds are used as well. Cameras have always defined the image frame as such. Paper comes cut in a rectangular format. Even computer screens and mobile devices render images using a vertical or horizontal rectangle.

These formats will govern the balance of a composition. You might not have thought of it that way before, but it's true. If you've ever had to reformat an image, you know that it requires rethinking and usually doesn't function the same. In the modern age of vertical video on phones, ask video editors how they like reframing a 16:9 video into 9:16.

These rectangles have what we call an "aspect ratio." This refers to the relationship of the length to the width. When Oskar Barnack made the first Leica, he used a 3:2 aspect ratio, which has carried through to the digital sensors we use today.

Euclid, an ancient Greek mathematician, spoke of the golden ratio in geometry. This golden ratio is dividing a line into two segments so that the ratio of the whole to the longer segment is the same as the ratio of the longer segment to the shorter segment.

In the twentieth century this ratio became known as phi.

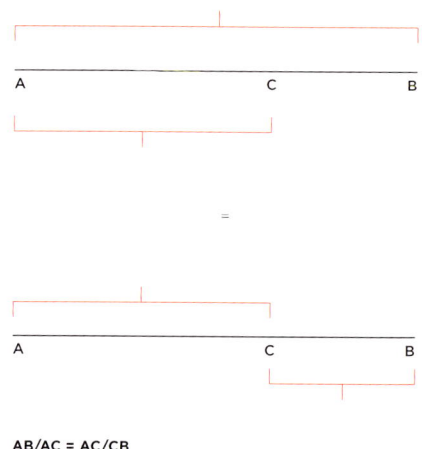

AB/AC = AC/CB

We can also apply phi to give us what we call a golden rectangle.

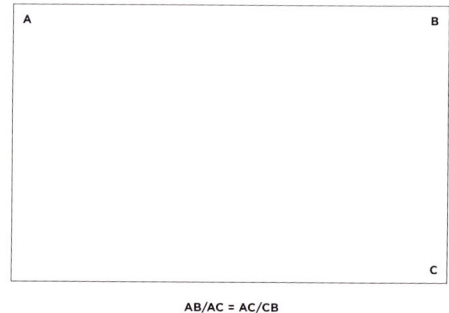

AB/AC = AC/CB

Back to the idea of aspect ratio. The aspect ratios I've already mentioned are all rational numbers—3/2 and 16/9.

The golden rectangle is difficult to express because it is an irrational number. As a fraction it is expressed as $1 + \sqrt{5}/2$. If we render this to a decimal, it comes out to 1.6180339887498 . . . I actually can't write the entire number because the trailing decimals go on indefinitely.

The important thing we can do with a golden rectangle is perfect division. A golden rectangle is a rectangle that can be divided into a square and a second golden rectangle. The aspect ratio is such that we can now take this second rectangle, divide that into a square and rectangle, and the process will repeat ad infinitum.

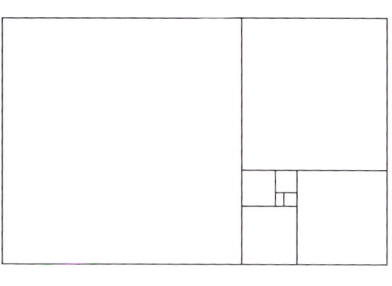

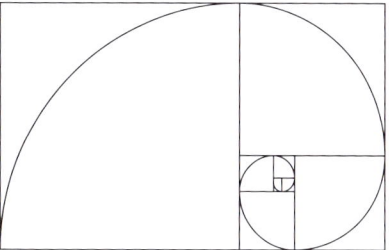

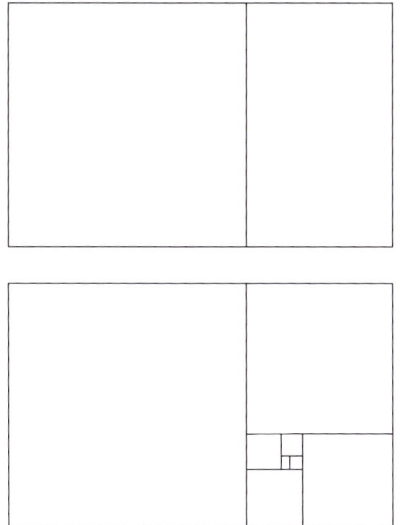

Now, if we draw an arch that connects the corners of each square section, we render what we call the Golden Spiral, which has visual associations with things found in nature, like the nautilus shell.

I should note, if you actually look at different nautiluses, you'll see that they are logarithmic, but there are many variations. None of them actually equal phi or can be measured as a true golden ratio. I'm pointing this out because it's easy to start thinking that

nature or even art are exact mathematical formulas. They are not. While a concept like phi can certainly guide an idea, nature and art are rarely about absolute perfection.

Visual composition is an art, not an equation. Centuries separate today from ancient Greece. While these concepts are all valid, using them as rationale to govern the idea of "beauty" and to create art doesn't make sense. We have evolved in so many ways since early human culture that it is nearly impossible to apply a governing rule when trying to superimpose the ideas of an earlier time into a medium that represents the contemporary era.

Henri Cartier-Bresson was probably the most well-known photographer who was influenced by this type of thinking. He studied painting in the late 1920s with André Lhote. Cartier-Bresson had a strong interest in the Renaissance masters, which is evident in his later work as a photographer. His compositional training clearly shows his knowledge of the ancient Greek geometric concepts of division and line. And this is in part what makes his compositions so great. They are not clinical or exact, and I don't think Cartier-Bresson ever intended them to be. This aspect of his work is what makes him such an incredible link between the past master painters and Modernism.

Rule of Thirds

Chances are you've heard of the "rule of thirds." The rule of thirds is a simplification of phi that gives us more versatility as a guide for breaking up symmetry in a composition. It works like this.

If you take any image ground and divide it into equal thirds, both horizontally and vertically, you will get a grid like in the exam-

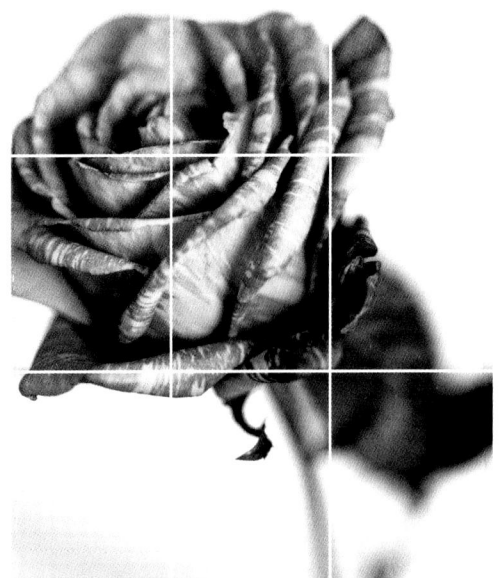

ple shown. This is the phi grid. The rule of thirds indicates that points of interest occur at the points of line intersection. Most cameras today allow you to see this grid on the viewfinder so you always have a template to work with. The same could also be said for long horizontal or vertical subjects. You'll have more interest lining these up to the third division.

As simple and overused as this concept is, I still consider it to be a very valid way to begin learning composition. It does two incredible things for any photographer. First, it gets you off the center of the image. Getting off the center starts to create interest in the figure/ground relationship. Second, it gets photographers to start thinking about placement and composition. While it may be simple, using the rule of thirds does work, and I think it has a place in any photographer's development. Just don't make it the only concept you use.

Rule of Odds

Photographs can contain multiple points of interest. But the more you have in a composition, the more chance you have for chaos. Our brains will attempt to group what we are seeing once that number goes beyond a certain point. For example, if you have a portrait of three people, you will see and perceive them as individuals. If you have a group portrait of fifteen people, your brain is less interested in the individuals because there are too many. The brain will see these as one group. You could divide the group in half visually and your brain would see it as two groups.

Arguably, the threshold is around five points of interest. Any more than this and your brain

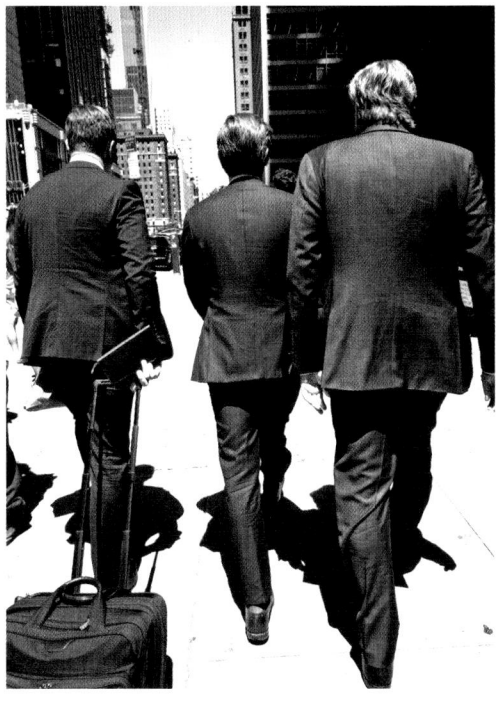

grid formulas mentioned previously. The rule of space is important when we start to look at the implication of motion or direction in a photograph. This is what ultimately can make or break a sense of balance (both equally important skills).

First, let's consider the idea of negative space. This is where we have a larger area of low impact that contrasts with a small area of high impact. We'll simplify this to a main subject and an empty background. Placement of the subject is important, as is the direction your subject might be looking or even moving. The rule of space simply means that the subject should have that larger, low impact area in front of them. If the head is turned, it should be facing the space. This gives a feeling of visual balance.

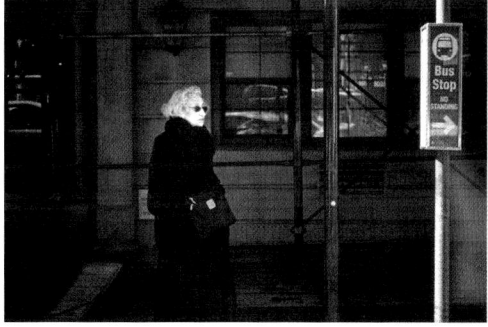

starts to group them. The rule of odds implies that odd numbers will provide more interest than even numbers. If you can control it, three points of interest is the better choice than two or four. The argument is that even numbers create less interest by virtue of being balanced and symmetrical. Of course, if balance and symmetry are the intention of your composition, then I would argue for breaking this rule.

The rule of odds can be problematic because the visual relationships between objects or points of interest is more important than the number. But this is still an essential principle to note and understand.

Rule of Space

Lastly, I want to talk about the rule of space. This rule can be applied to any of the other

This rule can also be applied to moving subjects within a picture. If your subject appears to be moving toward the greater space, you've created the feeling of moving into the picture. If the subject is moving away from the greater space, then you're creating the feeling of moving away from the picture.

CHAPTER 16

COMPOSITIONAL
TECHNIQUES

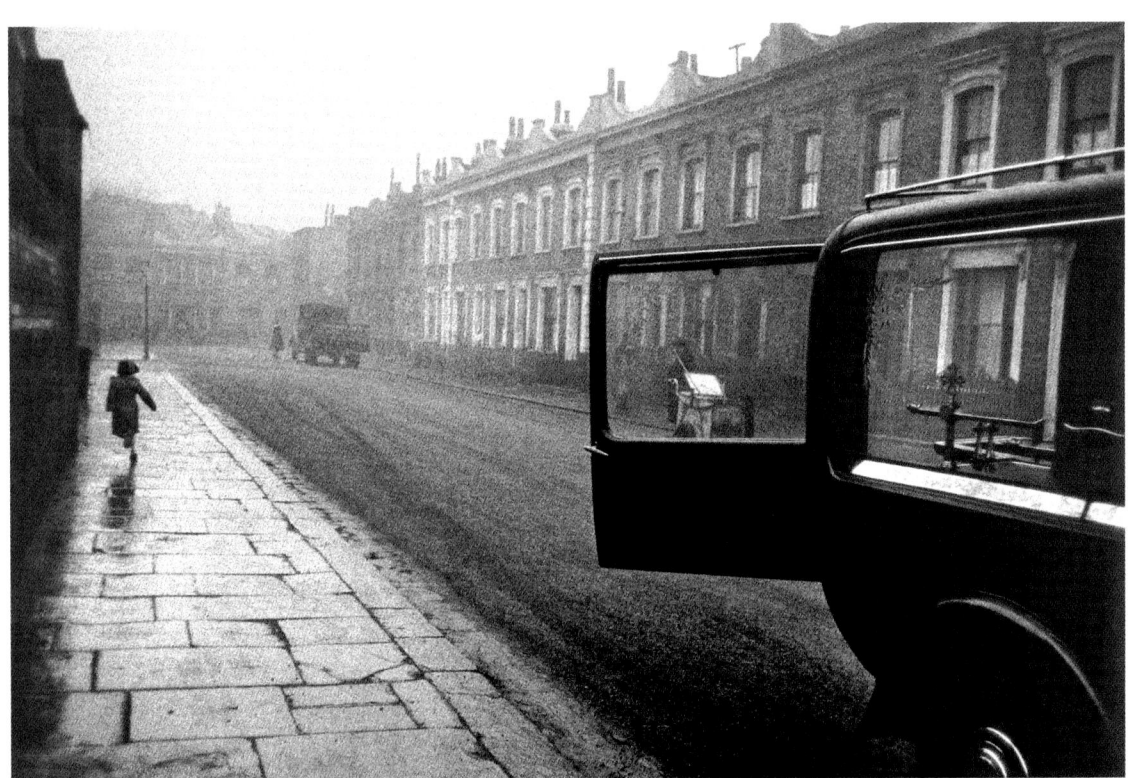

London (Hearse), 1951 by Robert Frank ©The June Leaf and Robert Frank Foundation.

LET'S EXPLORE several techniques that can add complexity to your visual compositions. This is not meant to be an exhaustive list. These are various techniques photographers have used across a wide range of genres and decades. A couple draw heavily on my music background. As I've said in this book before—crossing art forms and media is going to give you new perspectives on how to think about your craft.

Subframing

Subframing is a technique I first observed in the work of Robert Frank. *Hearse, London* is an early image he made in 1951. It's a street scene of a hearse with the rear door open. You see a young girl running off on the left. It's a powerful image, suggesting the spirit leaving after death. On the right-hand side of the image, framed in the window of the open door, a man with a cart is observing.

What makes this image work is the bringing together of three complex subjects that relate to one another, but each live in their own part of the composition. They're not grouped together. The hearse represents death, the girl on the left represents the spirit, and the man on the right is the witness.

There is no more powerful way to frame this up. The hearse is not obvious if the door is not open. The girl has been given plenty of negative space to demand attention. The man on the right would have possibly been distracting to the overall image had he not been perfectly framed in the rear door of the hearse.

The first time I saw this, I was taken back by the power of framing up something within the composition with another element to draw emphasis. This is exactly what we see here—a picture within a picture.

What's particularly impressive is that the girl is absolutely integral to this image. The subframing doesn't replace or distract from her. It simply puts an accent on a third figure standing by a truck in the distance, shrouded by fog—perhaps saving him for you to notice later. This is extraordinarily powerful. There is no way that Robert Frank could have composed this on the street. He did, however, react to the visual unfolding and framed up his camera. The visual concepts are internalized by an artist on this level. He's improvising by speaking the language.

I should also note that Robert Frank was about twenty-seven years old when this image was made. Let this impress you but not deter you.

I've used subframing many times in my own work. One of the things that gets me about the Frank image is how composition supports content. Using this technique to bring attention to the main subject is easy. Doing it with the tertiary subject combined with the secondary, as Frank did, is several levels above that. This image constantly reminds me of how far I still have to go to develop the complexity of my own skill. He was simply one of the best in the most subtle manner.

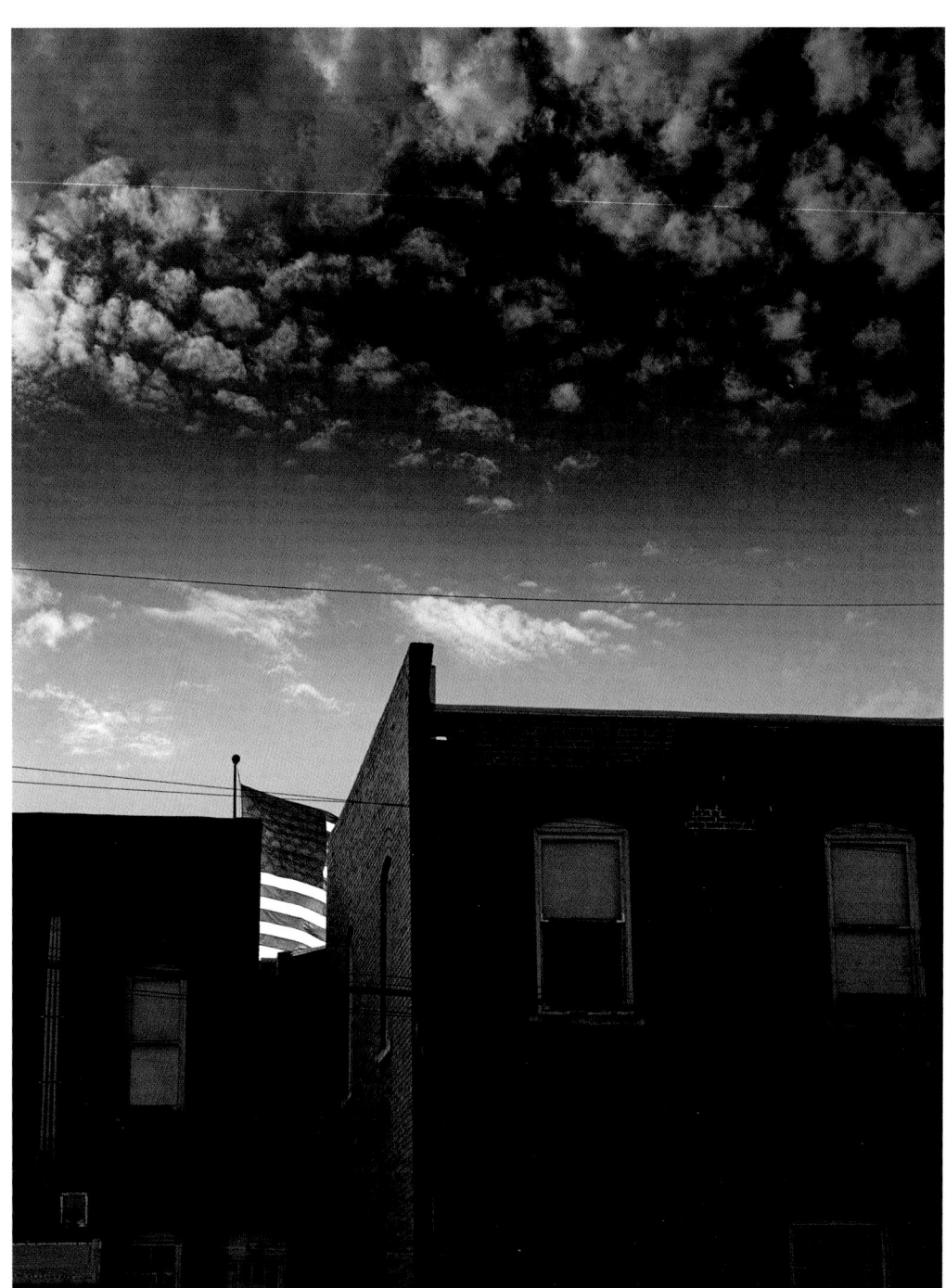

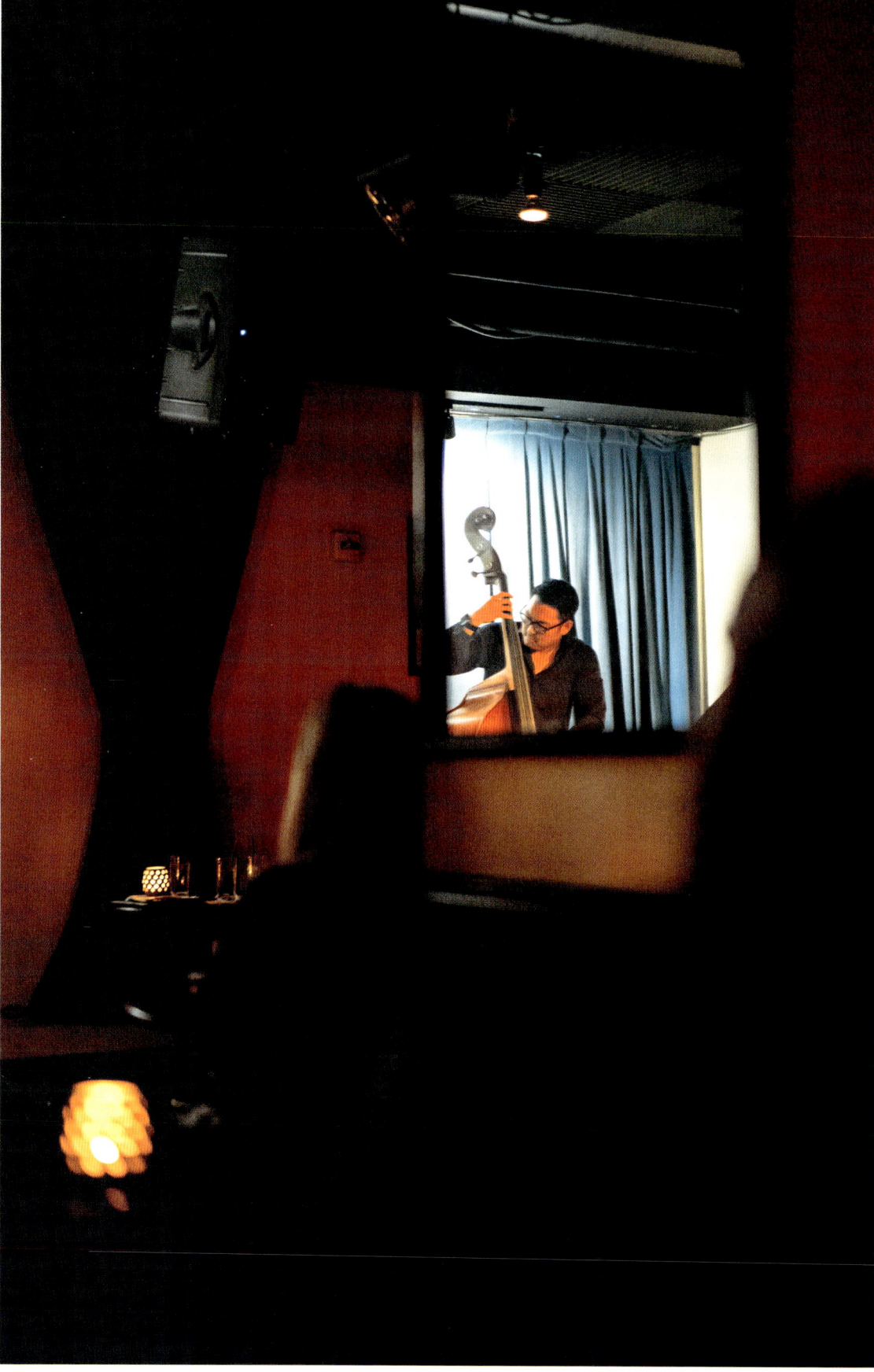

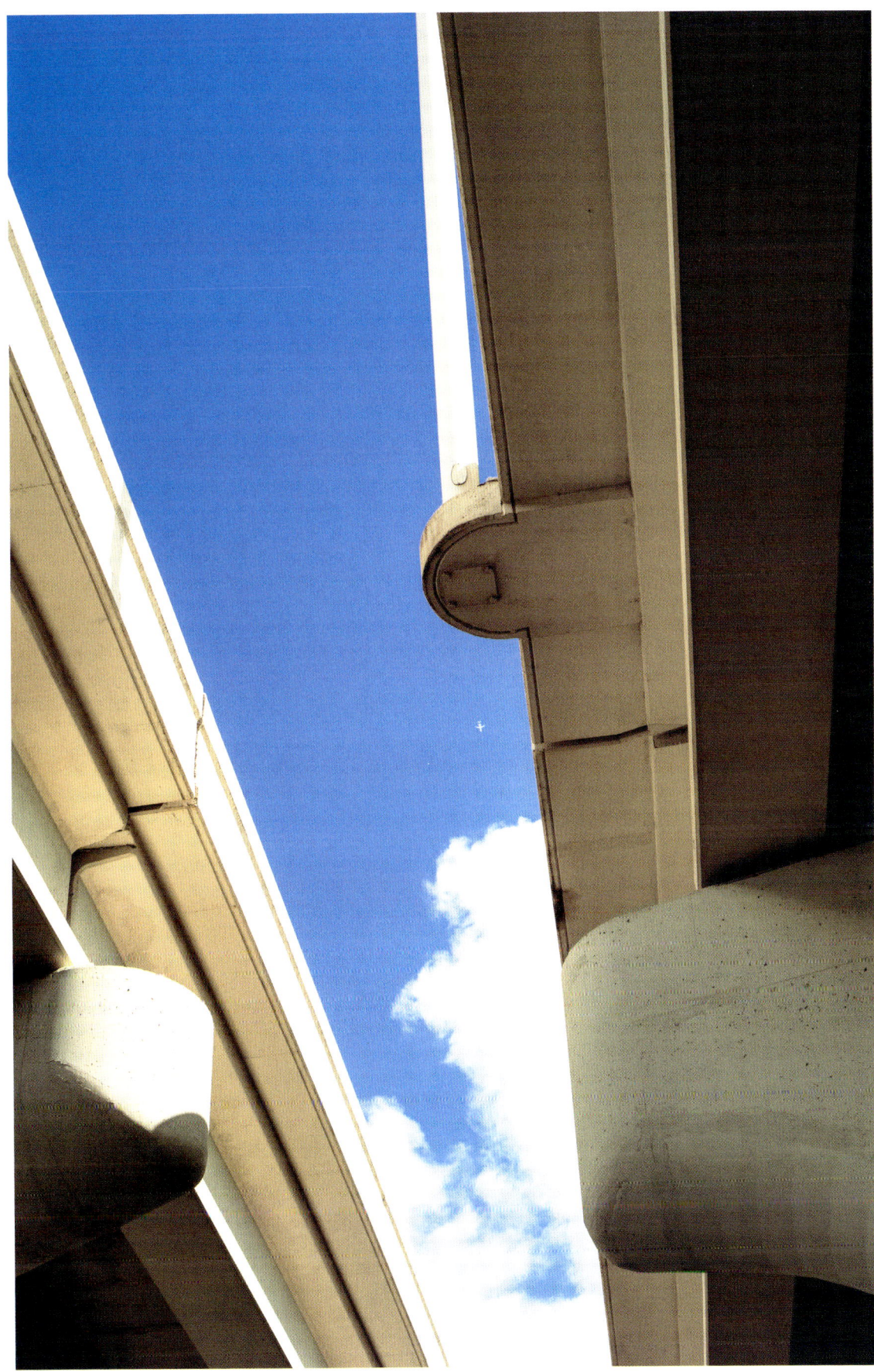

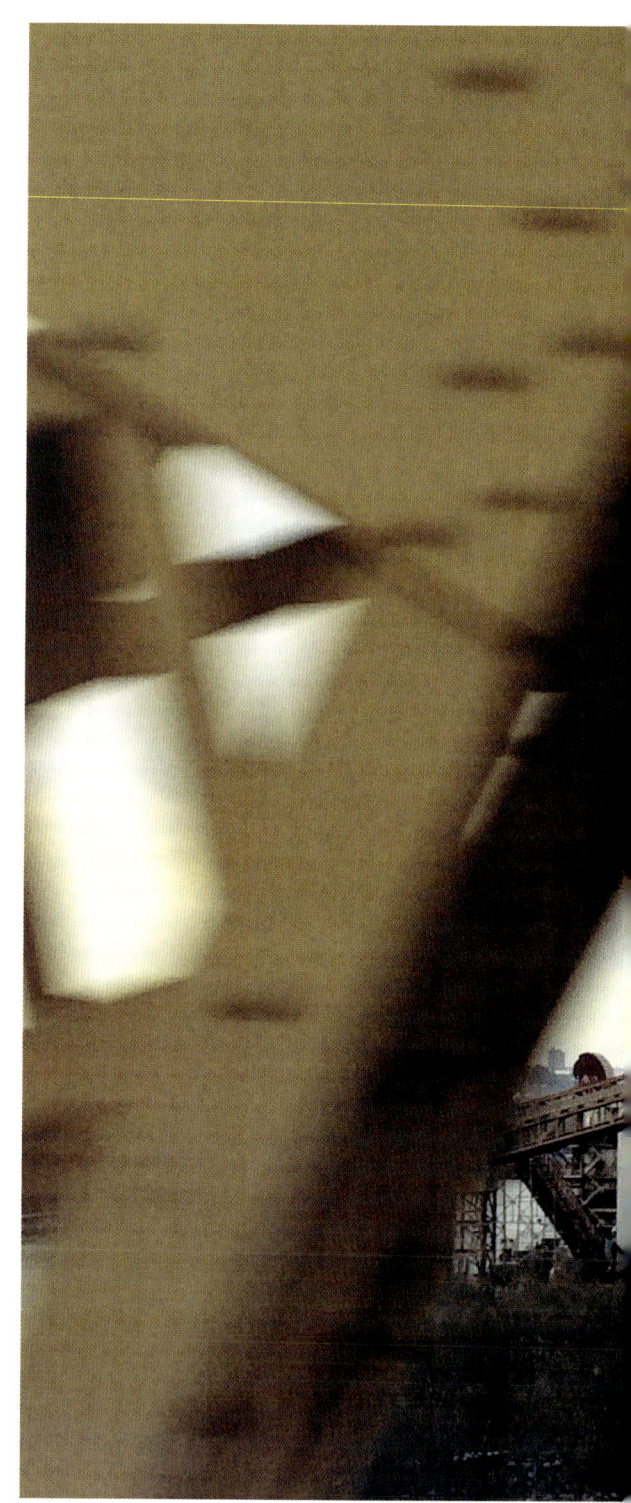

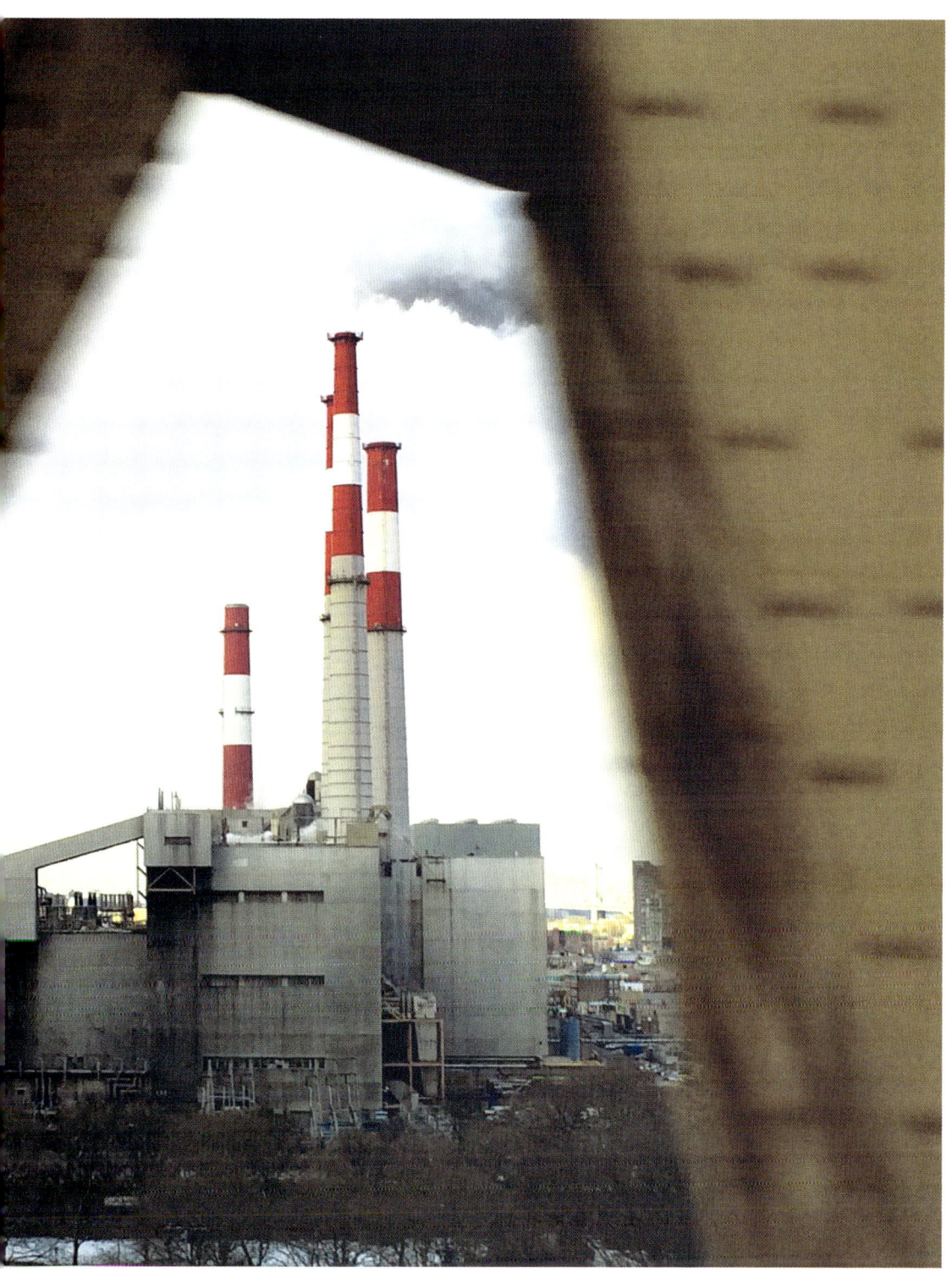

Rhythm

Rhythm is a musical idea that gives the listener a division of time. A rhythm with little variation becomes too predictable and boring so we also have a concept called syncopation. Syncopation occurs when unexpected accents are imposed over a predictable rhythm. This creates interest. It is at the heart of many forms of music, beginning with African and Indian music and used as the foundation of jazz. Today many forms of music incorporate this, from groove metal to hip hop.

So, how can this be expressed visually? In a visual composition, any repetition at even intervals creates rhythm. How can we interrupt this to suggest syncopation? This is a fairly intuitive technique in a studio set up and with patience can be applied to improvised photography.

Rhythm is a simple technique, but think about how it can be applied to more complex compositions as well. This is about finding the predictable and introducing something that is not. When overused it can distract from a composition, but subtleties can take an image to the next level.

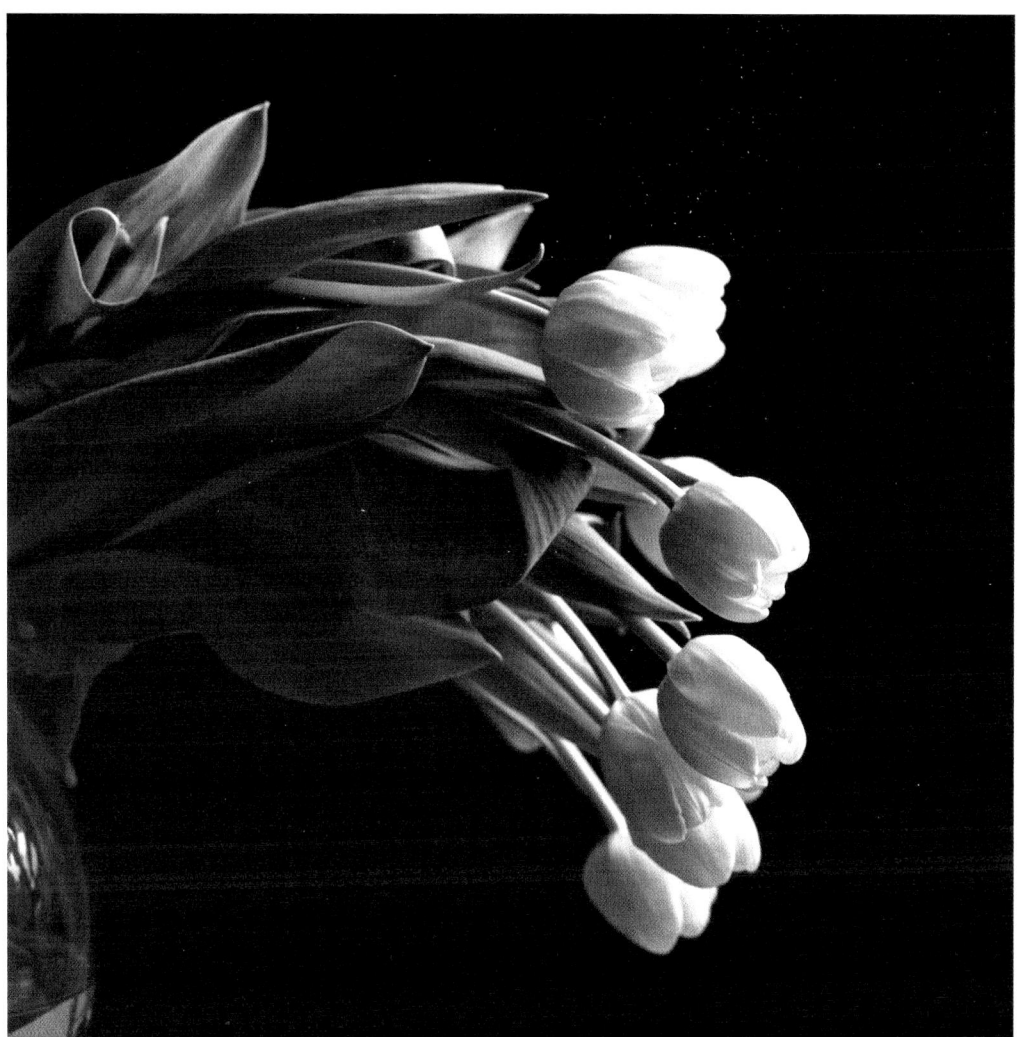

Tempo

If we can define rhythm as dividing patterns into something predictable, the next question should be "at what speed?" This is again borrowed from music. As you've likely experienced through music, faster tempos have a higher energy to them in contrast to the lower energy of slow tempos. Both fast and slow tempos can be dramatic and interesting.

When I was in college, I took a series of jazz arranging classes. Dr. Paris Rutherford was a teacher for whom I had immense respect. He was extremely thoughtful in the way he explained any concept. The class centered around arranging for jazz big bands. This is a genre that's sadly diminished in music today, but it's still taught in schools where there are enough musicians to fill out a large ensemble. If you've never seen a big band live, it's incredible. They are as loud as any rock band. Hearing an incredible arrangement from the few practitioners today, such as Maria Schneider, is an incredibly moving experience. And the same can be said of the "old guard," the likes of Stan Kenton, Buddy Rich, Count Basie, and Duke Ellington.

One of the core concepts that Dr. Rutherford taught me was, if you had higher energy, you needed less harmony. Less energy required more complex harmony. This makes sense when you think about it. At high tempos when the music is flying by, this is mostly achieved in unisons or octaves. Slower melodies require a deeper harmonic support to create interest. It's all about the contrasts.

Visual tempo is exactly the same. How much energy is being shown in a photograph? If it's high, then it follows that the subject matter or area of interest must remain simple for the photograph to be effective. Ori Gersht (see page 89) comes to mind. There's so much visually happening with the exploding flowers that the simple color scheme becomes highly effective. This gives the viewer an anchor in all the chaos. It gives you something to grab on to in a visually complex image.

Motion blur inherently has a high impact on energy in a visual composition as well as an obvious implication of speed. Ironically, modern cameras strive to eliminate motion blur by compensating with sensitivity, autofocus speed, and other techniques.

In 2018, Sony invited me on the press trip for the introduction of the Alpha 7 III. I was on a set with forty other photographers. All of us were shooting dancers under flowing water. The sound of fast shutters firing freaked me out from a creative standpoint. Each photographer was getting the same shot. Perhaps Sony was not amused, but I went the opposite direction and started taking single shots with slower exposure times of half a second. I heard about it later, but amazingly in a positive way. They liked what I was shooting.

You do have to be aware of composition with slower shutter speeds that incorporate blur. Be careful. If there is too much blur, the subject matter becomes unrecognizable.

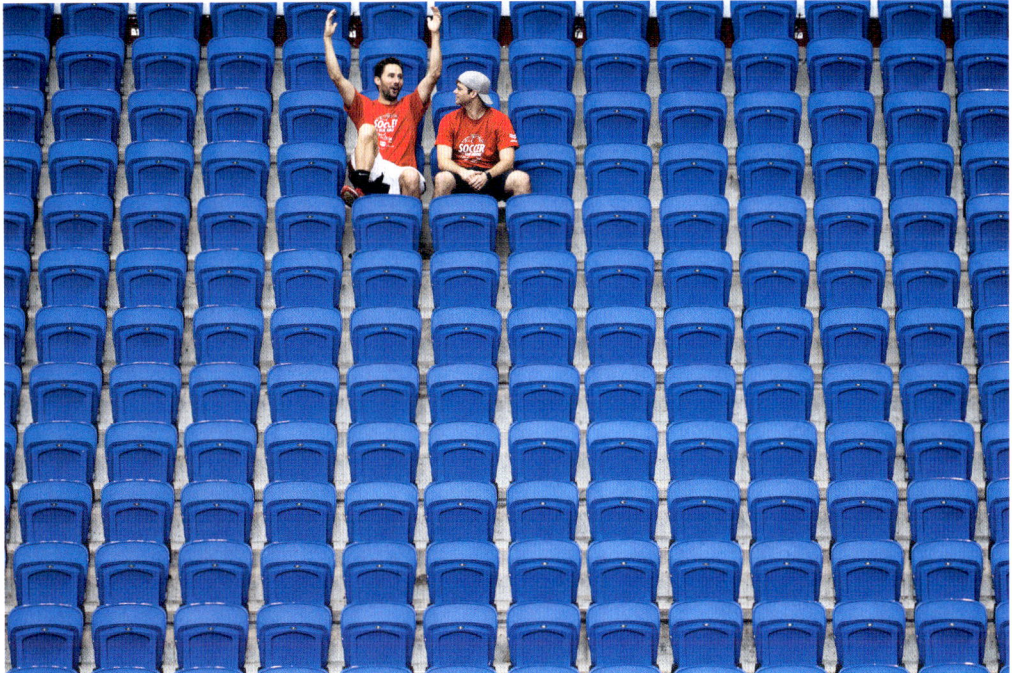

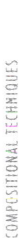

Layering

Working in layers is probably one of the most powerful techniques in rendering a visual composition. Composing in layers requires defining a foreground, middle ground, and background. Layering is the embodiment of depth by dividing the composition. In photography, this is complex because you have to deal with the possible optical limitations of the camera. Where is the focus point? What is the subject? There are realities that work against the aesthetics of your camera lens.

Placing emphasis on the middle layer is where this compositional technique performs at its best. This will achieve a true "three-field composition." Arguments can be made for emphasizing the background or even the foreground, but you run the risk of the two non-emphasized grounds seeming to be the same. If you emphasize the foreground, how will you prevent the middle and back layers from blending together?

There are two photographers that I admire for their mastery of layering. They are Gianni Berengo Gardin and Arthur Meyerson. Both artists are incredible in their own styles and techniques, yet they are very different. Gardin was a major voice in the Italian Neorealism movement of postwar photography, and Meyerson is an American colorist with a long career both in the commercial and fine art worlds.

There are five ways to create layering in a visual composition.

Horizontal layering—the foreground, middle ground, and background are divided parallel to the horizon line.

Vertical layering—the same concept as horizontal layering, but this time we divide the image perpendicular to the horizon line.

Diagonal layering—a further variation, where we divide the picture diagonally.

Mixed layering—more complex in that we are now using a combination of two or more of the previous techniques.

Breaking the fourth wall—using the third dimension and shooting through a texture or surface to divide the composition completely between the viewer and the subject.

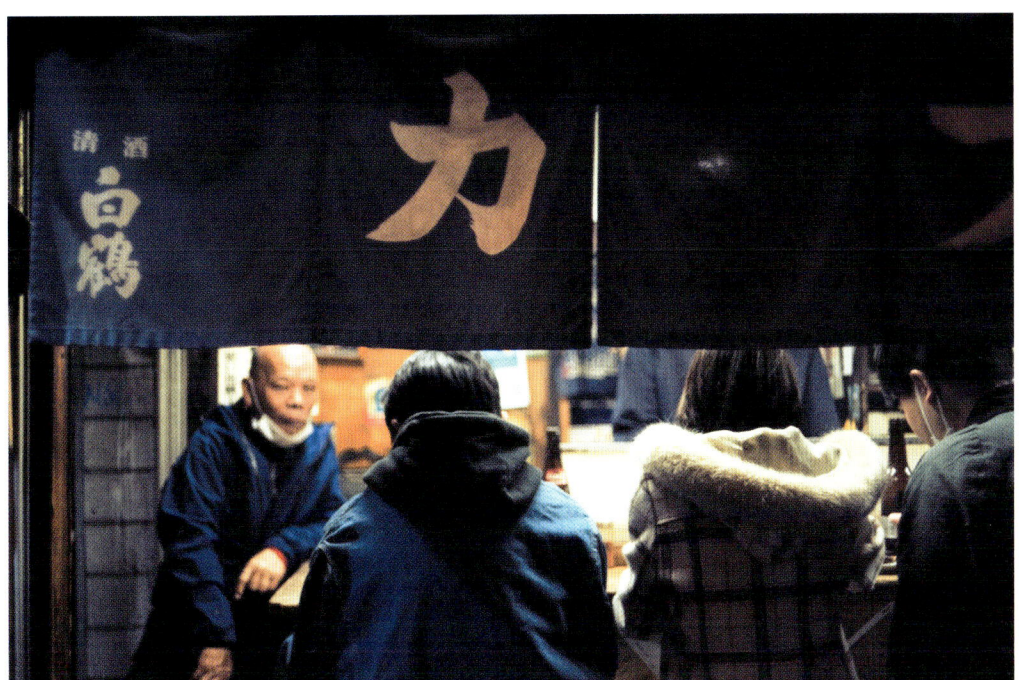

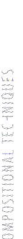

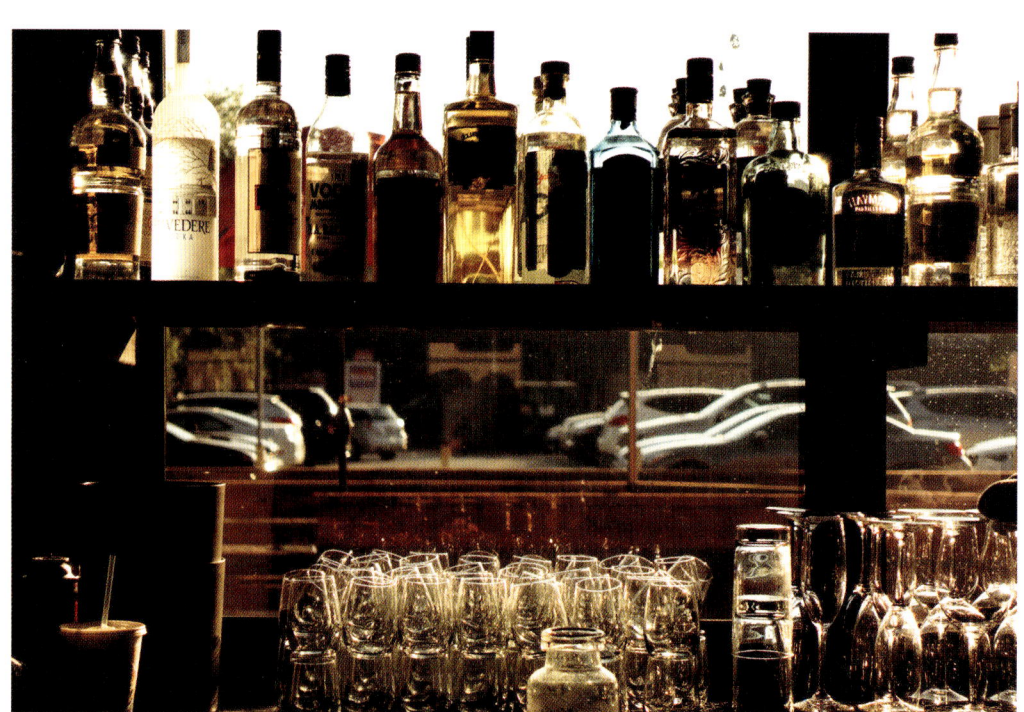

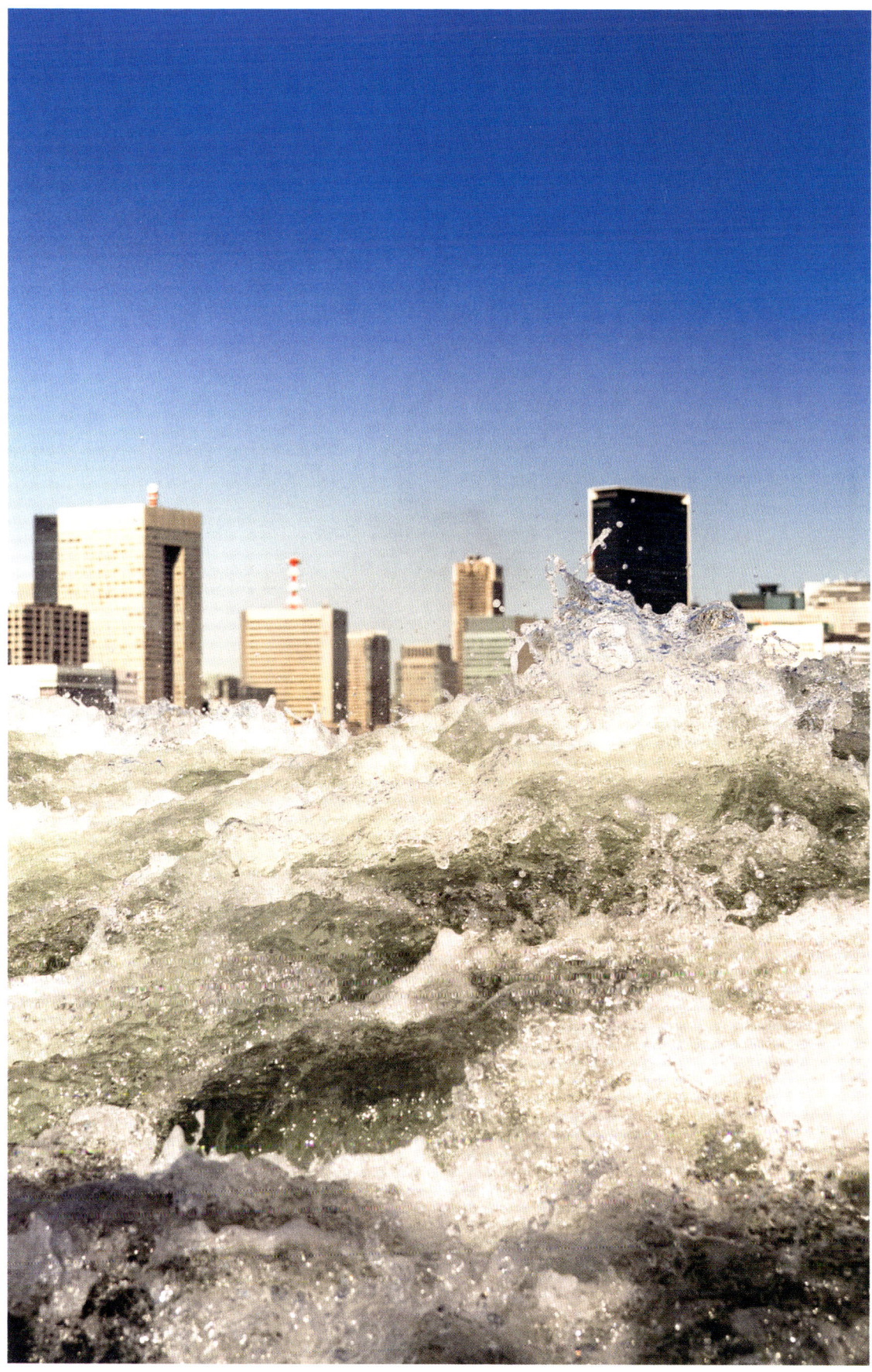

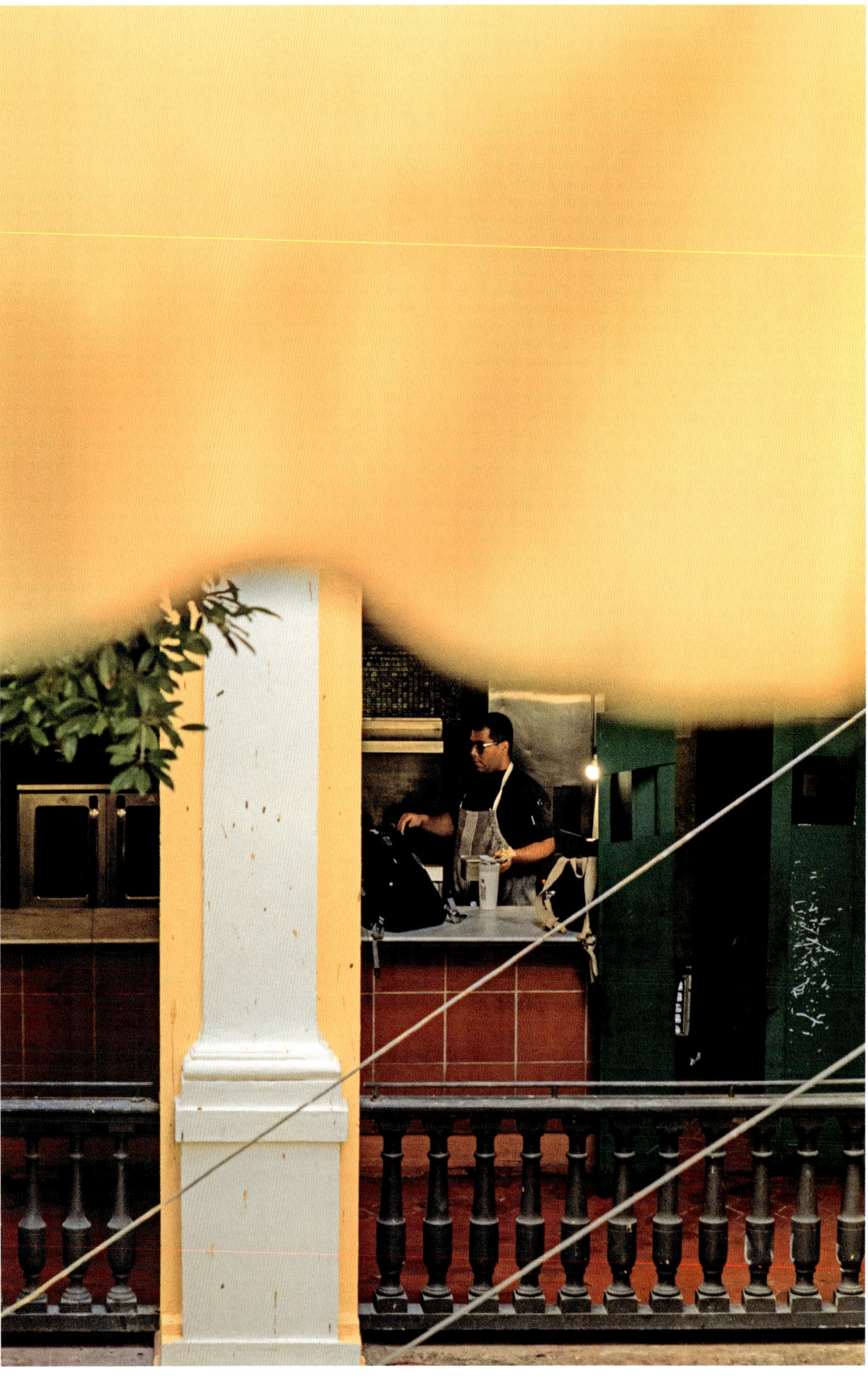

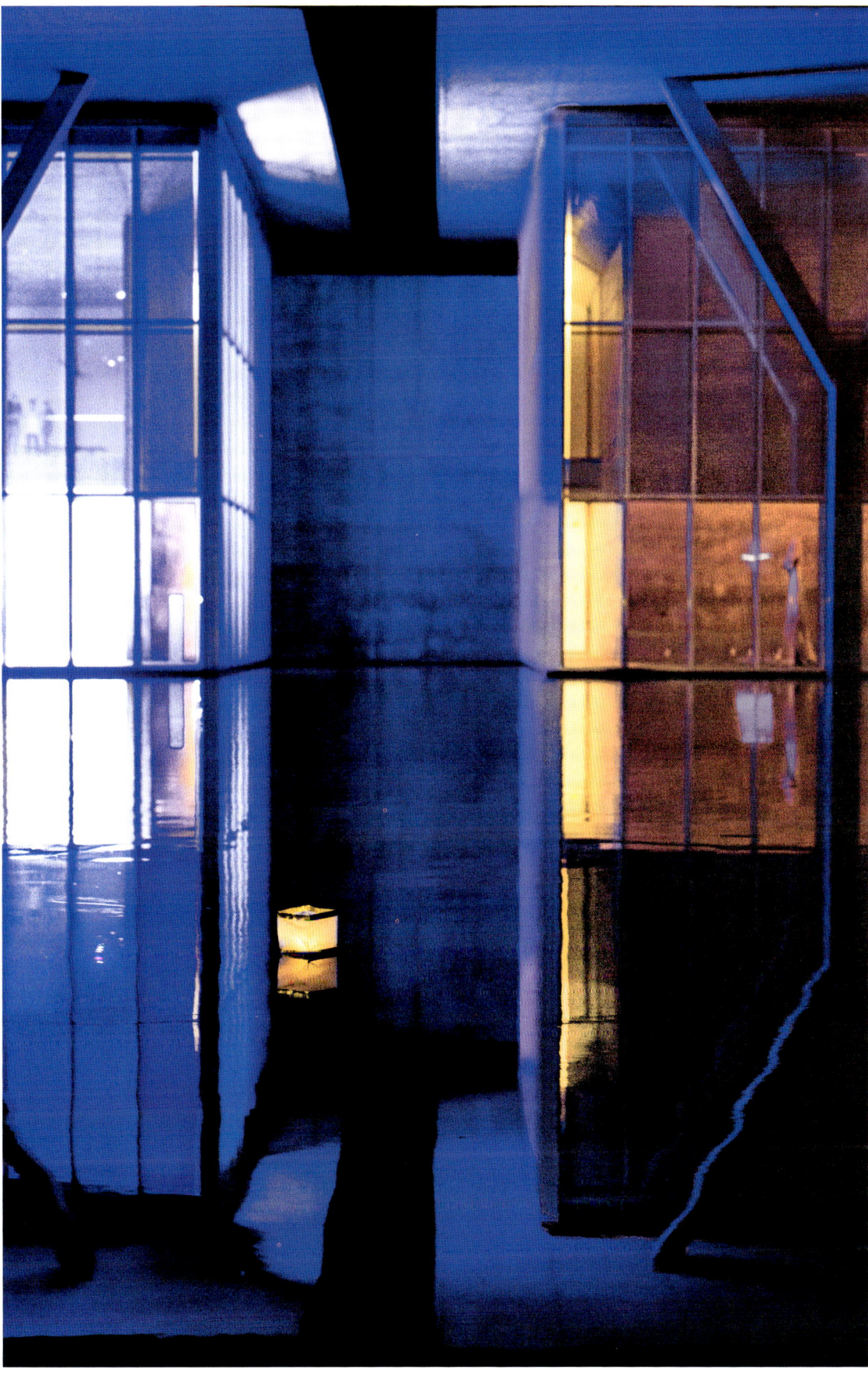

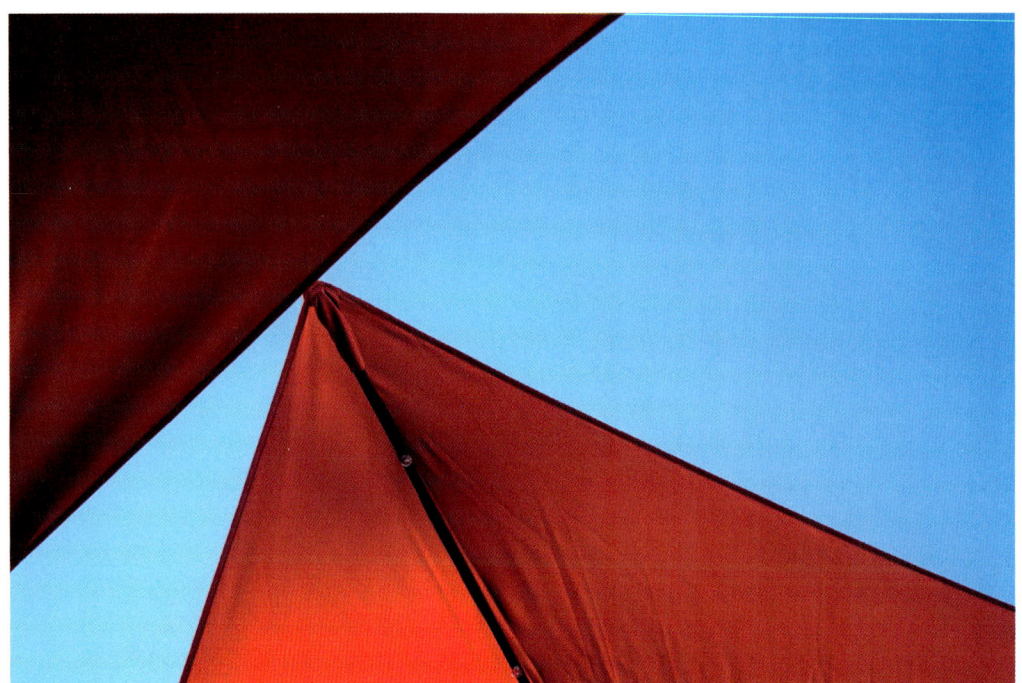

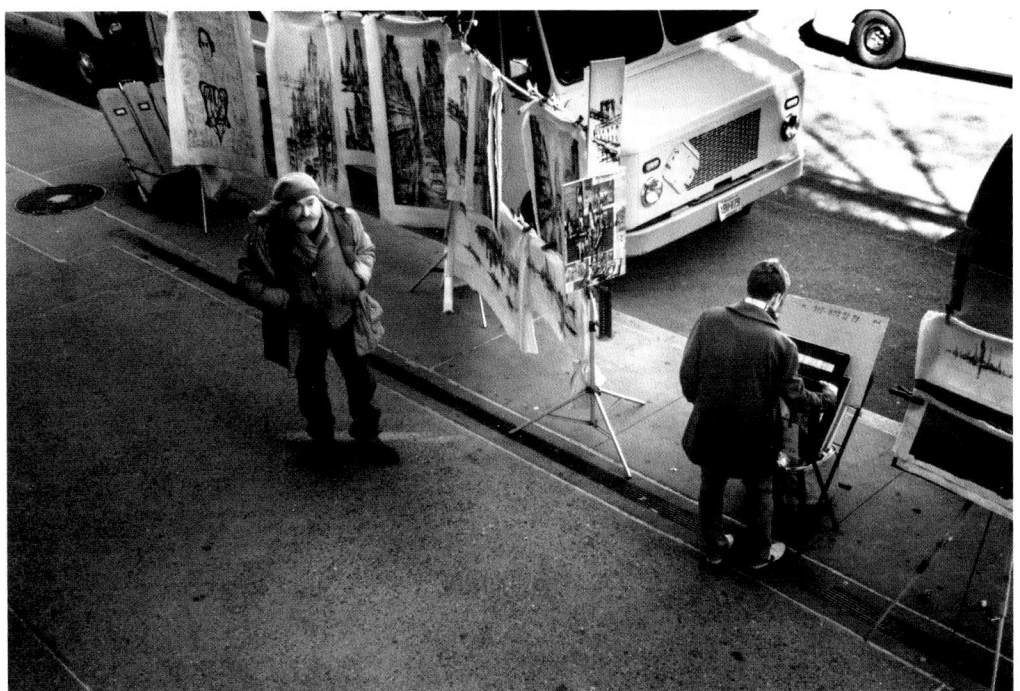

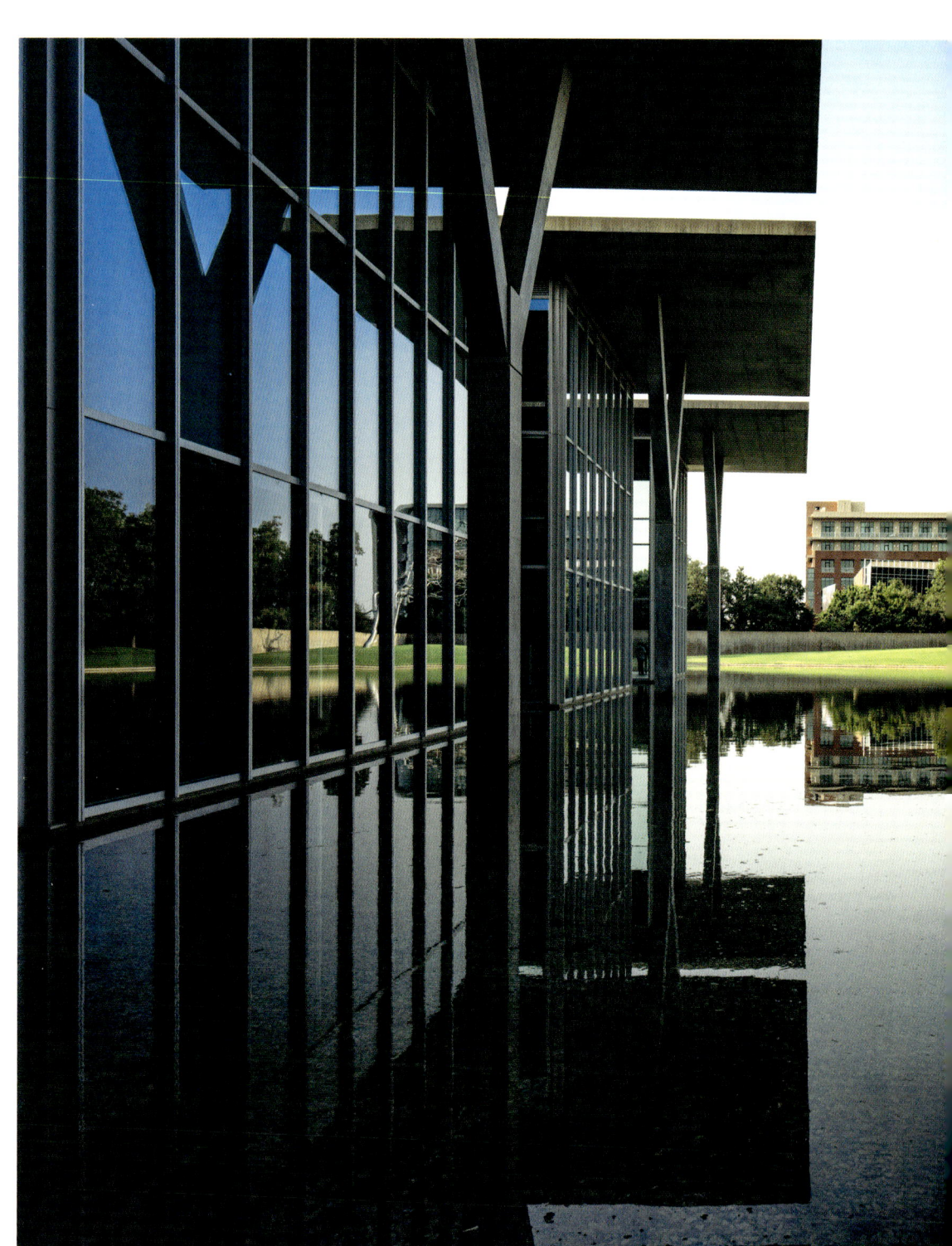

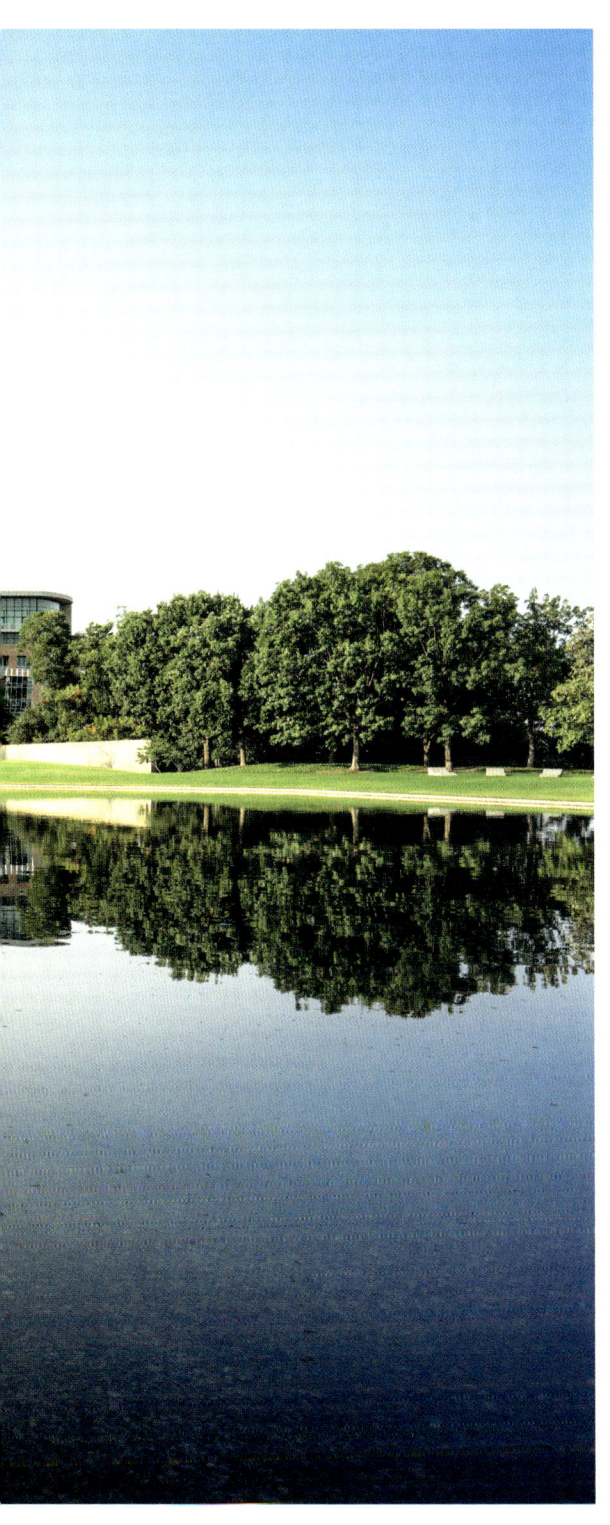

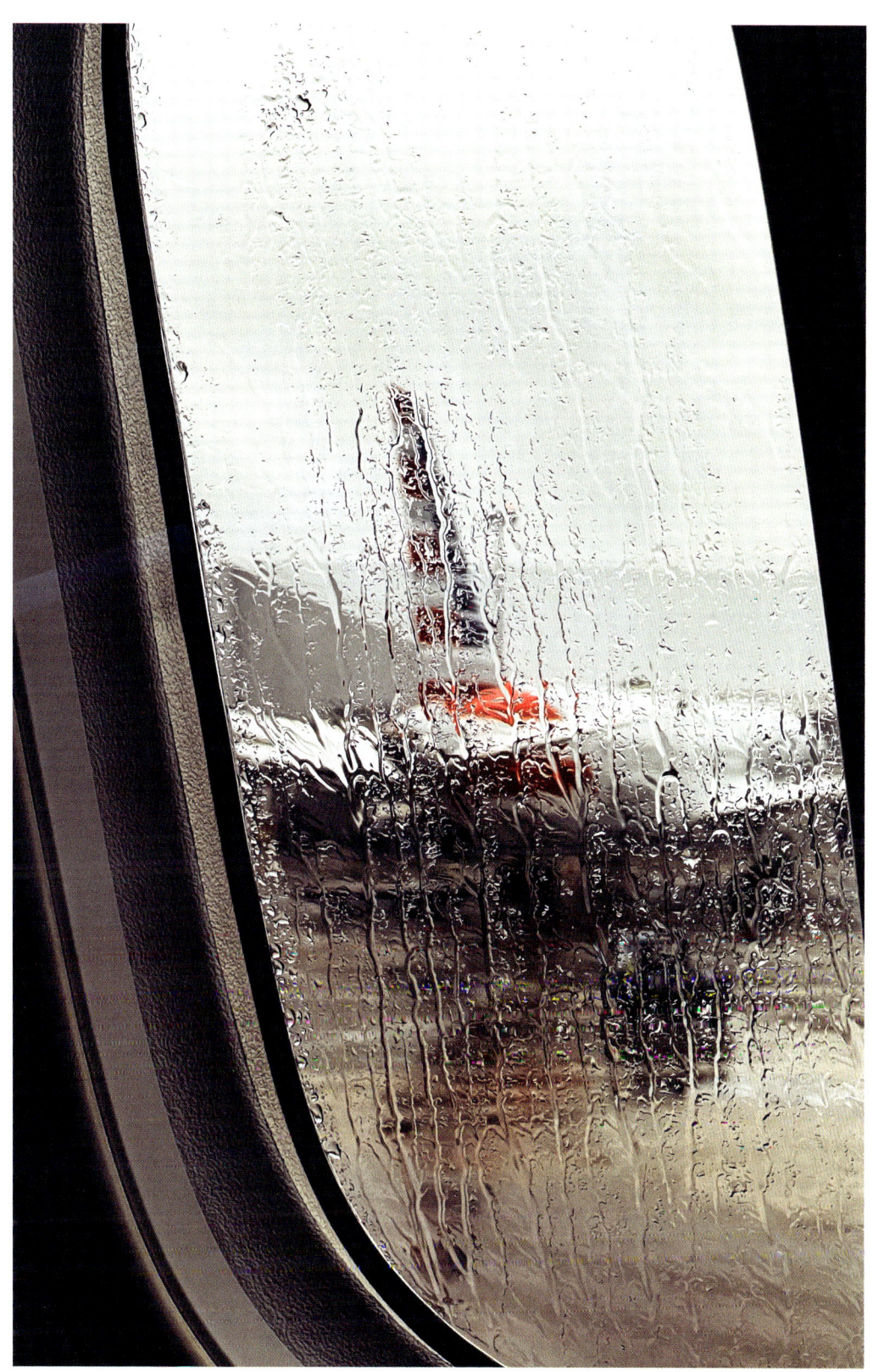

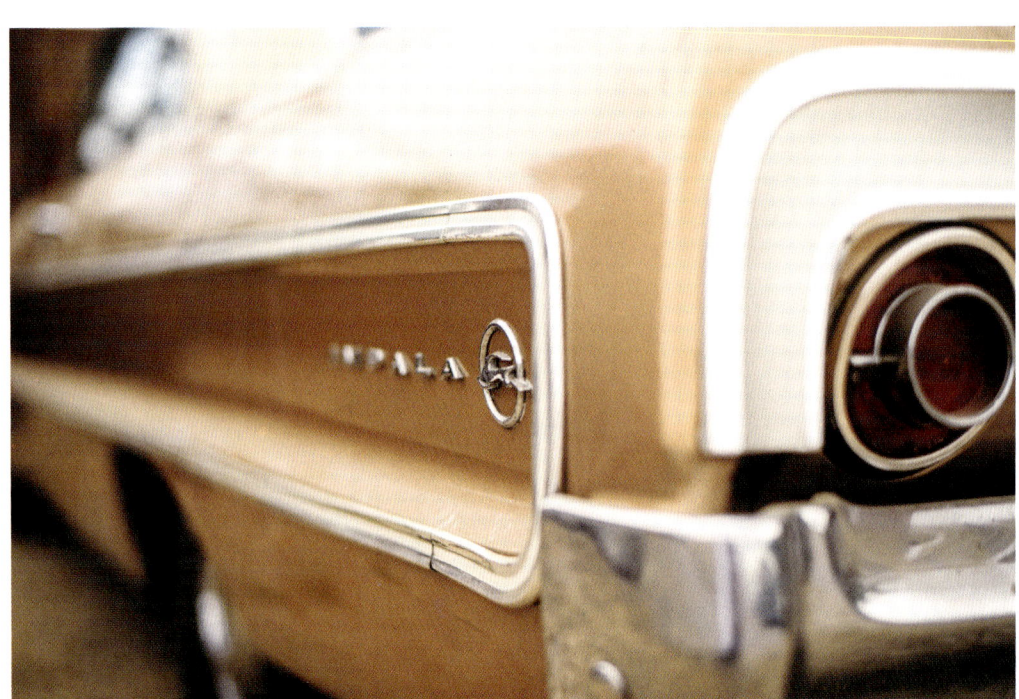

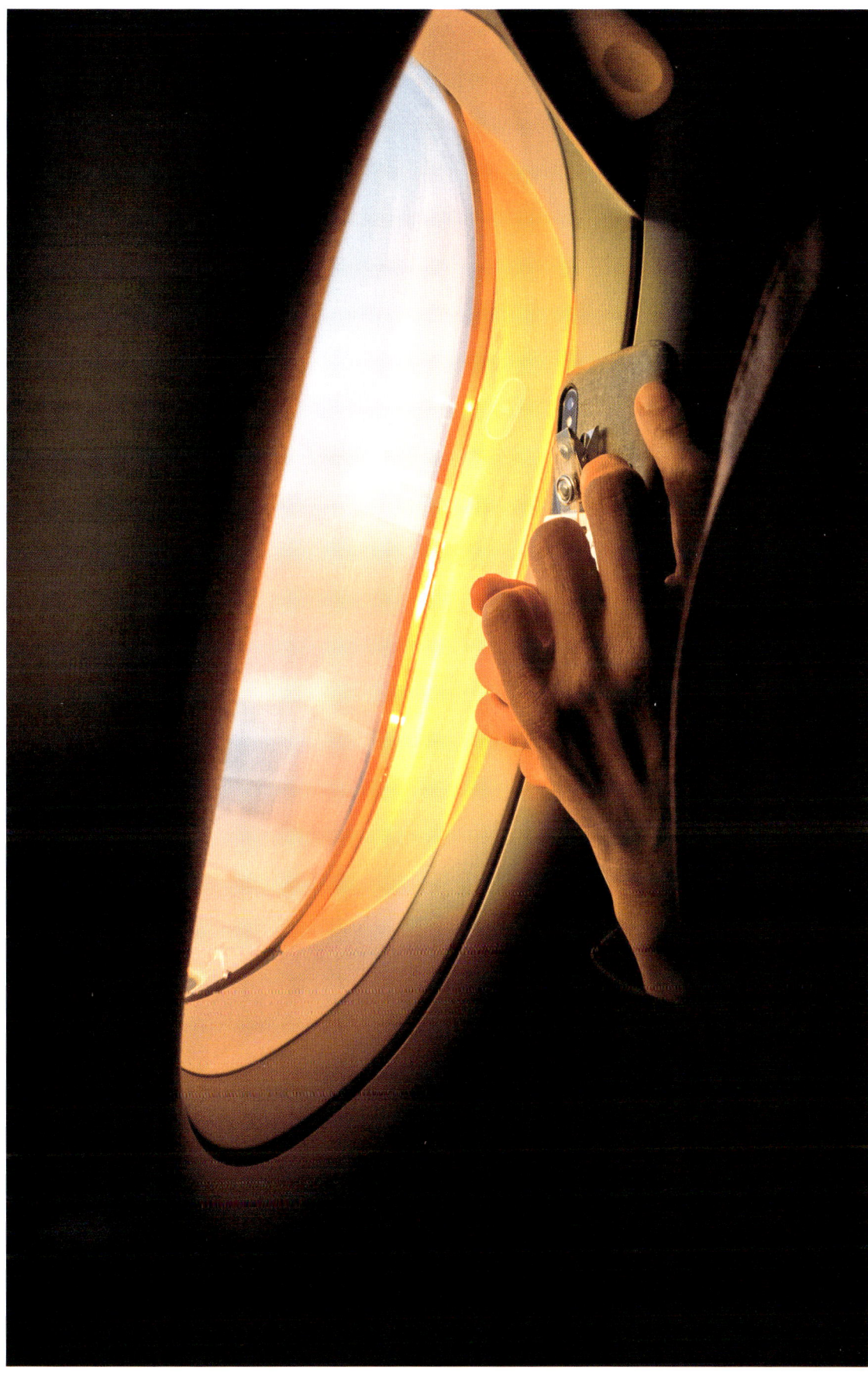

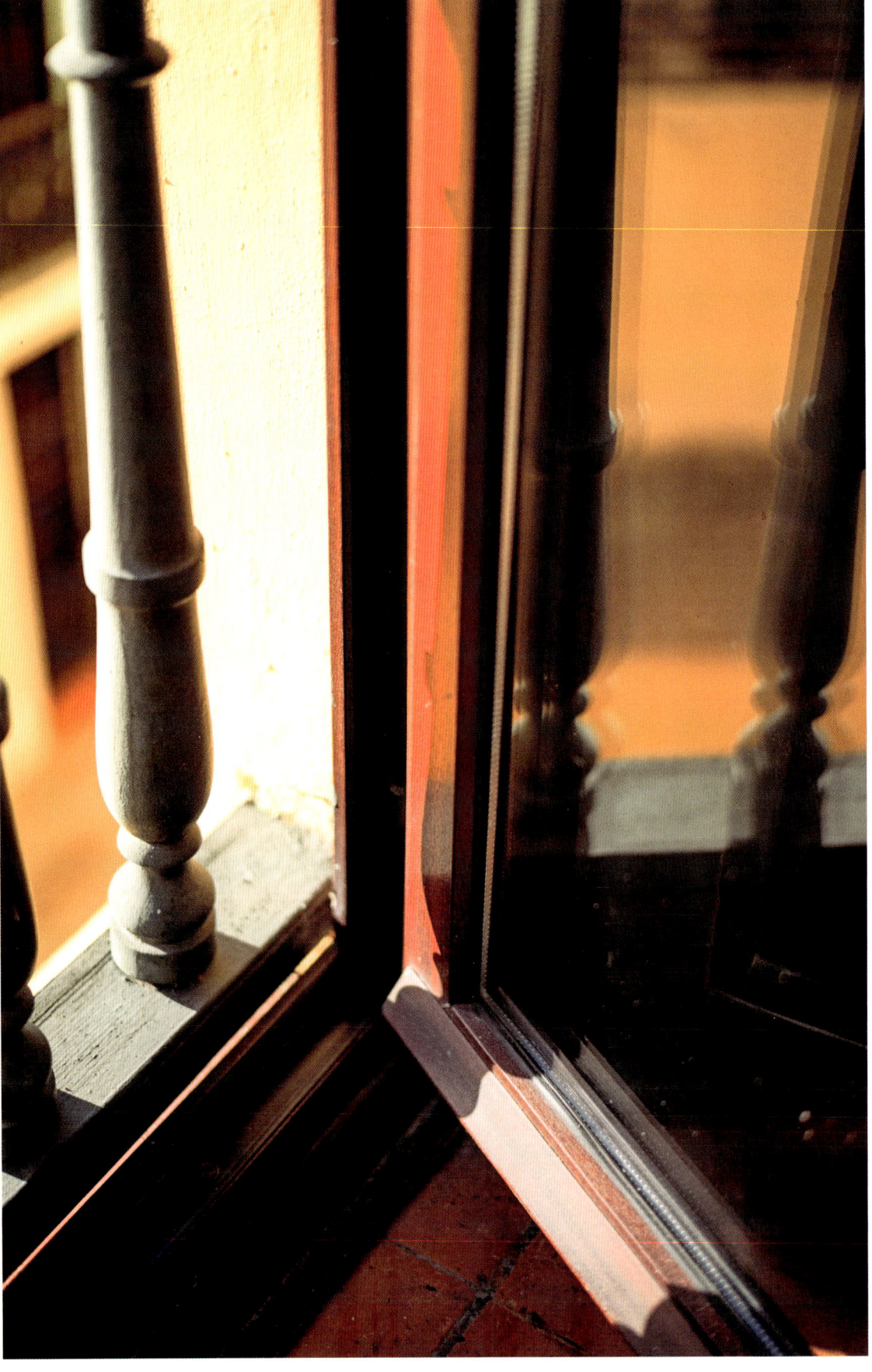

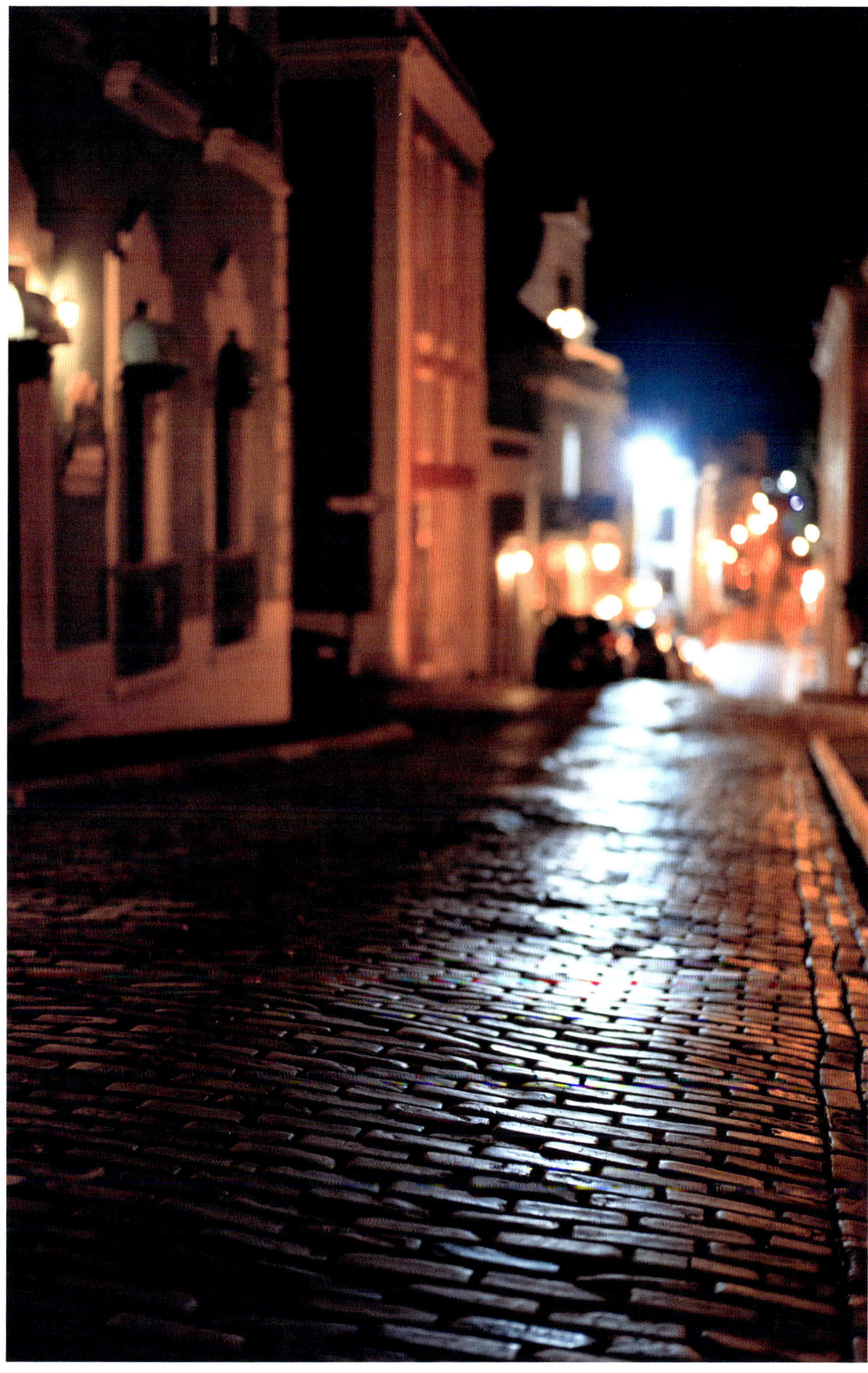

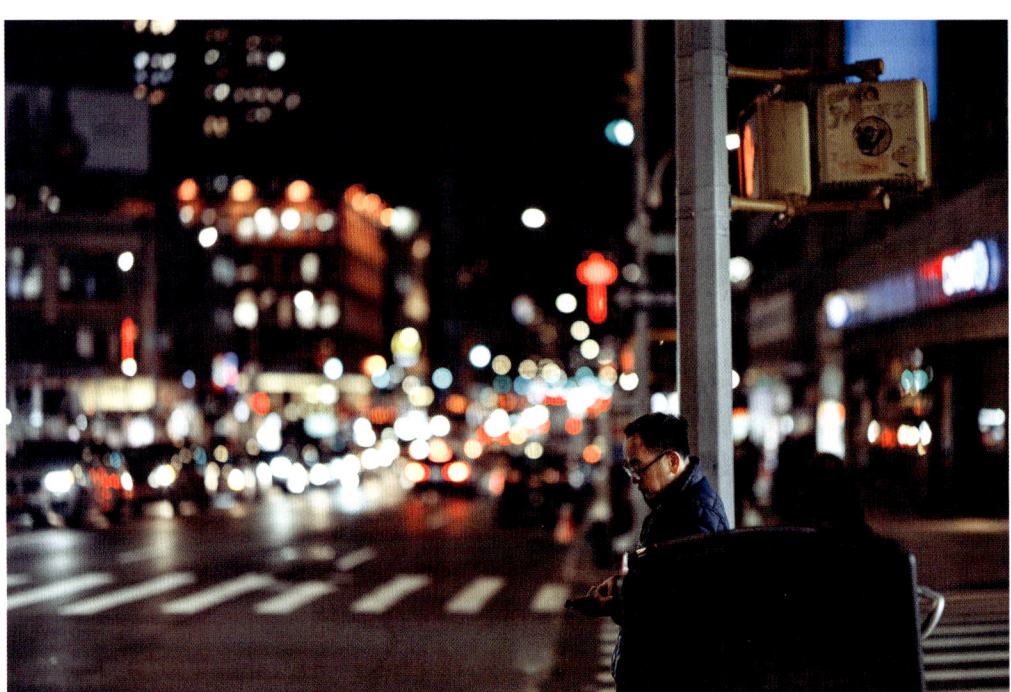

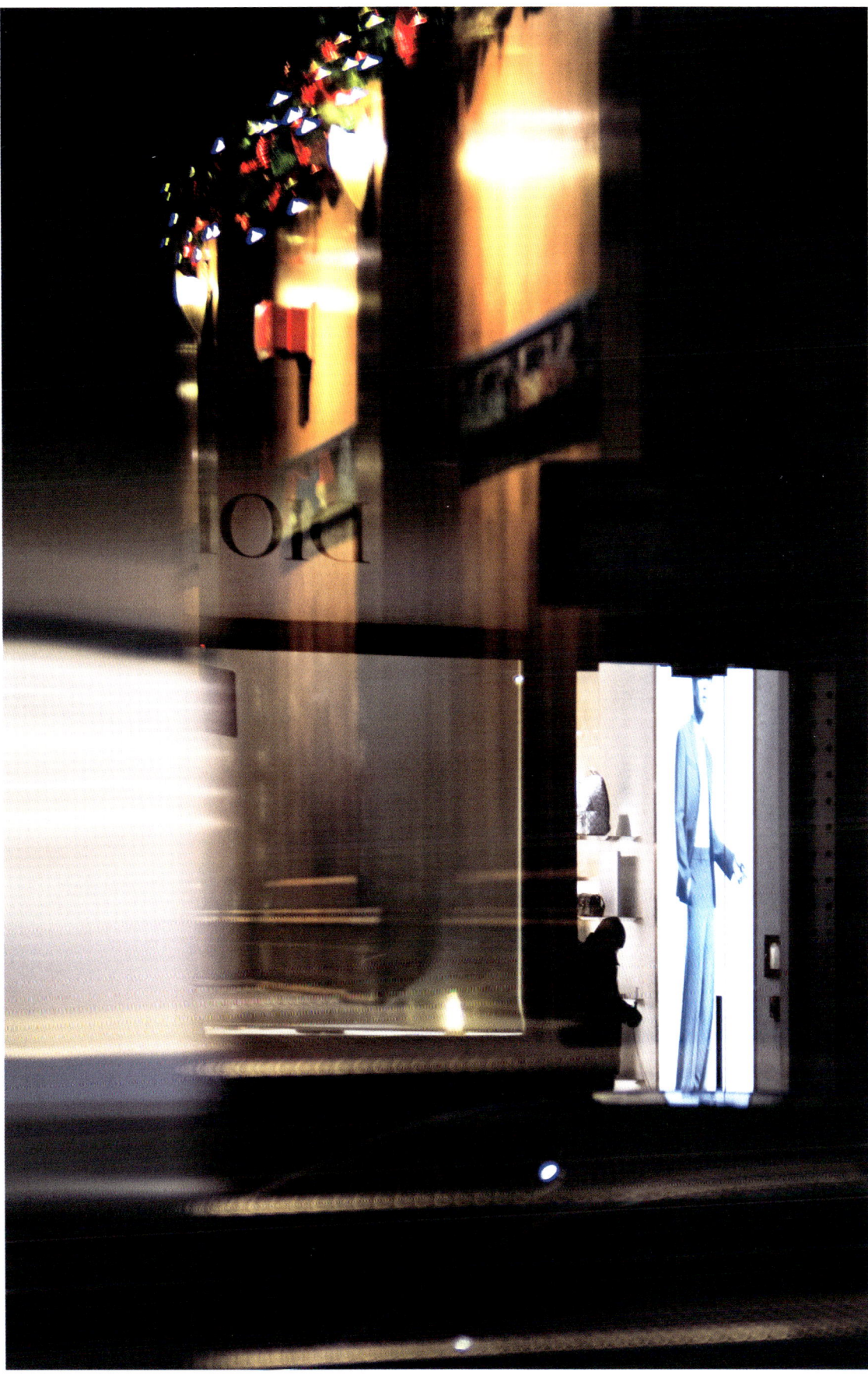

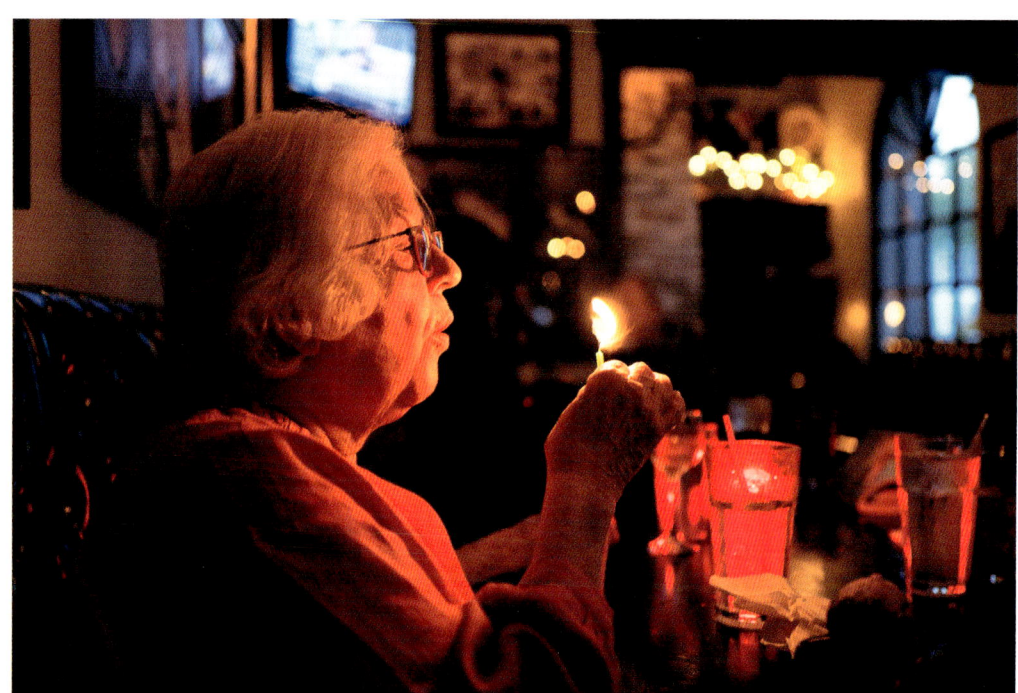

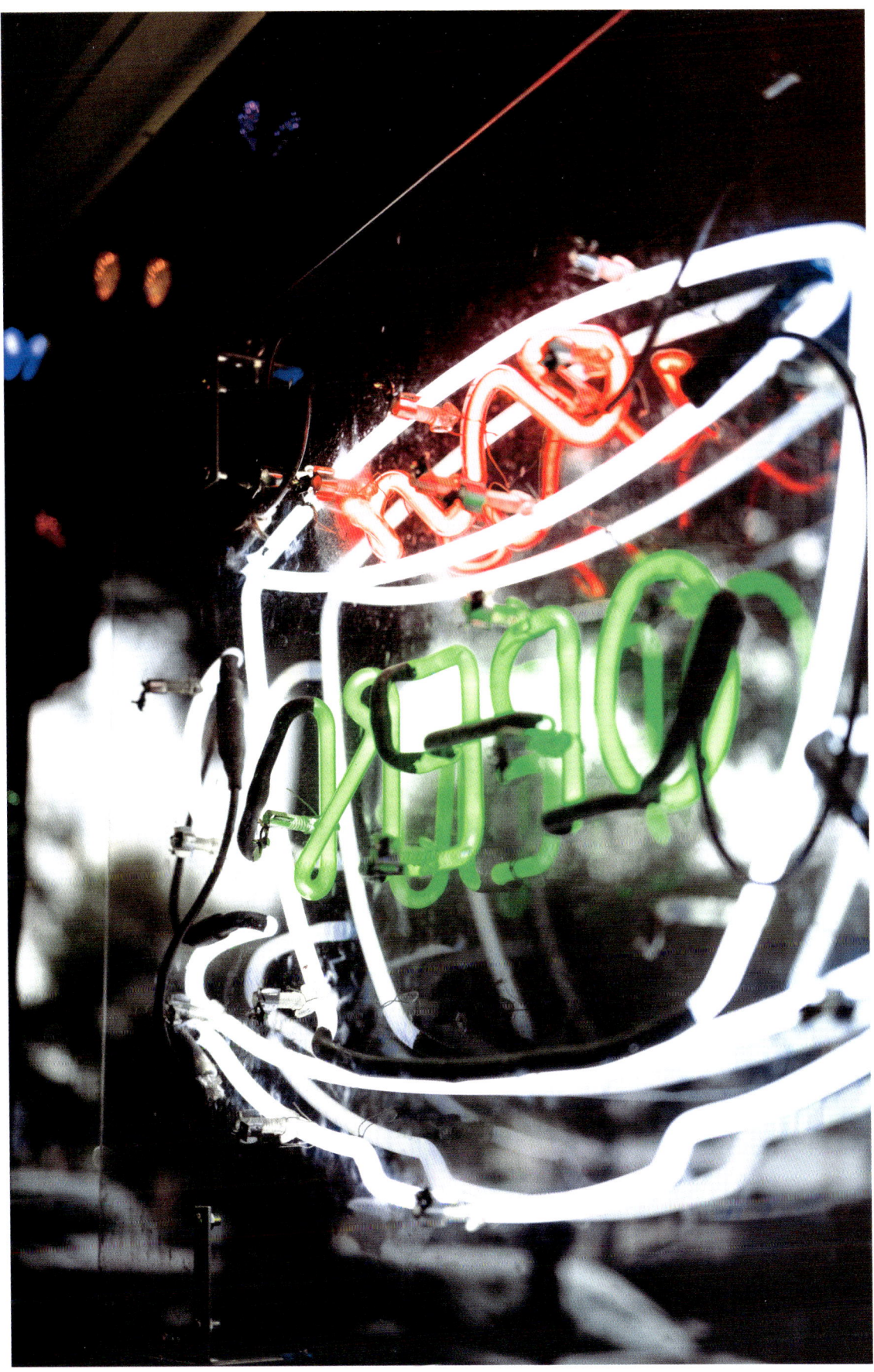

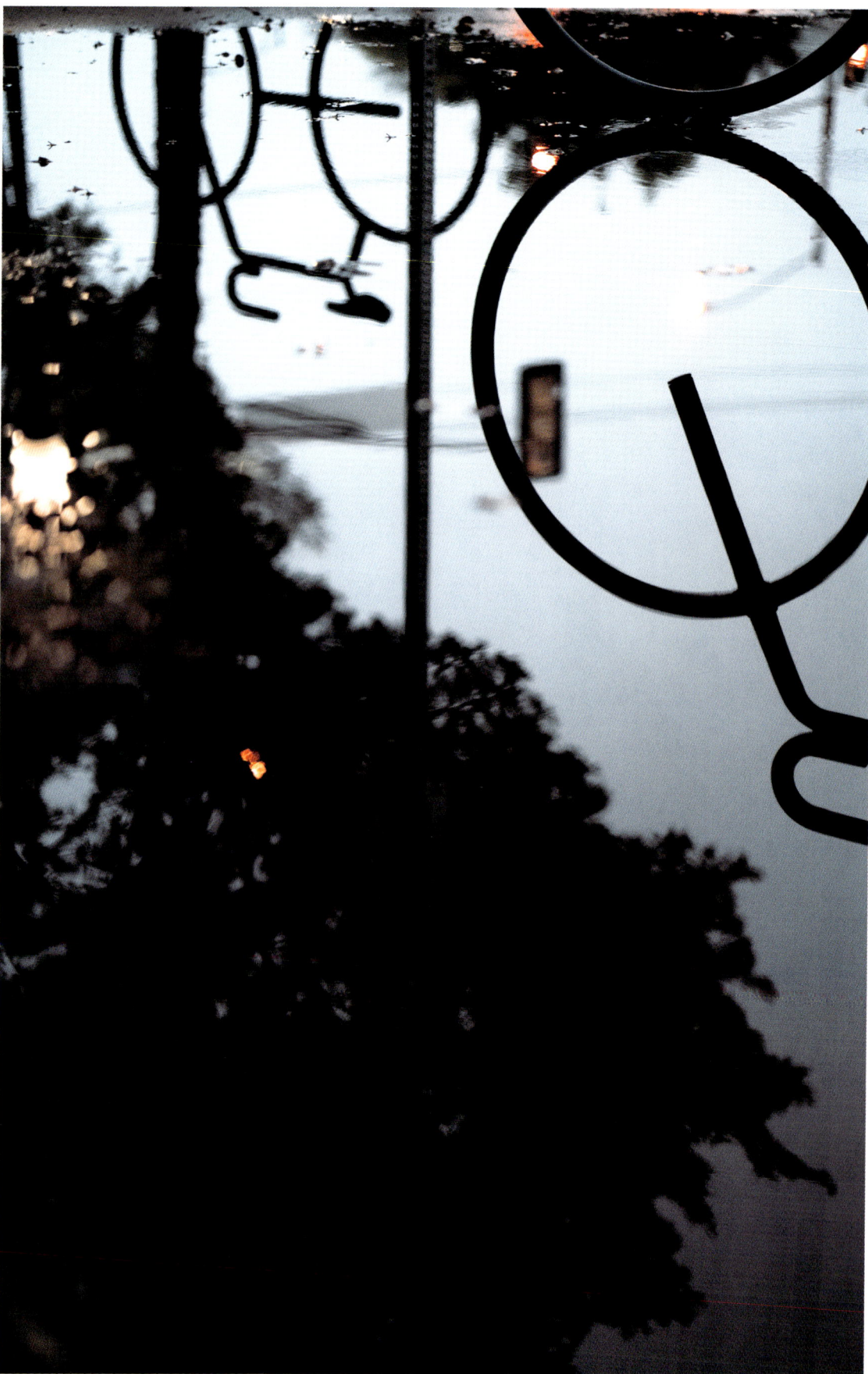

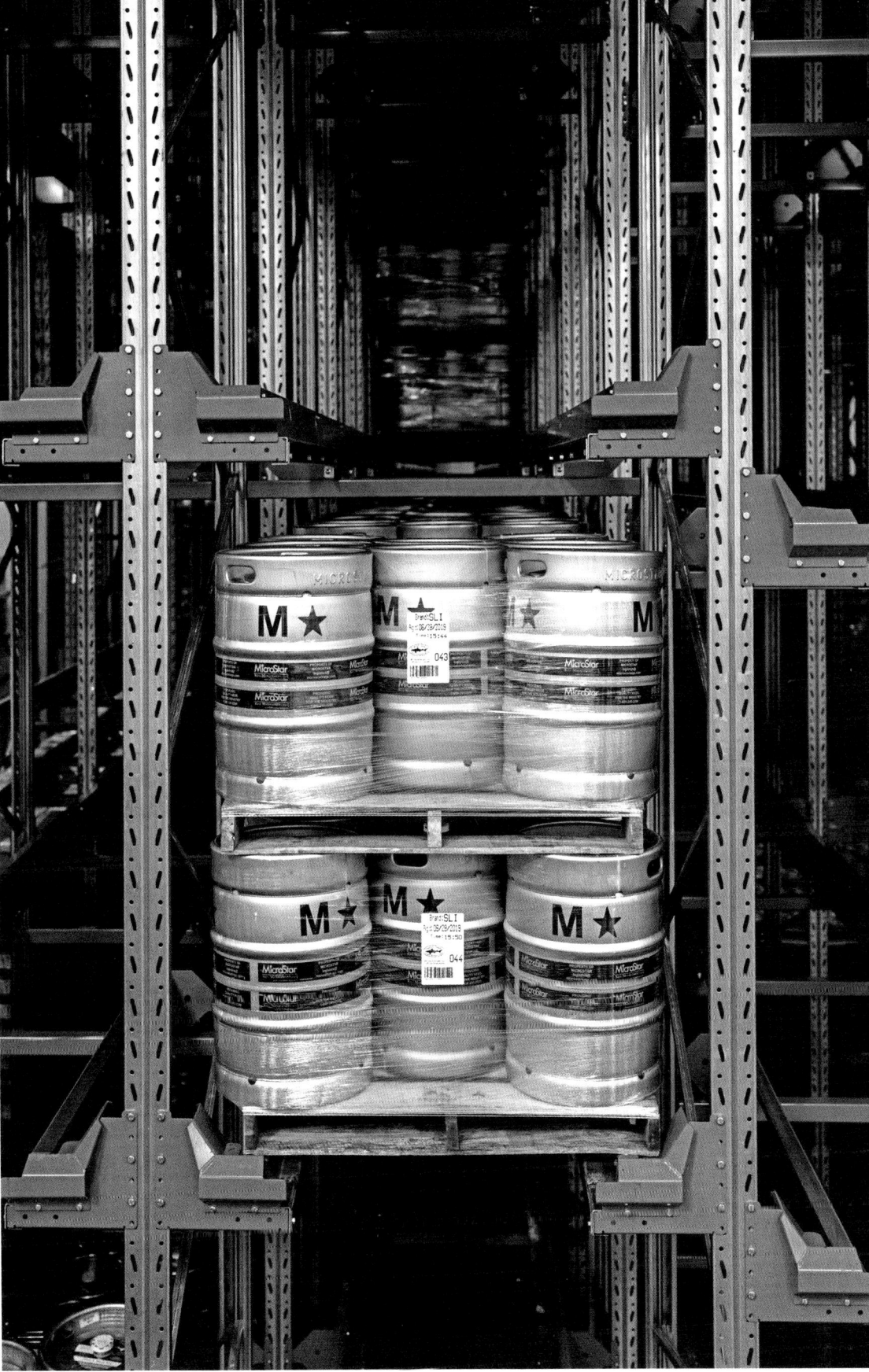

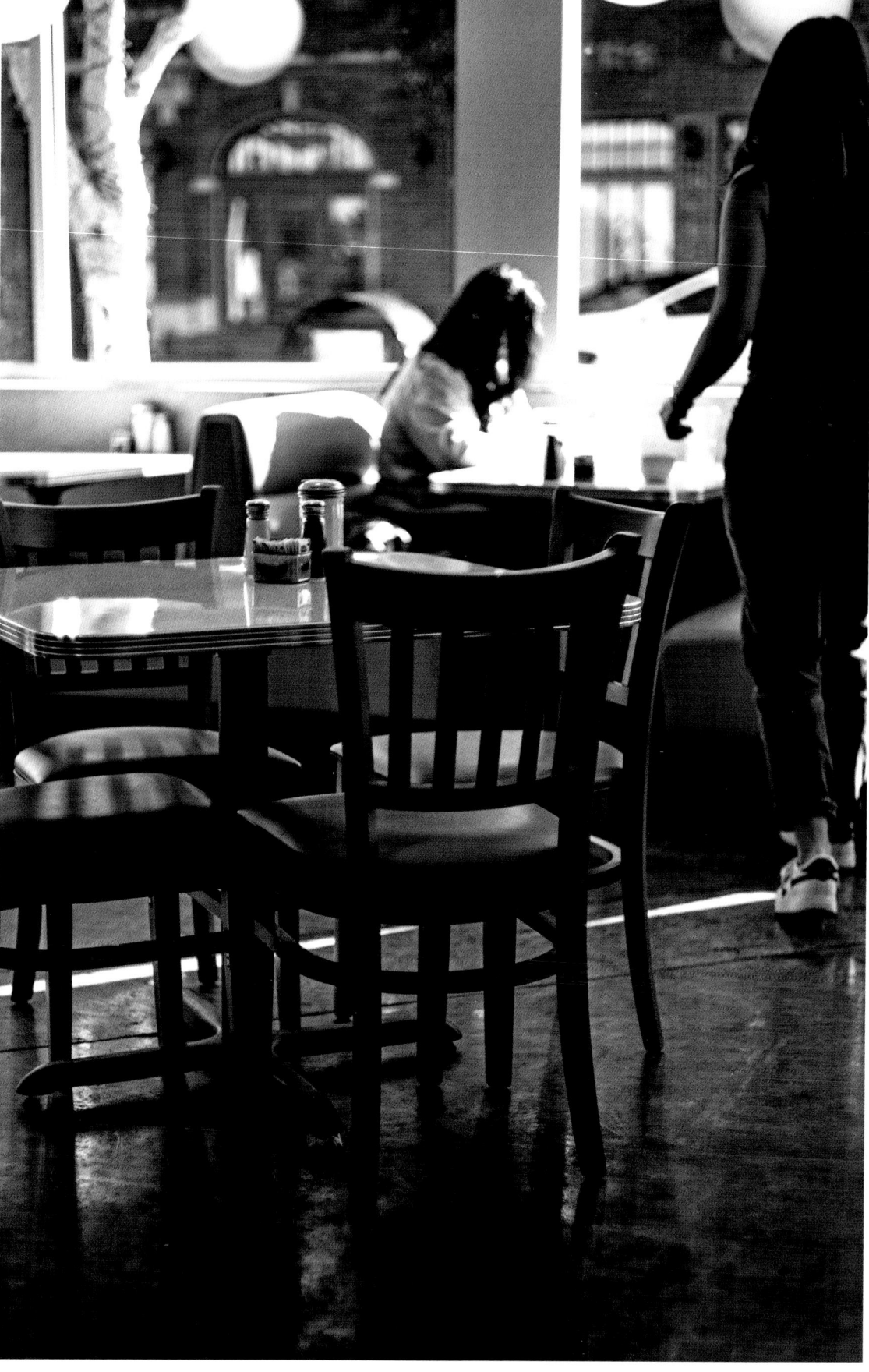

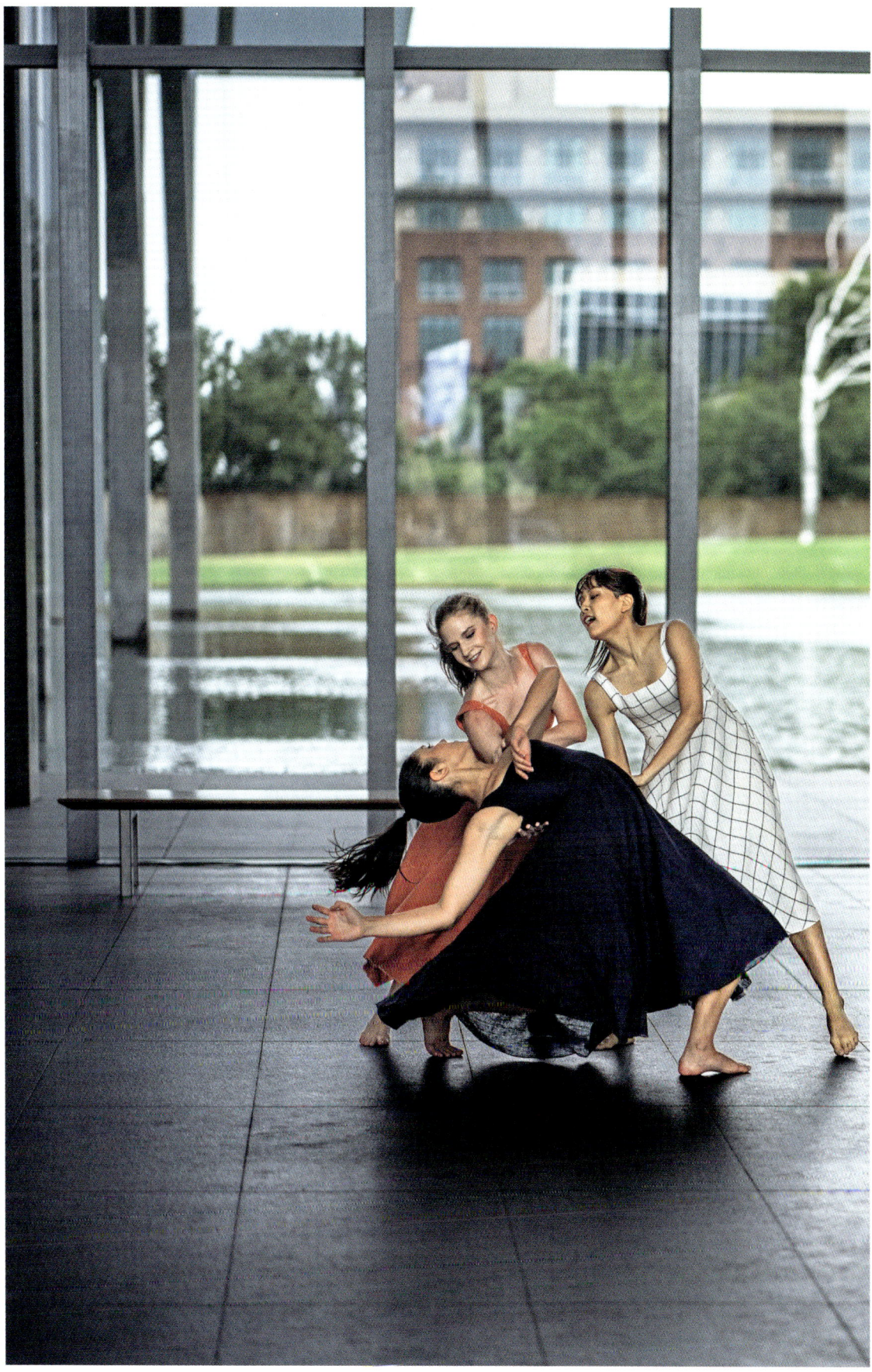

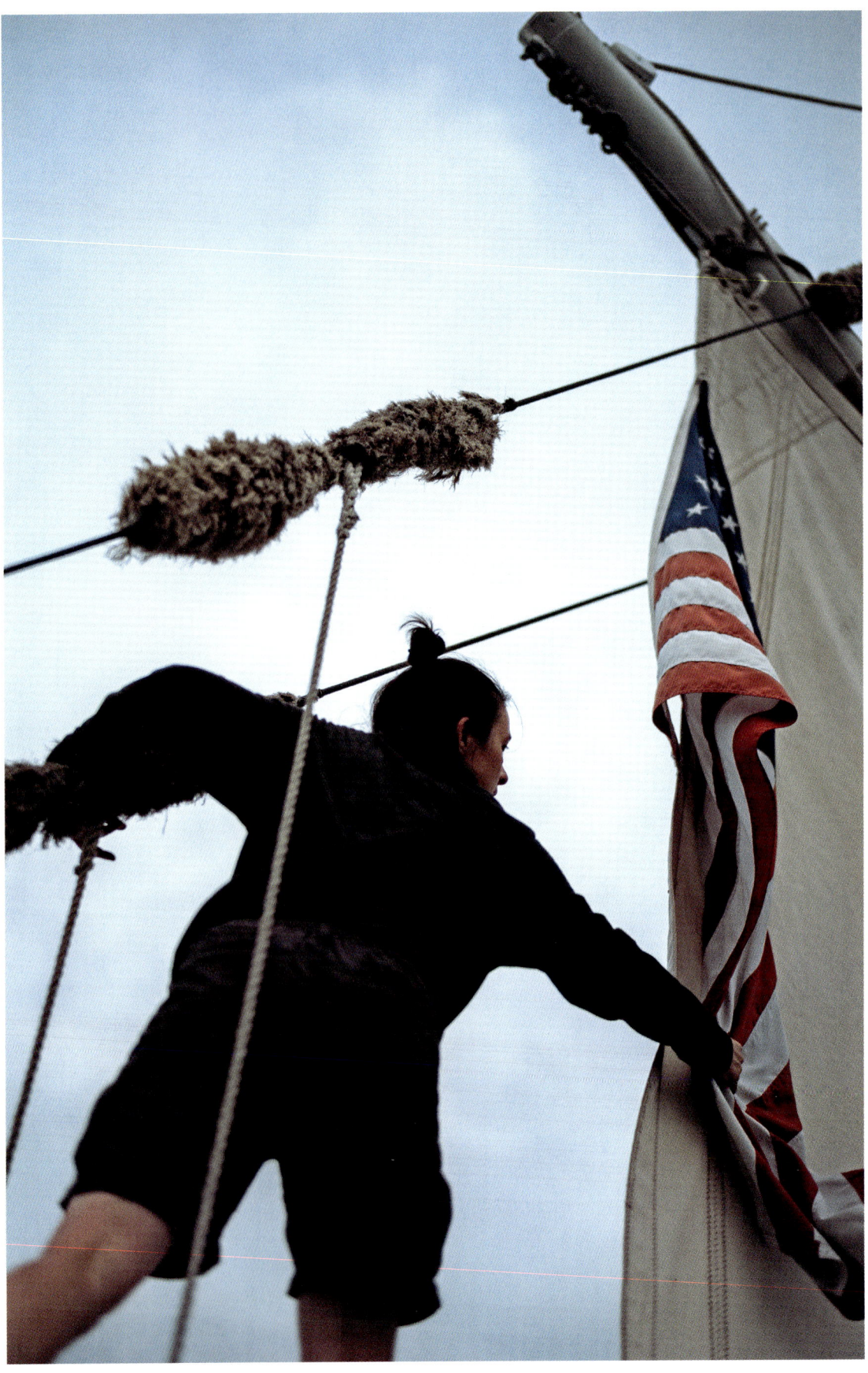

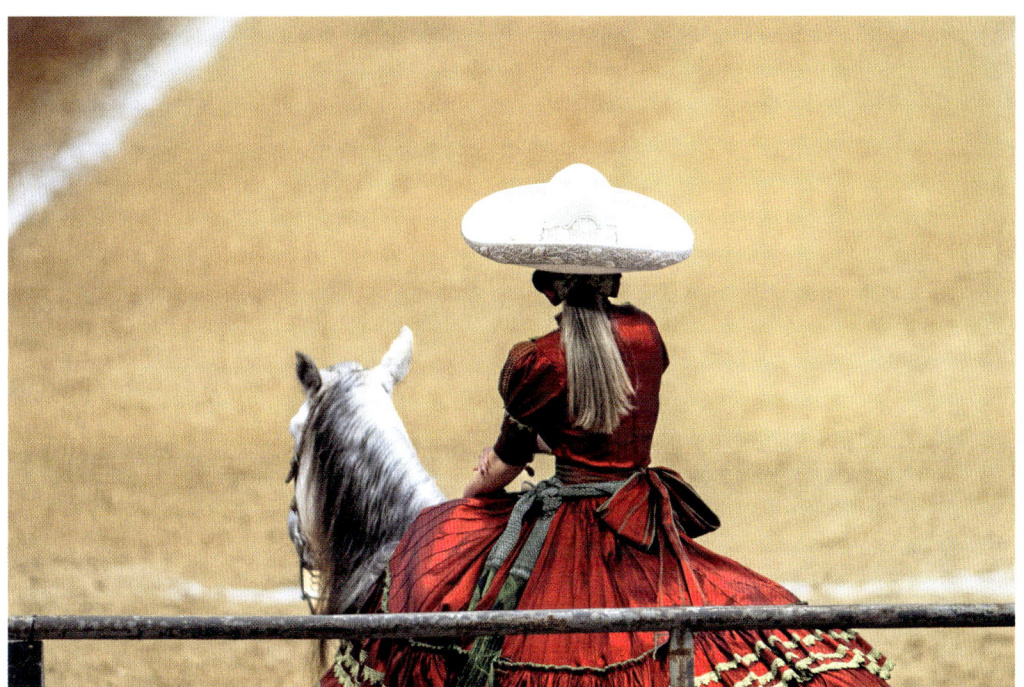

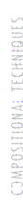

CHAPTER 17

SYMBOLISM
AND METAPHOR

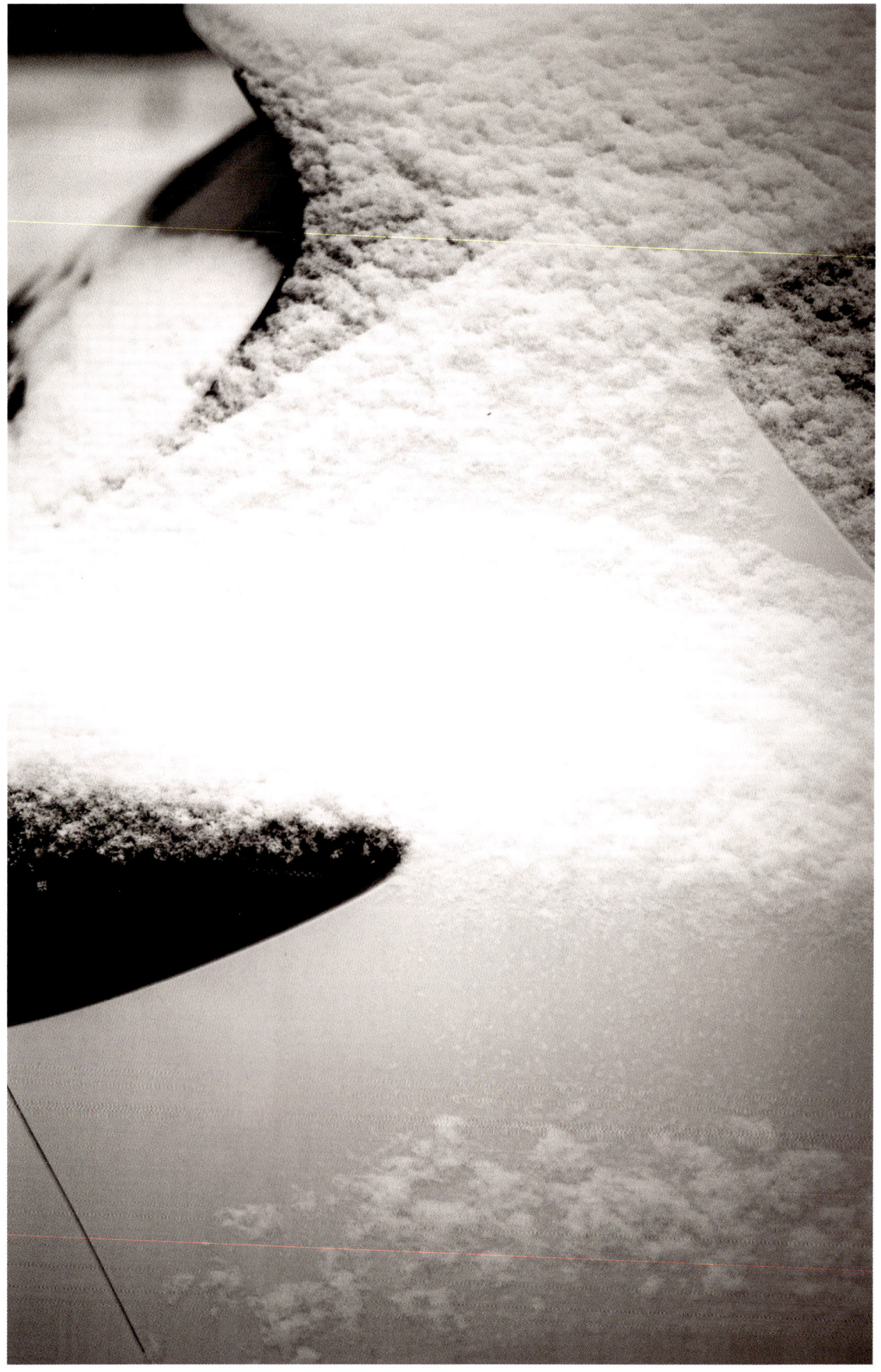

SIMPLY PUT, SYMBOLISM IS THE IDEA that one image or visual element can represent another thing. The color blue can symbolize the sky, cool temperatures, calm, or sadness. Symbolism is a long-established concept not limited to just art. It appears throughout religion, science, and literature as well. Iconography is the term often used when referring to the study of images and symbols in visual compositions. Symbolism can be a powerful, nonliteral communication tool.

In a lot of photography, the concept of "nonliteral" is difficult to define. Let's consider a photograph of a tree in a field. The specific type of tree may have some universal symbolism or meaning. Additionally, this image might mean one thing to you and another to me based on our own life experiences. This can expand interpretation. But even though you and I might see this tree differently, it's still a static image of a tree in a field. If you change the context, the perception can change. For example, consider the tree in a fishbowl instead of a field. This challenges our logical thinking. Now that the tree has potential to mean something else, we are communicating on a nonliteral plane. This becomes very powerful.

Think of advertising. The essential purpose of any advertisement is to pitch. Advertising is used to create awareness, but it is also used to sell an idea, product, or service. Don Draper in the TV series *Mad Men* taught us that the real power of advertising is not necessarily the product, but the person you could be if you used the product. It's not just a slide projector, it's a carousel of life's moments. It's not a shade of lipstick, it's a personal way for a woman to "mark her man." Effective advertising embraces symbolism—symbols of wealth, symbols of power, symbols of value, symbols of happiness, even symbols of empathy. You get the idea.

In 1959, Volkswagen had hired the advertising agency Doyle Dane Bernbach (DDB) to do a series of ads for a new small, ugly compact car that had ties to Adolph Hitler. It was a serious challenge to the public at the time, and they pulled off arguably one of the best ad campaigns in the history of advertising. A series of one-page ads with lots of negative space, a simple photo, a headline, and well-written copy—and the designs were something nobody would approve of today. But the taglines "Lemon," "Think Small," "It's Ugly but It Gets You There," and many others are not only remembered today, but they've been copied countless times. DDB reinvented the identity and symbolism for Volkswagen. They turned a negative association into a practical and desirable one.

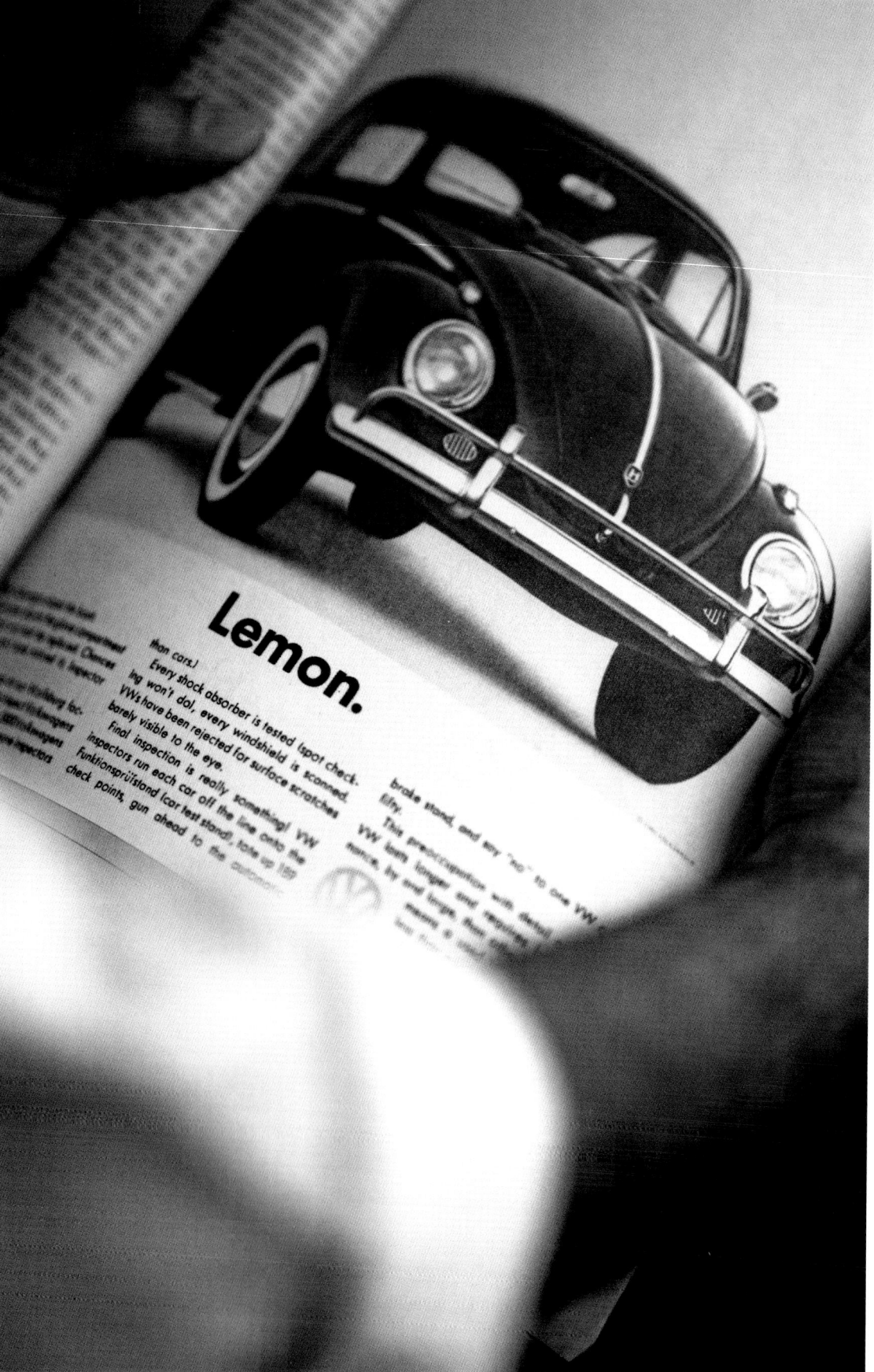

Metaphor is closely associated with symbolism. It is a literary concept that involves substituting a word or phrase that is not literal but brings emphasis to the original intent. Sometimes elements of abstraction or absurdity are used with metaphors to make the point:

The cold wind has turned my hands into blocks of ice.

My brother is the black sheep of the family.

The photo exhibition was on fire!

None of these statements is literal. My hands are cold but certainly not frozen; I'm not actually related to a sheep; and if the photo exhibition caught fire, that would be a bad situation. But each of these statements is made using metaphors to heighten the effect of the statement.

In visual communication, metaphor is using one subject that suggests or looks like another. Symbolism can be fairly broad and open in its visual interpretation, but metaphor is used more precisely to accentuate or exaggerate the main intention.

CHAPTER 18

CONTEXT

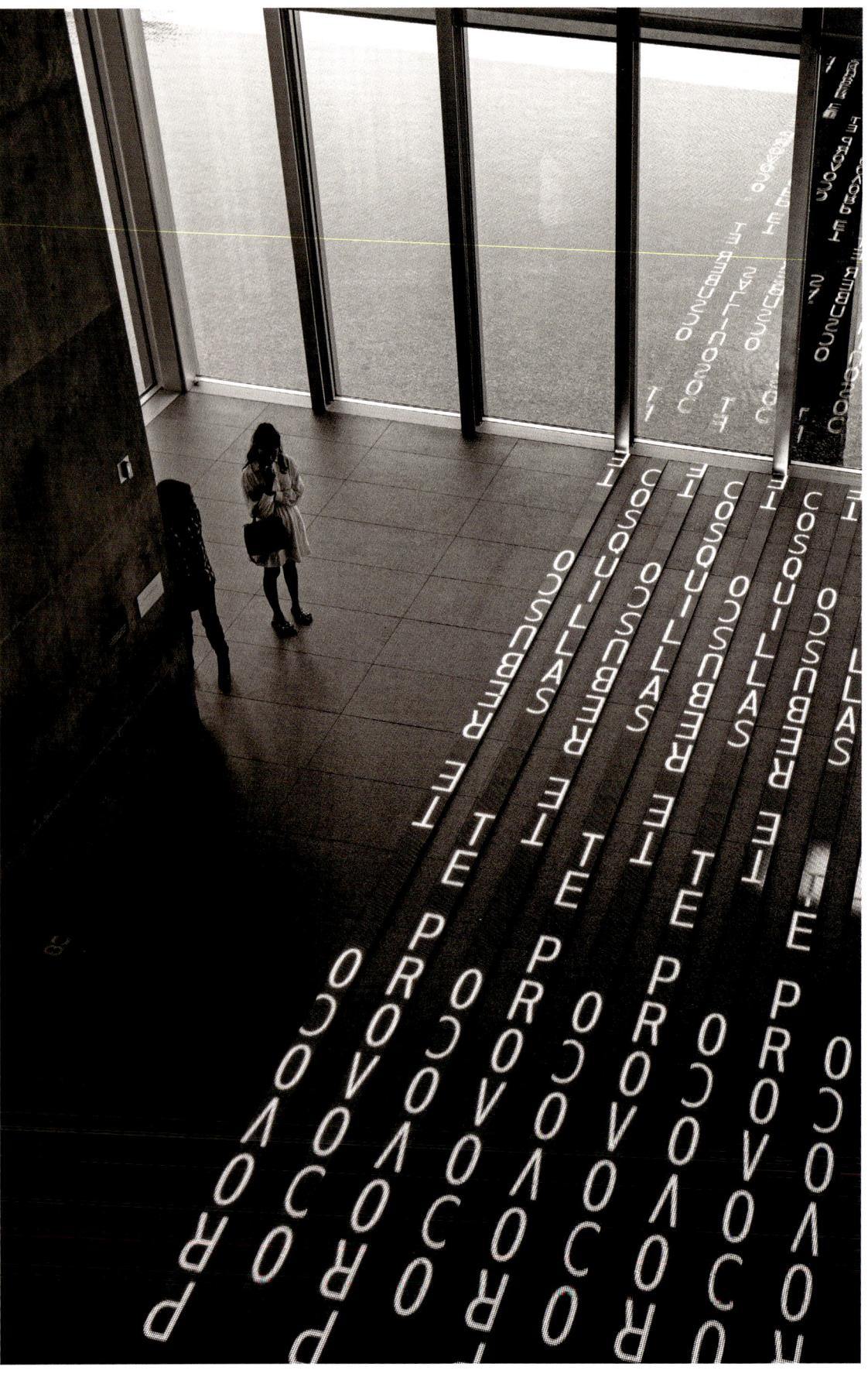

ANOTHER IMPORTANT ASPECT of photography today is the idea of context. This is becoming increasingly overlooked with newer generations of photographers, likely because of the modern photographic process of the digital medium. Before digital photography the only way to see your photographs was to print them or project them onto a wall. Today people make images, then view them instantly on the device used to create them. Images can be quickly shared, as everyone else can view them on their own devices as well. As a result, few people ever think of their photographs outside the context of a digital screen.

If you're serious about photography and you care about a viewer having an experience with your work, context should be as important to your process as actually making the image. I've seen many great photographs suffer from this oversight.

Context is the viewing experience. It's important to consider the medium to ensure your photography is successful in its intention. Most people are sharing images on their phones, which is absolutely great, but it's only one context. If you're going to print an image and put it on a wall, then you have to consider your options: How large should the print be? Should you use glossy or matte paper? If you print on glossy paper and put it under glass, can you actually see the image on the wall or does it reflect the gallery lighting?

The photo book is a medium, or context, unto itself. In 2010, I began talking quite a bit on my YouTube channel, The Art of Photography, about books. People who regularly watched my videos started sending me their work. As a result, I began to share the prints, books, and zines sent to me. My feeling was, if someone went to the trouble to make something, the least I could do is reward that by sharing it. I feel like it encourages more people to take on projects with their own work.

I've received hundreds of photo books and zines from a wide range of photographers, from beginners to professionals. I share them all equally, as I value the beauty of making, no matter how experienced or amateur it may be. Many viewers are making books for the first time, and it's fairly obvious they're dealing with challenges they've never considered.

For example, I get a lot of work that is mostly shot in a horizontal, landscape format. The book makers want to make their images as big as possible. Online printing services like Blurb have a variety of templates that generally encourage poor design choices. The result too often is a super long, oversized book that is nearly impossible to hold comfortably. A vertical book design format is much more natural, and the images presented in this format still speak, even if they are smaller.

I also see photographers who want their images to appear "full bleed" throughout an entire book. This means the edge of the image is the edge of the page. The effect is a book that looks more like graphic design than a photography showcase. And the bigger issue is that too many photographers don't consider the gutter, or the middle of the book. All books are bound, and if you have a two-page spread, the middle portion of the image is sucked into the book's gutter with the binding. I've seen the subject of the photograph literally sucked into the middle of a book. This spoils the experience and doesn't do much to encourage someone to continue paging through the book.

Another common oversight is book size. This is an important aspect of the user experience, if you want someone to spend time looking at your work. I remember, in the late 1990s, seeing an oversized Ansel Adams book on a clearance shelf in one of my favorite bookstores. The price was under $10. I purchased the book and I still have it. I think I flipped through it once. The experience was so disappointing. I absolutely love Adams's prints. One of my gripes is that his images don't reproduce the same in books as they do on gallery walls. I could almost forgive the print quality. It wasn't terrible, just not what I was looking for. I was hoping this posthumous release would be different. Two things were learned here: bigger does not equal better; bigger is really difficult to hold for more than a few minutes.

You can see that the context of the photo book is extremely important. You have to start thinking of your images in a different way when presenting them in book form. What is the flow of images from page to page? Are there too many images on each spread? Does the sequencing work to hold the viewer's interest? Is the work communicating in book form?

Now consider how a gallery exhibition changes the context again. In a gallery context, spacing around and between images is critical. You might have a large wall that tempts you to fill or clutter it with images. Photographs presented close together tend to start losing impact. How will sequencing be considered? This changes from the book concept. With a book, people typically explore in one direction—front to back. Galleries tend to be open spaces with no real starting or ending point. How is the viewer's experience affected if they start on the right side or the left side of the room?

Probably the most popular context for viewing photography today is also overlooked—the context of social media. The high use of social media is largely due to the optimization for mobile phones. So how does your work appear in the context of a smartphone? The default orientation is going to be vertical and the phone already has some major size limitations, so horizontal images become very difficult. The issue becomes being able to see detail. Vertical images fill the screen and get you a considerable bump in real estate.

There is no right or wrong answer. I've seen photographers be successful with either format, but it is something to consider. If your work requires the rendering of fine details, a horizontal format is going to work against you to some degree in the context of social media and phone viewing.

The best way of understanding context for your own work is experience. If you're working in social media, look at how successful photographers you respect display their work. Ask yourself what works and what doesn't. Experiment.

If you want to create photo books, you need to look at books. Ask yourself why a book is a certain size, or why one layout works better than another. Ask for advice from designers who work in the medium.

Context is important. There's more to photography than just shooting the images. You have to understand that you made the work, and it's up to you as an artist to control how it is displayed. It's up to you to be the champion and steward.

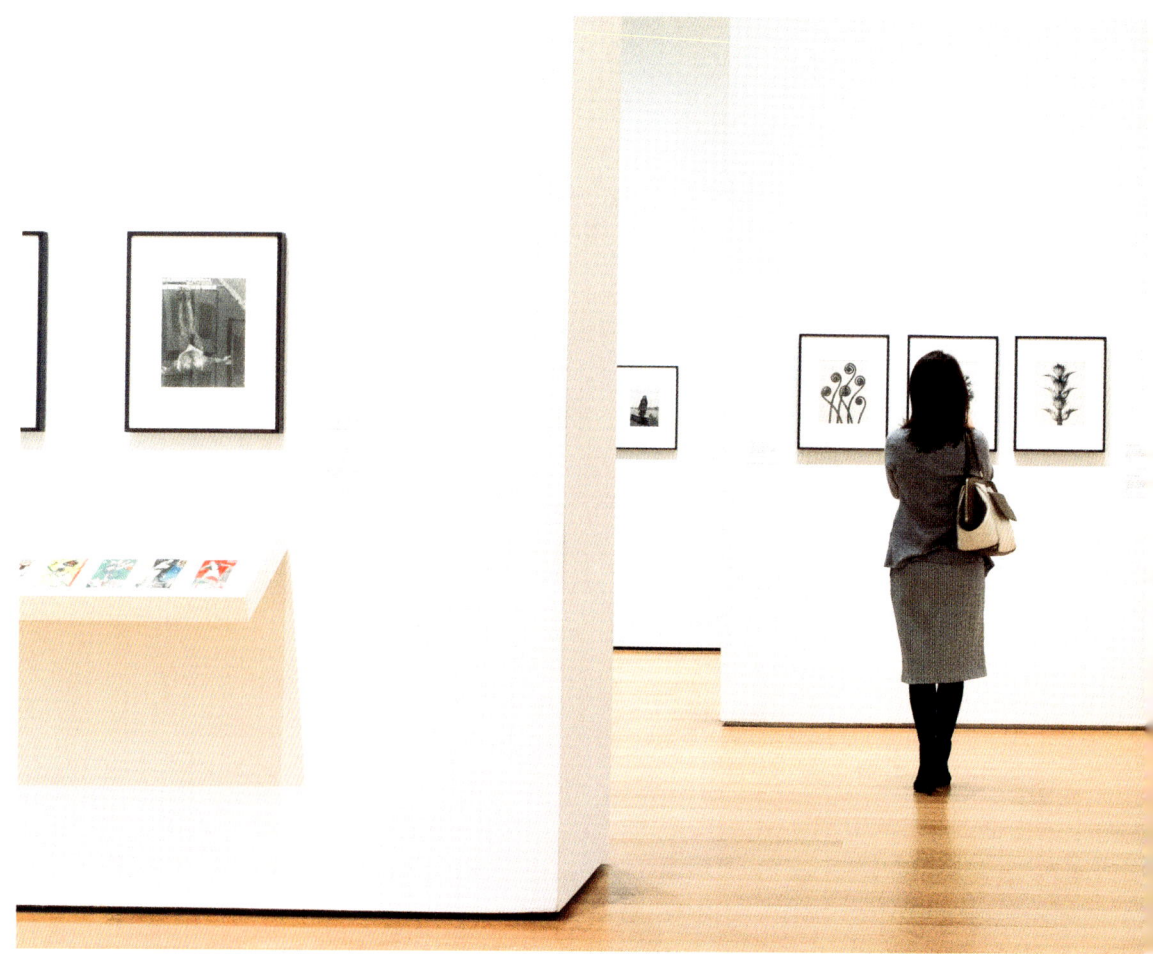

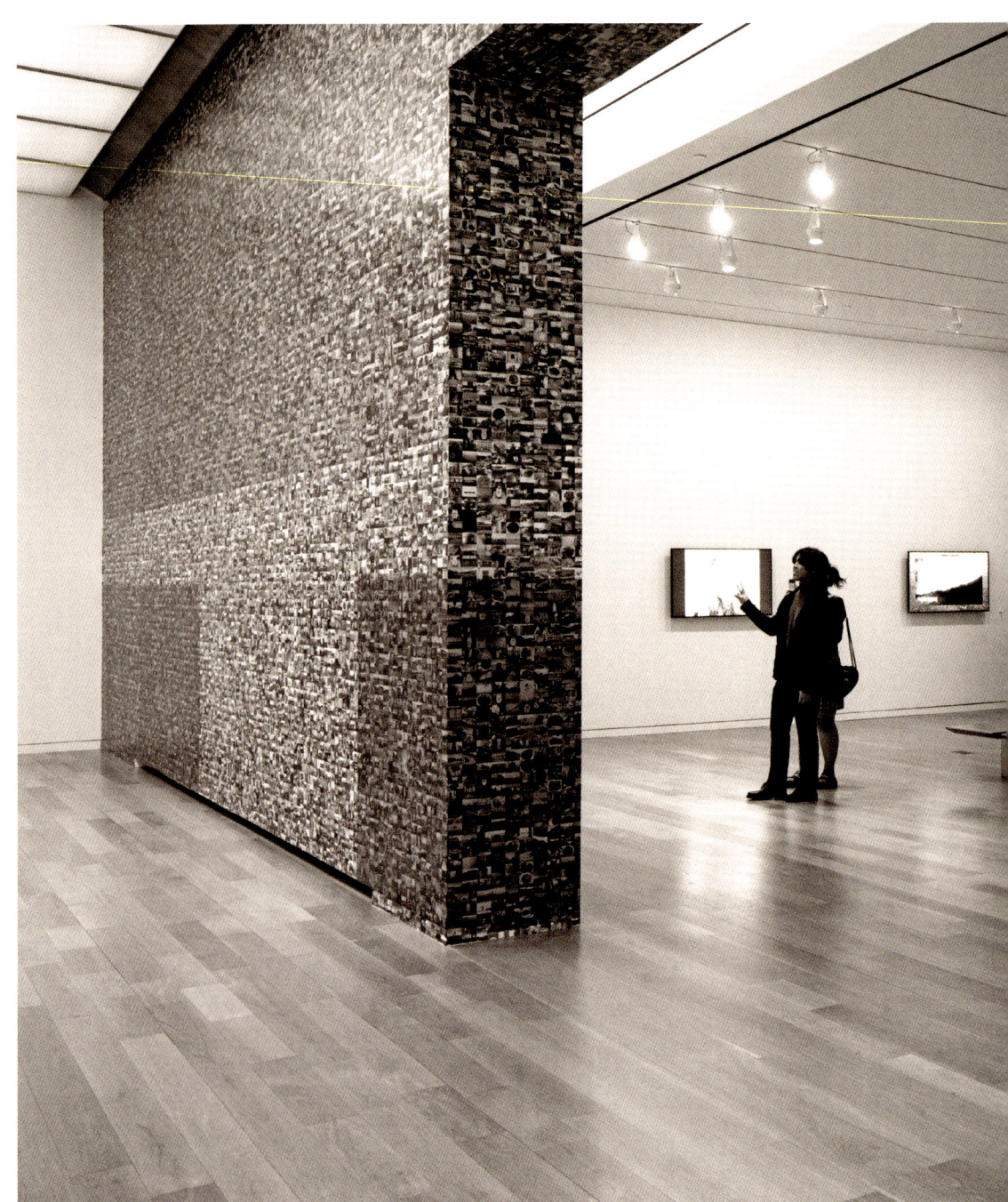

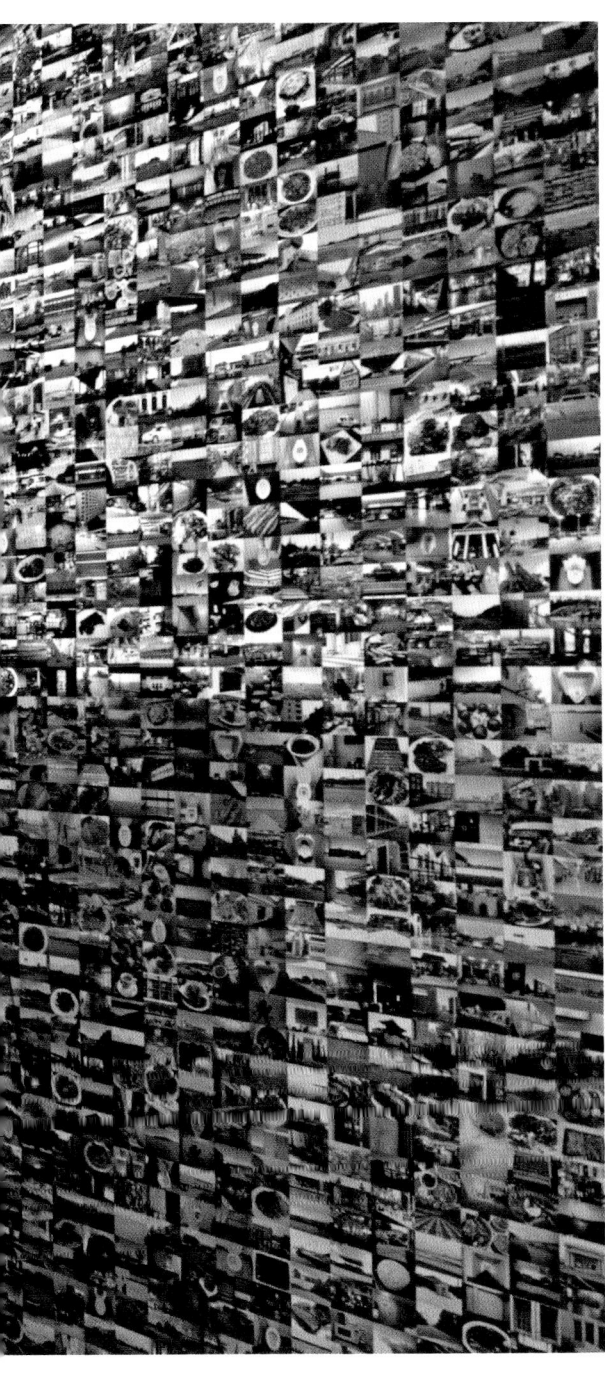

CHAPTER 19

FINDING YOUR
OWN VOICE

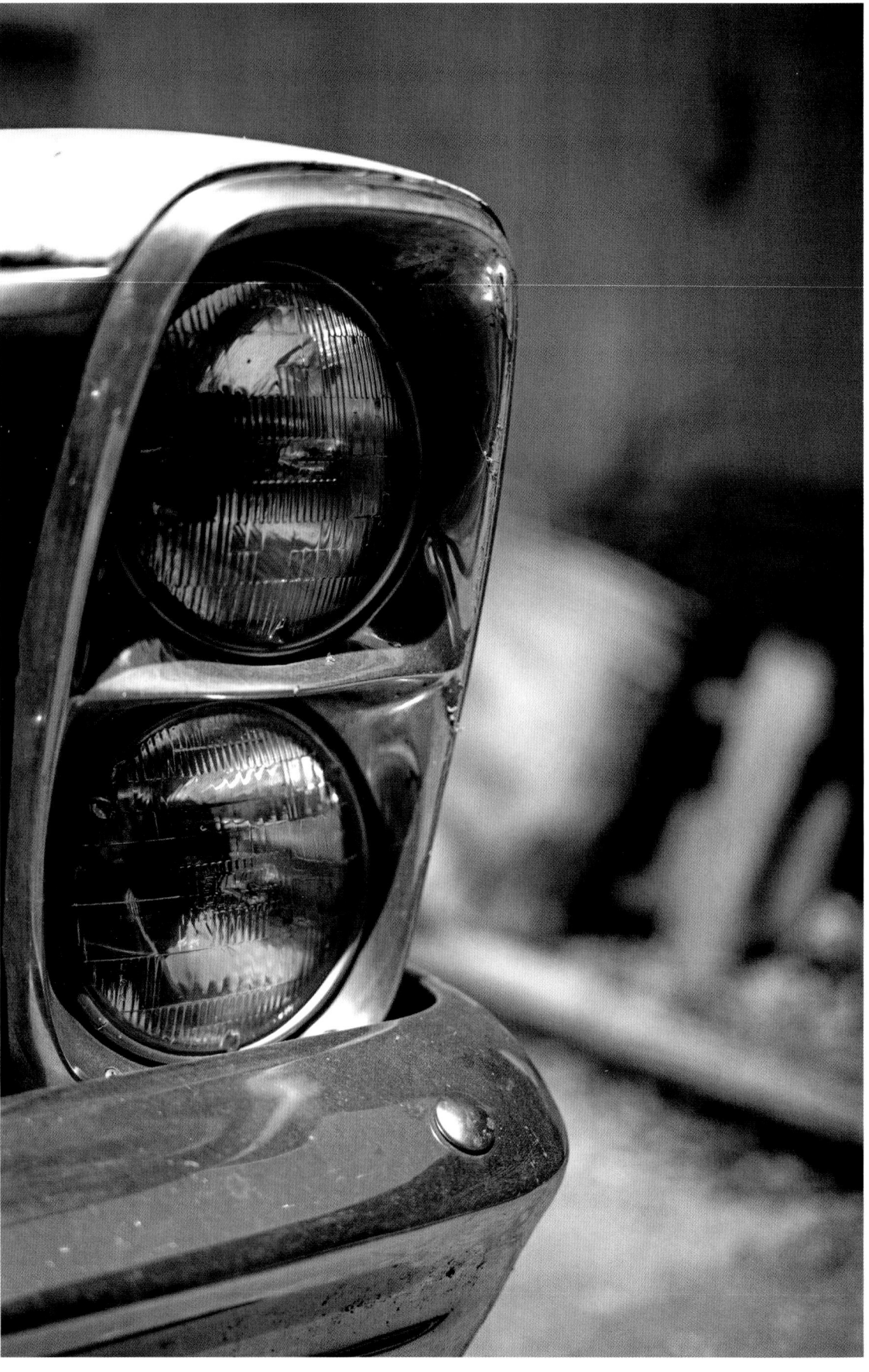

UP TO THIS CHAPTER, this book has been about the fundamentals for visual communication in photography. These concepts and ideas give us the tools and structure to understand the visual components of a picture. We use these concepts as a structure for what we are trying to do creatively. We might follow these structures or break away from them completely, as long as it supports the intent of what we want to say as photographers.

My objective here has been to teach you my thoughts, philosophy, and approach to photography. These concepts, ideas, and devices are all absolutely fundamental to understanding the craft. If used properly, they give you the ability to communicate in the visual language. However, if you're really serious about taking your talent as far as you possibly can, this chapter is one that cannot be skipped. It is perhaps the most difficult part of the book to write.

How do you develop your own visual voice?

What makes this difficult is that the originality is something that can't be taught. If you could follow a formula, then it wouldn't really be original. I can't say, Follow these steps and you'll find a unique voice in photography. I can't tell you what *your* voice even is because we are not the same person. We are all highly unique individuals. I can't tell you how to become you. I can't even tell you how to express yourself. This is a road you have to travel alone. There will be victories and there will be failures. Hopefully you will develop a vision along the way of how *you* want to work and what it takes to accomplish just that.

I once had the opportunity to hear actor Matthew McConaughey speak. He's a talented actor who started out being largely typecast. Over time he's turned into an excellent actor with an impressive range of roles. He's a fellow Texan for whom I have great respect. During the talk, McConaughey was reflecting on his work as an actor, and he said: "All art is self-expression, but not all self-expression is art. If that were true it would mean every teenage diary was on the level of Shakespeare."

This statement couldn't be truer. As artists, we start out "expressing ourselves" only to find that the work is beginner level, carries little substance, and in many cases is a metaphor for "our teenage diaries." It's the natural law of order. Being an artist requires a long journey of dedication, study, and practice.

Any art form has trends and styles that come and go. I've seen it happen many times. A good photographer gets hot for about five minutes while something is popular, and then they vanish as if they were never there. I've also seen artists get so good at looking, creating, or sounding like someone else that they become sort of a "cover band" of the person they're copying. It's beyond rare to see someone become respected in their field for imitating someone else.

My father is an artist. He currently works as a painter but spent the years of my childhood and youth working as a very successful commercial illustrator. Sadly, illustration is an art form and business that has shrunk today to almost nothing. My dad was there during its heyday, from the 1960s to the 1990s.

Now my father is my hero. He's absolutely incredible. He's my mentor and best friend. I am extremely fortunate to have grown up in an artistic household and observe one of the most successful and artistically thoughtful individuals in his profession. People will say to me, "It must have been great growing up in a house that encouraged art." I have to say it's not that simple. My parents definitely encouraged visual art and music, but they also knew the difficulties of having a career as an artist. They knew firsthand; my mother is an interior designer and my sister is a graphic designer.

My parents talk openly about art. They have very strong opinions about what is good and what is mediocre. Many of my parents' friends were also creatives in various disciplines—I was exposed to a lot of very talented people growing up. I had no idea one day this would be so valuable, but today it's one thing I am very thankful for.

My father spent nearly forty years working in illustration, until one day he decided he wanted to shift careers. The illustration business was changing, and my dad had always wanted to paint his own compositions and transition into the gallery world. At the time it seemed like a natural move that made a lot of sense. I didn't really realize the complexity of changing one's career after so many years. The process involved reinventing his style and artistic vision. Looking back, that's an impressive tightrope to balance on with no net, to say the least.

During the course of writing this book, I've bounced a lot of my ideas off my dad. I told him about wanting to include this chapter, and he got very interested. We had a long talk about pursuing art and the idea of being the best you could possibly be. You begin by learning the fundamentals. You practice. You create work. You experiment. You make mistakes and you learn from them. Talent mixed with ambition and determination will make you a very capable artist or photographer. But the really great artists and photographers have that

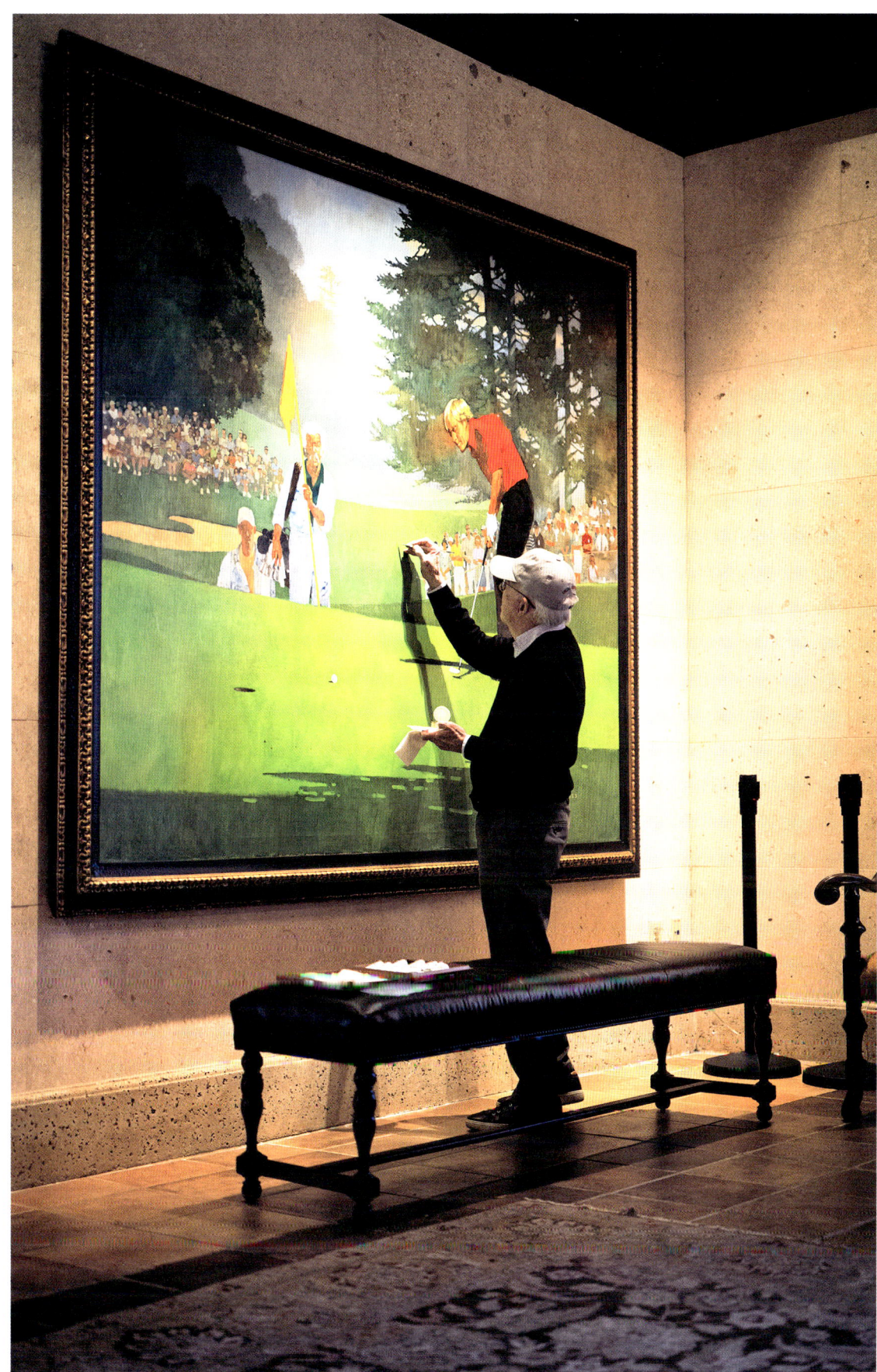

visual voice. They go above and beyond what everyone else is doing and produce work that is truly special and unique.

In any art form, there are trends. There are things that become popular and the world tends to chase them. We call this the herd mentality. There are trends that become popular in contemporary art, and this is what patrons and collectors more or less expect. In commercial art, there are trends that clients and ad agencies want to see. The entertainment industry is like this, too, with both film and music. We see similarities in social media. I see it all the time in the YouTube world.

So there is what seems like an opportunity in this cultural tendency. If you deliver what's in the current style or trend, it's only logical that your chances of success improve. And that's true to a degree. You probably will have some success. If you're okay with the herd mentality and just being "part of the crowd," then this is the path to take. You won't be considered a leader; you won't have the respect of being original. Your visual identity is defined by the herd.

What is originality?

Creating work that is original is inherently challenging because you're not deriving it from anything. In fact, you're intentionally creating a direction in which nobody else is heading. And simply having an original idea doesn't guarantee that it will gain attention.

Originality is more than finding something nobody else is doing. You need an understanding of what has come before you and what is going on now, and you have to take that in a new direction. It has to be good, and you also have to believe it's good.

As my father and I continued our discussion, I brought up his friend and colleague Mark English. Mark was another top illustrator working at the same time as my dad. There's an interview with Mark where he talks about moving away from New York City early in his career and completely changing his style. Both of these ideas would have been deemed career suicide back in those days. But the brilliant thing is that it worked for Mark. He evolved as an illustrator and his career went in an exciting, new direction.

Mark actually did this three or four times. It's what kept him relevant and attributed to a huge amount of his success as an artist. He later moved into doing abstract gallery work, which freaked out the gallery dealers—they couldn't sell it because it looked so different! But eventually that work even found its path.

My dad said to me, "You have a choice. You can find something unique that's really good and take the risk, or you can be like the thousands of other artists that all look alike that nobody remembers." He's right.

Ralph Gibson in many ways has been a big influence on me. I had the opportunity to study with him at one point and it turned into a friendship that we carry forward today. I've known Ralph's work for years and have always been inspired by his command of the image, his approach to book layouts, his suggestion of the abstract, and the intelligence that he displays through observations of the world.

Ralph is very conscious of his own work. Every picture has intelligence, intention, and thought behind it. I've never met anyone so aware of what they do and possessing the ability to communicate well about how they do it. I moderated a conversation with Ralph after he was awarded the Leica Hall of Fame award in Wetzlar, Germany. I've interviewed him a number of times on my channel.

But what I will do is give you a few observations I've made. First of all, Ralph works harder than anyone I've ever known. I know him pretty well, and I can tell you that he's never been handed anything on a plate. It's the exact opposite. He's fought tooth and nail for every single opportunity that he's had. His entire career happened because he willed it so. And he's delivered on every one of those opportunities. Ralph Gibson literally created Ralph Gibson.

Ralph is also a consummate champion of photography. He understands the history inside out. His first industry job was printing images for Dorothea Lange. He knew many of the great names of the 1960s and 1970s personally. He used to check in on André Kertész on a regular basis. He knew the great Henri Cartier-Bresson and assisted Robert Frank early in his career. Ralph also understands art outside of photography. He reads, studies, and is constantly learning and thinking.

I've said before that photography will reward you with what you are willing to put into it. Ralph is living proof of this. He's worked extremely hard.

Ralph is also a dedicated student of music. This is another thing we have in common and discuss often. Having a second craft brings new perspective and ideas into your primary craft.

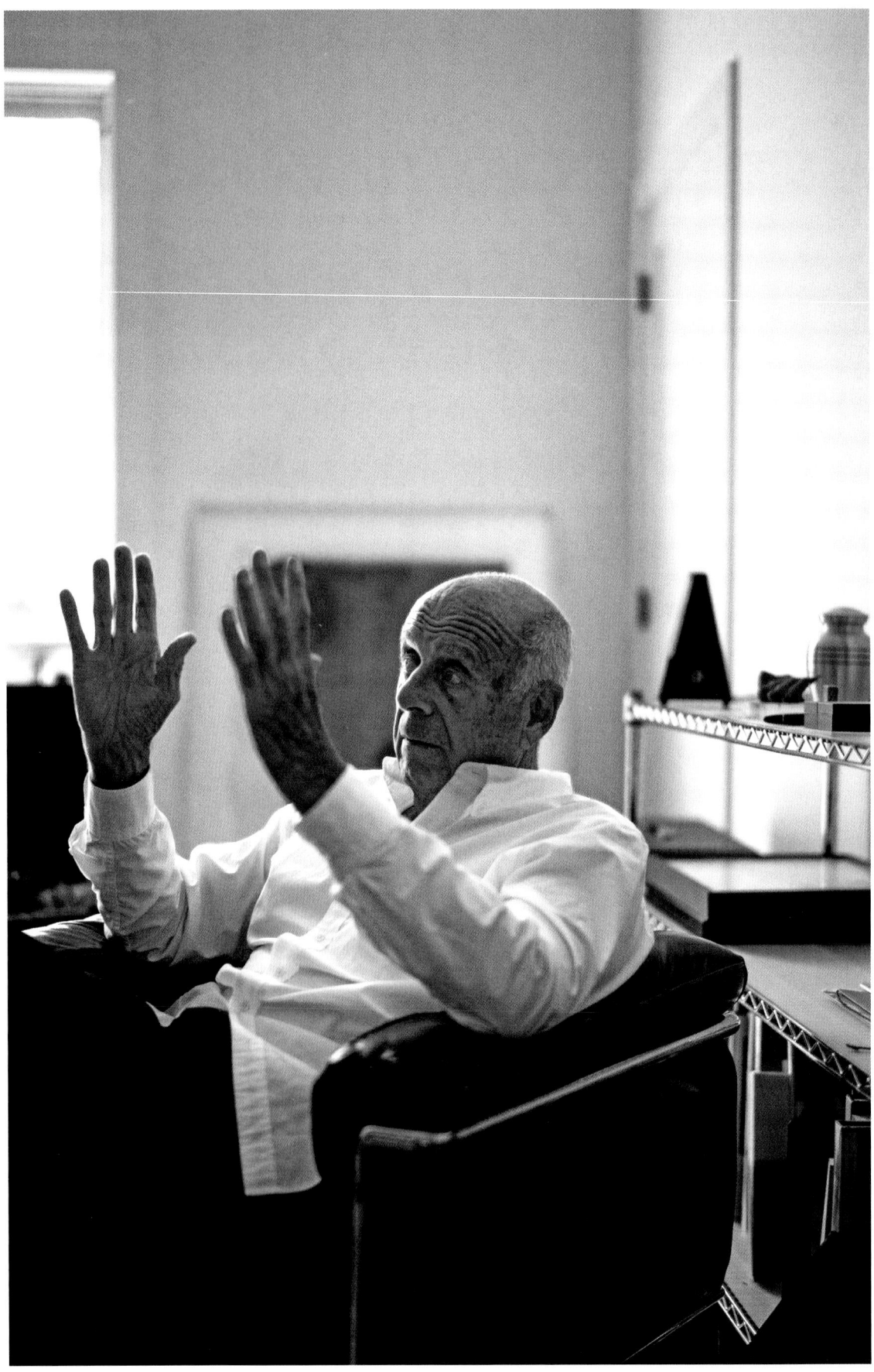

And my final observation—Ralph fully understands the proximity effect. This means, if you want to be successful, you need to be around people who are doing it. Ralph moved to New York in the early 1960s and knew everyone. He lived in the Chelsea Hotel, knew all the major photographers, and was even recommended to Magnum by Bruce Davidson. This is the proximity effect. Being around great photographers is an important part of one's own development in any art form. Of course this only works if you're also putting in the time, work, and dedication to your craft, but it is something I've actually seen really talented photographers skip over.

It's also important to understand that in the modern world, this proximity isn't necessarily New York City. The world has changed a lot since the 1960s and, really, today you can be anywhere and still associate with your colleagues all over the world. I talk to Ralph about once a week—I'm in Texas and he's in Long Island. It doesn't matter. Make connections with the people you aspire to be on level with.

My last piece of advice in your journey as an artist is, don't forget to enjoy the process. Learning is a beautiful gift. So is being able to use a camera and create images that express your vision of the world. Remember to savor that along the way. The journey is full of highs and lows, but it all adds up to something beautiful.

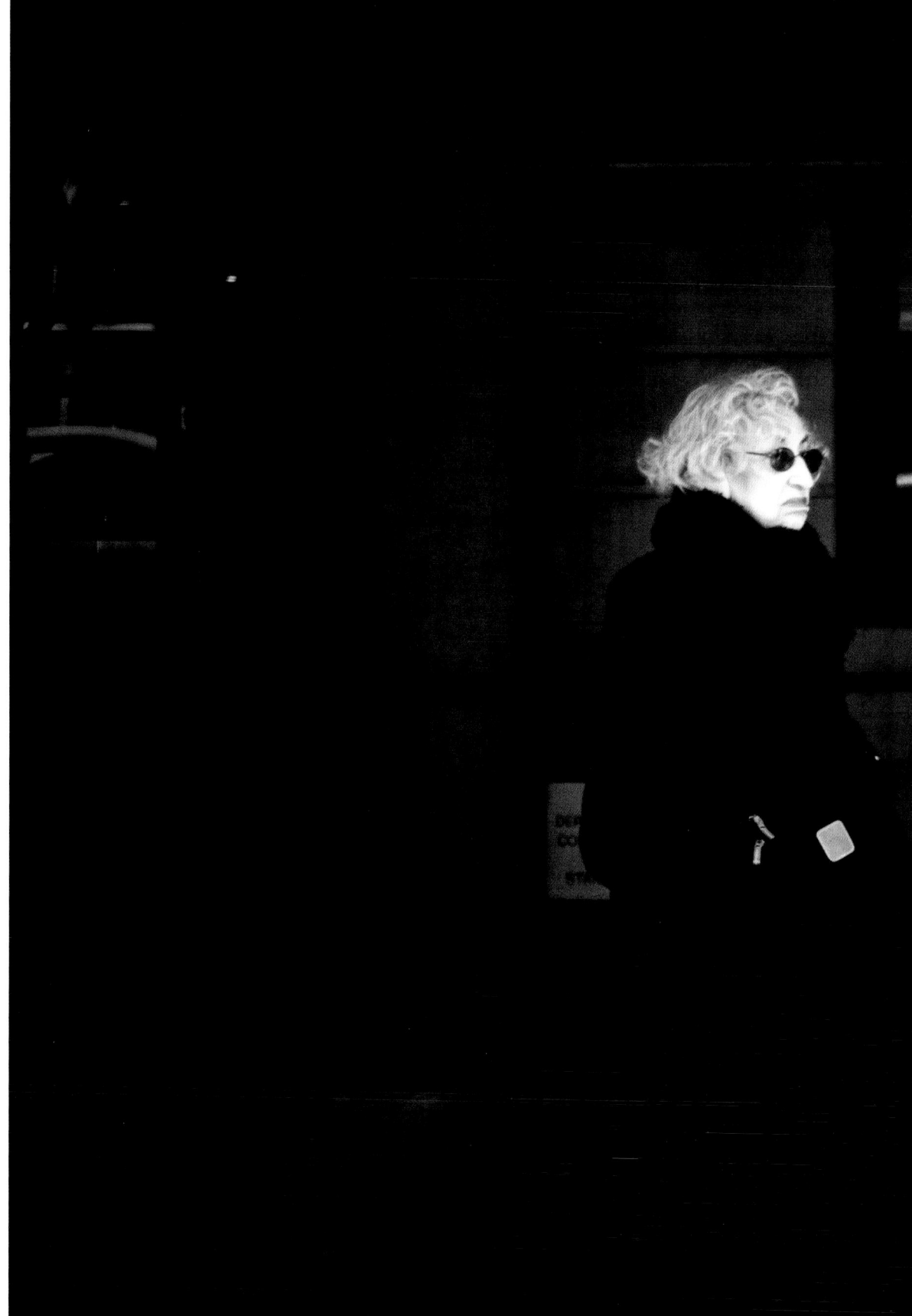

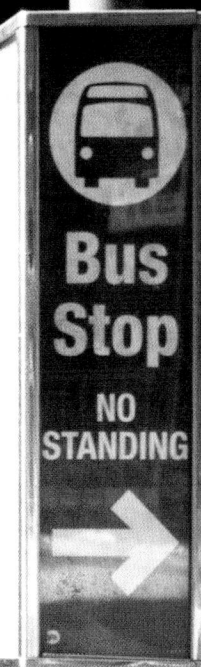

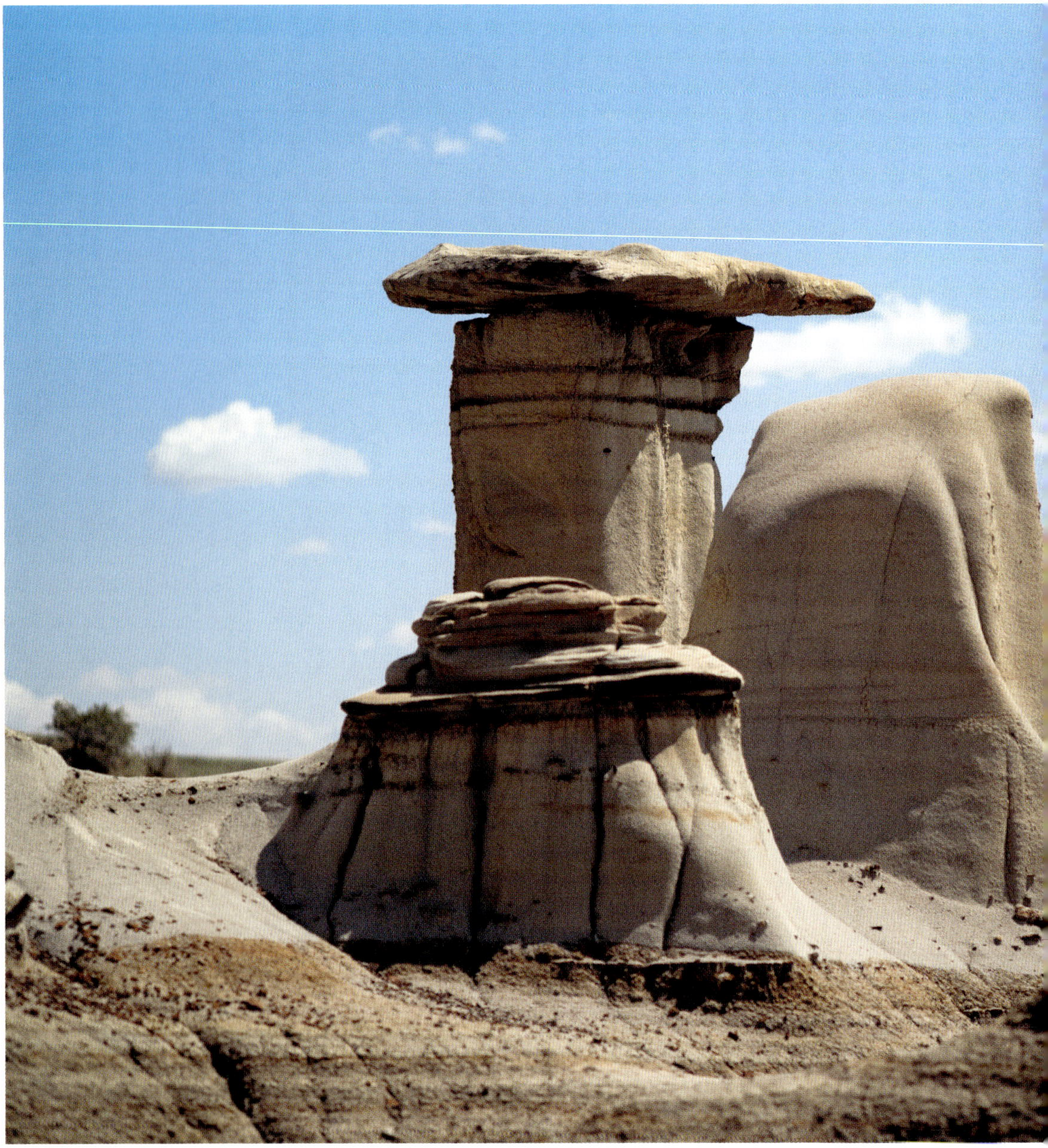

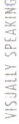

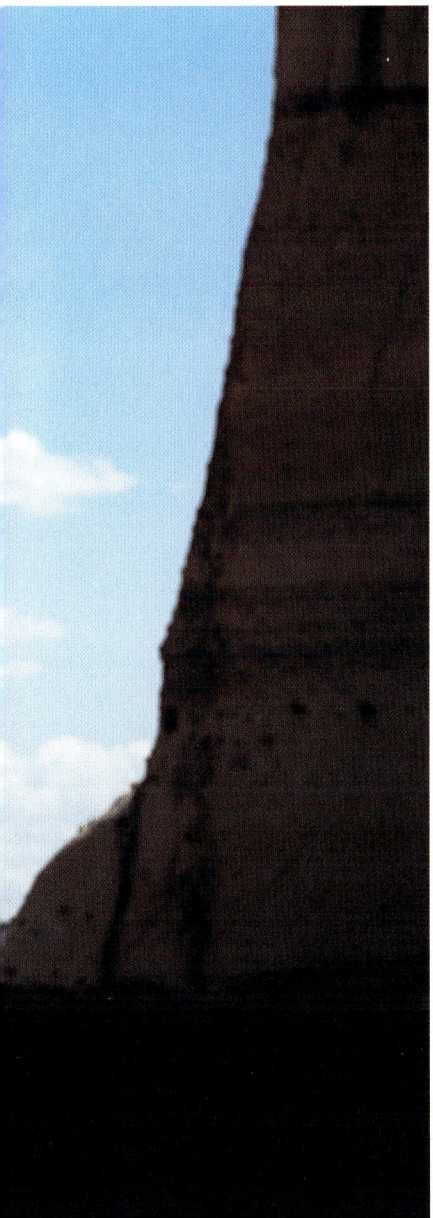

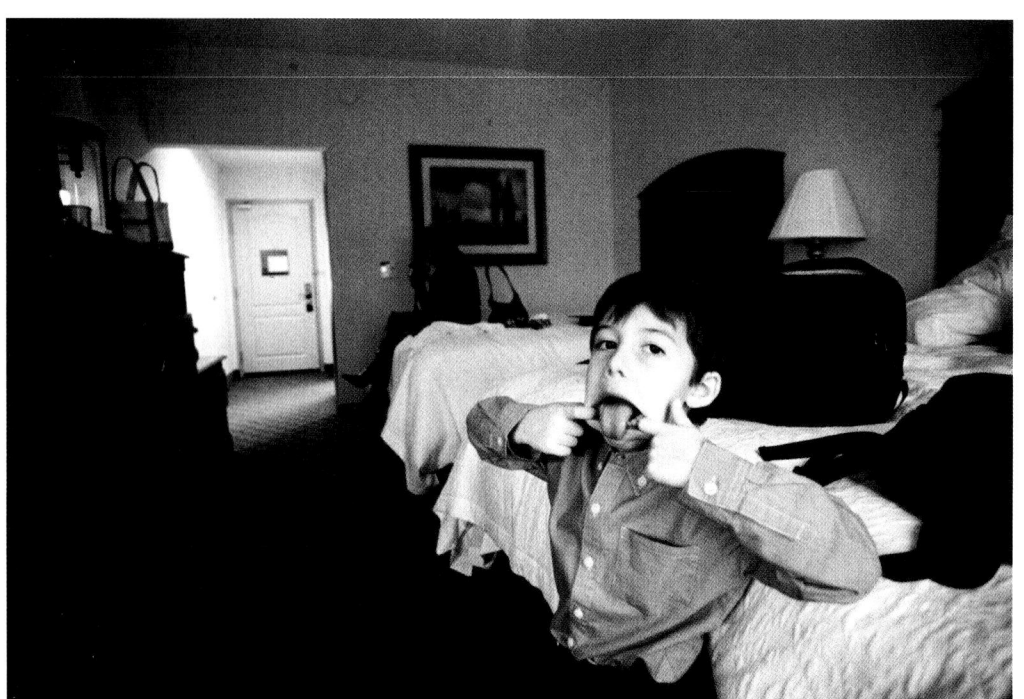

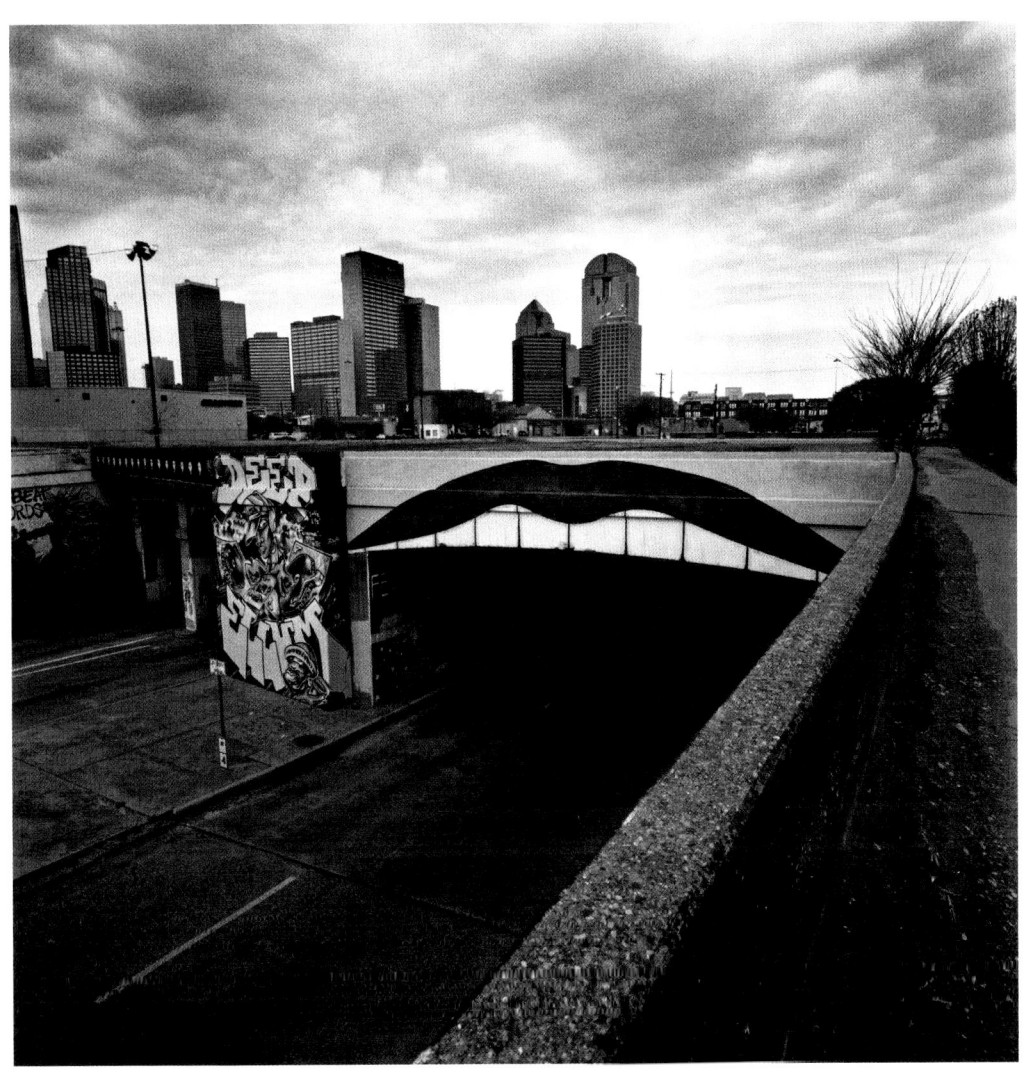

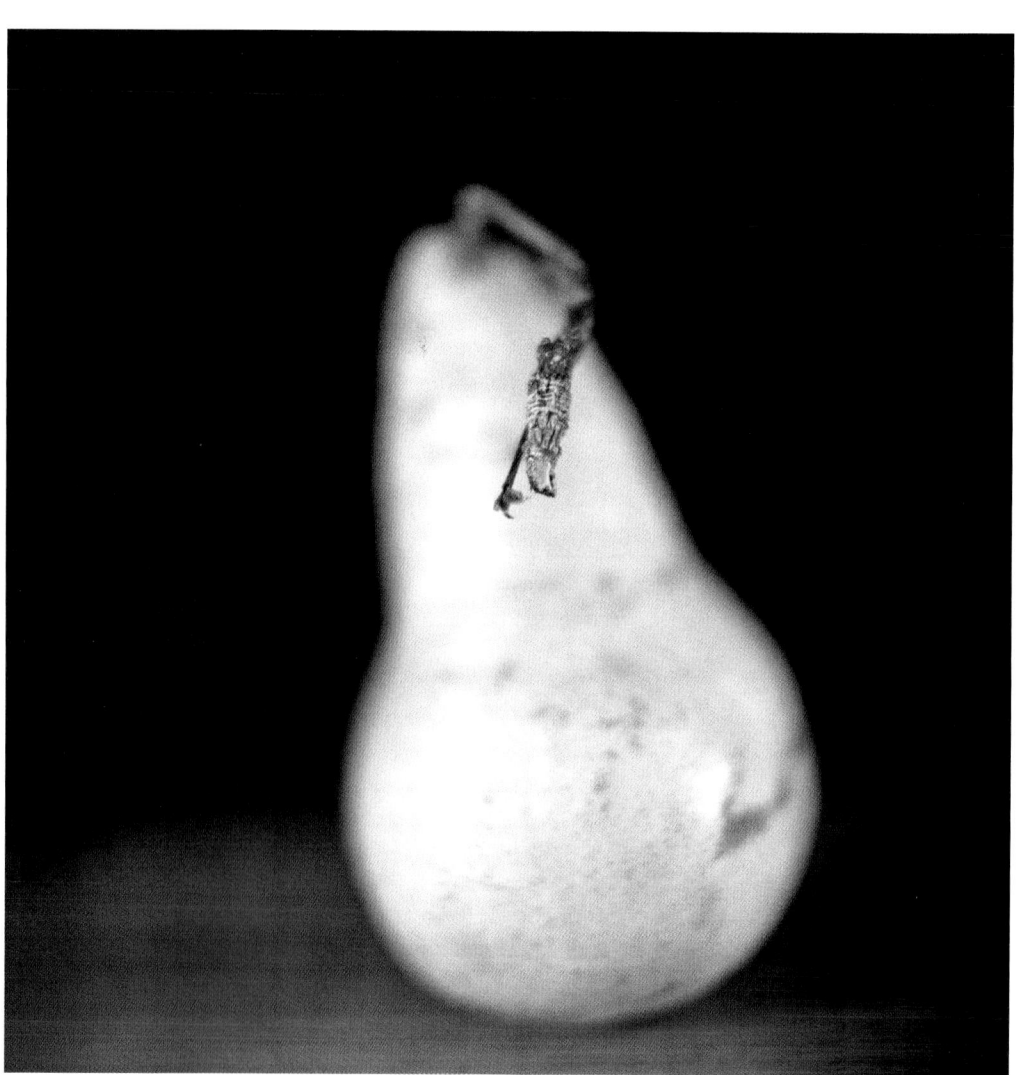

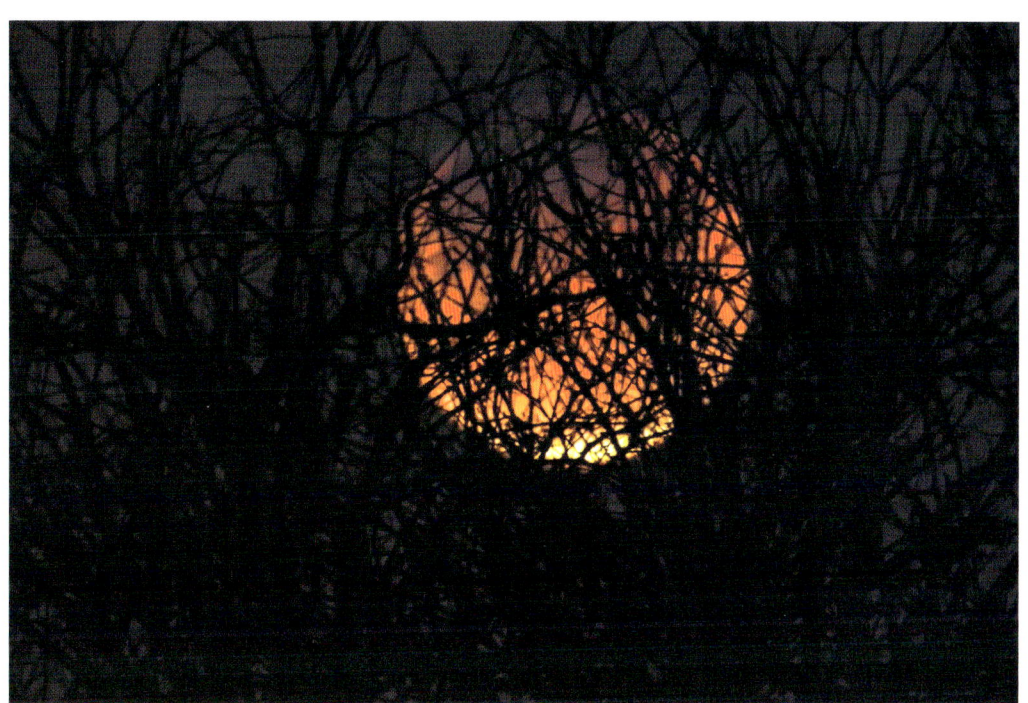

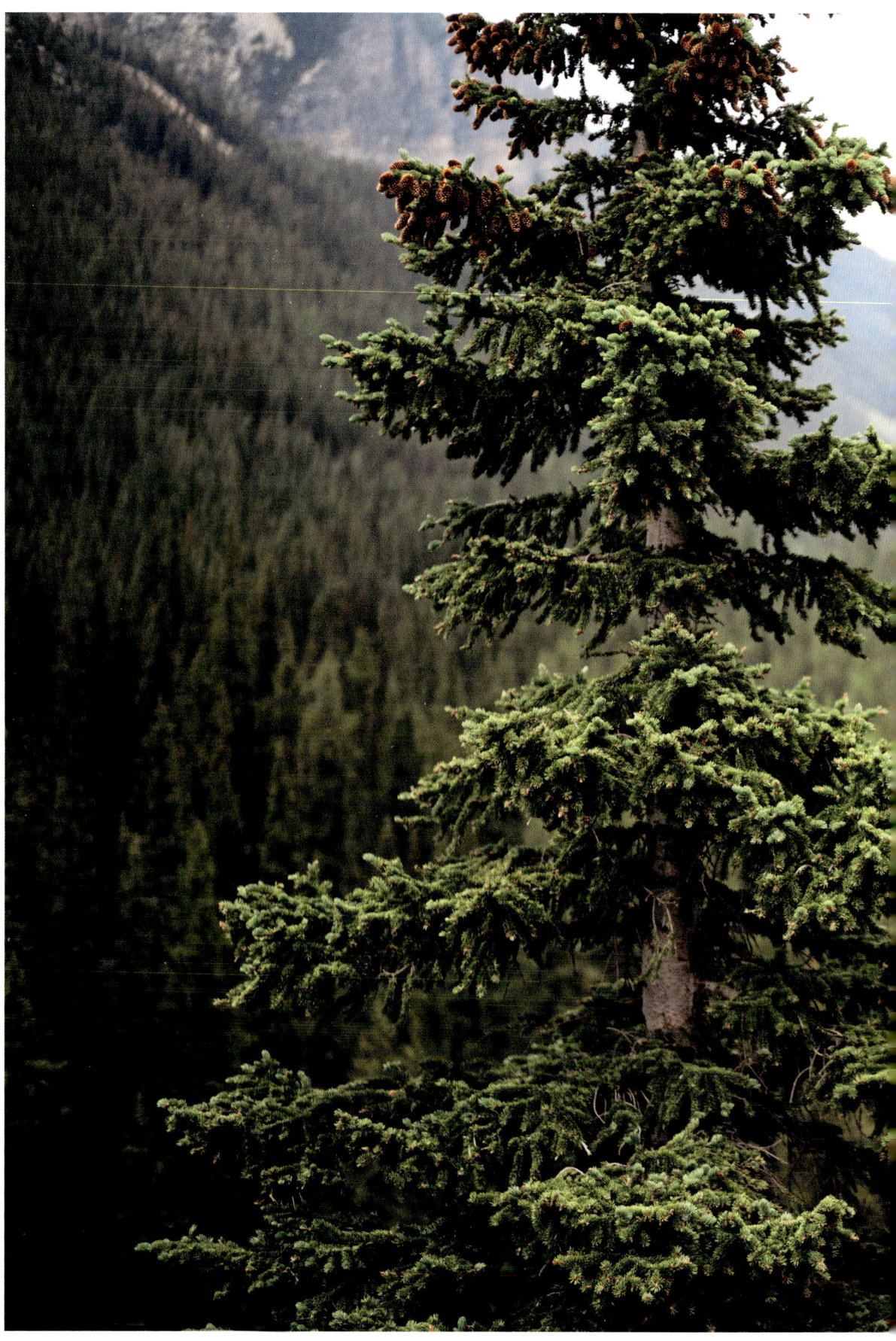

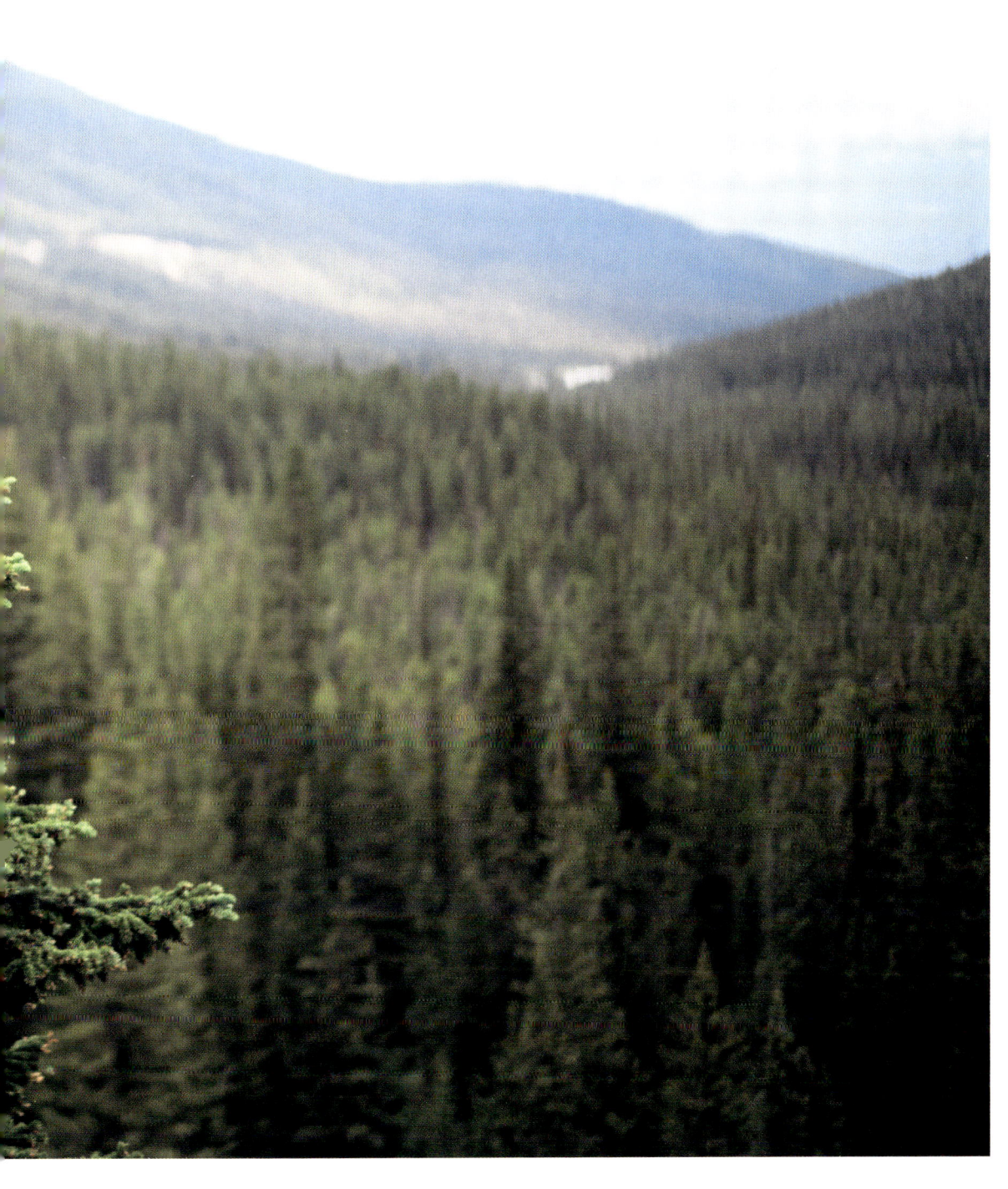

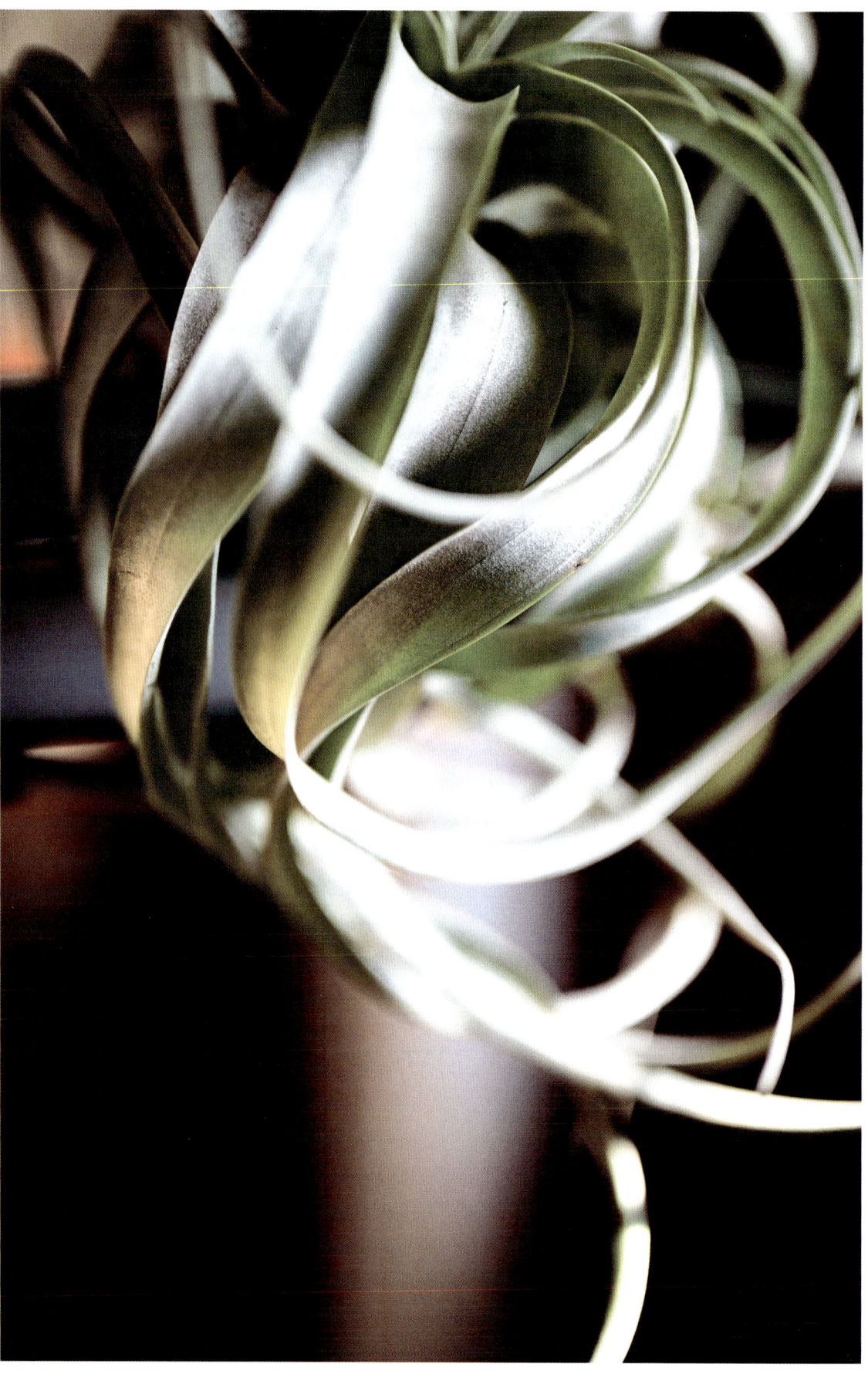

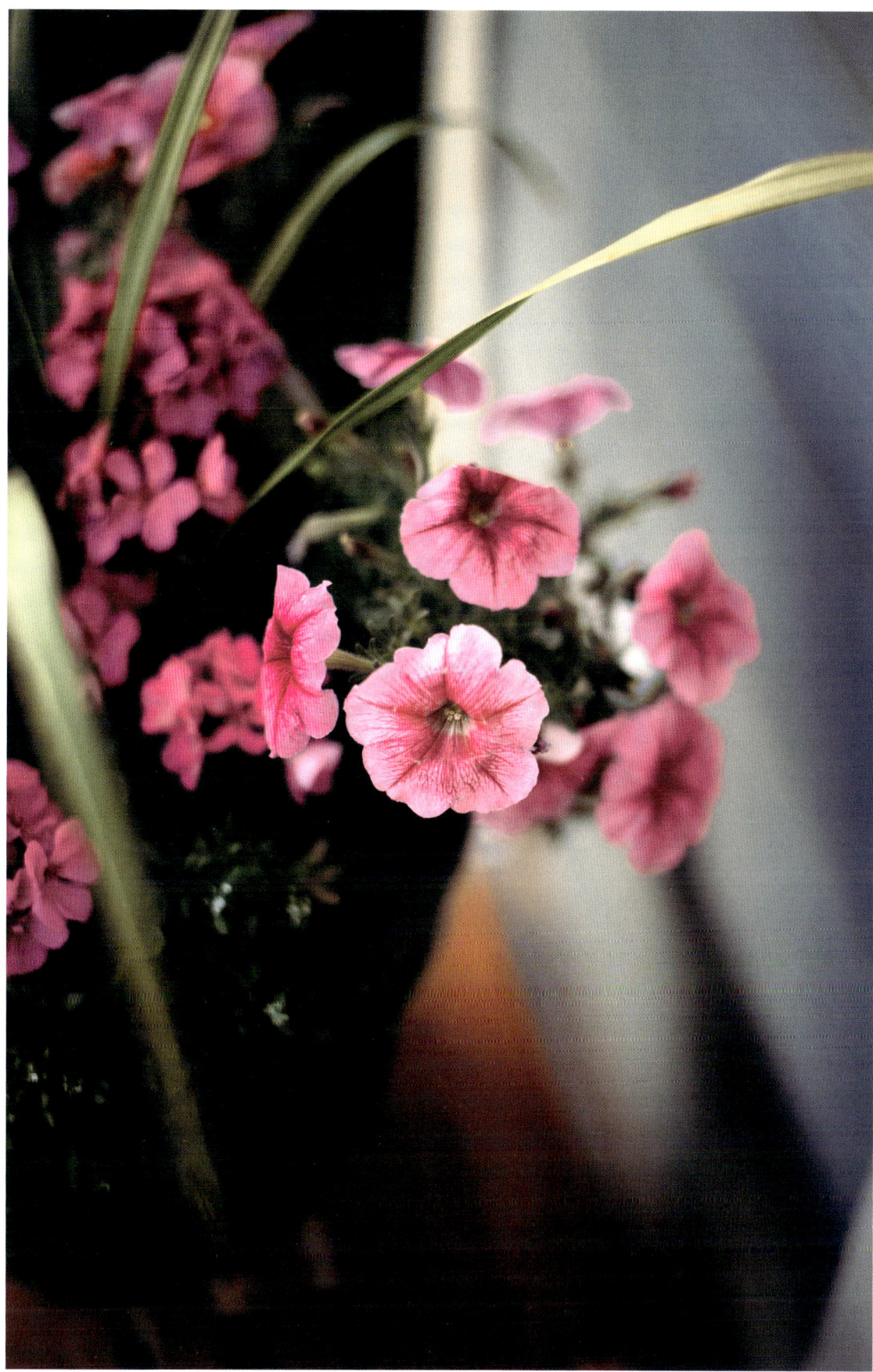

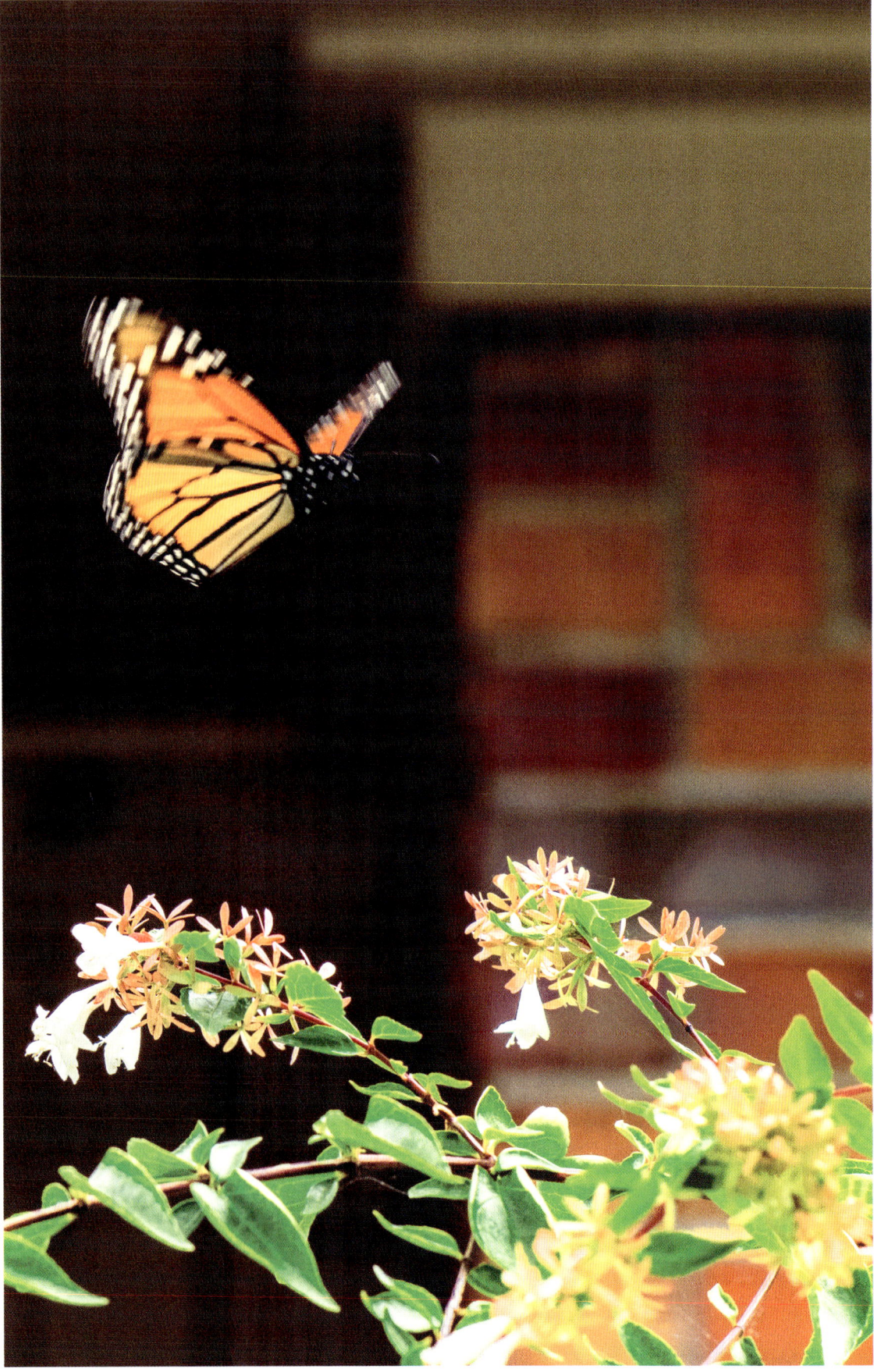

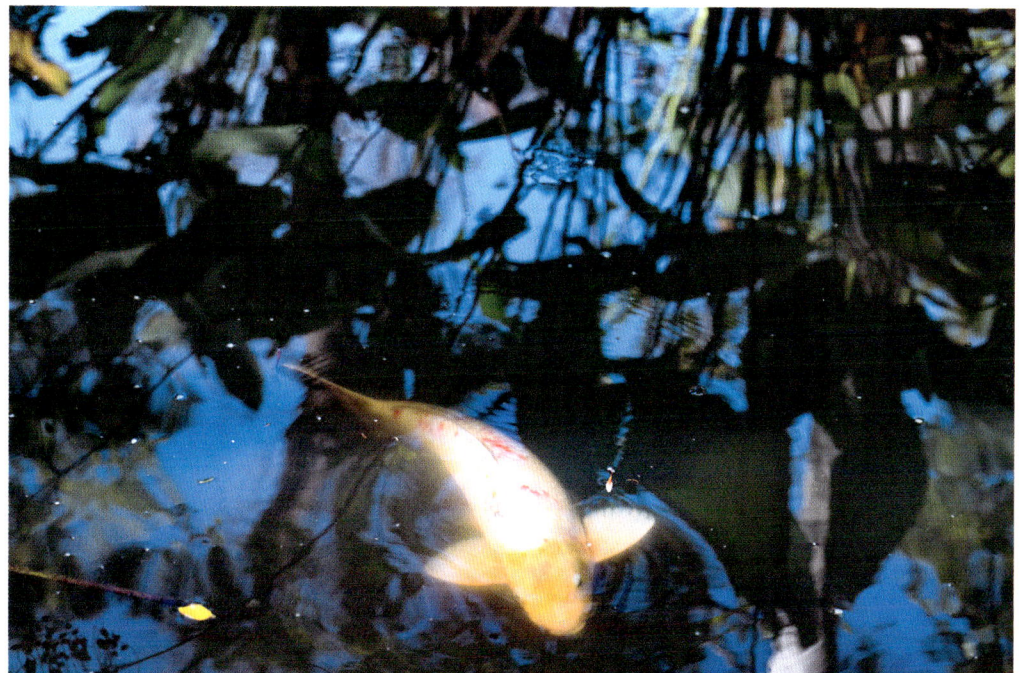

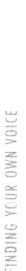

CHAPTER 20

COMMITMENT TO
THE PRACTICE

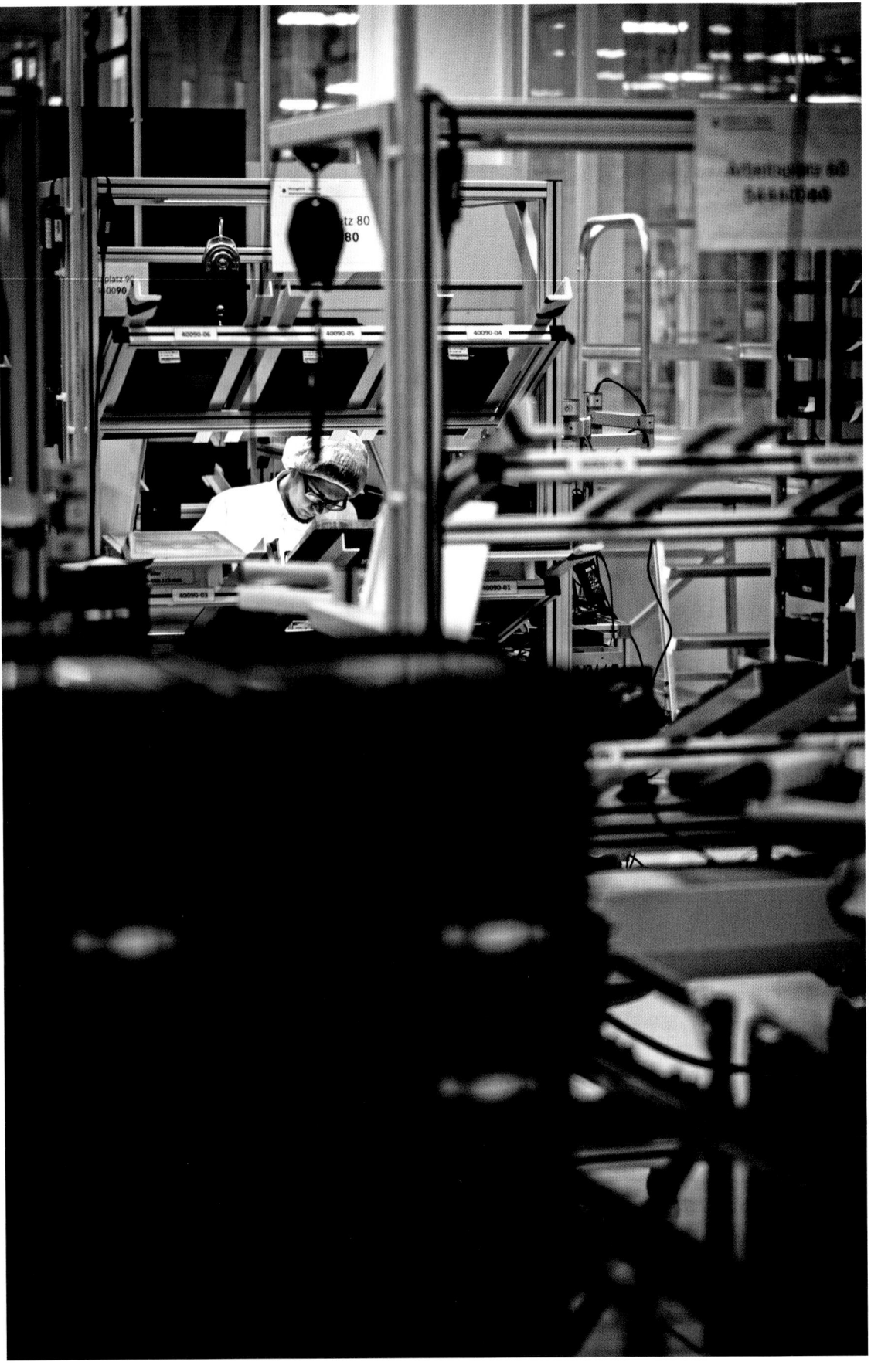

YES, THIS BOOK CONTAINS A LOT of information. I want to stress that it's important to remember you are on a photographic journey that requires dedication, commitment, and practice. Everyone's journey is different, just as everyone's personal style is different.

Those of you who speak multiple languages might agree that the best way to learn to speak a new language is a concept called "full immersion." In other words, being forced to hear and speak only the language you're trying to learn will yield much faster results than books, audio, or videos. This is because you're forcing yourself into practical use and not trying to find ways to remember small details.

The visual language of photography is no different. It comes in two parts. First, you want to be around other creatives and develop friendships. Secondly, you want to be photographing all the time. The camera doesn't ever go back on a shelf; it stays with you at all times.

I was lucky enough to grow up in an artistic family, so I was always around family and friends who understood creativity. They both supported and nourished it. But when I eventually grew up and became self-dependent in my professional life after college, I found myself alone creatively. I had to start somewhere, so I signed up for some local classes and later joined a professional organization that hosted monthly meetings for professionals in the visual arts. It was slow at first, and awkward, but I eventually made a few lunch plans with people. I got invited to get coffee and go to happy hour. I would invite others to have coffee or go to happy hour. Eventually I made friends that now, over twenty years later, I'm still very close to. We still go to lunch, seek creative opinions on work, or just enjoy the fact that we are on similar creative journeys.

Developing friendships with other creatives is essential. These relationships will push and inspire your own creative ambitions. They don't have to be local either. Over the years I've met people online, at conferences, and through professional connections, and none of us live in the same city. I have a small network of people who understand me as I understand them. It's very difficult to live in a vacuum.

As you're building your creative community, remember the importance of practice. You should be photographing every day—even if it's just for a few minutes or an hour you are able to set aside. The only way to get good at making photographs is to make photographs. I've found that always having a camera with me is the best way. Some days will be more prolific than others. Some days will feel too busy, but I've found that when the camera is at home on a shelf, I miss shots, I miss inspiration, and I miss opportunities. The camera lives with me. This is one of the reasons I prefer shooting a rangefinder. It was designed for that type of portability.

Always be looking and ready to shoot.

Photography is about discovery and learning how to see things. Remember, in painting you create the whole scene, but in photography you have to find it. You have to previsualize. You have to be very perceptive. In my day to day, I'm constantly looking and seeing the world as a possibility for a picture. The amazing thing about photography is that it only exists in a moment. That moment is unique and will never come along the same way again.

I remember one day, a few years ago, I was driving home from the studio. It was early February in Texas, so the days were still fairly short and the sunsets were dramatic that week. We'd had a brief snow and the skies had finally cleared.

My route home includes a long stretch of road that runs alongside train tracks. There's a small derailment point along that stretch where tank cars are left for distribution. That day, the sun was almost down, but there were stray clouds above the tank car silhouettes. The clouds were reflecting the most beautiful orange sunset from the other side of the sky and looked like nothing I'd ever seen. They were almost like mirrors. I thought maybe I should pull over and make the photograph, but there was a lot of traffic. It was also cold, I was tired . . . you know what happened here. I got lazy and thought to myself that I'd be ready the next day.

That scene has never looked the same again. I know. I've driven by it every single day since, and it continues to haunt me. I'll think about it tonight when I go home. I've pulled over many times when I thought the light was interesting. It has never been the same, not even close. I let that shot get away.

I've told this story many times to friends. In return, I usually get a similar story from them. I actually love this. The shots we miss are the ones we have to describe in great detail, and I always imagine the most elegant photograph when I hear these stories. The stories are beautiful, but the photographs don't exist. Can you imagine if Ansel Adams had been tired and lazy and decided not to photograph *Moonrise Over Hernendez*? It's his most collected and famous image!

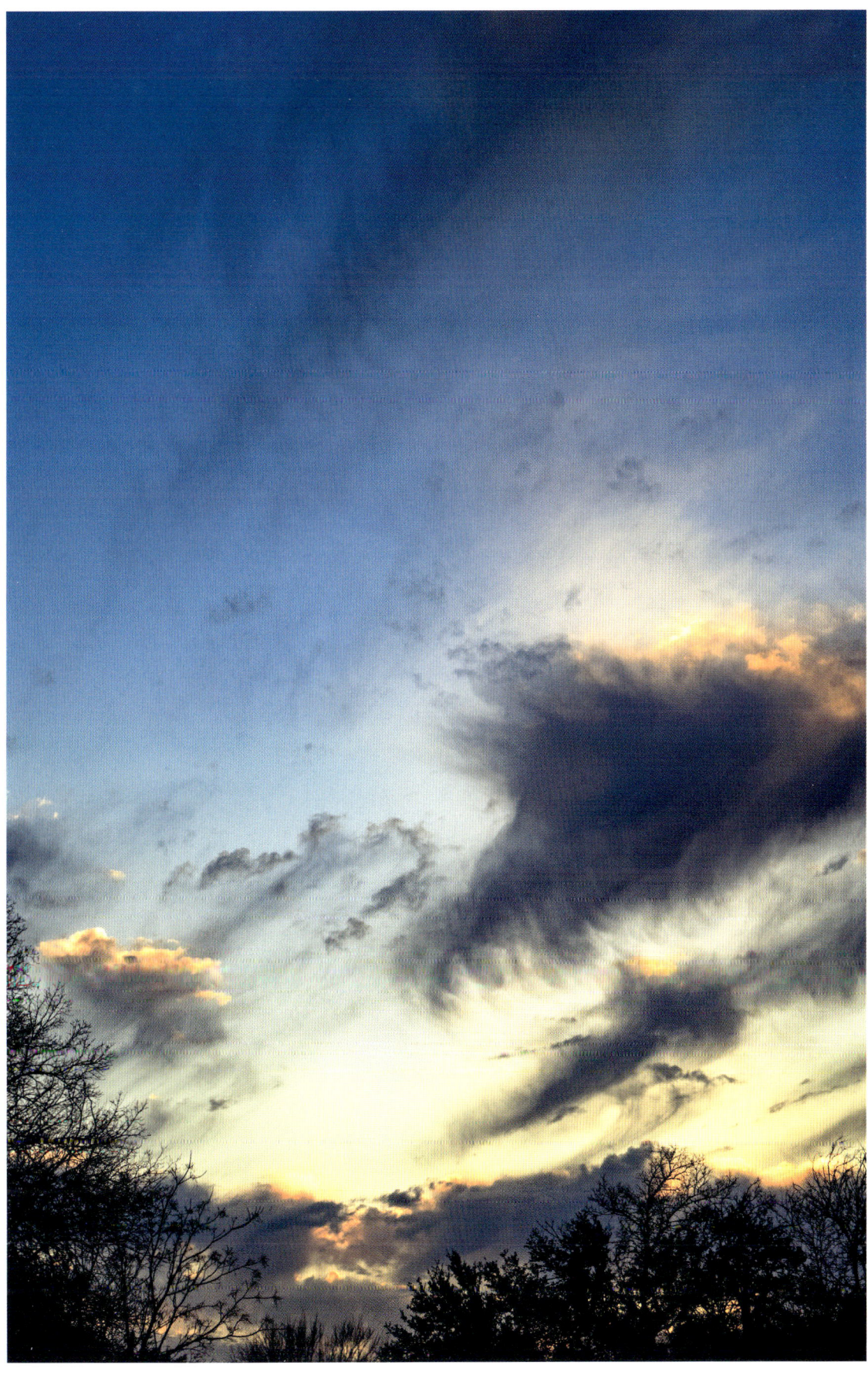

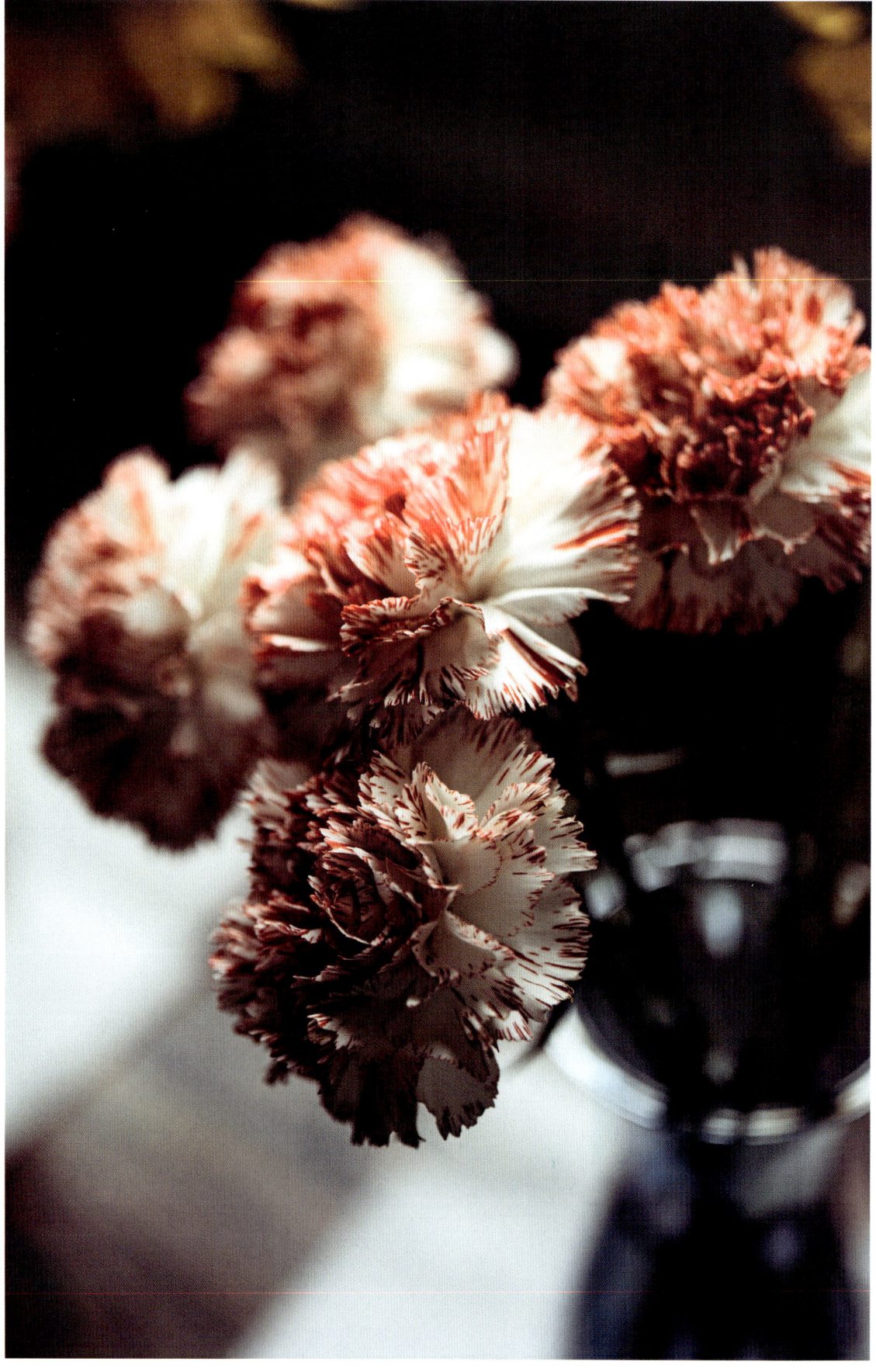

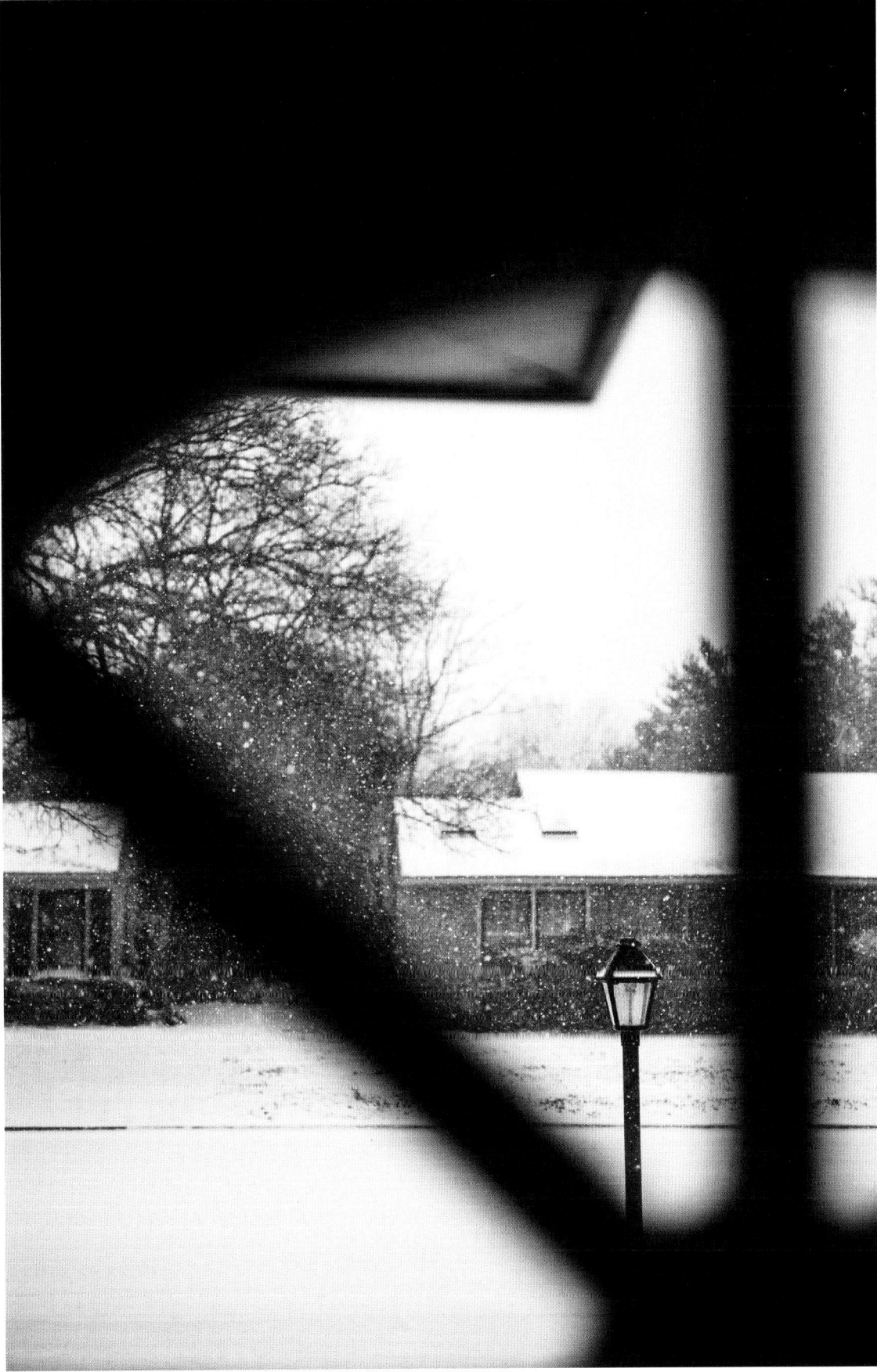

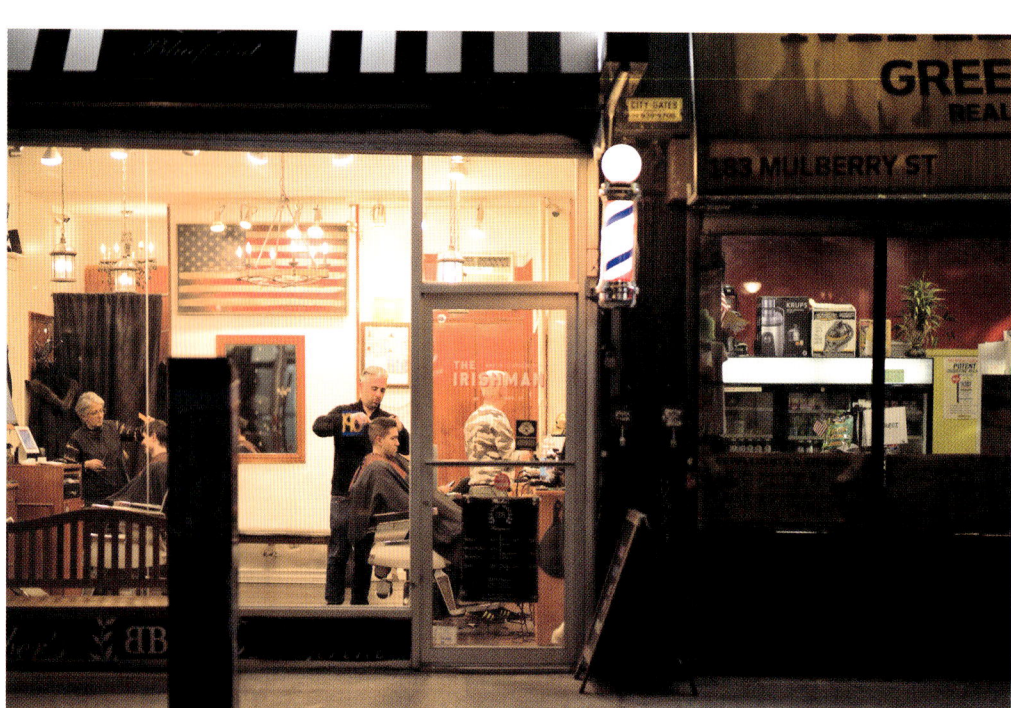

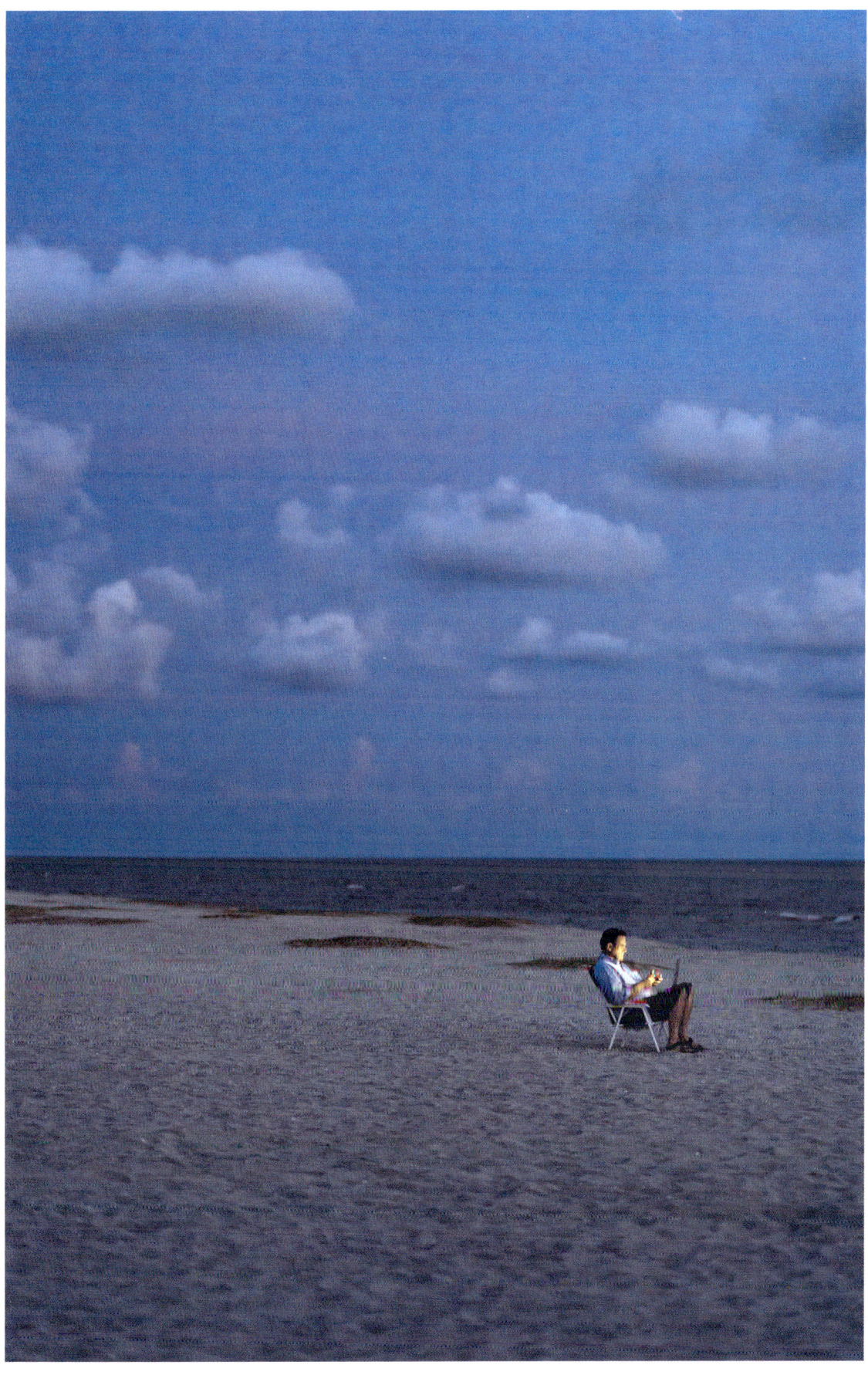

Sometimes it takes a careless mistake to learn a lesson. I'm no longer lazy with photographs. I'm looking and I'm ready to make the picture. Even if it's a miss, I must at least try.

When I was learning to play the guitar back when I was fourteen, my teachers would give me all kinds of things to practice. Scales, exercises, chord progressions, works by famous composers . . . all of the things any musician should be practicing.

For whatever reason photographers don't seem to practice in the same way that musicians do. My first mentor, Greg Booth, changed my thinking about this. He was the first photographer I knew who practiced.

This was back in the early 1980s, before digital photography and before autofocus. Greg was adamant about understanding the basic fundamentals of how his camera worked so they would be second nature. He also practiced composition through the viewfinder at all times. He used to tell me I didn't even need film in the camera—just go out in the yard and make yourself focus on something. Know where the lens is set and try to get it in the right focus position before the camera is up to your eye. Did I know where that was without looking at it? The technique of using your camera is just as important as the instrument to any musician.

This was a huge connection for me. Musicians learn the technique of their instrument. They know where the notes are without having to look. Why should photography be any different?

I still approach my camera the same way today. I am aware of where the focus ring should be. I understand if my exposure should be over or under. I understand the focal length of my lens and where I need to be to frame the composition. I know these things because I practice. I also study how other photographers approach a disciplined practice.

Henri Cartier-Bresson's text for the intro to *The Decisive Moment* offers a glimpse into the mind of a great photographer. He talks about his earliest memories of picking up a camera and how the moment he began to "use it and think about it." he became serious.

Saul Leiter spent decades and the better part of his commercial career shooting personal work on color slide film. His East Village neighborhood in New York City was the primary site for this body of work, which remained largely unknown until his association with Howard Greenberg Gallery in the 1990s.

Another approach to practice is something I came across from William Eggleston. If he was out with his camera, he didn't shoot multiple frames of the same thing. His rule was one image only. His reasoning is that multiple shots just makes things more confusing when he is editing his work. So he forces himself to think, raise the camera, make the image, and then move on to something else. I've always loved that philosophy. Eggleston is a master of visual language.

Every great photographer practices. Amateur photographers try to get great photographs. Great photographers are ready for them.

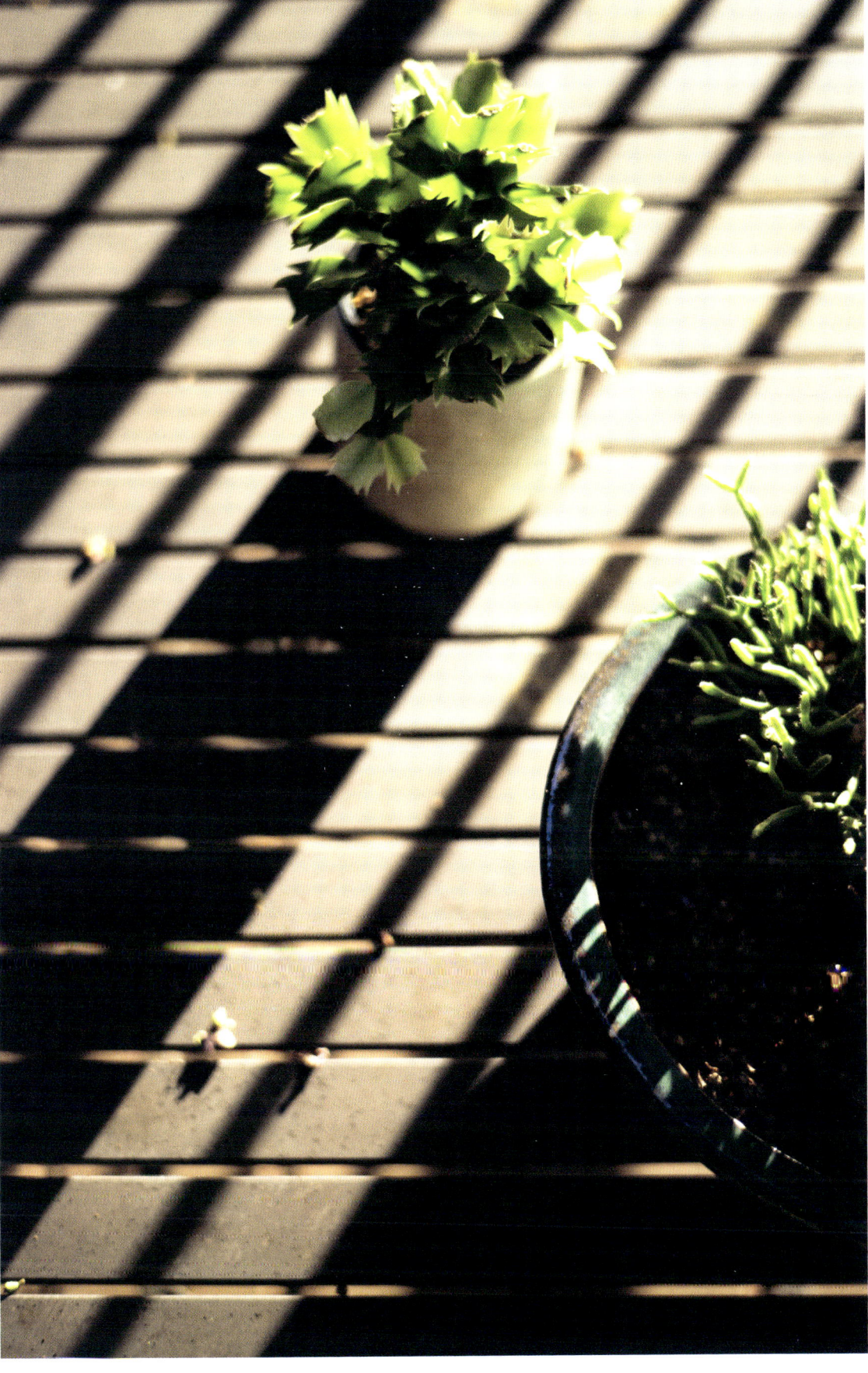

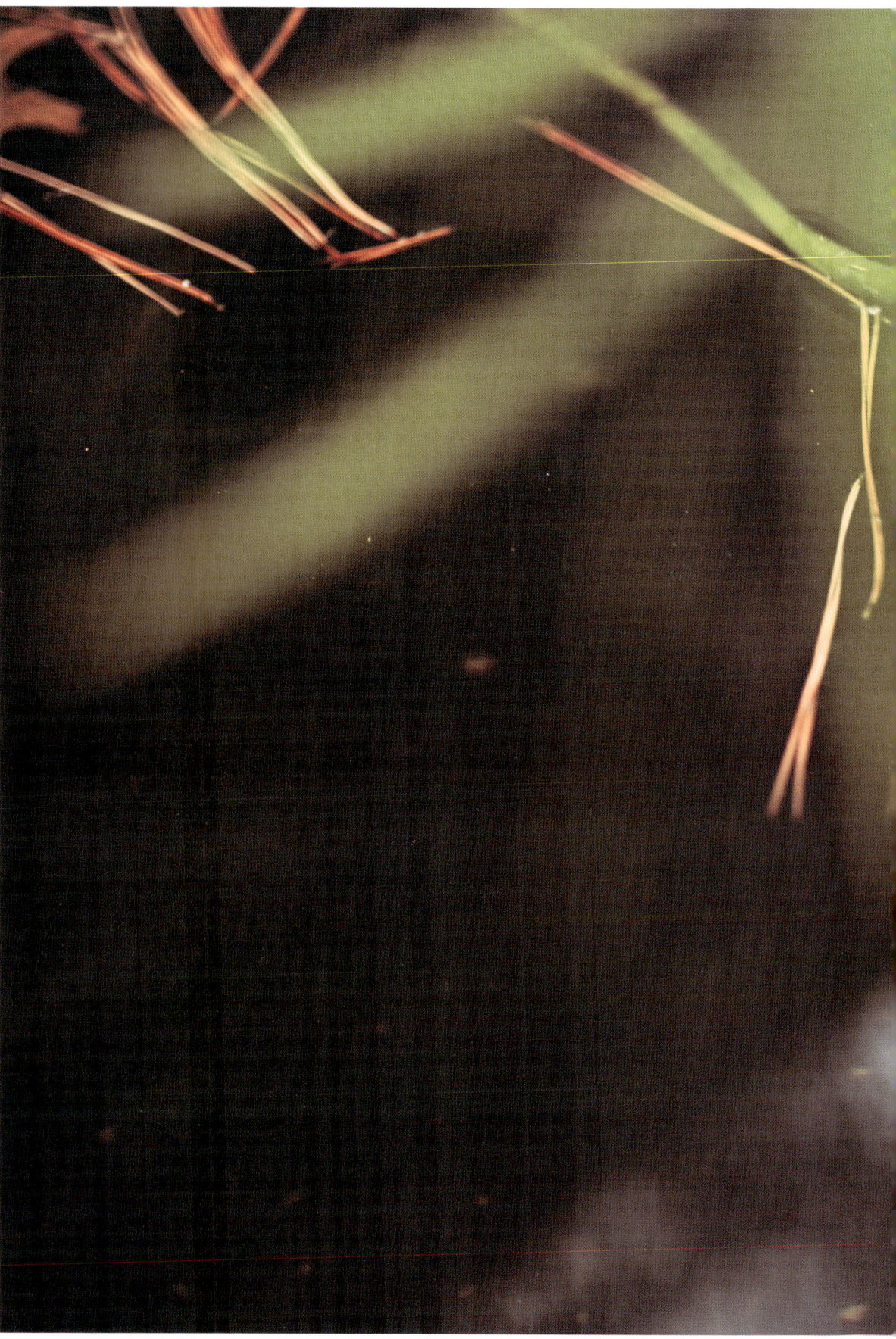

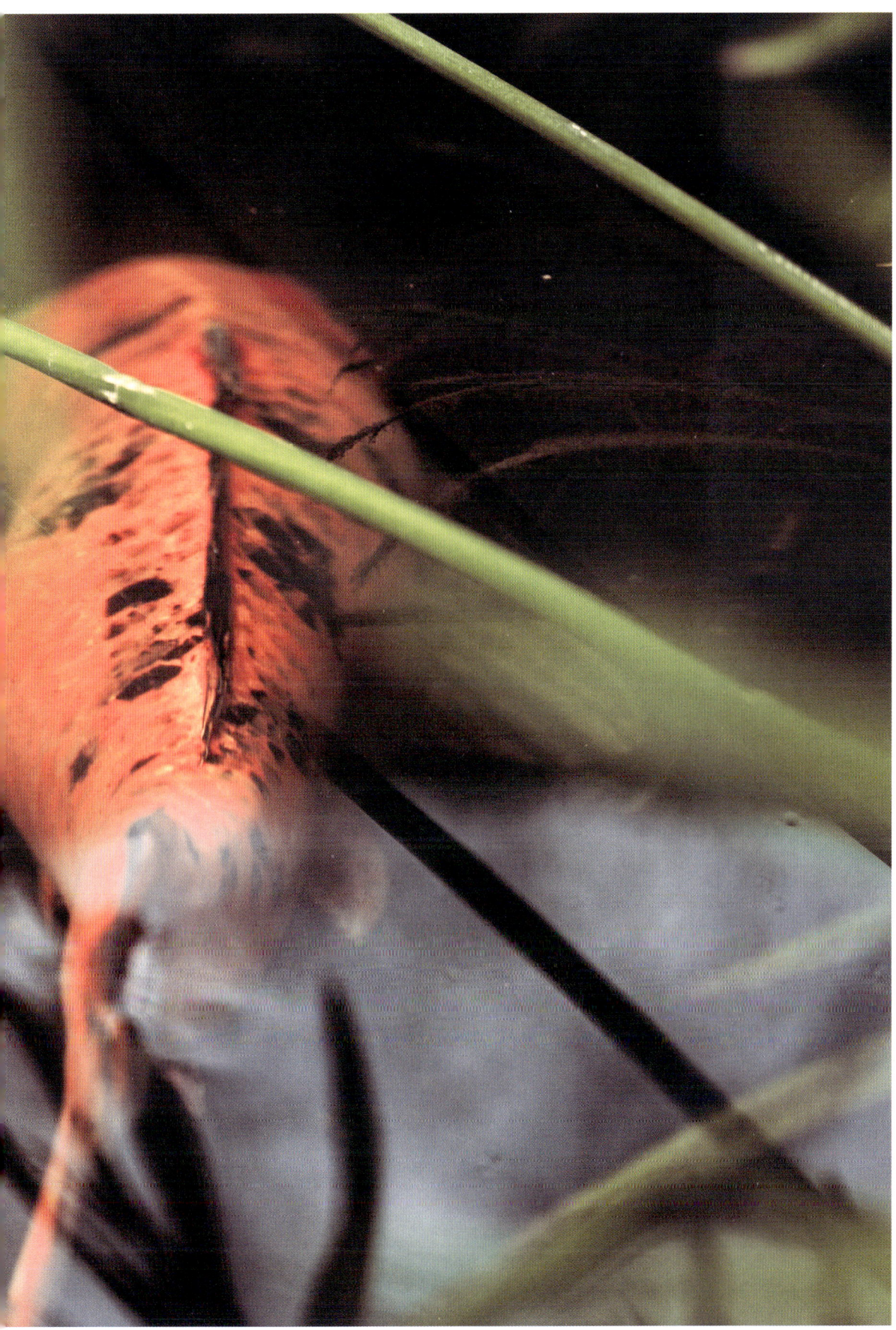

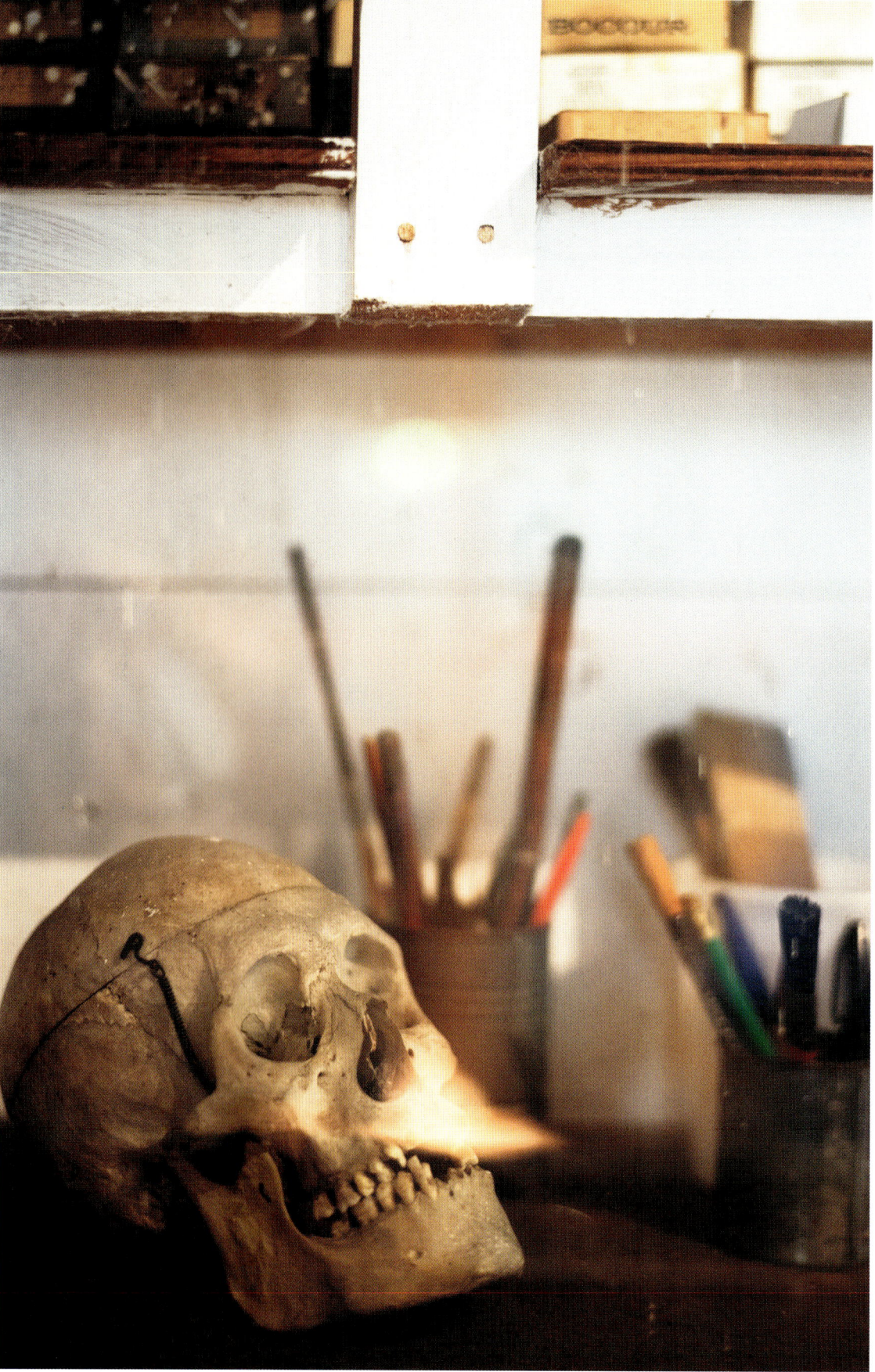

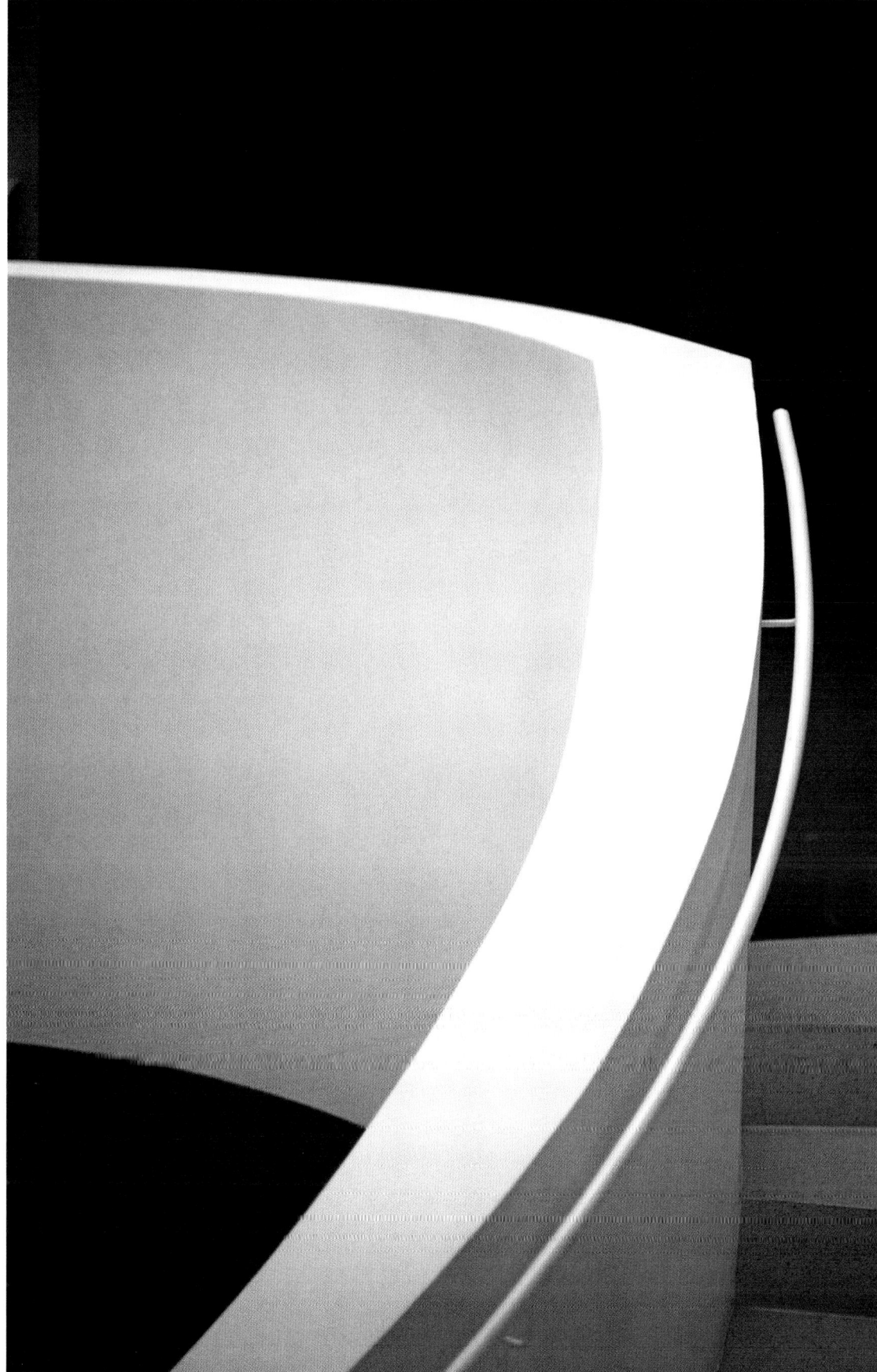

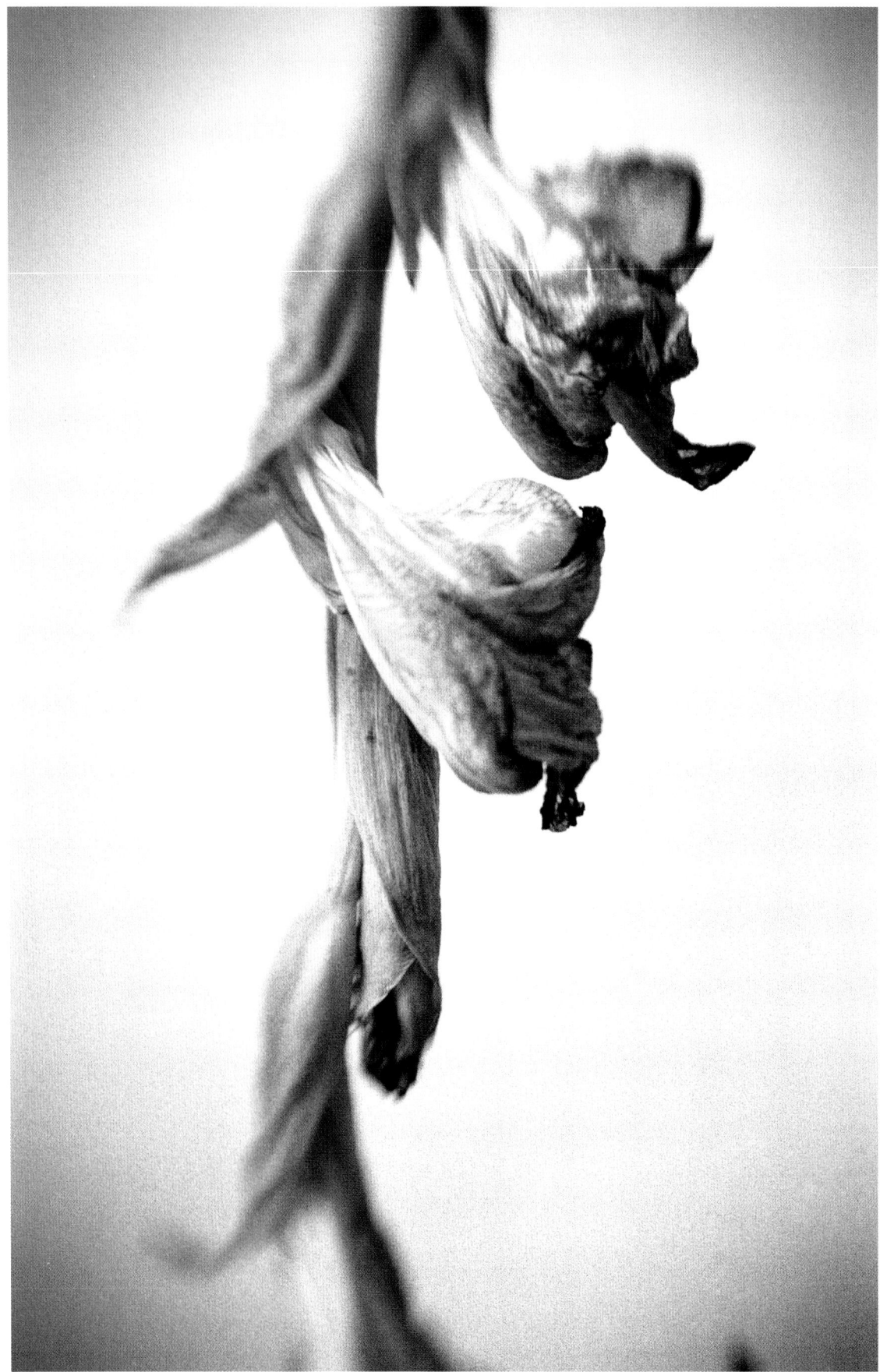

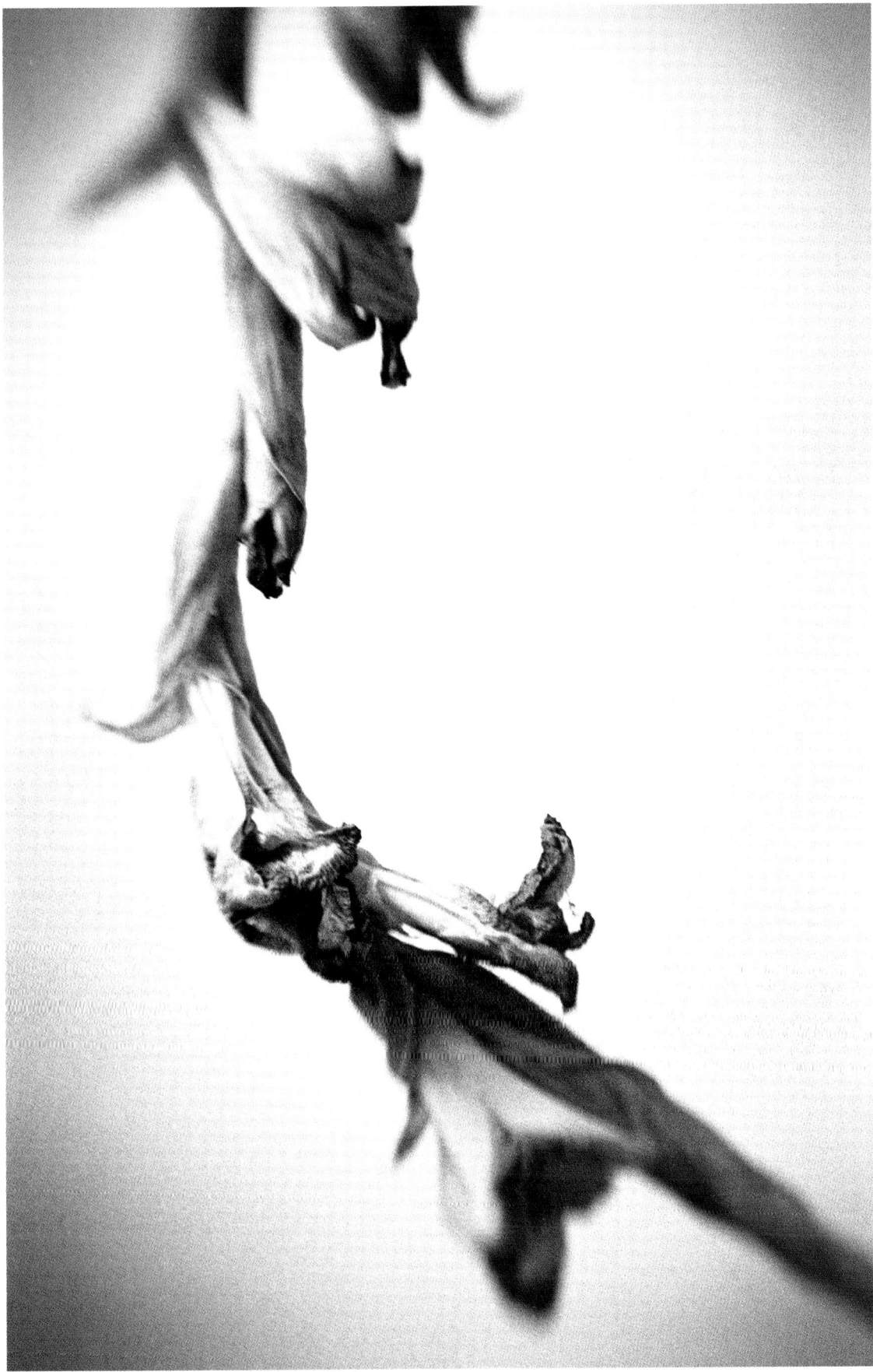

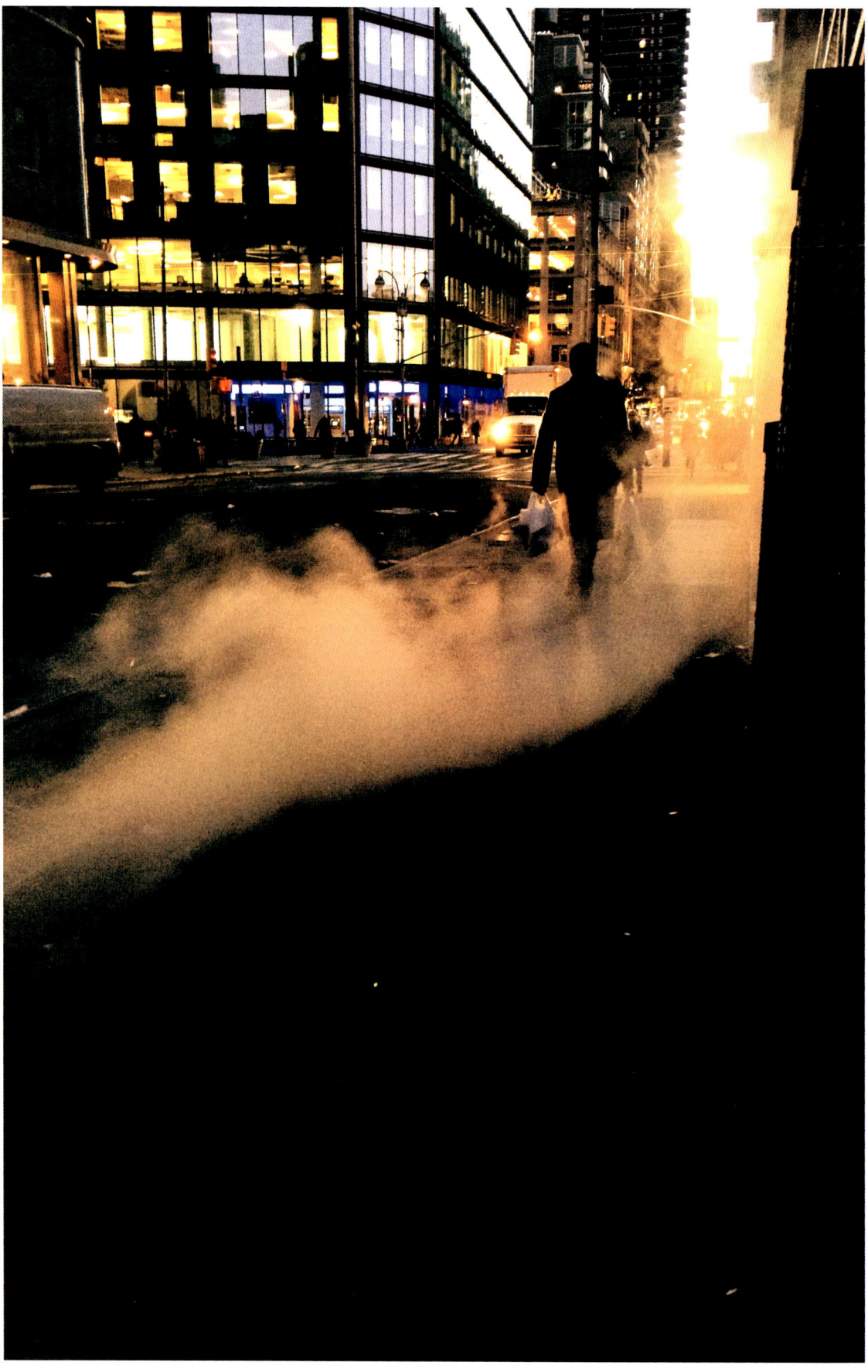

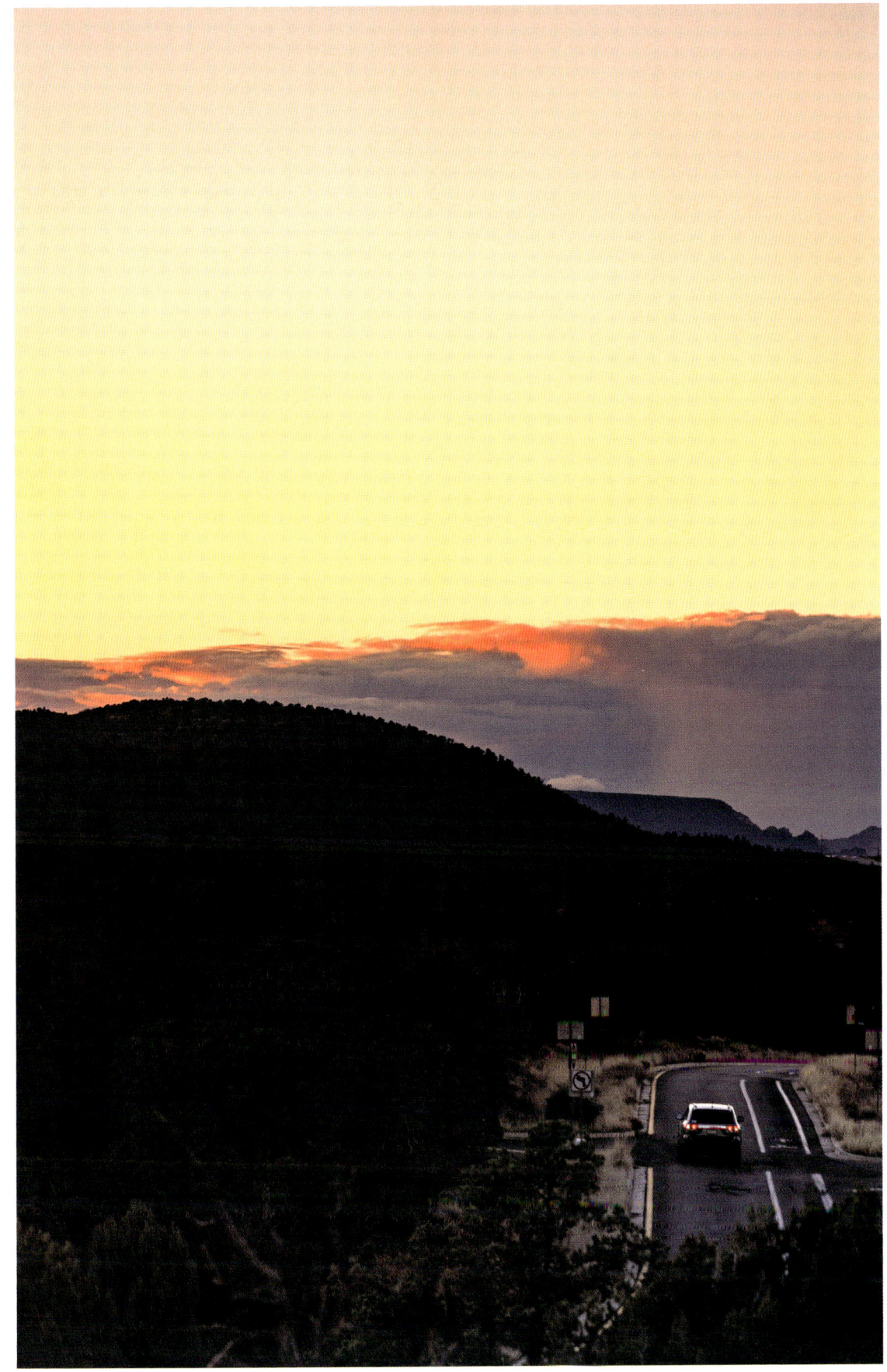

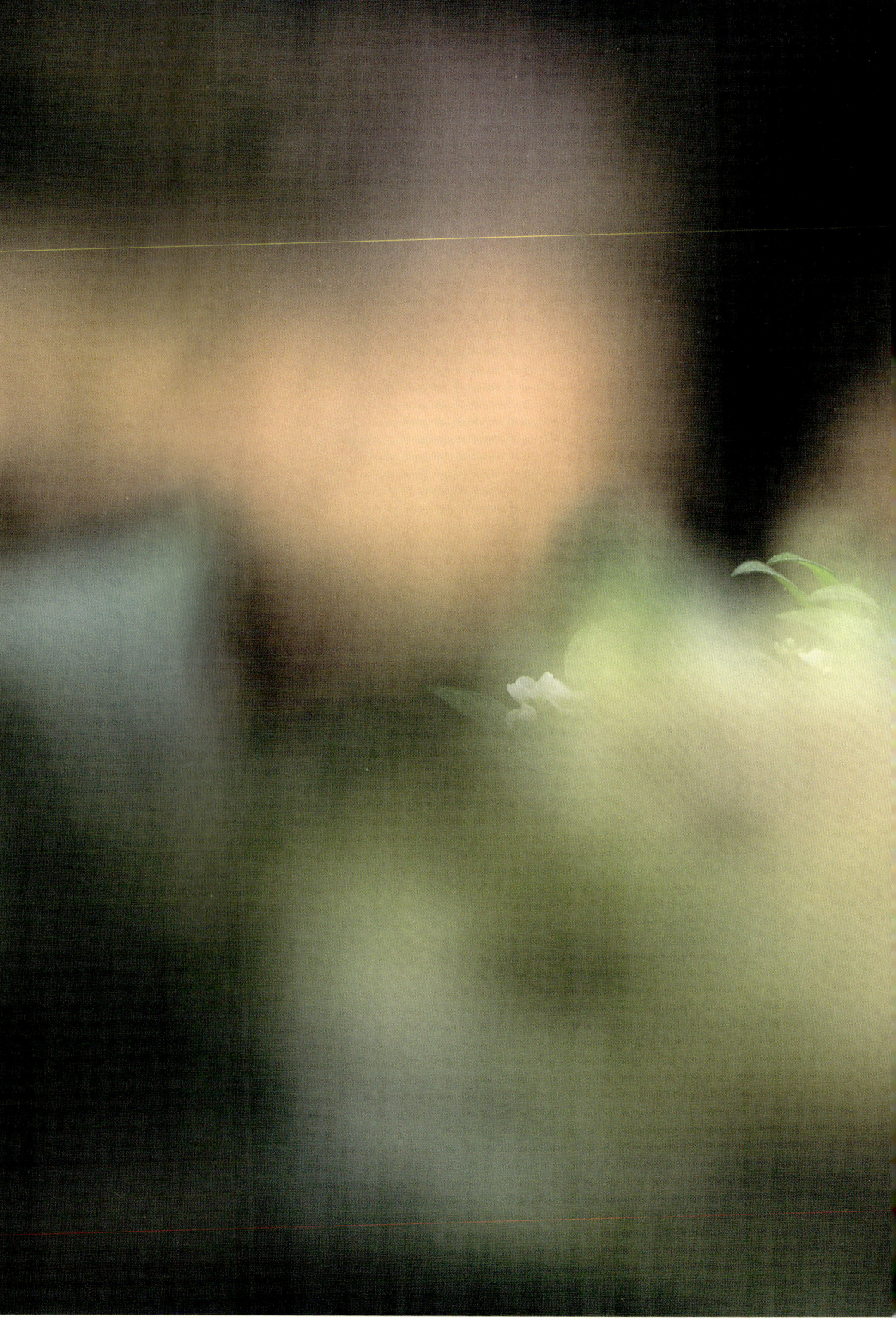

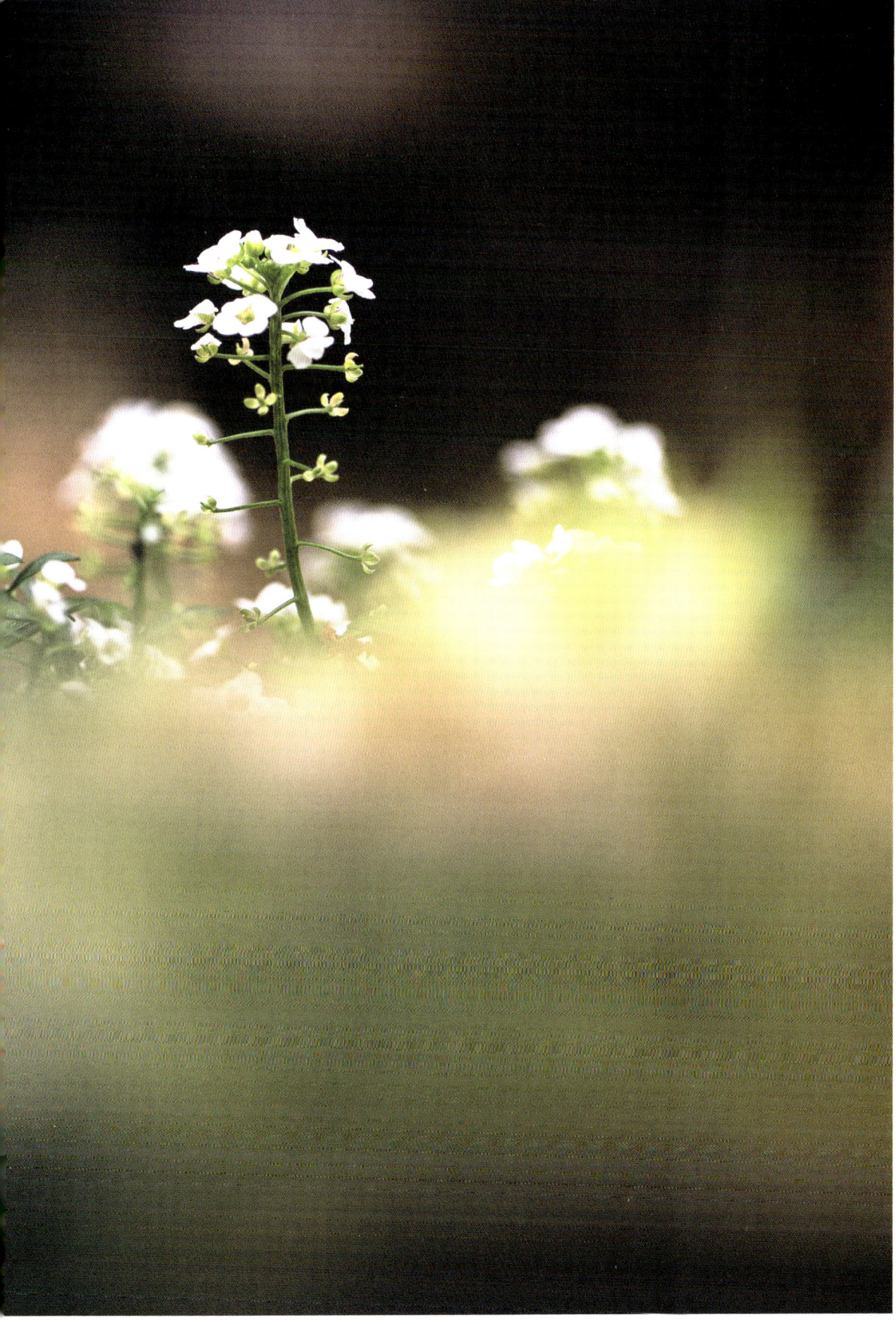

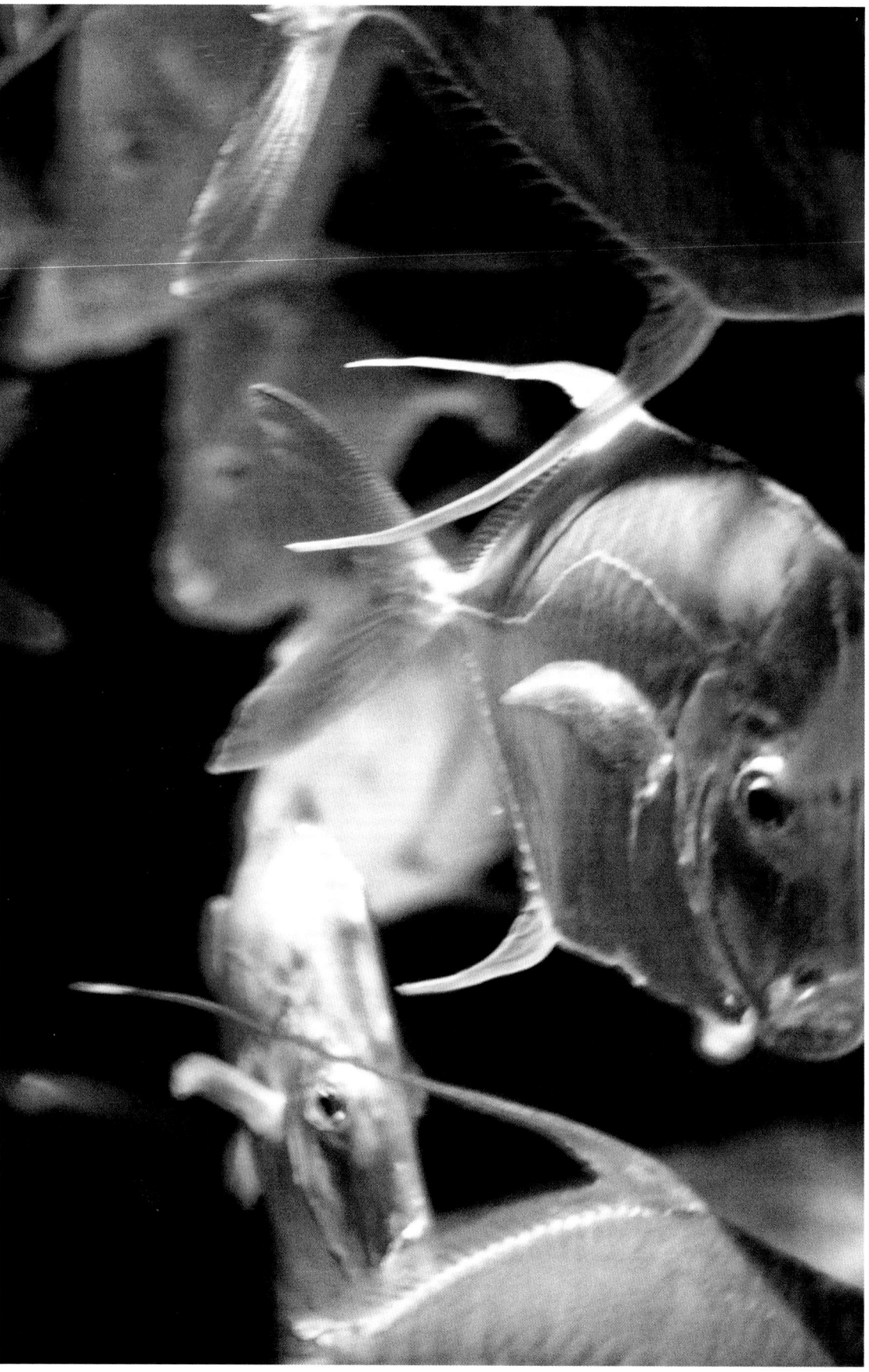

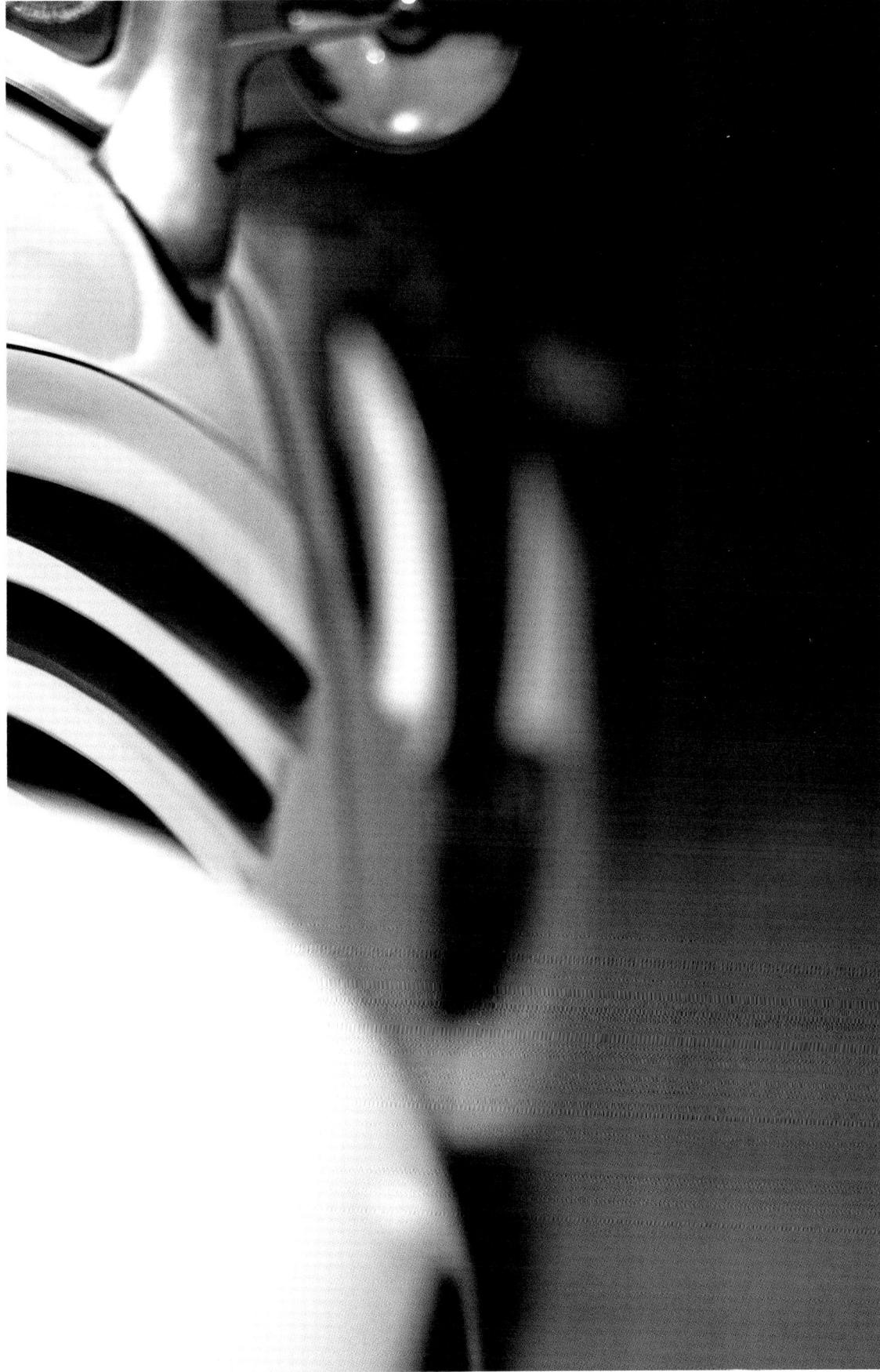

CHAPTER 21

AMATEURS, ARTISTS,
PROFESSIONALS,
AND LEGACY

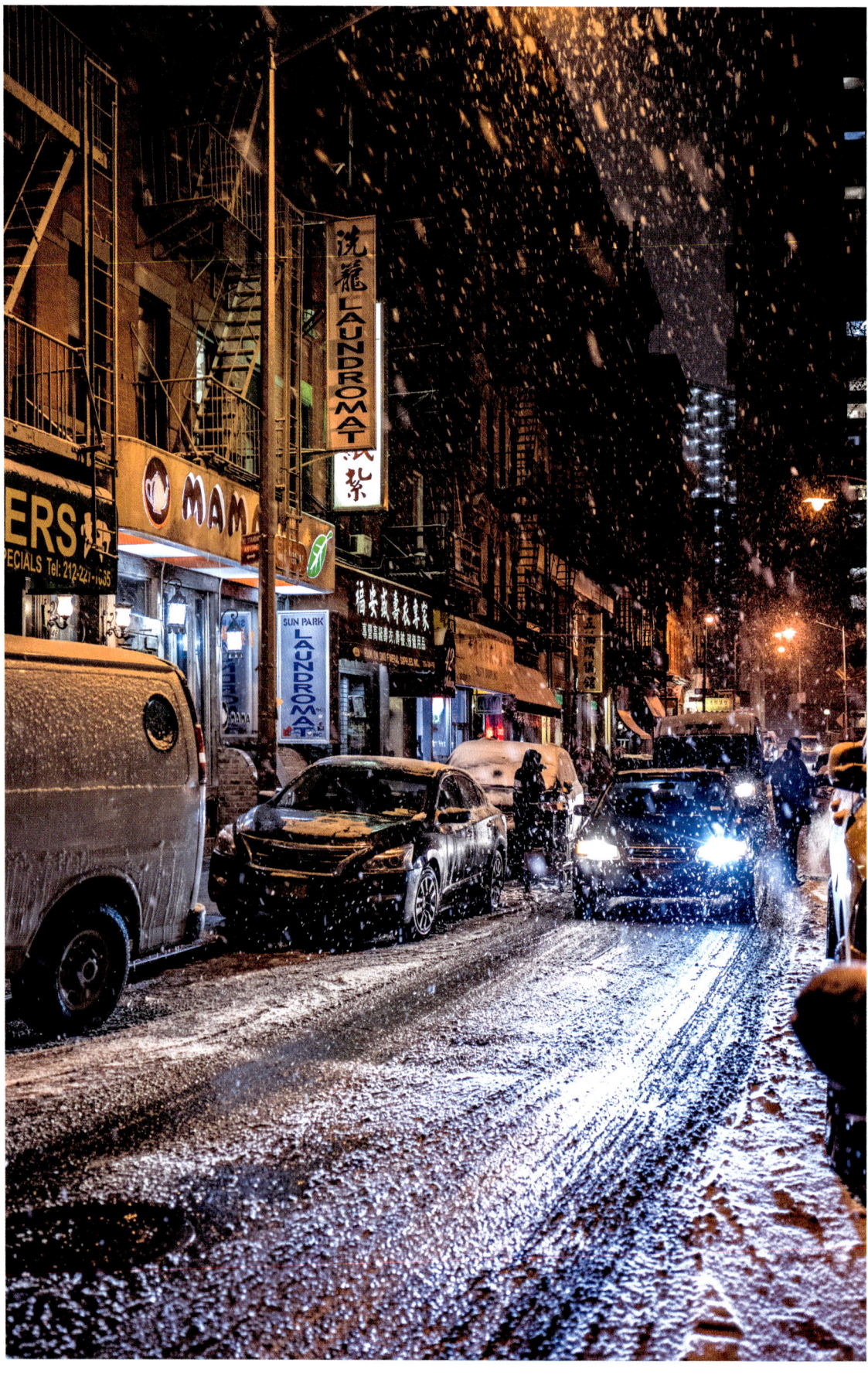

ON OCTOBER 6, 2010, a small, unknown app called Instagram opened up to the public. Within two months, one million people had accounts for this new photo-sharing app. Two years later, with over ten million accounts existing, the app was purchased by Facebook. At the time I'm writing this, there's a lot of controversy about new features on the app and the push away from photography for a more video-centric platform. But early on, Instagram was a benchmark in the history of photography as the next step in the smartphone era.

In those early days, the most beautiful part of it, for me, was how the platform embraced visual communication. The internet has a long history of being largely text-based through blogs, websites, Twitter, and even Facebook. Sure, images were combined with words, but Instagram was an image-dominant platform. And just like everyone having a camera on their phone, now everyone was using it to communicate on Instagram. Ironically, the users that struggled to do well were traditional photographers. I saw friends and colleagues complain that the speed of information cheapened their serious work. At the same time, I saw my family and non-photographer friends use this new platform to communicate daily what was going on in their lives. Put the idea of "internet celebrity" aside—early Instagram users were largely people communicating within small circles. They were not professional photographers; they were using their phone cameras.

I found it, and still find it, very beautiful to see people communicating largely with images. One couldn't write long political rants or bizarre stories. The image-based format required you to *show* what you wanted to say visually. Of course, over time, this started to sour, with the clutter of advertisements, memes, internet-famous celebrities, and the questionable practice of making one's life look different than it actually is. But for that brief few years, we turned a massive corner in favor of visual literacy.

I'm also of a generation that has witnessed photography both before and after the advent of the internet. The trends aren't over—more things will come and go. It might be interesting to the reader years after I've written these words. Will they even know what Instagram is, or will they care?

But early Instagram represents something bigger that's been coming to the surface over the last twenty years. As a culture, we now embrace the idea of visual communication, and there are platforms to put images in front of an audience. The line dividing amateurs and professionals has changed.

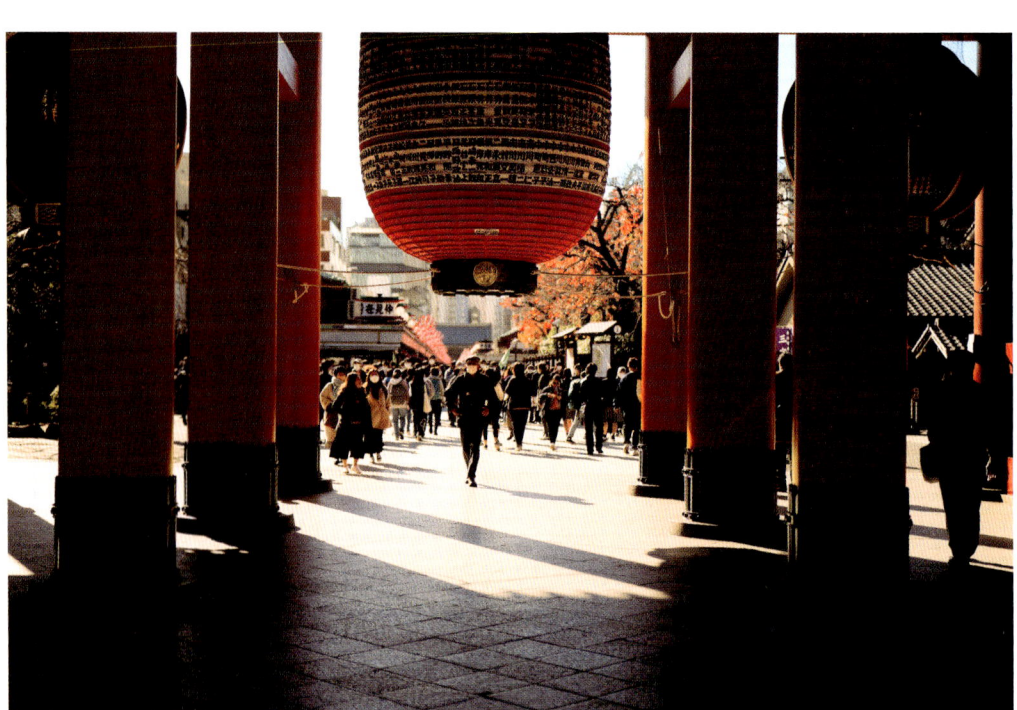

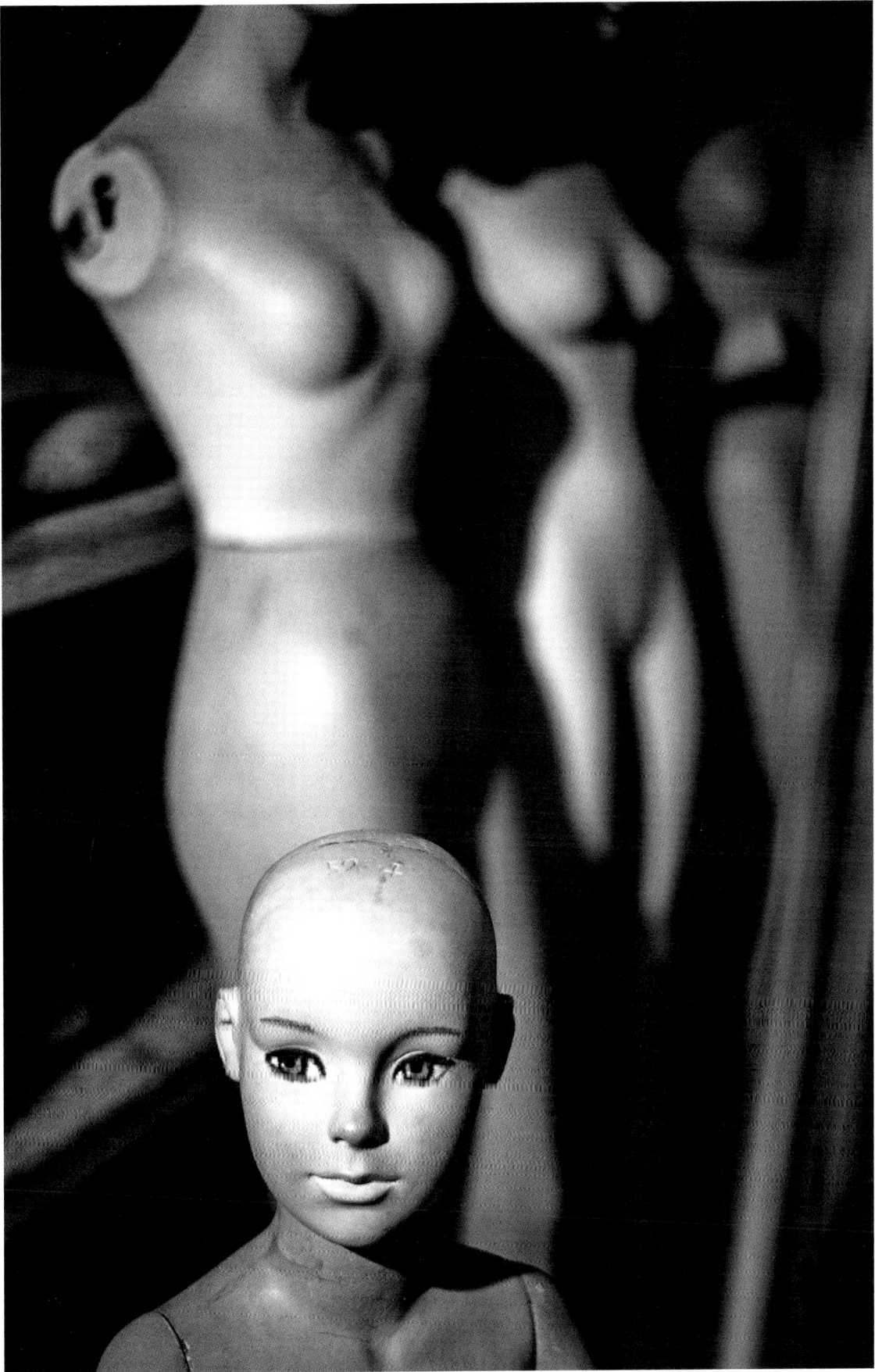

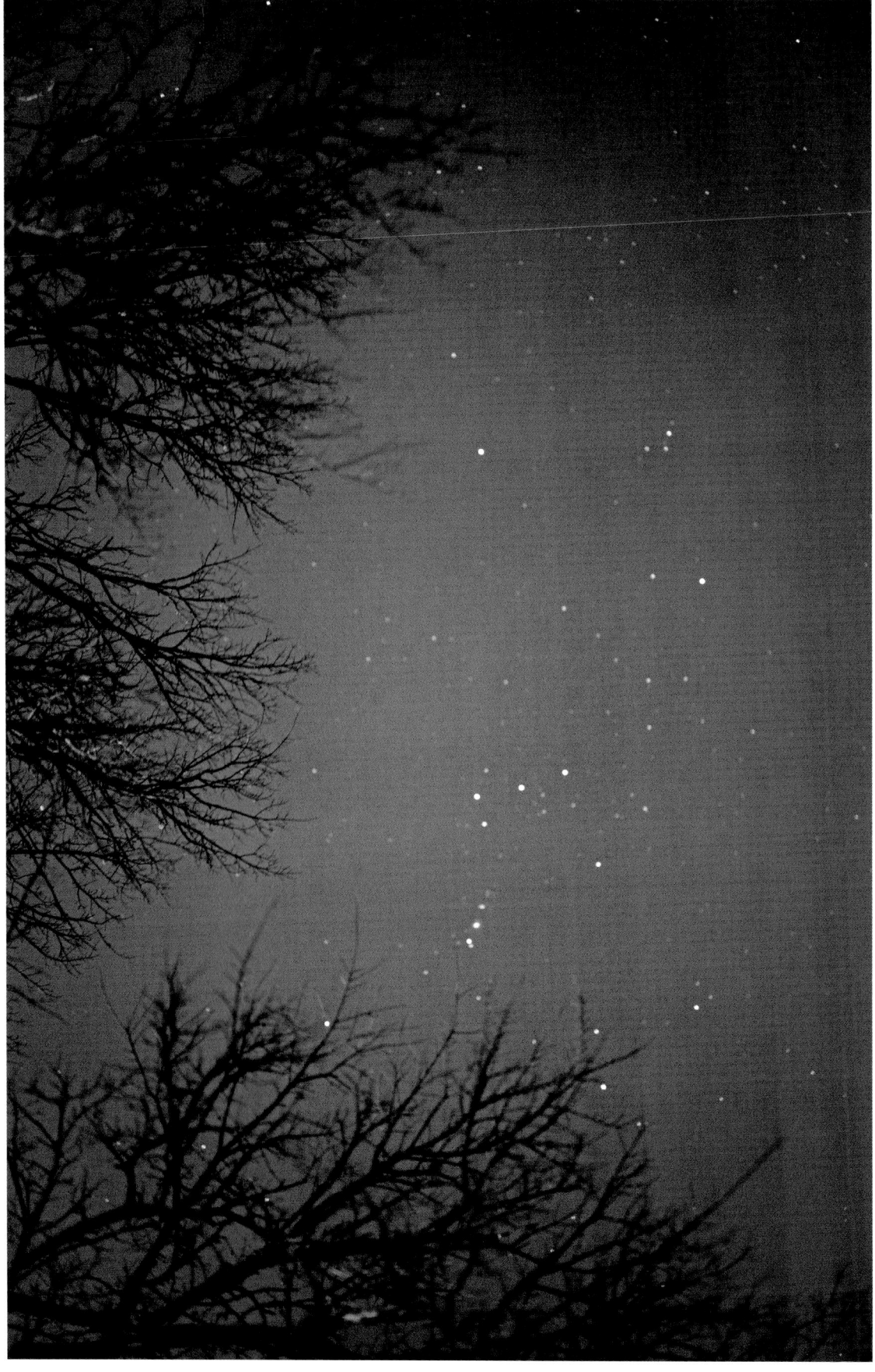

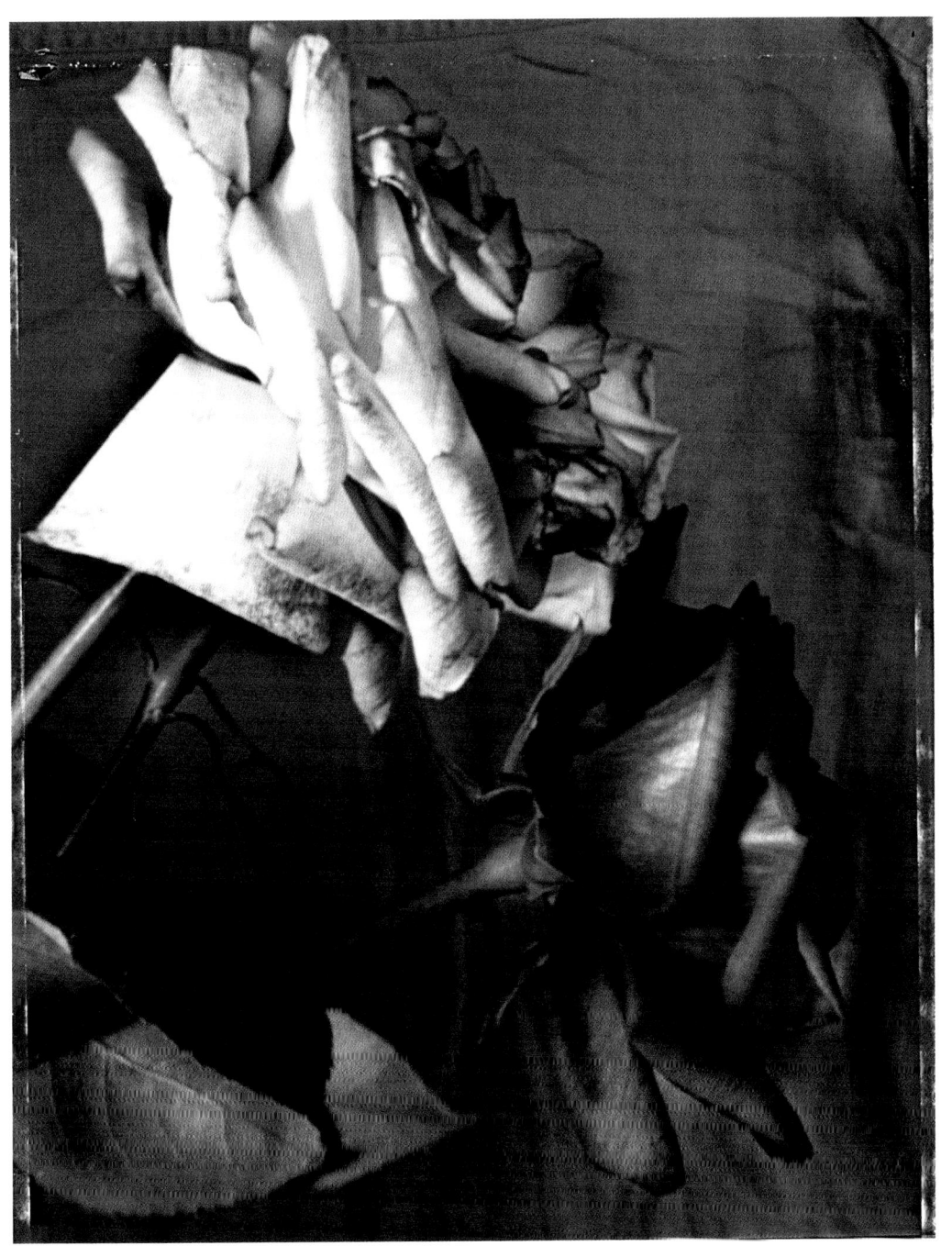

WHEN I WAS A KID, I was conditioned to think that the best photographers were always "pros." I always assumed when I was younger that they spent all their time with photography. It was their vocation—it was only natural that they would be the very best. This is actually not true at all.

In fact, I can tell you today, my perception is almost the opposite. There is some very exciting and courageous work being done today by photographers with no professional ambition whatsoever. They're good because of the passion that drives them, not recognition or validation from commercial sources.

It's an even playing field, and I can tell you that in photography, you'll get out of it exactly what you put into it. Some people want to make a living from their abilities, some don't. That has nothing to do with the strength of the work produced.

A common declaration that we've all heard over and over is, "What's the use? Everyone is a photographer." My response? That might be true, and so what? This should bring light to the evolution of photography, not destroy it. And it should inspire you to push harder, explore more, and find a true passion and love for this art form. Do you take photographs because you want praise and attention? Or is making photographs something that you must do? Sure, we all want recognition. Seeking attention or reward as a priority is a dangerous proposition.

My photography journey has included a broad range of experiences. I've had the fortune to work with and in many cases get to know various artists at many different levels of success, ability, and talent. This has led me often to ask the question, "What does it mean to be an artist?"

You become an artist by deciding that you are one. It's quite easy actually—no test to take, no license, no education required, just decide. Fortunately, medical doctors can't do the same.

That's not exactly a fair comparison. Photography doesn't regularly save lives (though I might argue it most likely has). It's not really like the medical profession, which is regulated. It's up to us to make it as great as it can and should be. I'd also argue, because we're not held to oversight, that we have a great deal of freedom in what we're able to explore and do with our artistic output.

I believe your legacy should drive you. I've noticed this commonality among the artists that I respect—they are driven by legacy, and I use this to fuel my own fire. When I look back at my journey, I want to see that it was something I loved and respected. I want to also see that I improved and changed overtime. We all have the opportunity to shape our own legacies. Think about what you want to leave behind. What defines you as an artist?

And remember, being an artist doesn't mean those behind the camera who "pull the trigger." I've known artists who are great editors, printers, writers, curators, teachers—photography provides a vast number of highly creative opportunities that many don't ever consider. I realized years ago that there was an opportunity to create YouTube videos that would start a conversation about photography. Nobody else was doing it back then, and I jumped in to share my voice. I've developed a whole career through making videos, talking about photography, and building The Art of Photography community. This career didn't exist back when my high school counselor had me in his office asking me what I was going to do with my life.

Visually Speaking is the culmination of thoughts and practices that I've learned and realized over the years that my artistic journey has unfolded. They are by no means the end or even the only way to understand visual communication. My journey continues and so does yours. Thank you for indulging me and reading. I hope you take this to a higher level by adding your own thoughts and discoveries. Maybe you even take it in a completely different direction and forever change the medium. Whatever you do, make time to practice, be thoughtful, and fall in love with the greatest art form of them all.

Now go make your next great picture.

Ted Forbes
Fort Worth, Texas
2023

A Guide to the Author's Photographs

Acknowledgments

A special thanks to some people without whom you would not be reading this book:

Greg Booth

Greg was a close friend, my mentor, and the reason I love photography today. In fact, the sole reason I became interested in photography was through Greg—a story I have shared in this book. He always encouraged me. He even bought a print from the first show that I did. It was my first sale ever. He was my first client when I built his first website.

I was privileged to know Greg in his short time on this planet. He died in 2008, and there has not been one day that has passed that I don't think of him in some way. I constantly wonder, "What would Greg have done?" or, "What would Greg think of this?" One of his Hasselblads sits on my desk. There have been so many moments in my career that I share with him, if only in my mind—in a spiritual sense. I miss him terribly.

Bart Marantz

Bart is an extraordinary person who I met when I was in high school. Bart was my band director. He's one of the most selfless people I've ever met. The man sacrificed so much to care for me and many others who were too young to realize what we had in him.

I still speak to Bart today. Now retired from education, he's an avid photographer. A lot of information in this book originated from Bart, but it was never intended that way. It was the language of jazz music. I don't have a formal art education, so I had to adapt my music education to make sense out of the visual world. Bart is to thank. He gave me opportunities and opened my eyes to a world of music that I've carried over into the photographic medium.

Bart and Mary Jo Forbes

I call them Mom and Dad, but Bart and Mary Jo are the greatest people in my life. They always have been. They supported me and encouraged me for many years. They've never given up on me. I love you both.

Nicole Forbes

My wife, partner in crime, and co-owner of our business. She puts up with my strange career, laughs at my stupid jokes, lets me honk the horn when she's driving, supports everything I do, and makes the best pizza you've ever had in your life. I love you darlin'.

Thank you to John Whalen for watching The Art of Photography and initiating the conversation that made this book possible. The WSE team—with special thanks to Buzz Poole and Steve Cooley—is greatly appreciated for their work on this project.

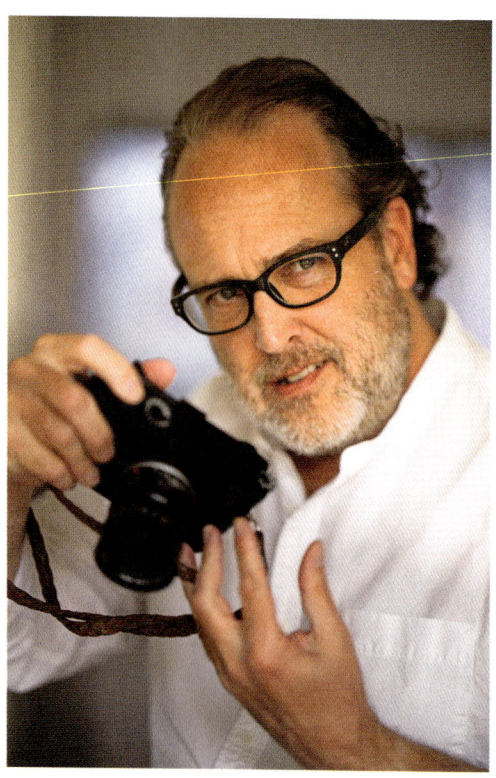

TED FORBES is a photographer and YouTube creator. He has reached international acclaim with his channel, The Art of Photography.

Using his platform as a way to inspire and educate, Forbes has created over 1,000 videos since 2008 that have generated over 75 million views covering topics from composition and technique to technical reviews and optics.

In 2017 he produced "The Artist Series" (on Amazon Prime) which comprises two seasons of short films documenting the best living photographers working today including William Wegman, Alexey Titarenko, Laura Wilson, Graciela Iturbide, Keith Carter, David Brookover, Lourdes Grobet and Pedro Meyer.

Forbes has also used his platform to encourage and inspire a younger generation of photographers as well. In his biweekly "Mail Time" videos, he's featured over 300 prints, books, and zines sent in by aspiring photographers for sharing and critique.

After a seven-year tenure working with the Dallas Museum of Art, Forbes left to pursue his own career. He regularly collaborates with Leica, Hasselblad, Sony, Canon, Nikon, and Fujifilm.

Originally from Dallas, Forbes studied at the Booker T. Washington High School for the Performing and Visual Arts and holds a music composition degree from the University of North Texas.

He currently lives in Fort Worth, Texas.

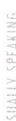

Visually Speaking

Copyright © 2024 by Ted Forbes.

This is an officially licensed book by Whalen Studio Editions.

All rights reserved under the Pan-American and International Copyright Conventions.

No part of this book may be reproduced in whole or in part, scanned, photocopied, record-ed, distributed in any printed or electronic form, or reproduced in any manner whatsoever, or by any information storage and retrieval system now known or hereafter invented, without express written permission of the publisher, except in the case of brief quotations embodied in critical articles and reviews.

The scanning, uploading, and distribution of this book via the internet or via any other means without permission of the publisher is illegal and punishable by law. Please support authors' rights, and do not participate in or encourage piracy of copyrighted materials.

13-Digit ISBN: 978-1-64643-435-0
10-Digit ISBN: 1-64643-435-8

Books published by Whalen Studio Editions are available at special discounts for bulk purchases in the United States by corporations, institutions, and other organi-zations. For more information, please contact the publisher.

Whalen Studio Editions
501 Nelson Place
Nashville, Tennessee 37214

Typography: Nimbus D, Futura PT

Printed in China

25 26 27 28 29 DSC 6 5 4 3 2

Whalen Studio Editions is an innovative publisher dedicated to celebrating visual artists and their work. We partner closely with photographers, painters, and other creatives to publish exceptional books—including special editions, slipcased volumes, and collectible editions with high-end prints—that embody the immense talents of our artists.

WHALEN
—————
STUDIO
—————
EDITIONS